CHURCH AND DENOMINATIONAL GROWTH

CHURCH
AND
DENOMINATIONAL
GROWTH

David A. Roozen
C. Kirk Hadaway

ABINGDON PRESS
NASHVILLE

CHURCH AND DENOMINATIONAL GROWTH

Copyright © 1993 by Abingdon Press

This book is printed on acid-free, recycled paper.

Library of Congress Cataloging-in-Publication Data

Church and denominational growth / [edited by] David A. Roozen,
  C. Kirk Hadaway.
    p.   cm.
  Includes bibliographical references and index.
  ISBN 0-687-15904-0 (alk. paper)
    1. Church growth. 2. Evangelistic work. 3. Choice of church.
  I. Roozen, David A.   II. Hadaway, C. Kirk.
  BV652.25.C478   1993   93-16698
  254'.5—dc20   CIP

Church and Denominational Growth: A Supplemental Appendix contains additional tables and technical definitions. It is available from the Center for Social and Religious Research, Hartford Seminary, 77 Sherman Street, Hartford, CT 06105.

93 94 95 96 97 98 99 00 01 02—10 9 8 7 6 5 4 3 2 1

MANUFACTURED IN THE UNITED STATES OF AMERICA

CONTENTS

PART THREE

INDIVIDUALS AND THE CHURCH CHOICE

David A. Roozen and C. Kirk Hadaway **241**

CONTRIBUTORS

Peter L. Benson, President, Search Institute, Minneapolis, Minnesota

Reginald W. Bibby, Professor, Department of Sociology, The University of Lethbridge, Lethbridge, Alberta Canada

Jackson W. Carroll, Ph.D., Professor of Religion and Society, and Director of the J. M Ormand Center for Research and Development, The Divinity School, Duke University

Michael J. Donahue, Research Scientist, Search Institute, Minneapolis, Minnesota

Norman M. Green, Jr., Director, Office of Planning and Resources, American Baptist National Ministries, Valley Forge, Pennsylvania

Bruce A. Greer, Ph.D. Candidate, Sociology Department, University of Massachusetts, Amherst

C. Kirk Hadaway, Secretary for Research and Evaluation, United Church Board for Homeland Ministries, Cleveland, Ohio

Dean R. Hoge, Professor of Sociology, Catholic University of America

Kenneth W. Inskeep, Director, Department of Research and Evaluation, The Lutheran Church in America, Chicago, Illinois

Mary Johnson, S.N.D., Lecturer in Sociology, Emmanuel College, Boston

Conrad L. Kanagy, Ph.D. Candidate, The Pennsylvania State University

Paul W. Light, Director of Research and Development, National Ministries, American Baptist Church, Valley Forge, Pennsylvania

Penny Long Marler, Assistant Professor of Religion, Samford University, Birmingham, Alabama

Hart M. Nelsen, Professor of Sociology, The Pennsylvania State University

Daniel V. A. Olson, Assistant Professor of Sociology, Indiana University South Bend

Wade Clark Roof, J. F. Rowney Professor of Religion and Society, University of California at Santa Barbara

David A. Roozen, Director, Center for Social and Religious Research, Hartford Seminary

Marjorie H. Royle, Research and Evaluation Coordinator, St. Joseph's Hospital and Medical Center, Paterson, New Jersey

Wayne L. Thompson, Assistant Professor of Sociology, Weber State University

Michael R. Welch, Associate Professor of Sociology, University of Notre Dame, Notre Dame, Indiana

FIGURES

9

TABLES

APPENDIX TABLES

Chapter One

Denominations Grow as Individuals Join Congregations

David A. Roozen

*A seismic shift has been occurring and
continues in American religion.*
Martin Marty, 1979

Seismic shifts rarely catch public attention except at the most dramatic moments of disjuncture. For American denominational religion that initial jolt into consciousness came in 1965 when the membership trends of most "mainline" Protestant denominations turned from growth to decline. Yet unlike the immediate awareness and response typically related to an earthquake, it was not until the mid-1970s that the mainline decline was widely accepted as a serious "new" reality that demanded attention. And it was not until 1979 that the first comprehensive collection of research on the decline was published: *Understanding Church Growth and Decline: 1950–1978* (Hoge and Roozen).

Marty's conclusion that a seismic shift was occurring drew heavily upon the empirical research reported in *Understanding Church Growth and Decline*. The shift dealt not only with "the mainline yin"—the major focus of that book, but also, "consistently if implicitly, with the evangelical yang" (Marty, 1979:12). In this way Marty called attention to the now familiar divergence of mainline and evangelical membership trends. As is evident in Figures 1.1 and 1.2, the trend lines present a powerful visual image of the situation. And indeed, coupled with other widely read books of the period such as Kelley's *Why Conservative Churches Are Growing* (1972), this visual image was "translated in the public imagination as a simplification: religious and spiritual revival was occurring in the conservative churches, and spiritual decay had overtaken the mainline churches" (Hunter, 1987:203).

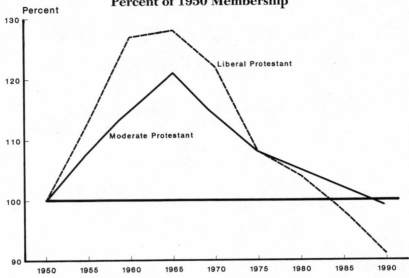

FIGURE 1.1
**Membership of Selected Denominational Families as a
Percent of 1950 Membership**

Percent

Liberal Protestant

Moderate Protestant

Source: Appendix Table 1.1

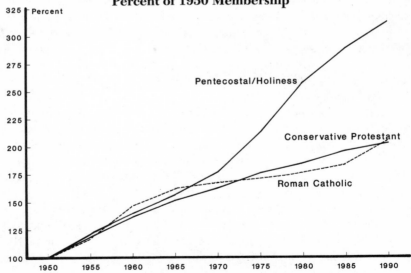

FIGURE 1.2
**Membership of Selected Denominational Families as a
Percent of 1950 Membership**

Percent

Pentecostal/Holiness

Conservative Protestant

Roman Catholic

Source: Appendix Table 1.1

With the hindsight of recent research we now know that the conclusion of revival and decay was a rather grievous oversimplification. Focusing on the mainline movement from membership gains to membership losses, the research of the 1970s—including much of our own—missed several important points. First, the growth of the mainline did not suddenly turn downward in the 1960s. It was already slowing in the 1950s! (See Figure 1.3.)

Second, while the popular perception was of a shift in vitality from mainline to conservative denominations beginning in the late 1950s, the reality is reflected in the following facts:

- The growth rate of all Protestant denominational families slowed during the 1950s.
- This slowdown intensified during the 1960s for all Protestant families except Pentecostal/Holiness.
- The growth rates of both moderate and liberal Protestantism have improved since the mid-1960s (although still negative), while the growth rate of conservative Protestantism has continued to slow (although still positive).

FIGURE 1.3
Five-Year Membership Growth Rates by Denominational Family

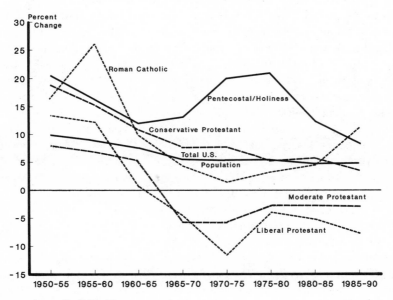

Source: Appendix Table 1.2

- The Pentecostal/Holiness surge of the late 1960s and 1970s cooled off considerably during the 1980s.
- To the extent membership growth rates are indicative of denominational vitality, Roman Catholicism led the way into the 1990s.[1]

As Marty (1979:10) reminded us as he called attention to the seismic shift occurring in American religion: "While church growth and decline are far from being the only ways of measuring religious health, they give at least some indication of how citizens are voting with their bodies." In this spirit, two purposes of this new collection of research on church growth and decline are: (1) to expand our understanding of the changes that were occurring in American religion during the 1960s and early 1970s, and (2) to chart the direction these changes have taken in the decade and a half since the publication of *Understanding Church Growth and Decline: 1950–1978.* In doing so, the book provides a window from which to view the changing fortunes of American denominational religion. But the book's primary purpose is more focused and more pragmatic.[2] It seeks to present a comprehensive collection of the most recent, comparative social research on the dynamics of church growth and decline. It does so in the hope that an increased understanding of these dynamics will lead to more effective responses on the part of religious leaders in American churches and denominations.

Given the avalanche of "church-growth-how-to" books, newsletters, and leadership seminars appearing in recent years, it is puzzling that there has not been a similar outpouring of published empirical research on the subject. Indeed, since *Understanding Church Growth and Decline: 1950–1978*, a rigorous, book-length "church growth" study spanning more than a few congregations or a single denomination has not appeared in print. This is not meant to imply that the "how-to" literature is devoid of wisdom. Yet some of it is quite superficial, and much of it is more motivational than programmatic. Nevertheless, the reservoir of "church growth" techniques that have worked somewhere for someone is, if anything, overflowing. What is less clear is why (or in what settings) a given technique works; and why (or in what settings) a given technique does not work. The type of social research reported in this volume provides an insightful journey into the underlying principles that should inform specific programmatic decisions.

I also do not want to minimize the positive contributions of the more probing church growth research focused on single denominations. *The Mainstream Protestant "Decline": The Presbyterian Pattern* (Coalter, Mulder and Weeks, 1990) and *Church Growth Principles: Separating Fact from Fiction* (Hadaway, 1991) are exemplary in this regard. Indeed, the collection of church growth research you are about to read is, in many respects, an extension of such work—a collection of research findings that moves across liberal and conservative, and black and white Protestantism, as well as Roman Catholicism. Before turning to this research, however, overviews of denominational membership trends in the last half century and changes in the broader religious climate should be helpful.

Membership Trends: An Overview

If one's only measure of American church membership trends since the 1950s was national public opinion poll data, one would be perplexed by all the fuss over church growth. According to the Gallup poll (Princeton Religion Research Center, 1992) the percentage of Americans who are church members was virtually the same in 1991 as it was in 1978 (68%), and is only 5 percentage points lower than poll readings from 1952 and 1965 (73%). The aggregate membership trend for the twenty-six denominations used in Figures 1.1 to 1.3 shows a remarkably similar pattern: the total market share of these denominations (membership as a percent of the total population) dropped only 5 percentage points from the mid-1960s to 1980, and was virtually static from 1980 to 1990 (see Appendix, Table A1.1). In light of this stability, especially during the last decade, the "fuss" over church growth only appears understandable as either: (1) a theologically driven shift toward an increased emphasis on "the Great Commission," or (2) a pragmatic awareness that American denominations had to work harder just to keep up. The research reported here suggests that it is a combination of the two.

Denominational Differences

The combination of theological and practical motivations for the increased concern over church growth and decline comes into clearer focus when it is further noted (as suggested in the language of seismic shift) that it is not the aggregate national trend in church membership that made it a center of attention. Rather, it was that some denominations were growing in members and others were declining. And as noted above, recent research shows that even the identification of winners and losers is more complicated than suggested by earlier assessments of mainline decline and conservative growth. A more nuanced interpretation is required, in part, because we now know that the mainline vs. conservative dichotomy obscures increasingly important divisions within the "Protestant house." But it is also required because we now know that different ways of measuring membership growth illuminate different aspects of its dynamic.

That the former Protestant mainline has moved "to the sideline" is an almost taken-for-granted assumption of recent commentary on the restructuring of American religion. Indeed, phrases such as "the third religious disestablishment" are not uncommon on the lips of American church historians. But the possibility that the old line splintered into sidelines received less consideration. Roof and McKinney's *American Mainline Religion* (1987) makes a strong case for this possibility. Their book shows that in terms of demographics, social and personal values, religious belief and practice, relationship to the mainstream of American culture, and future prospects for institutional viability there are significant differences between what they call the liberal and moderate families of former establishment Protestantism. Within the liberal family they include such denominations as the Episcopal Church, the United Church of Christ, and the Presbyterian Church (U.S.A.). Within the moderate family they include The United Methodist Church, the Evangelical Lutheran Church in America, the Christian Church (Disciples of Christ); and the Reformed Church in America.

Following Roof and McKinney's classification, Figure 1.1 shows the aggregate forty-year membership trend for a sampling of denominations in each family.[3] The membership trends for the two families have much in common, most notably the mid-1960s tipping point from growth to decline. Nevertheless, there is one highly suggestive difference. In regard to both the ascent and subsequent declines of the 1950s, the movement of liberal Protestantism is more extreme.

The Presidential election of born-again Southern Baptist, Democratic Jimmy Carter in 1976, and the co-mingling of television evangelists and conservative Republican politics beginning in 1980 did more to pique America's interest in conservative Protestantism and its internal diversity than did the mainline Protestant declines of the 1960s. But regardless of the source, along with a new curiosity in the public consciousness came a steady stream of scholarship that has greatly enhanced our understanding of the changing nature of this formerly quiet, but deep stream of American denominationalism. As is typically the case with probing inquiry, simplistic old stereotypes give way to more nuanced distinctions. In the case of conservative Protestantism, this process is still unfolding and no single schema of classification has yet to gain general acceptance.

Nevertheless, some consensus is emerging that there are at least two major conservative Protestant families. Both families place a strong emphasis on biblical authority, a conversionist approach to evangelism, and "traditional" American values. For one family this is combined with an emphasis on authoritative doctrine (Hunter, 1983; Ammerman, 1987); for the other, an emphasis on sanctification and the present-day operation of the Holy Spirit

(Quebedeaux, 1983; Poloma, 1989). The most prominent denominational representative of the former family, to which for present purposes I restrict the label "conservative Protestant," is the Southern Baptist Convention. The most prominent representative of the latter family, which for present purposes I call Pentecostal/Holiness, is the Assemblies of God.[4]

The significance of the conservative vs. Pentecostal/Holiness distinction for understanding recent trends in church membership is illustrated in Figure 1.2. Like Figure 1.1, it charts the aggregate forty-year membership trends for a sampling of denominations in each family.[5] The figure speaks for itself. From 1950 through the mid-1960s the growth trajectories of the two families are nearly indistinguishable. By the late 1960s, however, Pentecostal/Holiness growth noticeably begins to outpace conservative growth. The divergence accelerates dramatically throughout the 1970s. During the 1980s the Pentecostal/Holiness surge slows, and by the end of the decade its growth trajectory returns to near parallel with that of the conservative family. Figure 1.2 also shows the forty-year membership trend for Roman Catholicism. With a few minor deviations, it closely resembles that of the conservative Protestant family.[6]

No portrait of American denominationalism is complete without including the historical black denominations. Unfortunately, no membership trend data exist for this important and sizable family. Recent estimates suggest that black Baptists alone include nearly 7 million members (*Churches and Church Membership in the United States: 1990*). There are some national public opinion poll trend data on black church involvement, and the Nelsen and Kanagy chapter in this book reports on a portion of it. The conclusions reached by Nelsen and Kanagy are consistent with the findings of *The Black Church in the African American Experience* (Lincoln and Mamiya, 1990)— the first major study of the black church in over thirty years. Black church membership appears to have held its ground in the last decade or so, except among young adults in the inner cities of the industrial North.

New Measures, New Perspective

Figures 1.1 and 1.2 present membership trends in terms of absolute numbers. The data answer the question: are there more or less members from year to year? From the perspective of institutional maintenance and resource management, this is arguably the best measure of membership trends. It was also the clear pattern of decline within mainline Protestantism on this measure, beginning in the mid-1960s, that initially caught the public's attention. But there are two other approaches to measuring membership growth that provide different angles of vision. One focuses on "market share," the other on "growth rate." Both have been briefly introduced above—the former in the discussion of membership trends as measured by national public opinion surveys; the latter in the initial discussion in Figure 1.3.

Market Share and Opportunity. When applied to church membership, "market share" typically refers to membership as a percentage of the total population. It views membership in relation to the total pool of persons available to be members. Or, to put it yet another way, market share measures growth relative to contextual opportunity. From such a perspective 10% membership growth in an area with 5% population growth is better than 10% membership growth in an area with 20% population growth. Given that the total population of the U.S. has grown throughout the postwar period, the liberal and moderate declines in number of members since the 1960s shown in Figure 1.1 take on added significance. In the last twenty-five years these denominational families actually lost members during a period of increasing opportunity!

But a market share perspective also tempers our interpretation of the continual growth in members of other denominational families. Indeed the membership market share of conservative Protestants and Roman Catholics has not changed since the early 1970s, and the market share of the Pentecostal/Holiness family has only inched upward—from .08% of the U.S. population in 1965, to 1.3% in 1990 (see Table A1.1 in the Appendix).

Of course, the membership of most denominational families is more concentrated in some regions of the United States than others and different regions of the country have different rates of population growth. Putting these observations together led some scholars to suggest that a large portion of the difference in membership growth among denominational families may be due to the concentration of low growth families in low growth regions of the country (e.g., Hutchinson, 1986). Figures 1.4 and 1.5 challenge such an interpretation. They compare 1980 and 1990 membership change for each denominational family with the change in the U.S. population by region of the country.

The two most notable patterns in the figures are that liberal and moderate Protestantism are losing members in all regions, even those with the greatest population growth; and that the Pentecostal/Holiness family is increasing market share (that is, membership growth is greater than population growth) in all regions. Roman Catholicism is gaining market share in all regions except the mountain states. Its increasing market share is especially dramatic on the Pacific coast, where it is apparently capitalizing on its historical relationship to Hispanics. Conservative Protestantism is gaining market share in three of the five regions. One of the regions in which it is losing market share, however, is its "home base" in the South; the other is the most rapidly growing region of the country—the Pacific coast—where it is losing out to both Roman Catholics and the Pentecostal/Holiness family.

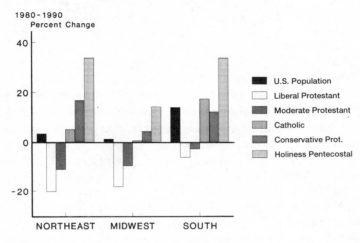

FIGURE 1.4
1980–1990 Membership Change by Region by
Denominational Family and Total U.S. Population

1980-1990
Percent Change

Legend:
- U.S. Population
- Liberal Protestant
- Moderate Protestant
- Catholic
- Conservative Prot.
- Holiness Pentecostal

NORTHEAST   MIDWEST   SOUTH

Source:
Quinn et al. (1982); Bradley et al. (1992)

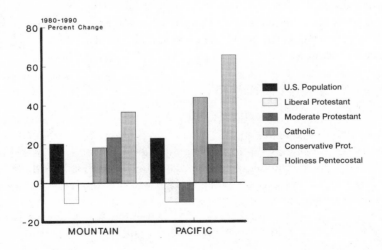

FIGURE 1.5
1980–1990 Membership Change by Region by
Denominational Family and Total U.S. Population

1980-1990
Percent Change

Legend:
- U.S. Population
- Liberal Protestant
- Moderate Protestant
- Catholic
- Conservative Prot.
- Holiness Pentecostal

MOUNTAIN   PACIFIC

Source:
Quinn et al. (1982); Bradley et al. (1992)

Growth Rates and Internal Resources. Still another perspective on growth is provided through an analysis of growth rates. In its simplest form a growth rate is the percent change in membership across some period of time. In contrast to market share which, as noted above, is membership change relative to external opportunity—the pool of possible members; growth rates measure membership change relative to internally available resources—the pool of existing members. In terms of membership growth, growth rates are the statistical equivalent of the biblical adage that to whom much is given much is expected. The use of growth rates also, as already noted in our initial discussion of Figure 1.3, dramatically changes old stereotypes about differences in membership growth among denominational families.

Figure 1.3 shows the trend in five-year growth rates from 1950 to 1990 for the five denominational families and the U.S. population. Many of the salient patterns visible there have already been noted, but two additional observations deserve comment. First, the growth rate of conservative Protestantism has been moving downward since at least 1950, and in the late 1980s it actually dropped below the growth rate of the U.S. population. The latter is significant because it means that the continuing slowdown in conservative Protestant growth has now reached the point of decreasing national market share.

Second, the growth rate trends for conservative and moderate Protestants are the least volatile of any denominational family. Since these two families are arguably the least culturally extreme within American Protestantism, the relative stability of their growth rate suggests that the closer a denominational ethos is to the underlying mainstream of American culture, the lower the risk of steep decline on the one hand, but also the lower the possibility of dramatic growth on the other.

Growth Equals Additions Minus Losses. There is one additional perspective on membership growth and decline that has generated much discussion, especially concerning the numerical declines in mainline Protestantism. This perspective draws attention to the simple fact that numerical membership change is the total of membership additions minus membership losses. All denominations, like most congregations, have both additions and losses every year. Numerical growth, of course, is the result of having more additions than losses; and numerical decline is the result of having more losses than additions. But it is important to remember that numerical decline can result from either an increase in losses or from a decrease in additions.

One of the predominant myths about mainline declines in the late 1960s is that they were the result of increased losses. More specifically, the popular rhetoric of the time suggested that the declines were primarily due to members leaving because of denominational involvement in social action. Many people still believe this today. Nevertheless, *Understanding Church Growth and Decline: 1950–1978* (Hoge and Roozen, 1979) clearly showed that the mainline membership declines in the late 1960s and early 1970s were more a result of fewer people joining than of members leaving. But this isn't the final word on the story.

Greer's chapter in the current book suggests that social justice advocacy did have some detrimental effect on membership growth. But consistent with Hoge and Roozen, this was not because people went away mad. Rather, it was because the shift in theological priorities toward social justice concerns pulled resources away from recruitment/evangelism and new church development.

Greer's chapter also indicates that each of the four mainline denominations examined reemphasized evangelism and new church development during the 1980s. Juxtaposed with the evidence from Figure 1.3 that mainline declines moderated somewhat during the 1980s, one is tempted to conclude that the improvement must be because of increased additions. Resist the temptation. Although a comprehensive study of mainline additions and losses over the last twenty-five years has yet to appear, our preliminary examination of data from several denominations suggests that the relative improvement of growth rates in the last decade is due more to decreased losses (despite increased deaths related to the aging of the mainline membership), than to increased additions. Indeed the data show that additions have decreased steadily since at least the mid-1960s.

The Independent Sector

The focus of this book is American denominational religion, and the introductory discussion of membership trends thus far has been limited to that. But the high visibility of new religious movements during the 1960s and more recent impressions of a proliferation of nondenominational (i.e., independent) congregations are helpful reminders that the American religious marketplace is broader than denominationalism.

Until 1990, national membership figures for independent congregations were nonexistent. Thanks to a cooperative effort between the International MegaChurch Research Center directed by John Vaughan, and the steering committee for *Churches and Church Membership in the United States: 1990* (CCM:90; Bradley, et al., 1992) we now have a baseline of independent church membership data for every county in the United States. The data have some limitations, most significantly in identifying only independent congregations with "memberships" of 300 or more, and primarily such congregations in metropolitan areas with a population of 20,000 or more. The data, therefore, are clearly an undercount, and not a count of members per se, but more closely akin to a count of what the CCM:90 calls "adherents." Additionally the data are only for 1990 and therefore preclude a direct confirmation of the widely shared perception that both the number of independent congregations and the total membership of independents has increased dramatically in the past ten to twenty years.

Its limitations notwithstanding, the CCM:90 data provide an instructive first look at churches' independent sector. Even given the undercount, the 2,001,327 total adherents reported in CCM:90 for independent congregations makes the independent church sector larger than all but eight U.S. denominations. It pegs the independent church sector as just a little smaller than the Assemblies of God and Lutheran Church, Missouri Synod, and just slightly larger than the United Church of Christ.

Like most denominations, independent church membership is not evenly distributed across the United States. Figures 1.6 and 1.7 show the regional distribution of independent church adherents, comparing it with that of the three denominations noted above. These three denominations are used for comparative purposes not only because they are roughly equal in overall size, but also because each represents a different denominational family. Two patterns in the figures stand out. First, the independent church sector is less regionally concentrated than any of the three comparative denominations. Second, to the extent that there is a regional tilt in the independent church sector it is from relatively low concentrations in the northeast to increasingly higher concentrations as one moves south and west.

The only differentiation the CCM:90 makes in its count of independent church adherents is between adherents of charismatic and noncharismatic congregations. Figure 1.8 presents this breakdown, again by region and for the nation as a whole. Overall, CCM:90 reports half again as many adherents of noncharismatic than charismatic congregations. But this overall figure masks significant regional differences. In New England and the South Atlantic noncharismatics outnumber charismatics by two to one; and in the East North Central and East South Central, by more than three to one. But in the mid-Atlantic states charismatics outnumber noncharismatics by two to one; and in the West South Central, Mountain, and Pacific regions the two groups are roughly equal in size. Figure 1.8 also shows that charismatics are strongest (in terms of market share) in the West South Central. This also is the region of greatest strength for the Assemblies of God (see Figures 1.6 and 1.7). Both groups also share relative strength in the Mountain and Pacific regions of the West.

FIGURE 1.6
Total Adherents as a Percentage of the Population by Region for Independents and Selected Denominations

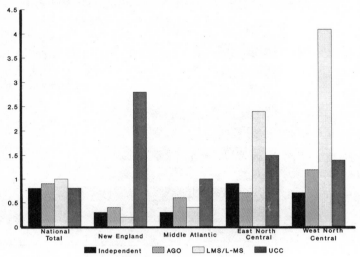

FIGURE 1.7
Total Adherents as a Percentage of the Population by Region for Independents and Selected Denominations

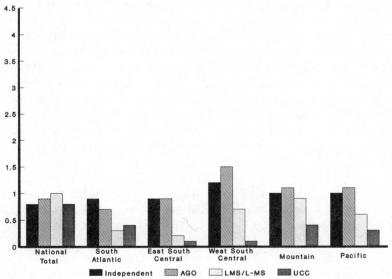

FIGURE 1.8
Charismatic and Noncharismatic Independent Adherents as a Percent of the Population by Region

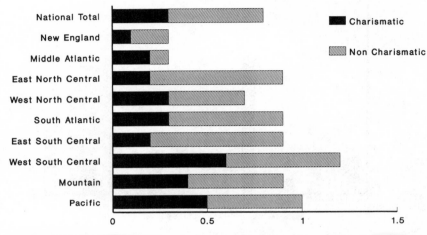

The new religious movements that rose around the edges of the countercul-ture during the 1960s were more sect-like than church-like, but they did attract a good number of church dropouts. We now know that their increasing visibility during that time was greatly disproportional to their numerical growth. Partici-pants in the movements were almost exclusively young adults and even within this segment of society, primarily college students. Scholars tend to concur, however, that the movements' high visibility contributed an important symbolic dimension to the more general cultural upheaval of the 1960s. As Robbins, Anthony, and Richardson (1978) note, the new religious movements were of two general types: mystical-therapeutic and neo-fundamentalist. The former synthesized scientific, psychological, and religious (particularly Eastern mysti-cal) themes in a quest for personal meaning. The latter mixed cosmological dualism and traditional morality in a protest against the relativism and permis-siveness of modern society. Of the two types, the mystical-therapeutic was numerically the largest. The symbolic significance of the two streams, according to Wuthnow (1988), was to broaden and refine the outer limits of religious respectability. The mystical-therapeutic pushed to the left; the neo-fundamentalist pushed to the right. Although the "new" movements of the 1960s are still among us, both their visibility and their energy have dissipated. The dis-sipating wake of the mystical-therapeutic appears to have merged in the 1980s as a part of the amorphous "New Age" movement. The neo-fundamentalist stream of the movement appears to have been co-opted into the more established net-works of conservative, and especially Pentecostal/Holiness, Protestantism.

The Broader Context of Religious Change

Many people agree with theologian Robert Hudnut's (1975) assertion: "Church growth is not the point." But even if one disagrees on theological grounds, Hudnut's statement is a helpful reminder that church membership and participation are just one of several dimensions of individual religiosity, and membership growth is only one of many priorities competing for denominational and congregational attention. From the perspective of church growth these "other" dimensions of religiosity and denominational attention provide the broader context of religious change that shapes and is shaped by membership trends.

National public opinion polls provide a helpful reading of trends in individual religiosity and perceptions of organized religion since the 1940s. Indeed, since the early 1970s the amount of public opinion poll data on religion is almost overwhelming. Fortunately for present purposes, the Princeton Religion Index (Princeton Religion Research Center, 1990) provides a concise summary of the extensive and extended religious soundings of the Gallup poll. To the extent that a single "best" empirical barometer of the United States' religious climate exists, it is the Princeton Religion Index. The index is a composite of several measures of individual religious belief and practice, self-perceived saliency of religion in one's life, and attitudes toward organized religion. Figure 1.9 includes a listing of the different items included in the composite. More importantly, Figure 1.9 shows both the fifty-year trend in the index, and a more focused look at the trend during the 1980s.

The most dramatic image in the index's fifty-year trend, and perhaps the most important perspective it adds to our understanding of membership trends, is that the 1960s represent a profoundly transitional decade for religion in the United States. The tipping of mainline Protestantism from growth to decline in 1965 is only one manifestation of a much broader seismic shift in American religion.

As noted in the discussion of market share as a measure of contextual opportunity, the percentage of the U.S. population who are church members has only declined five percentage points since the 1950s. In comparing this to the index's fifty-year trend, a second helpful perspective on membership trends emerges. Church membership has declined considerably less since the 1950s than has the overall religious climate. The scale of the index distorts the visual magnitude of the comparison to some extent, but the general point is still true. The overall religious climate as measured in the index has declined about twice as much as church membership since 1950.

FIGURE 1.9
Fifty-Year Trend in the Princeton Religion Index*

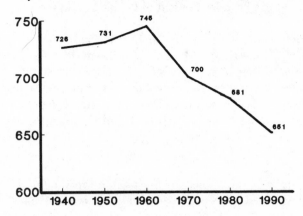

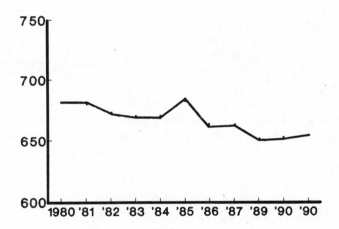

* PRINCETON RELIGION INDEX
IS A COMPOSITE OF:

Belief in God
Having a Religious Preference
Believing Religion Can Answer Today's Problems
Church Membership
Confidence in Organized Religion
Feeling Clergy are Honest
Viewing Religion as Very Imoportant in One's Life
Church/Synagogue Attendance

Switching to the index's trend through the 1980s, one sees that the traumatic plunge of the 1960s has given way to a plateau of stability. But like the membership trends for the 1980s seen in Figure 1.3, and despite a few minor blips up and down, the overall pattern is one of creeping decline. Nevertheless, a careful comparison of the index trend for the 1980s to the overall trend in church membership for the same period suggests that even during the 1980s the slowing of membership growth rates was slightly less than the downward movement in the broader religious climate.

Research of the late 1970s was quite specific in locating the major source of the religious reversal of the 1960s. It was a unique set of social and cultural changes carried along by the baby boom generation's movement into young adulthood. This now taken-for-granted fact is documented in the research literature with chart after chart showing how dramatically less religious the boomer cohort was from previous generations on just about every measure of religion for which data were available (see, for example, Hoge and Roozen, 1979).

Given the centrality of cohort differences for understanding the religious reversal of the 1960s, it is interesting to look at how cohort trends in religion have played out since then. Figures 1.10 and 1.11 do just that, the first for prayer and the second for worship attendance. Each figure includes the trend for five cohorts ranging from those born prior to World War II to those born after 1965 (post baby boom). Each figure also includes the total population trend (i.e., all cohorts combined). Each figure is based on data from the National Opinion Research Center's General Social Survey series. One covers the period 1975 to 1990; the other covers the period 1983 to 1990.

A few summary comments must suffice. First, in comparison to the dramatic divergence in cohort religious belief and practice during the 1960s, the trend lines in Figures 1.10 and 1.11 are strikingly parallel. That is, the cohorts all tend to move up or down together. The dynamics of religious change in the 1980s have affected all cohorts equally. Second, looking at just the 1990 level of prayer in Figure 1.10 and worship attendance in Figure 1.11 for each cohort, one finds the cohorts arranged in exactly the same order—the youngest cohort at the lowest level and the oldest cohort at the highest level. This is in stark contrast to the situation in the early 1950s, when age differences in religion were minimal (e.g., Roozen, 1979). One result of the religious transition of the sixties, therefore, appears to be the creation of an enduring stratification of religious expression by age.

Third, in Figure 1.11 one sees a pattern that is important to the argument of several chapters in this book. There is more movement in each of the cohort trends than in the overall trend. Indeed, the upward movement for each cohort is distinct; but the overall trend barely moves at all. The overall

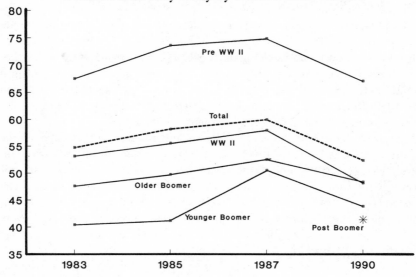

FIGURE 1.10
Percent Who Pray Daily by Cohort: 1983–1990

Source: NORC General Social Surveys

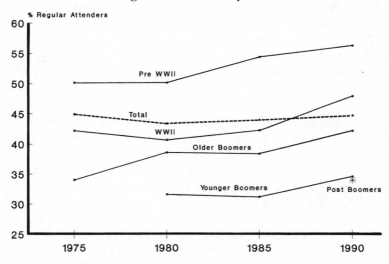

FIGURE 1.11
Percent Regular Attenders by Cohort: 1975–1990*

% Regular Attenders

•Regular attenders are those indicating that they attended at least
least two or three times a month

Source: NORC General Social Surveys

trend increases less than any of the individual cohorts because of the interrelationship between the age stratification in religion noted above, and what demographers call "cohort replacement." The specifics of cohort replacement are too complex to explain here.[7] The important point for now is that, as previously seen for church membership, if one only looks at the overall trend, one would miss significant movement among critical subgroups.

Finally, in both Figures 1.10 and 1.11, from the early to mid-1980s the "total" trend moves upward, consistent with the mid-1980s upward blip in the Princeton Religion Index (Figure 1.9). But from the mid-1980s to 1990, the total prayer and worship attendance trends move in opposite directions—prayer downward, worship attendance ever so slightly upward. As was suggested in the comparison of membership trends to the Princeton Religion Index's fifty-year trend, religious participation trends are at least somewhat independent from the trends in other dimensions of religiosity.

In the broad sweep provided by a comparison of the index's trend and that of membership since 1950, the independence of membership from the overall religious climate manifests itself through the fact that the downward trend in membership is less severe than that for the index. The significance of this fact comes into clearer focus when it is further noted that the index is weighted toward measures of traditional belief and commitment. The divergence in the two trends means, therefore, that an increasing number of church members are nontraditional in their belief and commitment. This may hardly seem like a startling observation, especially for church leaders in mainline Protestantism. But if Wuthnow (1988) is correct that the driving force in the restructuring of American religion is not an increasing polarization between the churched and the unchurched, or an increasing polarization between liberal and conservative denominations, but rather the increasing polarization between liberal and traditional church members within denominations; then the shifting balance of these two groups will be critical to the future of denominational religion.

A Framework for Understanding Church Growth

The organization of the chapters in this book follows from the simple fact: Denominations grow as individuals join congregations. Each one is a source of initiative or response in the overall growth equation. Accordingly, the reader will find three major sections in the book, each containing several chapters, each chapter reporting original research. The first section focuses on denominations; the second section focuses on congregations; and the third section focuses on the individual. Each section begins with a brief introduction that not only serves to set its chapters within the broader context of research related to the section topic, but also summarizes the major conclusions of each chapter.

The denomination-congregation-individual organization of the book should not be interpreted, however, to mean that the three are unrelated. Indeed, they form an interrelated whole in the overall growth equation—each shaping and shaped by the others. An exploration of church membership initiated at one level inevitably leads to questions about the others. The concluding chapter by Hadaway, therefore, does not attempt to summarize each chapter (this is done in the section introductions). Rather, it provides an integrated interpretation of the whole. It does so first from the perspective of the interrelationship among denomination, congregation, and social-cultural changes that enter the growth equation through individuals. It then uses this integrated perspective to address the possibilities for future growth within different denominational families.

Although we use the growth = denomination + congregation + individual equation to structure the organization of chapters, the reader will find another important framework for understanding church growth and decline very much in evidence. It is from *Understanding Church Growth and Decline: 1950–1978* (Hoge and Roozen, 1979), a book that is the inspiration for the current collection of research. As one of the first cross-denominational studies of church growth and decline, and the first major piece after Dean Kelley's *Why Conservative Churches Are Growing* (1972), *Understanding Church Growth and Decline: 1950–1978* received a good bit of attention—both positive and negative. But one thing that just about everyone found helpful was the book's broad conceptual framework for thinking about the multitude of factors that affect membership trends. The framework contained four categories developed by crosscutting two dimensions. One dimension ran from the local level (of the congregation) to the national level. The second dimension distinguished between those things largely outside the church's control, which were called contextual factors, and those things internal to the life of congregations or denominations that were more or less subject to their control, which were called institutional factors. The four categories produced by crosscutting the two dimensions, are:

- National contextual factors—pervasive social and cultural trends
- National institutional factors—denominational ethos, polity, and program
- Local contextual factors—unique social, cultural, and demographic aspects of a local congregation's immediate environment
- Local institutional factors—the ethos, structure, and program of local congregations

The research and interpretation in this book takes the Hoge and Roozen distinction between context and institutional, and applies it to each of our three levels—the denomination, the congregation, and the individual. The section on denominations, therefore, addresses the interplay between national contextual and national institutional factors. The section on congregations addresses the interplay between local contextual and local institutional factors. And the section on individuals addresses both how social and cultural forces (contextual factors), and how characteristics and perceptions of congregations and denominations (institutional factors) influence individual decisions about whether or not to become church members.

Part One

DENOMINATIONAL GROWTH AND DECLINE

C. Kirk Hadaway and David A. Roozen

A t the end of each year, denominational research (or yearbook) offices tally their total number of churches and the total number of members included in those churches. If the number of members added through new churches and through the growth of existing churches exceeds the number of members lost, the denomination grew. If losses through declining churches and through the closing of congregations exceeds the number of members gained, the denomination declined. Then the good news (or bad) is handed over to anxious denominational executives.

Interestingly, less than two percentage points separated the growth of the Southern Baptist Convention and the decline of The United Methodist Church in 1988. Spread among over seventy-five thousand churches in the two denominations, that difference is minuscule. So comparing a typical Southern Baptist church with a typical United Methodist church does not sufficiently explain the growth of one denomination or the decline of the other.

The complex equation that results in growth or decline at the denominational level is the subject of the chapters in this section. Why do some denominations grow and others decline? As we see it, denominational growth is heavily affected by the national context. Denominational growth is also affected by what Hoge and Roozen (1979) call national institutional factors. These factors include denominational character (what a denomination *is*) and denominational actions (what a denomination *does*). And although the three (context, character, and actions) are separated for purposes of discussion, they are very much related.

Denominational Growth Is Affected by the National Context

All three chapters in this section underscore the strong link between denominational membership trends and changes in the national context. The chapter by Marler and Hadaway shows that a profound "period effect" influenced most denominations over the past thirty years. This leads to our first point.

FIGURE P1.1
Membership Change in Six Conservative and Eight Mainline Denominations

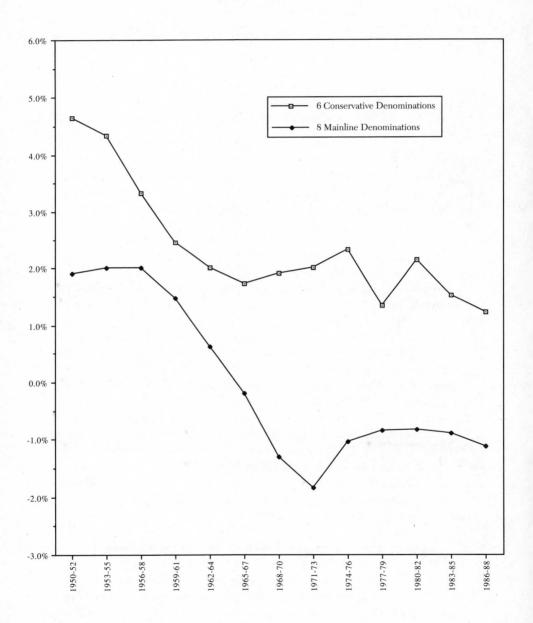

> **Major mainline and conservative denominations share virtually identical patterns of membership change.**

Denominations, mainline and conservative alike, experienced rapid growth in the 1950s. But as early as the mid-1950s average rates of percentage membership growth began to decline. This decline was steady and drastic until it reached a low point in 1972. At that point, growth rates bottomed out, rebounded slightly, then fell more slowly. With the notable exception of smaller Pentecostal/Holiness groups (see chapter 1), there was no conservative resurgence in the 1970s. Conservative church growth paralleled the decline of the mainline. This pattern can be seen in Figure P1.1.[1]

Why did diverse denominations experience similar patterns of membership change? Part of the answer is demographic. And the link of demographic transitions to church membership trends is clear and direct. Rates of membership growth dropped along with the birthrate and population growth. The proportion of young children in the population also declined. This leads to our second point.

> **Denominational growth is heavily influenced by the birthrate.**

As shown in Figure P1.2, the link between the white birthrate and membership change is particularly strong. Why? Obviously, the relationship is tied to the supply of young children of "baptizable" age. Denominations tend to grow as the supply of potential members increases. Interestingly, however, the correlation between the sheer supply of young children and membership change is lower than the correlation between the birthrate and membership change. The birthrate is especially important because it reflects changes in social attitudes regarding children and families *and* changes in the supply of young children. Churches are for families—particularly families with children (or families that used to have children) (Marler, 1992). Mainline and conservative churches do better in eras when having children is perceived as important.[2] Demographic studies show that the birthrate dropped during the 1950s and 1960s. Further, the proportion of married couple households with children also fell, and continues to fall. The economy, the movement toward two-income households, and the passage of the baby boom generation through the family life cycle all influenced this change. The extent of these demographic changes is also tied to changes in the general culture. Smaller families become the norm, rather than the exception, and being single loses much of its social stigma. The church was affected both by demographic and cultural change.

FIGURE P1.2
Period Effect and White Birthrate: 1950–1988

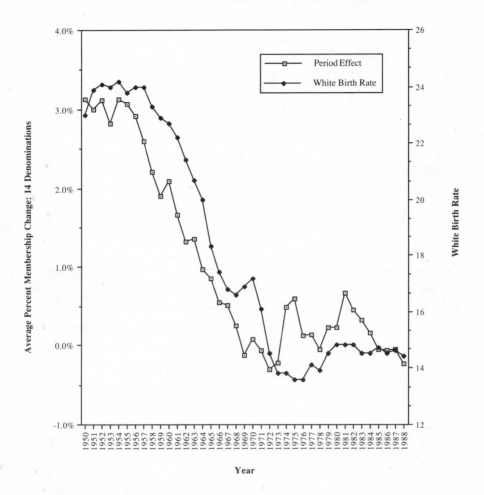

Cultural shifts affect denominational growth through changes in priorities.

Cultural change affects what people see as important. Priorities change. One of the ways that cultural change affects the church is through denominational structure and actions. As shown by Greer, particularly, and also by

Green and Light, denominational priorities changed as the culture did. This is especially true for the mainline. To some extent, new denominational priorities were necessary because of new socio-economic realities. For example, new churches were more costly and more difficult to start in the 1970s. Nevertheless, most of the change in structure and policy can be traced to changing ideology. In the case of the American Baptist Churches, Greer notes that "evangelism which aimed solely for individual conversion was (seen as) too narrow and simplistic, failing to challenge all of society with the full claims of the gospel." Evangelism was redefined and "a new church development famine ensued" as "other priorities concerned BNM (Board of National Ministries) staff, including the political and cultural upheaval of the nation."

Denominational Growth Is Affected by Denominational Character

A shared national context explains parallel patterns of decline in percentage rates of membership growth, but it does not explain continuing differences in the numerical "bottom line" between conservative and mainline denominations. Conservative denominations may have experienced slower growth at the same time that the mainline experienced decline—but conservatives remained "in the black." This gap existed in the 1950s and persists today.

> *Conservative denominations are still growing; the mainline is still in decline.*

The pattern of conservative denominational growth and mainline decline has been constant since the mid-1960s. And as Marler and Hadaway point out in the first chapter of this section, conservative denominations were growing faster, on average, than mainline denominations—even in the 1950s. Some of this growth differential was due to demographics. Indeed, conservative denominations have higher birthrates on average than mainline denominations (Roof and McKinney, 1987). Conservative denominations also have younger constituencies, and some are concentrated in growing areas of the nation. Yet these differences alone do not explain the numerical gap between conservative and mainline denominations.

> *Conservatism is related to growth, but not to strictness.*

Dean Kelley's *Why Conservative Churches Are Growing* set the stage for research, controversy, and confusion over the sources of church growth and decline among conservative and mainline denominations. Kelley's book is more about denominational growth than it is about the growth of local churches, and it is more about institutional vitality than it is about growth. In fact, in a later article Kelley noted that a more appropriate title of his book would have been, "Why Strict Churches Are Strong."

Research has provided little support for what has been called "the Kelley thesis." Conservative churches are more likely to grow than liberal/mainline churches (in most studies, but see Thompson, Carroll, and Hoge in this volume). Conservative denominations also are more likely to grow than liberal/mainline denominations. Strictness (Kelley's main point), however, is unrelated to growth within liberal or conservative families. Kelley's "theory" is best understood as one of sectarian survival—not congregational or denominational growth. The theory explains how sectarian groups maintain their viability in a culture that does not share their values. Yet it neither explains the growth of sectarian groups that are strict nor the growth of conservative, nonsectarian groups that are not strict. Even more telling is the fact that Kelley's theory fails to explain why strict, nonevangelical sects frequently experience very little growth.

What is it about conservatism that produces growth? Two factors stand out: (1) a higher level of ideological commitment to evangelistic action, and (2) a lower level of secularism. Conservative denominations tend to be evangelical, and this evangelicalism is related to growth-producing actions such as personal evangelism and new church development. Conservative denominations also are less secularized. Along with a stable, concrete set of traditional beliefs, they retain a greater sense of otherworldliness. As such, churches in conservative denominations are better able to maintain strong symbolic boundaries between what is religious and what is not (see Hunter, 1983). All other things being equal, this characteristic encourages growth because religious meaning separates churches from other voluntary, communal institutions.

Some conservative denominations are "resilient."

Marler and Hadaway suggest that some denominations act like social movements. Commitment is high and goals are widely shared. Leaders and members feel that they have a mission to convert the nation. As a result, growth-related actions are less affected by the context because great effort will be made despite the appropriateness of such actions. If the times (or the territory) discourage proselytizing, resilient denominations are usually up to the task. Whether twenty or a hundred calls are needed to "harvest a lost soul," they will be made; whether a neighborhood is demographically "favorable" for growth or not, a new church is just as likely to take root and flourish there.

High levels of commitment and ideological fervor, however, tend to encourage volatility. In fact, churches in denominations like the Assemblies of God have a "boom or bust" quality. Large numbers are growing, but large numbers also are declining. And unlike mainline denominations or older conservative denominations, the Assemblies of God has fewer stable churches.

In some ways, more resilient, movement-like denominations are similar to older conservative denominations, and in some ways, they are very different. As shown by Marler and Hadaway, groups like the Southern Baptist Convention and the Lutheran Church, Missouri Synod have large numbers of stable, plateaued congregations. In this respect, these traditionalistic conservative denominations look more like the mainline. One feature that groups like the Assemblies of God and Southern Baptists share, however, is the fact that much of their growth comes from large entrepreneurial, independent-minded congregations. Mainline denominations have fewer congregations of this type.

Denominational Growth Is Affected by Denominational Actions in the Case of the Mainline

Mainline denominations were hurt by changes in the national context, and they have neither an evangelistic ethos nor organizational resilience. This may explain the declining growth rates of the mainline in the 1950s and the parallel trends in mainline and conservative growth rates in the 1960s, 1970s, and 1980s. But it does not completely explain why the mainline actually lost members from 1965 to the present. Marler and Hadaway's research suggests that mainline membership trends are related to denominational priorities. This link is important, because as seen in the other two chapters (particularly the chapter by Greer) there were major shifts in denominational priorities during the 1970s.

Mainline priorities changed.

In some mainline denominations the meaning of evangelism changed. Greer points out that in other mainline denominations evangelism and new church development retained their historic meaning but lost personnel, budget dollars, and organizational visibility. Other priorities—particularly those related to ecumenism, organizational restructuring, and social justice—came to the forefront. If programmatic emphasis on growth-oriented procedures is related to growth, then it is not surprising that mainline denominations experienced more difficulties than conservative denominations.

Conservative denominations were not immune to the changes that affected the priorities of mainline agencies. In the Southern Baptist Convention during the 1970s, traditional approaches to new church development were replaced with experimental techniques in a few areas. While there was increased emphasis on social justice concerns in some conservative denominations, there was never a complete reorientation of denominational priorities, however. Traditional evangelism and new church development efforts continued to receive the lion's share of denominational mission funds.

> **Changed denominational priorities produce new (and unexpected) challenges.**

What denominations do at the national level makes a difference. This is seen clearly in Green and Light's case study of the American Baptist Churches. Changing denominational priorities resulted in a policy of racial inclusion. New African-American churches were started and existing African-American churches were invited to join the ABC. Other denominations had similar emphases, but none were as successful as the ABC. The result is a significant shift in the racial balance of this traditionally white denomination.

Without adding black churches, the membership trend for the ABC would look much like that of the UCC or the Presbyterian Church (U.S.A.). By adding black churches, the ABC avoided severe membership losses. Yet radical change in the policies and constituency of the ABC led to an unexpected consequence. It has accelerated the loss of white churches and white members. Further, differences in assumptions regarding denominational support place a greater and greater financial burden on the remaining white churches in the ABC.

A change in denominational priorities in all mainline denominations resulted in fewer new churches. This is clear in all three chapters in this section. Staff cuts and declining interest in new church development combined with higher start-up costs and decreased success rates to produce this effect.

Mainline membership trends are tied to denominational priorities.

Marler and Hadaway conclude that mainline denominational growth is related to goal-directed planning. All other things being equal, mainline denominations increase their chances for growth when they place a high priority on growth-related tasks. Mainline denominations are affected by the culture and the birthrate. But the evidence suggests that they could grow, or at least moderate their declines, by re-emphasizing evangelism and new church development.

From a sociological perspective, we have a relatively good grasp of what helps and what hinders growth. But what price are denominational executives (and their loyal congregations) willing to pay to change their priorities? Talk of "price" and "priorities" raises the issue of base commitments and ultimate concerns. And rightly so, for behind convenient sociological solutions, this question tests deeper, soteriological convictions.

Re-energized growth programs must compete for dollars and priority.

To some extent, mainline denominations have re-emphasized church growth. Yet Greer shows that funding levels for church growth have *not* kept pace with inflation. As a consequence, staff cuts have reduced new church development efforts to minimal levels. Evangelism and new church development now compete with many other programs for money and clout. While these programs are no longer considered "embarrassing" by mainline denominational officials, they have not regained their former prominence. In an era of slow population growth, high divorce rates, high building costs, and increased competition for time, denominations must work harder than ever to prevent membership loss. For the mainline, church growth efforts to date have not been sufficient to reverse numerical decline.

Chapter Two

New Church Development and Denominational Growth (1950–1988):

Symptom or Cause?*

Penny Long Marler and C. Kirk Hadaway

*If you want to grow something to last a season—
plant flowers.
If you want to grow something to last a lifetime—
plant trees.
If you want to grow something to last through eternity—
plant churches.*
Anonymous, quoted in Hesselgrave (1980:38)

S tatistics from several American Protestant denominations provide unprecedented opportunity to explore the impact of new church development. An analysis of the post-World War II period is especially critical as these several decades have witnessed a veritable "boom and bust" in both new church development (hereafter NCD) and denominational membership growth. Indeed, data are rich, if not perfect, enabling us to examine a few older theories and some newer hunches.

In a recent survey of twentieth-century Presbyterian new church development, Bullock (1991:27) concludes:

New church development is a necessary but not a sufficient condition for overall denominational membership growth. Vital denominations will engage in new church development and expand, regardless of the economics. Churches that lack a core vitality will decline. The lack of a strong new church development program, therefore, is as much a symptom of deeper underlying problems as it is the cause of denominational decline.

So, Bullock has determined that NCD is more likely a "symptom" of membership growth or vitality across a denomination. The inference is that simply

47

beginning an aggressive program of NCD will not guarantee membership growth in a given denomination. Instead, NCD appears to be just one component—albeit an important one—of a denomination-wide growth trend. While this claim seems plausible, Bullock provides little evidence of the specific factors that contribute to overall denominational "vitality."

Bullock argues that the slowdown in NCD (and membership growth) is the direct result of: (1) changes in denominational priorities from evangelism and church extension to social justice issues; (2) the rising costs of new churches; and (3) in general, an increasingly specialized and fragmented denominational bureaucracy (see also Brooks, 1990). His observations are similar to those voiced years earlier by Ezra Earl Jones, a prominent United Methodist executive. Jones named high building costs, the over-churching of the suburbs in the 1950s, and the failure to meet the church development needs of racial and ethnic groups in the inner cities as the sources of denominational woes (Jones, 1976:10ff.).

However, even growing denominations—like the Southern Baptist Convention and the Assemblies of God—started fewer churches from the mid-1960s to the mid-1970s. Membership growth rates also declined among these evangelical denominations. During the same period, NCD in the mainline dropped perilously, and declines in membership followed. Several commentators point to the general social and political turmoil of those years as the source of the overall slowdown (Towns, Vaughan, and Seifert, 1987). Perhaps, but as Jones (1976) hints, it is also likely that past church extension activity and racial unrest were at least indirectly related. The white, middle-class suburbanization of the 1950s (and the accompanying "churching" of the population in these areas) exacerbated the social and economic problems of inner cities and their largely racial/ethnic populations (Winter 1962). Symptom or cause?

In response to a denomination-wide pinch during the 1960s, mainliners retreated to a "survival-goal" theme (Perry, 1979; see also Metz, 1967:103-16). The focus of denominational activity narrowed to institutional survival. And, in the push-and-pull of a number of interest groups, church extension was explicitly or implicitly adjudged too costly, too tainted by white, middle-class stigma, or too "evangelical." Consequently, rates of NCD plunged—and so did overall denominational membership.

Evangelicals, on the other hand, translated membership declines as a lack of evangelistic zeal. They responded with increasing attention to personal witnessing programs, church planting, and the burgeoning "church growth" movement (Amberson, 1979; Brock, 1981; Chaney, 1982; Hesselgrave, 1980; Hodges, 1973; McGavran and Arn, 1974, 1977; Moorhous, 1975; Towns, 1975; Redford, 1978; Starr, 1978; Tidsworth, 1979; Wagner, 1976). The results in most cases included increases in NCD and renewed membership growth—although percentage gains for most evangelical denominations began a downward turn in the 1980s (despite continued programs of church extension).

What is the lesson of the post-World War II period? Denomination-watchers conclude that economics, priorities, and careful planning are important. But most agree that something more is at work in denominations that thrive numerically in spite of adverse social, geographic, institutional, and economic circumstances. Bullock (1991:27) calls it vitality; Schaller (1991:229) dubs it "Great Commission Growth"; Melvin Hodges (1973:25-27), an Assemblies of God spokesperson, unabashedly calls it the Holy Spirit. Descriptively, the characteristic might be best labeled "resilience": the organizational ability to recover from or adjust easily to misfortune or change.

Happily, Schaller (1991), provides some handles for quantifying the complex relationship between NCD and denominational growth. These are measurable "hunches" that flow from his wealth of practice wisdom:

1. Newer denominations grow faster and start more churches than do older denominations.
2. Denominational growth is strongly related to two factors: new church development and growth in average congregation size.
3. Growing denominations have started at least 20% of their churches within the last twenty-five years.
4. New churches grow faster if they start larger, that is, with at least 200 at the first worship service.
5. Churches tend to grow fastest in high population areas experiencing rapid rates of in-migration.

Fortunately, the data on hand allow us to test Schaller's hypotheses—and even to extend them. For example, the growing number of racial/ethnic church starts and racial/ethnic affiliations raises questions about their contributions to denominational growth. On the subject of congregational size, Schaller's observation about increasing size is at odds with a hunch that the presence of a "superchurch" suppresses the number of new church starts in a given locale. These and other provocative possibilities are pursued in this study.

Because of our explicit interest in denominational growth and decline, NCD is examined with an eye to this larger relationship. With clear indebtedness to Schaller and others, the following analysis tests three primary assumptions:

Assumption 1. Growing denominations have higher rates of NCD and an increasing average congregation size.

Assumption 2. Growing denominations plant churches in areas that are "geographically favorable"—that is, in areas of high population growth, high in-migration rates, and/or unchurched people groups.

Assumption 3. Growing denominations demonstrate *resilience* to the degree that they adapt to changing social conditions and sustain growth across congregational age, size, and location factors.

Findings Related to Assumption Number 1: Rates of NCD, Average Congregation Size, and Denominational Growth

New Church Starts: Trends

The first step in unraveling a possible relationship between NCD and denominational growth is to examine trends in NCD in several denominations from 1950 to 1988. Our purpose is to show whether there is any discernible pattern to NCD activity in various denominations over time; and if there is, we wish to determine if such a pattern parallels trends in denominational growth over the same period. To accomplish this task, yearly data on NCD were collected from denominational agencies and matched with denominational yearbook data on membership. Complete information was obtained from five denominations.[1]

FIGURE 2.1
New Churches for Five Denominations: 1950–1988

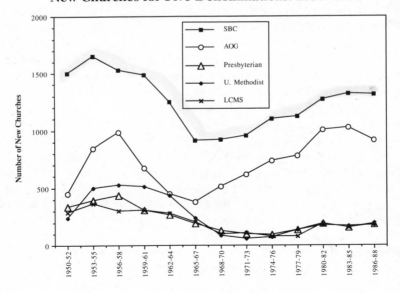

As can be seen in Figure 2.1, there *is* a definite pattern to NCD activity over the past twenty-eight years. For evangelical and mainline denominations alike, the late 1950s were very good years for NCD. By the early 1960s, however, NCD activity was beginning to subside. For the two evangelical denominations (the Southern Baptist Convention and the Assemblies of God) the low ebb was reached in the mid- to late-1960s, with the years 1965-67 recording the lowest levels of NCD. For mainline denominations, the decline began at the same time, but rather than turning around in the early 1970s, NCD levels continued to decline well into the 1970s.

In the two evangelical denominations, NCD rebounded strongly in the 1970s. In recent years NCD activity in the Southern Baptist Convention has almost reached the levels recorded by this denomination in the 1950s. The Assemblies of God has done even better. This denomination started more new churches in the 1980s than it started in the 1950s.

New church development among mainline denominations also rebounded—although it took longer to do so. However, levels of NCD in the 1980s remain far below those recorded during the 1950s and the first half of the 1960s. In fact, the mainline denominations seem to have converged on about the same number of new churches to start each year (even though these denominations vary widely in size, and presumably in resources available for NCD).[2]

Trends in Denominational Membership

For anyone who has observed denominational trends over the past several decades, it should be apparent that the downturn in NCD occurred at about the same time that mainline denominations began to plateau and then decline in membership (see Kelley, 1977:3-8; Roozen and Carroll, 1979:22-25).[3] In Figure 2.1, it can be seen that membership problems began in earnest around 1965-68 for the three mainline denominations that are included. The decline among United Methodists (UMC) and Presbyterians (PCUSA) began earlier than for the Lutheran Church, Missouri Synod (LCMS); it also has continued longer, and has been more serious in magnitude among these two mainline bodies.[4] The two evangelical denominations, on the other hand, have grown during the entire twenty-eight-year period displayed in the figure. For Southern Baptists (SBC), the growth has been slow and steady, while for the Assemblies of God (AOG) it appears rapid and fitful. It should be noted, however, that the abrupt shifts in 1971 and 1979 for the Assemblies of God were statistical adjustments rather than one-year surges in membership growth.[5] Even if we ignore the two artificial jumps, growth still has been impressive for the Assemblies of God.

FIGURE 2.2
Membership for Five Denominations: 1949–1988

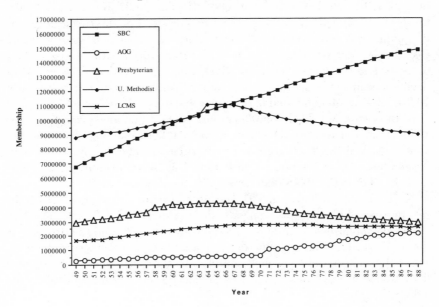

Mainline decline, when compared to continued evangelical growth, has led some observers to suggest that evangelical denominations have grown at the expense of the mainline, or that there has been something of a conservative resurgence during this period (see Roof and McKinney, 1987:23-25). The membership curves seen in Figure 2.2 show what seems to be steady growth—growth that was not affected by the social and cultural changes that devastated mainline denominations during the same period. This is misleading, however, because the figure does not show what happened to the *rate* of membership growth among evangelical denominations. Growth continued, but these denominations grew less rapidly than before. In Figure 2.3, for instance, it can be seen that the rate of membership growth for the Southern Baptist Convention declined almost unabated from 1950 to 1970. Southern Baptist churches avoided decline at an aggregate level, but the SBC certainly experienced no true resurgence during the past three decades. In fact, SBC growth is now at its lowest level ever.[6] Clearly, the social and cultural changes affecting the mainline also affected evangelical denominations.

Another interesting twist to denominational membership trends over the past several decades is that changes in the average size of congregations precisely parallel the membership curves shown in Figure 2.2 (see Figure 2.4

FIGURE 2.3
Membership Change in the SBC by Year: 1950–1988

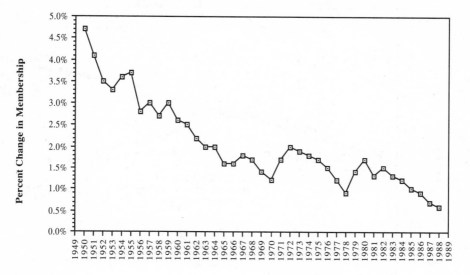

for trends in average size). As noted earlier, Schaller (1991) hypothesized that growing denominations should experience increases in average congregational size. His hypothesis is confirmed, and perhaps this should not be too surprising—since average congregational size is simply the total membership of a denomination divided by its number of churches. Still, the similarity between the patterns seems rather amazing, because it does not have to be so close. A growing denomination could record all of its gains through the accumulation of new small churches, and thereby decline in average size. On the other hand, a plateaued denomination *could* experience an increase in the average size of its congregations if it was closing many smaller churches. However, it would appear that a drop in average size of congregations seems to occur along with: (1) overall membership losses; (2) declines in a denomination's number of congregations; and (3) drops in NCD. Conversely, the historical pattern for many denominations shows that overall membership growth is accompanied by growth in average congregational size. In fact, without this effect, membership growth would have eluded many denominations in years past because NCD rates were too low to keep up with the loss of congregations—much less to add to the rate of membership growth by increasing the total number of congregations.

FIGURE 2.4
Average Size of Churches in Five Denominations

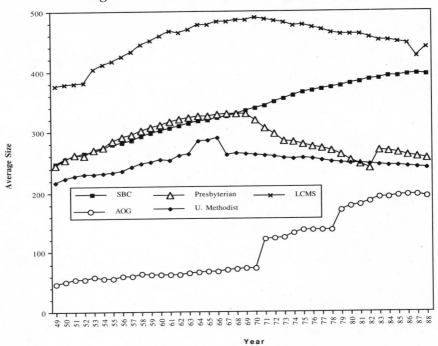

Membership Change Compared to Rates of New Church Development

If there is a link between NCD and denominational growth we would expect that the historical pattern of membership change since 1949 should look roughly (or precisely) similar to the pattern of new church starts. That is, percentage rates of membership growth should be high in the 1950s and early 1960s, decline in the mid- to late-1960s, continue to be low during much of the 1970s, and then rebound in the late 1970s or early 1980s. In the next series of figures we look at this relationship within five denominations.

In the Southern Baptist Convention it is obvious that the decline in denominational membership growth paralleled a drop in NCD from 1952 to 1973. Declines in the rate of membership growth were accompanied by declines in the new church start rate (new churches per 1,000 existing congregations), and when the decline in membership change bottomed out and began to increase slightly in the early 1970s, a similar pattern occurred in NCD. However, from 1973 to 1988, the patterns diverged. NCD continued at rather high levels, while membership growth dropped. A scattergram (not shown here) of the relationship between the NCD rate and denominational growth reveals a similar pattern—an almost perfect correlation through 1973, and virtually no correlation thereafter. Schaller's hypothesis that growing denominations start more churches—regardless of social conditions—may be relevant here. However, there is some question as to whether this is a sign of "resilience" within the Southern Baptist Convention or an organized bureaucratic response to the slowdown in membership growth. (See Figure 2.5.)

FIGURE 2.5
SBC NCD Rate and Percent Membership Change

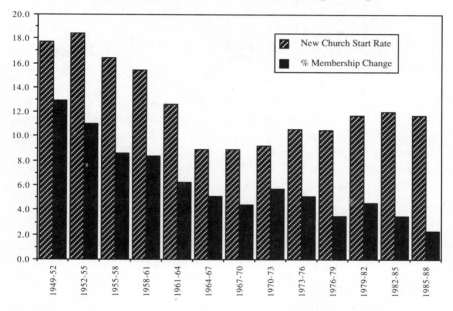

For the Assemblies of God the similarity between historical patterns of NCD and denominational growth is clear, but the erratic nature of membership change makes interpretation somewhat more difficult. However, if the odd fluctuations are ignored the two change curves seem remarkably similar. The best years were during the 1950s. Rates began to slow in the late 1950s and throughout the 1960s. The picture became more positive in the 1970s, especially in NCD, before sliding in both areas during the 1980s. Even though the directional pattern of change in both areas tends to be parallel for the Assemblies of God, the fluctuations in the growth rate should reduce the correlation between rates of NCD and percent membership change. (See Figure 2.6.)

FIGURE 2.6
Assembly NCD Rate and Percent Membership Change

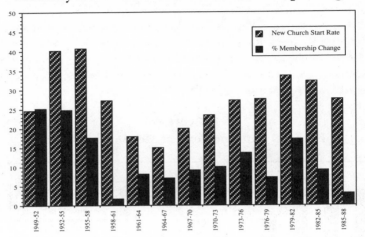

For the three mainline denominations, patterns of NCD and membership change also tend to co-vary. New church start rates were highest in the era of greatest denominational growth and lowest in the era of most severe denominational decline. Further, in more recent years (from the mid- to late-1970s and in the early 1980s) new church start rates have increased and membership declines have moderated.

FIGURE 2.7
Presbyterian NCD Rate and Percent Membership Change

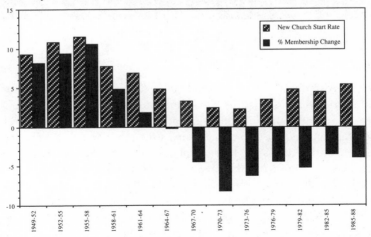

For the Presbyterians the declines in membership were most serious from 1970 to 1976, but losses have continued at a rather alarming rate into the 1980s. The new church start rate has followed the same pattern. The rate of NCD was highest in 1955 to 1958, as was the rate of membership growth. The lowest years of NCD came in 1970 to 1976, and it was during this six-year interval that membership losses were the greatest for Presbyterians. (See Figure 2.7.)

For the United Methodists, membership losses were most severe from 1967 to 1973. However, it should be noted that the severity of the losses (in percentage terms) has never been as great as for the Presbyterian Church. Declines have continued for the United Methodists to the present without much fluctuation. Like the Presbyterians, membership losses were most severe at the same time that the NCD rate reached its lowest levels—1967 to 1973. Both areas have seen slight improvements since then, but there is no sign that would suggest that a return to growth is imminent. (See Figure 2.8.)

FIGURE 2.8
Methodist NCD Rate and Percent Membership Change

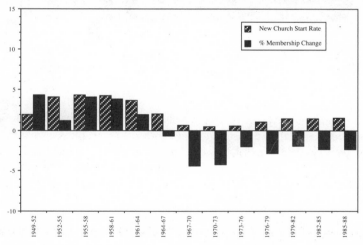

For the Lutheran Church, Missouri Synod, the transition from rapid growth to membership decline took longer. The membership growth rate began to drop in the mid-1950s and continued to slide into the late 1970s. The worst years of loss came in the 1976–79 period. This was during the period of schism. It has been estimated that perhaps as much as two-thirds of the decline over this three-year period resulted from the loss of churches during the denominational conflict.[7] The LCMS gained members over the next six years, before losing again in the latest three-year period (1985–88).

NCD was highest in the 1950s—higher in terms of the *rate* than the Southern Baptist Convention during this period. A long, steep decline followed, however, before the NCD rate reached its low ebb from 1973–79. Not surprisingly, this low point in NCD coincided with the years of greatest membership loss in the Lutheran Church, Missouri Synod. (See Figure 2.9.)

FIGURE 2.9
LCMS NCD Rate and Percent Membership Change

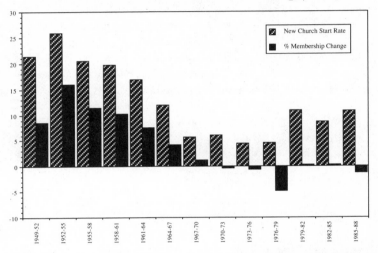

In the previous series of figures we also see evidence that the late 1980s have not been kind to American denominations. In fact, rates of membership change worsened in four of the five denominations during the last three years of study. Only The United Methodist Church avoided this pattern, but even here the rate of membership decline remained unchanged—it did not improve.

The Correlation Between New Church Development and Denominational Growth

It should be apparent that NCD rates and denominational membership change are highly correlated—even if a causal connection cannot be established. In order to measure the extent of this correlation we computed the rate of NCD as well as percent membership change for each year from 1950 to 1988.[8] The NCD rate was computed by multiplying the number of churches started in each year by 1,000 and then dividing this total by the number of churches in the denomination in the previous year. This gives the number of new churches started per 1,000 churches in the denomination.

When all denominations are combined, the correlation (Pearson's r) between the new church start rate and percent membership change was .76—a very strong correlation. Given the similarity in trends shown in the last series of charts, an even stronger correlation may have been anticipated. Part of the reason that the correlation was not higher might be traced to meaningless yearly fluctuations in the rates. However, when we recomputed the correlation based on three-year intervals, the Pearson's r coefficient was raised only slightly to .82. The major reason for the suppression in the correlation can be found in denominational differences.

For individual denominations the correlation between percent membership change and the NCD rate was strongest in the Presbyterian Church and in the Lutheran Church, Missouri Synod (r = .89). It was also extremely high for The United Methodist Church (r = .86) and for the Southern Baptist Convention (r = .78). However, it was a surprise to discover that the correlation for the Assemblies of God was much lower (only .46). The Pearson's r coefficients using one- and three-year intervals of measurement can be seen in Table 2.1.

TABLE 2.1
Correlation[1] Between Percent Membership Change and NCD Rate

	One-Year Intervals[2]	Three-Year Intervals
All Denominations	.76	.82
SBC	.78	.84
AOG	.46	.50
United Methodist	.86	.88
LCMS	.89	.94
Presbyterian	.89	.95

[1]Correlation coefficient is Pearson's r.

[2]Measurement of membership change and new church development was based on one-year intervals in this case. That is, percent membership change was computed from 1949 to 1950, from 1950 to 1951, and so forth. The new church development rate for 1950 was the number of new churches added to the denomination in 1950 per 1,000 existing churches in 1949.

It is interesting that the lowest correlations between new church starts and denominational growth are found among the two denominations with by far the highest rates of NCD. For the SBC, the slightly lower correlation can be attributed to the divergence of trends over the past decade. This denomination has continued to start churches at a rapid pace, while its membership growth rate has suffered. For the Assemblies of God this finding is somewhat harder to interpret. Even though the basic pattern of change among the two variables has been similar over the past twenty-eight years, the magnitude of change has been quite dissimilar in many of the years. In 1949 to 1952, for instance, the Assemblies of God had a relatively modest new church start rate (as compared to the rest of the 1950s for this denomination, not in comparison to other denominations), but grew dramatically in membership. New church development then rose substantially over the next six years. Membership growth remained strong from 1952 to 1955, but then fell off in 1955 to 1958. From 1958 to 1961 the NCD rate remained fairly high. However, membership growth plunged to a very low level. Similarly, in the 1980s, levels of new church development remain high, but denominational growth has slowed dramatically. This erratic pattern produced the lower correlation among the Assemblies of God. It should be noted, however, that a correlation of .50 is not low, by any standard. Still, it is in great contrast to coefficients among other denominations that approach a perfect correlation.

This "low" correlation among the Assemblies of God seems odd in light of the fact that their rate of NCD has been much higher than any other denomination. Further, in 1988, 21.7% of Assemblies of God churches reported a date of organization within the previous ten years. This is in contrast to 8.3% of SBC churches, 5.6% of Presbyterian churches, 4.7% of American Baptist Churches, and only 2.5% of United Church of Christ churches. The Assemblies of God is a young denomination, which is composed of newer churches. So it is clear that new churches are a major source of growth for the Assemblies of God. Why is the correlation not higher? It is possible that for the Assemblies of God high levels of NCD are a sign of organizational resilience. A resilient denomination will start many new churches in periods that do not encourage this activity and are not conducive to denominational growth.

For mainline denominations and for the Southern Baptist Convention, a high correlation between NCD and denominational membership change was expected and found. The meaning of this correlation is not readily apparent, however, because the actual number of members added through high levels of NCD or lost through low levels are not enough to explain the growth of the SBC or the declines of the mainline. One possible explanation for the high correlations is that rates of NCD may be a "barometer of the times." When the times are favorable to American churches, denominations will plant new churches, but when times are bad, few new church starts will be attempted. Is it possible that a "period effect" exists that may explain changes in NCD *and* changes in membership growth? To test this idea we computed an average membership change for each year from 1950 to 1988, based on fourteen denominations.[9] The resulting graph is shown in Figure 2.10. Its basic shape should be quite familiar, given the figures shown earlier. We then computed a partial correlation between NCD and percent membership change for each denomination controlling for this period effect. This was an effort to determine whether rates of membership growth tend to be higher in years when the NCD rate is higher, irrespective of the general pattern of membership change among Protestant denominations in American society.

FIGURE 2.10
Period Effects (Based on Fourteen Denominations)

Zero-order correlations between the period effect and membership change ranged from a "low" of .64 for the Assemblies of God to .94 for the Lutheran Church, Missouri Synod. Because of these strong relationships it was no surprise that the correlations between NCD and membership change were reduced when the statistical control was in effect. However, it was something of a surprise that the greatest reduction in correlation was for the Southern Baptist Convention and for the Lutheran Church,

Missouri Synod. In fact, for the SBC the correlation was reduced from .78 to − .30. (NCD rates remained positively associated with membership change in the LCMS, but the correlation was reduced greatly.) This reduction occurred because the correlation between the NCD rate and percent membership change was weaker than the correlation between: (1) the period effect and membership change, and (2) the period effect and the NCD rate. So for these two denominations, levels of both membership growth and NCD seem to be a function of the times. They maintain fairly high rates of NCD because this activity is consistent with their conservative ideology. The primary motivation for NCD is outreach. New churches are a way of expanding into new populations and exposing them to a gospel witness. Fluctuations in this rate do not reflect changes in the strength of this ideology or hard work, but changes in the dominant culture. The motivation to start new churches is constant, but the feasibility and success of this activity is dictated by the times. And in recent decades, the shift away from the liberal values of the 1960s helped conservative denominations more than mainline denominations.[10]

The Methodists and Presbyterians were affected by the times as well. However, there was a residual effect, which suggests that new churches also may be a barometer of the degree to which these denominations are willing to work and plan for growth. Lacking the movement quality of the Assemblies of God and the conservative ideology of the Southern Baptist Convention (and LCMS), new churches must result from organized, bureaucratic efforts. Although greatly affected by the demographic and cultural changes in American society, the fortunes of these denominations lie in the direction towards which their efforts and resources are channeled.

For Assemblies of God the pattern is entirely different. The times affected their membership growth rate substantially, but the impact of this period effect was much lower on their rate of NCD. Further, the correlation between NCD and membership growth was reduced when controlling for the period effect, but the drop was not large. This denomination retains something of a movement quality that enables it to grow more than would be expected in "bad" times and to start more new churches than would be expected in good times or bad. In addition, its growth rate and NCD rate may drop in response to movement-related problems that are not reflected in the larger culture.[11]

New churches translate directly into large numbers of new members for the Assemblies of God, but the growth of this denomination in any given year results from many factors—not just NCD or a favorable cultural context. Unlike the other denominations considered here, the Assemblies of

God does not have a large group of stable, highly institutionalized churches that keep overall membership statistics smooth and even. Three-quarters of AOG churches are either growing or declining. Few are on the plateau (see Table 2.5). The precarious balance between the set of growing churches and the set of declining churches tends to make membership statistics erratic from one year to the next. The result is a relatively low correlation between rates of NCD and membership change, and it is a correlation that is reduced only slightly when we control for period effects.

The Impact of New Churches on Membership Change: 1983–1988

From an accounting perspective, new churches cannot logically hurt a denomination's rate of membership change. Unlike older churches that only add the difference in membership between, say, 1983 and 1988, new churches add their full membership to a denomination's total in 1988. Some of these new congregations may well be in decline by 1988, but this decline is not recorded—only their growth from zero to whatever their membership stands in 1988. So the question is not whether new churches help a denomination's "bottom line" in terms of membership, but how much they help.

To answer this question it was necessary to turn to a different source of data: the actual membership records of individual congregations (both old and new) in several denominations. Unfortunately, it was not possible to use the same five denominations analyzed above. Data tapes on all congregations were not available from The United Methodist Church or the Lutheran Church, Missouri Synod. So these denominations were replaced by the United Church of Christ and the American Baptist Churches. Tapes supplied by these two denominations (also the SBC, AOG, and the Presbyterian Church, U.S.A.) contained membership data, dates of organization, and other variables for 1983 and 1988. Subsequent analysis is based on data from these five denominations.

For the SBC, new churches (those organized from 1983 to 1988) added 214,120 members to the denomination. From 1983 to 1988 the overall denomination grew 4.7%.[12] Subtracting the members contributed by new churches leaves the denomination with a growth of 3.2%. Thus, the Southern Baptist Convention would have grown without its new churches, but the rate of growth would have been reduced.

For the Assemblies of God the impact of new churches was even more substantial. New churches added 97,805 members to the denomination from 1983 to 1988.[13] The total denomination grew by 11.3% over these five years. However, without new churches the growth of Assemblies of God congregations would be reduced to 4.0%. This suggests that not only did the Assemblies of God grow more (in aggregate percentage terms) through new churches than the SBC, but that older Assemblies of God churches were more likely to grow than were older Southern Baptist churches.[14] Indeed this is the case. Additional analysis shows that among churches that existed in 1983 and 1988, 38% of Assemblies of God churches experienced growth of more than 10%, as compared to 30% of Southern Baptist Churches.

Declining denominations are losing members in spite of the new churches that they organize. In the case of the American Baptist Churches, the overall membership loss was 1.7% from 1983 to 1988. New churches helped to moderate the declines experienced by older churches in this denomination. Without the 11,214 members added by new ABC congregations, the denomination's overall membership loss drops to −2.4%. Presbyterian losses were even greater. The overall loss was 5.5% from 1983 to 1988. Without new churches, this loss would have been 6.9%.

Calculating aggregate losses for United Church of Christ congregations in the same manner as for the other four denominations was not possible using the data available because churches that died or left the denomination between 1983 and 1988 were not included on the data tape. Thus, any losses that we compute should be substantially greater. Nevertheless, the UCC churches included in the data set lost 2.4% on an aggregate level. Without new churches this loss would have been 2.9%.

Findings Related to Assumption Number 2: NCD as a Denominational Growth Strategy

New Churches: A Way of Reaching into New Populations or of Keeping up with One's Members?

Denominations differ in the extent to which they are concentrated in certain regions of the nation. Of the five denominations for which we have individual church data, the Southern Baptist Convention is the most regionally defined. As can be seen in Figures 2.11A, 2.11B, and 2.11C, it is in southern states that the concentration of churches greatly exceeds the expected frequency.[15] Further, SBC concentration tends to be either extremely heavy or very light. Virginia provides the only exception to this rule.

FIGURE 2.11A

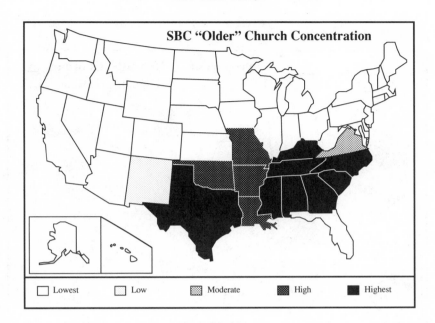

SBC "Older" Church Concentration

☐ Lowest   ☐ Low   ▨ Moderate   ▨ High   ■ Highest

FIGURE 2.11B

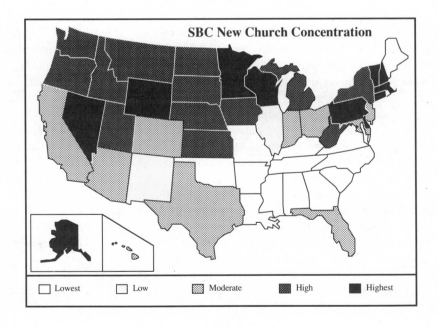

SBC New Church Concentration

☐ Lowest   ☐ Low   ▨ Moderate   ▨ High   ■ Highest

FIGURE 2.11C

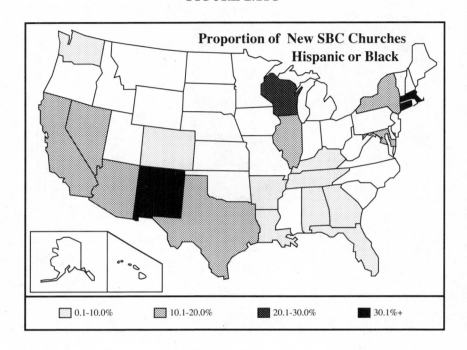

Where are Southern Baptists starting new churches? Rates of NCD are highest outside their region of concentration—Southern Baptists are starting churches "where they are not."[16] In some ways this should not be surprising, because the density of concentration in the South would seem to preclude a high rate of NCD in most southern states. Further, there is a new church development strategy operating at the national level to plant at least one church in what are called "unentered counties" and to concentrate church extension in the largest metropolitan areas of the United States—most of which are located outside the South. For these reasons, NCD rates are higher in nonsouthern states.

The Assemblies of God is much less regionally defined than the SBC. In fact, less than half of the congregations in this denomination are located in states shaded moderate to highest concentration, as compared to 80% of SBC churches (see Figures 2.12A and 2.12B).[17] Like Southern Baptists, Assemblies of God are also planting new churches "where they are not." However, they appear to have concentrated NCD efforts particularly in three rapidly growing western states, in growing "Sunbelt" states, and along the eastern seaboard from Maine to Florida.

FIGURE 2.12A

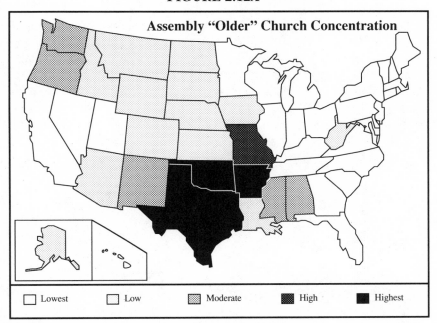

Assembly "Older" Church Concentration

Lowest   Low   Moderate   High   Highest

FIGURE 2.12B

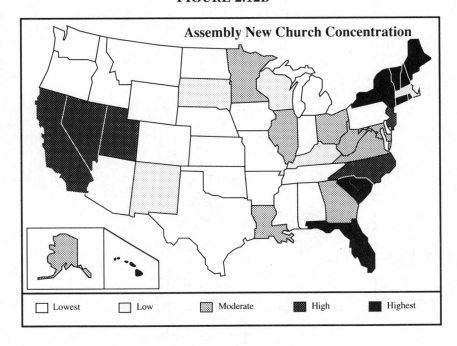

Assembly New Church Concentration

Lowest   Low   Moderate   High   Highest

For the American Baptists, the heaviest concentration of churches is in the Northeast and in the East North Central region of the United States (Figures 2.13A, 2.13B, and 2.13C). Because the American Baptists have not started many new churches in recent years, few states have high NCD rates (for a state to be shaded the denomination must have started at least two churches in that state from 1983 to 1988). Rates are highest in the Far West, where a relatively large number of new churches have been started, and in Missouri, where only a few have been started.[18]

FIGURE 2.13A

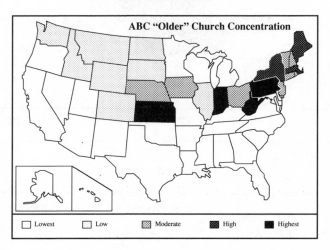

FIGURE 2.13B

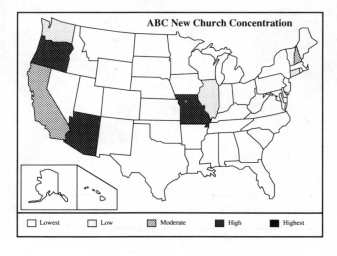

FIGURE 2.13C

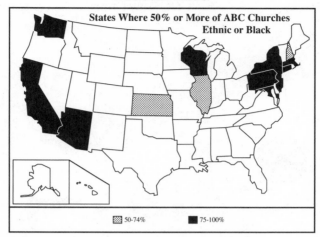

The United Church of Christ distribution reflects the peculiar nature of this denomination, which resulted from the merger of the Congregationalists (who were heavily concentrated in New England) with a Reformed body (which was concentrated in Pennsylvania and the Midwest). Thus, New England is shaded dark, along with Pennsylvania, Ohio, Wisconsin, Illinois, and Iowa (Figure 2.14A). New UCC churches are concentrated in areas far removed from the UCC "strongholds." The states shaded in Figure 2.14B also tend to be growing (see the population change map in Figure 2.16).

FIGURE 2.14A

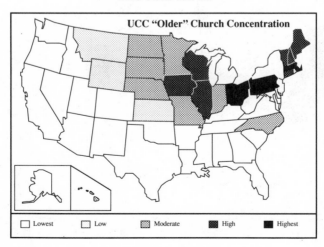

FIGURE 2.14B

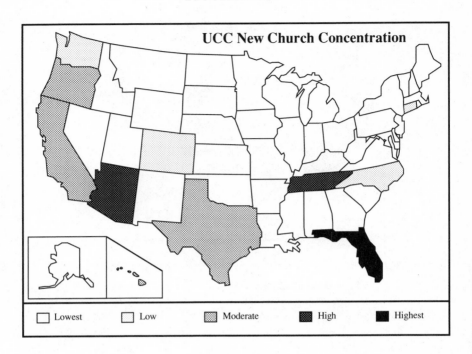

UCC New Church Concentration

Lowest Low Moderate High Highest

FIGURE 2.14C

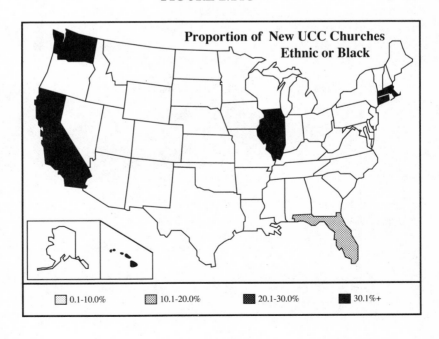

Proportion of New UCC Churches Ethnic or Black

0.1-10.0% 10.1-20.0% 20.1-30.0% 30.1%+

FIGURE 2.15A

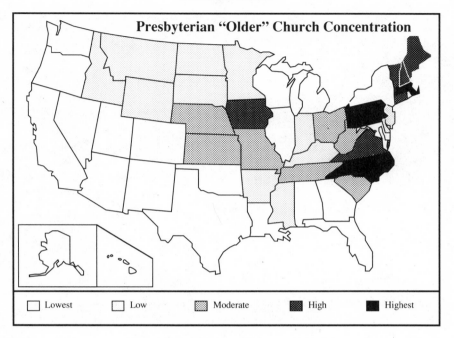

Like American Baptists and Assemblies of God, Presbyterian churches are dispersed across several regions of the United States (Figures 2.15A, 2.15B, and 2.15C). In fact, their pattern of concentration looks remarkably similar to that of the ABC, but with more of a Middle Atlantic-Southern shift. Relative to the population, Presbyterian concentration is highest in Pennsylvania, North Carolina, Virginia, and Iowa. New church development rates are highest in the Far West, the Sunbelt, and in scattered other states. Like the Assemblies of God and the UCC, it would appear that Presbyterians are combining efforts to start new churches "where they are not" with a growing state strategy.

Is there any pattern to regional rates of NCD? Specifically, are growing denominations like the Assemblies of God and the Southern Baptist Convention starting a disproportionately larger number of new churches in growing states or in states with higher levels of in-migration? The answer is yes and no, and in the case of the "yes" it is difficult to tell whether there is any strategy behind the trend. The correlation (Pearson's r) at the state level between population growth and NCD rates are .46 for the UCC, .43 for the Presbyterian Church, .30 for the

FIGURE 2.15B

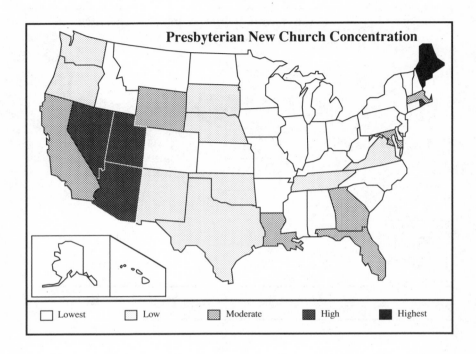

Presbyterian New Church Concentration

☐ Lowest   ☐ Low   ▨ Moderate   ▧ High   ■ Highest

AOG, .28 for the ABC, and .12 for the SBC. All five denominations have higher rates of NCD in states that are growing in population. Is this happenstance, strategy, or simply the fact that it is easier to start new churches in states where the population is growing? More than likely it is a little of each, with some denominations leaning more toward strategy than others. (See Figure 2.16.)

The relationship between levels of population mobility and NCD is less close. Again, the two denominations with the most severe declines in membership have the strongest state-level correlations (.28 for the UCC and .26 for the Presbyterian Church). For the denomination with the most rapid growth over the past twenty-eight years, the state-level correlation is the lowest: − .02 for the Assemblies of God. The correlation for the ABC is .24 and for the SBC it is .14. Few conclusions can be drawn from this state-level comparison. Further, Schaller's hypothesis concerning in-migration probably is more applicable to community levels of in-migration and to the ability of new churches to grow where they happen to be planted rather than to the tendency of a denomination to plant churches in states with high levels of in-migration. Unfortunately, this thesis could not be tested with the data on hand.[19]

FIGURE 2.15C

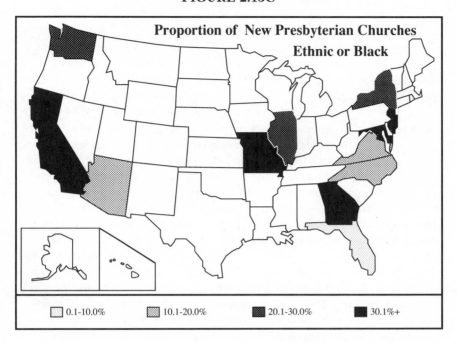

Proportion of New Presbyterian Churches Ethnic or Black

☐ 0.1-10.0%   ▨ 10.1-20.0%   ▦ 20.1-30.0%   ■ 30.1%+

FIGURE 2.16

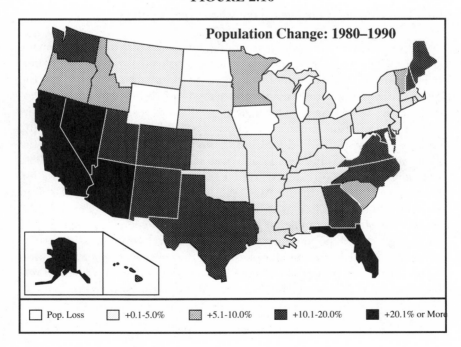

Population Change: 1980–1990

☐ Pop. Loss   ☐ +0.1-5.0%   ▨ +5.1-10.0%   ▦ +10.1-20.0%   ■ +20.1% or More

The fact that the UCC, the Presbyterian Church, and the ABC seem to be focusing their limited church extension efforts in states that are demographically "better" than other states raises the possibility that they are being more careful and intentional about where they start new churches than the Southern Baptist Convention. Indeed, most church extension guides produced by mainline authors emphasize the "careful" approach (see Jones, 1976). For the SBC the "quality" of a region has been irrelevant. Much more attention has been given to the degree to which an area has been "reached" with the gospel—with judgments in this area being based primarily on the existence of SBC churches, rather than on the proportion of the population that is "churched."

All denominations have targeted NCD outside their regions of concentration. So in this sense, NCD is a way of reaching into new territory (although not necessarily into new populations) for mainline and conservative denominations alike. However, the next question that can be posed is whether *new churches* grow better outside the region of concentration. The answer is no for all denominations except for the United Church of Christ. In the other four denominations newer churches (those formed in 1972 to 1982) in states of concentration are just as likely to grow as newer churches in states outside the region of concentration. However, among older churches (organized prior to 1972) there is a trend for churches to see more growth on average outside the region of concentration in all denominations, again except for the UCC.

New Churches and Community Population Characteristics

In the past, the acknowledged strategy for NCD was to target growing suburbs. Changing denominational priorities, as well as the growth potential of ethnic congregations have changed this approach somewhat, but the question remains whether new churches tend to be planted in demographically "better" areas. The answer is a definite yes, especially in reference to population growth. As shown in Table 2.2, for "older" SBC churches (those formed prior to 1983), the mean population change in the zip code where the church is located was +25.6% between 1970 and 1980. For new churches (organized from 1983 to 1988) the mean population change was +46.4%. In the AOG the percentages were +26.8% (older churches) and +37.2% (new churches). For the ABC, older churches saw an average of 9.6% population growth in their zip codes, as compared to an average 26.1% population gain for new church zip codes. For UCC churches and Presbyterian churches the differences were even more dramatic. The mean population change in zip codes surrounding older Presbyterian churches was +17.1%. By contrast the mean for new Presbyterian churches was +63.7%. For older UCC churches the mean population change was +14.3%, as compared to an average 61.9% gain for zip codes around new UCC churches.

TABLE 2.2
Average Percent Change[1] in Zip Code
Population for New Churches[2] and Older Churches[3]

	New Churches	Older Churches
SBC	46.4%	25.6%
AOG	37.2	26.8
ABC	26.1	9.6
UCC	61.9	14.3
Presbyterian	63.7	17.1

[1]Population change in zip codes surrounding churches was measured from 1970 to 1980.
[2]New churches were organized from 1983 to 1988.
[3]Older churches were organized prior to 1983.

Newer churches tend to be located in areas with newer housing, with higher housing values, and with a higher proportion of college graduates. On the other hand, newer churches were also more likely to be located in areas with a higher proportion of multifamily housing, a greater proportion of Hispanics, and a greater proportion of renters. For Assemblies of God, the American Baptist Churches, and the United Church of Christ (but not Southern Baptists or Presbyterians), new churches were more often found in areas with a greater proportion of African Americans. Zip codes surrounding new ABC and UCC churches were more likely to have a higher proportion below the poverty level than were zip codes surrounding older ABC and UCC churches.

So do new churches tend to be planted in demographically better areas for growth? Again, the answer is yes. In fact, in the ABC, even new African-American and ethnic congregations tend to be located in areas of greater population growth than do older African-American and ethnic congregations. However, these demographic findings do seem somewhat contradictory in some cases (e.g., higher housing values and more poverty). This is due, no doubt, to the fact that denominations are starting a variety of new churches. Unlike the 1950s, new churches in the 1980s (and 1990s) are no longer exclusively suburban. Many new churches are located in the inner city and are targeted to ethnic populations or designed for specific types of urban ministry.

New Churches Among Racial/Ethnic Groups

For predominantly white "Anglo" denominations, expansion into new populations has meant NCD among non-Anglo racial/ethnic groups as well as NCD outside their region of concentration. New ethnic churches have allowed denominations to find new sources of growth and to ameliorate the embarrassing legacy of segregation in their histories. For some denominations new African-American or ethnic churches have helped augment the slumping development of new Anglo churches. For other groups, new black and ethnic churches have become the dominant mode of NCD. In the ABC, for instance, 65% of the churches organized from 1983 to 1988 were ethnic or black.[20] This is in contrast to only about 20% of American Baptist churches organized prior to 1983.

A total of 31% of new UCC churches are black or ethnic, as compared to 26% of new Presbyterian churches and an estimated 28% of new Assemblies of God churches (up from around 22% ten years ago). For the SBC, reliable data were not available on the issue until 1990. Analysis among reporting churches indicated that 20% of new SBC congregations (organized from 1985 to 1990) were predominantly ethnic or black in membership). In all five denominations ethnic and black congregations are greatly over-represented among new churches. For the AOG the proportion of ethnic or black new church starts is about twice the proportion of non-Anglo churches in the denomination (although it may be higher). For the other four denominations the over-representation of black and ethnic churches is far greater. In Table 2.3 it can be seen that 5% of older Presbyterian churches are black or ethnic in comparison to 26% of new Presbyterian churches. Similarly, only 8% of older UCC churches are black or ethnic in comparison to 31% of new UCC congregations. And finally, 20% of new SBC churches are ethnic or black in comparison to only 5% of existing SBC congregations. Without new black or ethnic churches, NCD rates would be much lower in all five denominations.

In Figure 2.13C it can be seen that in ten states (and in Washington, D.C.) over three-quarters of new ABC churches are ethnic or black. For the other four denominations the proportion of non-Anglo churches is less than for the ABC. Nevertheless, a number of states have a high proportion of new churches that are ethnic or black. For instance, in Figure 2.11C it can be seen that in Massachusetts, Connecticut, Wisconsin, and New Mexico, a sizable proportion of new SBC churches are Hispanic or black. For the Presbyterian church, several states with high rates of NCD also have high proportions of new churches that are ethnic or black. These states include

California, Arizona, Georgia, and Maryland. Likewise, for the UCC, states with high rates of NCD and a large proportion of new black or ethnic churches include California, Hawaii, and Florida. In these states predominantly white denominations are expanding into new territory by NCD outside their region of concentration and among nontraditional populations. (See Figure 2.14C).

TABLE 2.3
Percent of Churches Black or Ethnic by Denomination

	New Churches	Older Churches
SBC°	20%	5%
AOG (est.)	28	14
ABC	65	20
UCC	31	8
Presbyterian	26	5

°Figures for Southern Baptist churches were based on the 1990 Uniform Church Letter. New churches were those organized from 1985 to 1990. For other denominations, new churches were those organized 1983 to 1988.

How much do new ethnic or black churches add to the growth of a denomination? And do new ethnic churches grow faster than new Anglo churches? We only have data on three denominations to answer these questions. Ethnic and black churches are more likely to grow than Anglo churches in all three denominations.[21] However, as shown in Table 2.4, the magnitude of the difference in the percentage of churches growing is not as large as might be expected between Anglo churches and black/ethnic churches. Still, the aggregate result of this relationship is rather substantial. In the ABC, older ethnic churches grew by 7.9% from 1983 to 1988. Older Anglo churches lost 6.8% over the same period. Thus, the growth of older black and ethnic churches combined with the addition of many new black and ethnic churches helped to moderate the decline of this denomination.

In the Presbyterian Church, older black or ethnic churches did not fare as well. They declined by 3.5% at an aggregate level. However, older Anglo churches did even worse, declining by 6.2%. When new ethnic churches are combined with older ethnic churches, the entire set of ethnic churches grew by 7.0% from 1983 to 1988. When new Anglo churches are combined with older Anglo churches, the entire set of Anglo churches declined by 5.0% during the same period. Thus, as for the ABC, ethnic and black congregations helped moderate the decline of the Presbyterian Church (U.S.A.).[22]

TABLE 2.4
Percent of Churches Growing[1] by Racial/Ethnic Status

	Older[2] Black or Ethnic	Older Anglo
ABC	23.6%	18.9%
UCC	29.8	17.0
Presbyterian	23.8	15.7
	Newer[3] Black or Ethnic	Newer Anglo
ABC	38.9%	58.5%
UCC	41.4	52.7
Presbyterian	48.	46.2

[1]Growing churches were those with over 10% increase in membership from 1983 to 1988.
[2]Newer churches were organized from 1973 to 1982.
[3]Older churches were organized prior to 1973.

Differences existed between denominations in the likelihood of *newer* racial/ethnic churches (those formed after 1972) to grow as compared to newer Anglo churches. As shown in Table 2.4, in both the ABC and the UCC, newer Anglo churches were more likely to grow than were newer black/ethnic churches. For the Presbyterian Church, however, newer black/ethnic churches were slightly more likely to grow than were newer Anglo churches. New churches tend to grow, whatever their ethnic makeup. After a church is no longer new, the prospects for continued growth seem to be better for non-Anglo congregations.

Findings Related to Assumption 3:
NCD and Denominational Resilience

Our final assumption concerns the relationship of denominational resilience to NCD and denominational growth. As indicated earlier, there are some intangible aspects to denominational growth, but we expected that these intangibles would have very tangible correlates. Schaller suggested that the churches in newer denominations would be more likely to grow than the churches in older denominations. As can be seen in Table 2.5, the "newest" of the five denominations (the Assemblies of God) has the largest proportion of growing congregations.[23] If we only consider the percent of churches growing, it is clear that this denomination probably has a larger share of "resilient" congregations. But the picture is more complex than that, because the Assemblies of God also has the second largest proportion of *declining* churches (after the Presbyterians).

Again we see evidence that the AOG is distinct from the other four denominations. It retains something of a movement ("boom or bust") quality. Churches are either growing or declining. Few are stable institutions on the plateau. For the SBC, on the other hand, the proportion declining is very low (only 18%) but the proportion on the plateau is huge. Clearly, the least resilient denomination of the five (as indicated by this criteria) is the Presbyterian Church. This denomination has the smallest percentage of growing congregations and by far the largest proportion of declining churches (42%). UCC churches tend to be on the plateau or declining, as do American Baptist churches.

TABLE 2.5
Percent of Churches Growing,[1] Plateaued,[2] or Declining:[3]
1983–1988

	Growing	Plateaued	Declining
SBC	30.5%	51.9%	17.6%
AOG	38.3	25.4	36.3
ABC	19	47	32.4
UCC	18.0	52.6	29.3
Presbyterian	16.2	41.4	42.4

[1]Growing churches were those with over 10% increase in membership from 1983 to 1988.
[2]Plateaued churches were those with between +10% and −10% change in membership from 1983 to 1988.
[3]Declining churches were those with over 10% decline in membership from 1983 to 1988.

We also have suggested that growing denominations may demonstrate organizational resilience to the degree that their congregations sustain growth across congregational age, size, and location categories. Do the churches in resilient denominations grow "across the board"? If the answer is yes, this would mean that the churches in such denominations are less affected by outside forces that tend to encourage or constrain the growth of most congregations. On the other hand, it is possible that in growing denominations each size, age, or location category will simply contain a larger percentage of growing congregations.

Previous research on the relationship between age of church and membership growth showed that among SBC churches, newer congregations were much more likely to grow than were older congregations (Hadaway, 1990:371). This observation led to the assumption that low levels of NCD would lead to a larger proportion of slower-growing older congregations in a denomination. Do these findings hold for other denominations as well? And what does this say about denominational resilience?

TABLE 2.6
Percent of Churches Growing by Date of Organization

	Oldest Churches	1928–47	1948–57	1958–72	1973–82
SBC	22.4%	27.9%	33.9%	42.7%	62.5%
AOG	34.8	34.8	36.0	40.9	48.8
ABC	17.8	20.3	25.3	27.0	46.1
UCC	16.4	21.4	18.9	24.5	47.5
Presbyterian	13.0	19.2	18.7	22.8	46.8

Data for the American Baptist Churches, the United Church of Christ, and the Presbyterian Church also reveal a fairly substantial, but curvilinear relationship between age of congregation and percentage of churches growing. As shown in Table 2.6, a smaller percentage of newer ABC, UCC, and Presbyterian churches were growing (46.1%, 47.5%, and 46.8%, respectively) than were newer Southern Baptist churches (62.5%). But all four denominations are similar in that there was a very large difference between the newest set of congregations (organized from 1973 to 1982) as compared to the next youngest set of congregations (organized from 1958 to 1972). For SBC churches the difference was 19.8 percentage points, while for ABC churches the difference was 19.1 percentage points. Similarly, the differences between the two youngest groups of churches in percent of churches growing were 24 percentage points for the Presbyterians, and 23 percentage points for the United Church of Christ. In these four denominations, new churches were very likely to experience growth. However, the positive effect of this "newness" does not last very long.

Among Assemblies of God congregations, the pattern was somewhat different. The relationship between age of church and growth was present, but it was also weak because newer churches were only slightly more likely to grow than older AOG churches. In other words, AOG churches were more likely to sustain growth across age categories. Newer AOG congregations were less likely to grow than were newer SBC congregations. On the other hand, older AOG congregations were more likely to grow than older SBC congregations. Age seems to matter less among AOG churches. Instead, resilience, as measured by percent of churches growing, is spread rather evenly among churches of different ages.

A similar effect is seen in the area of church size. For both Southern Baptists and Assemblies of God congregations there is something of a "U-shaped" relationship between church size and aggregate membership growth. Both smaller and larger churches tend to do better in terms of growth than do mid-sized congregations. For Southern Baptists, the smallest churches do the best (by far). Churches that had between one and fifty members in 1983 grew by an aggregate 20%. For Assemblies of God, the percentage gain was lower among small churches (+11%), but it was still substantial if compared to the American Baptists and Presbyterians. Small ABC churches declined by 12% overall. Likewise, small Presbyterian churches declined by 11%.

As can be seen in Figure 2.17, among both the AOG and the SBC, aggregate growth rises substantially among the *largest* churches in each denomination. This goes against conventional wisdom, because it is logistically (and statistically) easier for a small group of any kind to experience larger percentage gains than it is for a large group. In these two denominations, however, churches with over 1,000 members are more likely to grow and to experience larger aggregate gains than are churches with only a few hundred members. This suggests that for both the SBC and the AOG, denominational growth is dependent on the growth of both small (and often new) congregations and very large churches. Again, Schaller is supported. And this may point to yet another source of resilience because the presence of large, growing congregations—some of which are relatively young—provides models to entrepreneurial young pastors who would like to build large, growing congregations themselves. Further, the growth curve for the AOG is flatter than for the SBC. Size has less effect on the aggregate growth (and average growth) of AOG churches—providing more support for the resilience thesis.[24]

For ABC and Presbyterian churches the relationship is quite different. In the ABC, it is the smallest and largest churches that experience the largest aggregate declines. The largest ABC congregations collectively lost 9.4% of their members from 1983 to 1988. In addition, the smallest ABC churches lost 11.8% of their members. But among those churches that existed in *both* 1983 and 1988, the smallest churches were more likely to grow. This finding is not hard to explain. For growing denominations the smallest set of churches contains many new, growing congregations that will not be small for long. However, in a declining denomination, the smallest set of churches contains many dying churches that will not be with the denomination for long. Those that survive are more likely to grow, but their growth does not compensate for the loss of other small congregations.

A third pattern is evident for Presbyterian churches. Like the ABC, their smallest churches do poorly in terms of aggregate growth. However, decline is pervasive in this denomination. Congregations in the middle range do no better than smaller congregations in aggregate terms. Unlike the ABC, the Presbyterians retain substantial numbers of larger, prestigious churches. These churches allow the growth curve to inch into "the black" among those congregations with more than 3,000 members. But what is striking about the curve for Presbyterians is the fact that it is so flat. If pervasive resilience can produce a flat curve on some correlates of growth (as in the case of the AOG), then it is also possible for a pervasive lack of resilience to do the same.

FIGURE 2.17
Percent Change in Aggregate Membership by Size Category: 1983–1988

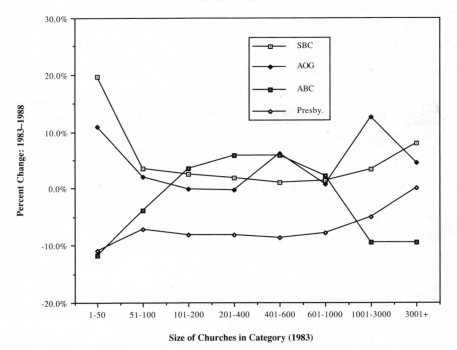

Size of Churches in Category (1983)

Additional Findings Related to Church Size

Among the many hypotheses outlined by Schaller (1991) in his book on new church development is the idea that new churches are more likely to grow if they are started larger—preferably with 200 persons or more attending the initial worship service. The logic is that such churches are able to bypass the "single cell" stage of organization and are less likely to become "stuck" at one of the typical points of plateau.

Unfortunately, it was not possible to test this hypothesis directly. We had no way of knowing worship attendance at the first worship service. As an alternative, we looked at membership growth from 1983 to 1988 among those churches organized in 1982 or 1983 by size category (as measured in 1983). Results indicate that in the Assemblies of God, the SBC, and the Presbyterian Church, growth was most likely among smaller churches. For the SBC and the AOG, growth was most likely in the category of one to fifty members. These denominations had very few *new* churches with 200 or more members in 1983 (3% of new AOG churches and 10% of new SBC congregations were this large in 1983). New Presbyterian churches were larger on average than new SBC or AOG churches (13% were over 200 in 1983), however, growth was most likely in the category of fifty-one to one hundred members (Presbyterians had very few *new* churches with less than fifty-one members in 1983). If one plans intentionally to become a megachurch, it may help to begin with over 200 members, but larger initial size (at date of organization) apparently is not required to predict the relative likelihood of growth among mainline and evangelical congregations.

A second hypothesis related to church size (not from Schaller in this case) is that very large churches may suppress NCD and the overall growth of the denomination in the area in which they are located. This hypothesis was not supported. We looked at counties that had churches with 3,000 members or more in 1983 (4,000 or more for the SBC). Results indicate that for the SBC, AOG, and ABC, the rate of NCD is substantially higher on average in areas with superchurches, as compared to the rate for the entire denomination. Further, it appears that while superchurches tend to show more growth than do the smaller congregations in their communities, the overall growth of a denomination's churches in a community with a superchurch is not hurt. In fact, aggregate percentage membership growth in such communities tends to exceed that of the overall denomination. This effect was marginal for Southern Baptists, a little stronger for American Baptists, but very strong for the Assemblies of God. AOG churches in communities with superchurches grew over three times faster than the national average.

Discussion

Growing denominations have higher rates of NCD. This is very clear. In the 1950s, all five denominations that were analzyed had relatively high rates of both NCD and membership growth. Further, membership growth tended to be greater in denominations with higher rates of NCD. In later years, all denominations experienced declines in NCD, and all denominations experienced erosions in their rates of membership growth. But not all denominations declined in membership. The two that avoided membership declines were those that maintained higher rates of NCD. Among mainline denominations, membership decline was least severe for the Lutheran Church, Missouri Synod—a denomination with a rate of NCD that has tended to be much higher than the Presbyterian Church or The United Methodist Church.

Growing denominations also have an increasing average congregation size. This has been true throughout the twenty-eight-year period of investigation. Southern Baptist churches and Assemblies of God congregations experienced increases in average size from 1950 to the present. On the other hand, the mainline denominations began to decline in membership at the same time that the average size of their congregations began to shrink.

All denominations tend to plant churches in areas that are demographically favorable and outside their region of concentration. This seems particularly true with regard to NCD and state-by-state patterns of population growth. It must be added, however, that new churches tend to be located in "geographically favorable" areas and among receptive populations *even in declining denominations.* The highest correlations between NCD rates and population growth were found for the Presbyterian Church and for the United Church of Christ—at both the state level and at the zip code level.

It is also true that all five denominations are making major efforts to expand beyond their Anglo base into African-American and ethnic populations. This push appears to be somewhat greater in proportional terms among declining denominations. However, it is possible that relatively little effort at the denominational level is involved in the ongoing business of racial/ethnic NCD. Once started, this activity may gain a life of its own and be carried by the ethnic populations rather than by denominational agencies. Further, the proportion of new churches that are ethnic or black be so high in mainline denominations because so few Anglo churches are being started—rather than because so many ethnic or black churches are being organized.

Even the most rapidly growing denominations experienced rather severe downturns in NCD during the 1960s. However, not all denominations were as drastically affected by the changes as were others. Apparently, some denominations have a certain resilience that helps them adjust more readily to the times. They experienced membership growth and started new churches—even when doing so was costly and the success rate was low. Oddly enough, among such denominations the statistical link between rates of NCD and rates of membership change is likely to be less tight. For particularly resilient denominations, the NCD rate may remain high even when membership growth is difficult. The net effect is a somewhat lower correlation between NCD and membership change.

Finally, it is clear that growing denominations have a larger proportion of growing churches and their churches tend to sustain growth across congregational age, size, and location factors. This was particularly true for the Assemblies of God. AOG churches were more likely to grow, even in those categories that discourage growth in most denominations. On the other hand, the growth pattern of SBC churches looked more like the growth pattern of mainline churches. The only difference was that for the SBC, the percentage of churches growing was greater in each category. The clear exception to this generalization was in the relationship between size of congregation and church growth. For both the SBC and the AOG, large churches were almost as likely to grow as small churches. Indeed, we can speculate that large, growing churches provide models that may inspire potential church planters. These examples show what is possible. But denominations that lack such models may find it difficult to encourage people to become church planters.

Conclusion

Earlier we referred to several statements by Bullock (1991) concerning NCD and denominational growth. His remarks led to our main research question: Is NCD a cause or a symptom of denominational membership growth? Our examination of the data suggests, simply—it depends. In some denominations, NCD is more a cause of growth. In others, NCD seems to be a symptom of something else—something deeper, and perhaps, less programmable.

The Assemblies of God is an interesting and instructive case. New churches have added more to its growth than to any other denomination. At the same time, the rate of NCD appears to be symptomatic of something else—a certain organizational resilience or movement quality (to which growth in membership is closely tied). So for the Assemblies of God, new churches are both a *cause* and a *symptom* of growth.

New churches also add something to the growth of the Southern Baptist Convention and the Lutheran Church, Missouri Synod. However, new churches do not contribute very many new members (in percentage terms);

and increases in the rate of NCD are not associated with increases in membership growth when period effects are controlled. The 1970s and the 1980s, in general, provided a favorable climate for these conservative, noncharismatic denominations—and they benefited from this climate. So, for these two denominations, NCD is more a *symptom* than a cause of denominational growth. In eras where membership growth occurs, these denominations start many new churches, but it is the *era* that makes both (membership growth and NCD) more likely.

When NCD is symptomatic of growth, evidence of a link between the two can be found in various places in a denomination. Growing denominations start more new churches and simultaneously, have increased numbers of "megachurches" (1,000+ members). Indeed, large, successful churches seem to give the needed stimulus for budding church planters. They provide inspirational models to follow. This has been important for growth among the Assemblies of God and the Southern Baptist Convention.

Finally, for mainline denominations, we have shown that little growth has come from new churches in recent years, because these denominations have simply started so few. However, growth has been enhanced in those eras in which they have started many—even when controlling for period effects. So for the mainline, new churches are more a cause of growth than they are a symptom of growth. When these denominations make the effort to start new churches, they tend to grow (or at least moderate their declines). When they do not make the effort, they tend to decline.

New churches are not the only answer for denominational growth. Yet they are important, both as a potential source of some growth, and as a barometer of other things that affect membership growth.[25] For some denominations, levels of NCD may indicate overall organizational resilience, for other denominations they may indicate hard work and success in reaching goals, and for still other denominations, they may reflect how "friendly" social and geographical conditions are to churches, both new and old.

Chapter Three

Strategies for Evangelism and Growth in Three Denominations (1965–1990)

Bruce A. Greer

The story of mainline Protestant membership trends since World War II is well known and much discussed. For the twenty years following World War II, riding on the crest of prosperity, suburbanization, a "baby boom," and all-time high church participation levels, the denominations of the Protestant mainline grew vigorously. From the mid-1960s onward, however, the graphs charting membership trends began to point downward rather than upward, at times to a frightening degree. The literature describing and analyzing these trends is voluminous; yet, there is a paucity of literature on the response of these same denominations to their decline. This is puzzling because since the mid-1960s, significant changes have occurred in mainline Protestant evangelism and new church development programs. In addition to these changes, the emergence of the "church growth movement" in the 1970s added a new dimension to church outreach and extension. Such salient developments undoubtedly are related to the membership decline that disturbed mainline Protestant leaders throughout the 1970s and into the 1980s.

This chapter examines the evangelism, church growth, and new church development programs of three historic, mainline Protestant denominations—the American Baptist Churches in the U.S.A. (ABC), the United Church of Christ (UCC) and The United Methodist Church (UMC)—and compares them briefly with the experience of a fourth, the Presbyterian Church, U.S.A. (PCUSA). All four denominations occupy an important place in American religious history. Each has been an integral part of the nation's religious establishment. Each experienced significant numerical decline in their white constituencies since the mid-1960s and responded in various ways to the decline through programmatic efforts in evangelism, church growth, and new church development. And, each is seeking to find their niche in a changed American religious marketplace (see Roof and McKinney, 1987:229-51 and Berger, 1967:137-47).

The findings of this study are based upon thirty face-to-face interviews with past and present national level denominational executives and staff in the ABC, UCC, and UMC. In addition, numerous books, articles, reports, and archival materials—most of which are not cited—were reviewed. "Informants" in each of the three denominations, each having worked in high denominational positions over a significant span of time, provided especially candid and useful insights about the theological and political nuances of their denomination. The interviews and materials reviewed point out striking similarities between the three denominations, and equally striking similarities between them and the PCUSA. From the findings of this study, a number of conclusions about evangelism, church growth, and new church development in the Protestant mainline are offered.

The American Baptist Churches

Unlike the other denominations examined in this study, the ABC is not the result of a series of mergers. It is, for the most part, a repository of more moderate Baptists, the result of two centuries of sifting through an unwieldy and fractious Baptist movement. Perhaps the most celebrated sifting of Baptists occurred in 1845 with the separation of northern and southern Baptists, primarily over slavery, a division that has never been overcome. Later schisms were more pointedly theological in nature. By the 1920s, the ABC had coalesced into three distinct theological categories: liberals, a large middle group of conservatives, and fundamentalists (Torbet, 1973:433). Caught in the middle of the fundamentalist-modernist controversy, the ABC lost members to separating fundamentalists in the first half of this century. Despite the departure of most fundamentalists from the ABC, making its median theological position more moderate, theological conflict continues.

Evangelism

Few positions of leadership in the ABC are the focal point of the continuing theological tension more than the Director of Evangelism. From 1936 to 1991, the ABC has had only three: Walter Woodbury (1936–56), Jitsuo Morikawa (1956–76) and Emmett Johnson (1979–91). Each one has had a significant impact on the ABC and served as an "antidote" to the emphases of his predecessor, dramatizing the dilemma of a denomination caught in the middle of an ongoing theological tug-of-war.

Walter Woodbury's method blazed a new path for ABC evangelism. Though he represented the conservative middle of the ABC, Woodbury's visitation evangelism method rankled evangelical traditionalists who were committed to clergy-dominated, revivalistic mass evangelism. Used for years in the ABC, his method involved going door to door to present the gospel to unchurched people through the use of flip charts, a method spawned in an era when door-to-door sales were commonplace. Though some in the ABC refer to the Woodbury method as simplistic, it was effective in three ways: (1) it enlisted lay participation, (2) it was meant for the local church, and (3) it kept close to the historic, evangelical roots of the ABC. Criticism of the Woodbury approach was tempered by the "theological correctness" of his goal: to "save" people from their sins and bring them into the faith and fellowship of the Christian church. The work of his department was described as "soul winning," a phrase near and dear to ABC evangelicals (Woodbury, 1956:299).

Both Morikawa's theology and method of evangelism were a quantum leap from Woodbury's, and altogether averse to the long-standing tradition of revivalistic mass evangelism. In the span of twenty years, the arena for ABC denominational evangelism would shift from tents, auditoriums, and churches to living rooms and the institutions of American society. Morikawa believed that evangelism that aimed solely for individual conversion was too narrow and simplistic, failing to challenge all of society with the full claims of the gospel. Morikawa pressed for a more comprehensive definition of evangelism. Evangelism is (1) God's mission and not the church's, (2) social, not simply individual, (3) sending the church into the world and not winning the world into the church (Morikawa, 1963:8-12).

Given this definition of evangelism, the ABC program moved in bold new directions. Evangelism meant Christians disbursed as leaven in the secular world with clergy (as "worker-priests") and laity alike ministering *within* secular institutions. The goal was to transform all institutions to the point of acknowledging the Lordship of Christ and participating in the kingdom of God. Evangelism became "evangelism planning," an "action-reflection" research model by which the church listened to the secular world—through the arts, and the social and behavioral sciences—before engaging in mission. Evangelism became everything the church did, and the evangelism department's job was to assist the ABC's Board of National Ministries (BNM) with strategic planning for mission.

Morikawa maintained a headlock on ABC evangelism until "Key '73," a major interdenominational evangelism emphasis for North America. Through this event, ABC conservatives who were alienated by Morikawa's theology and methods had an opportunity to advocate their form of evangelism. Though Morikawa reluctantly supported Key '73, he tailored it to his theological taste with a follow-up program called "Evangelistic Life Style." Despite the alleged failure of Key '73 (see Newman and D'Antonio, 1978), it reopened the evangelism debate in the ABC and Morikawa's critics were legion. In the words of one ABC leader, Morikawa "attempted to integrate his cosmic view of the role of the church into a church which had emphasized personal salvation and revivalism." "You can't baptize General Motors," was the criticism of another ABC leader. The conservative evangelical theologian Carl F. H. Henry criticized Morikawa's approach as "a 'contextual evangelism' which plays down gospel proclamation and emphasizes social action" (Torbet, 1973:479). On the other hand, most agree that Morikawa succeeded in generating serious debate on the meaning of evangelism (Hine, 1982:20).

The selection of Emmett Johnson to be the next Director of Evangelism made good political sense to the committee that labored for over two years to find a successor to Morikawa. The potential candidate had to emphasize traditional pietism, personal evangelism, and grass-roots programming suitable to the conservative middle of the ABC. The new director had to be able to communicate with "traditional people," meaning a more conventional, less controversial approach. Coming from the conservative, primarily Swedish, Baptist General Conference, Johnson had the right credentials as an evangelical. Both a successful pastor and evangelist, he described himself as a "left wing evangelical" committed to peace, civil rights, and conciliar ecumenism. In other words, his credentials would please two ABC constituencies—liberals and the conservative middle. His charisma and approach to evangelism found many supporters.

Johnson sought to reclaim personal evangelism, which had been neglected by the ABC's evangelism department for years. In doing so, he did not advocate a return to an old restrictive piety or old methods. He did, however, seek to maintain the long-standing ABC commitment to social witness. His task, as he saw it, was to fashion a "holistic" approach to evangelism, calling people to personal faith *and* mission in the world. Johnson's vision for evangelism was given a theological framework by the late George Peck, an influential ABC theologian and seminary president. In seeking to create "a theological environment for effective evangelism," Peck responded to Morikawa's theology of evangelism with six evangelistic objectives: (1) to make the gospel known, (2) to encourage the worshiping community, (3) to promote the growth of the church, (4) to ensure the quality of the church, (5) to prepare for service and action, and (6) to seek the conversion of individuals (Peck, 1983:21-29). Though affirming the importance of Christian witness through social service and action, Peck stressed the importance of personal evangelism.

During the Johnson era, evangelism was literally redefined with the assistance of the American Baptist Evangelism Team (an elite group of primarily national and regional staff) and officially adopted by the ABC. Evangelism was also vigorously promoted. National convocations on evangelism were held. Several seminary conferences on evangelism were offered at ABC seminaries, even those that did not offer a course on the subject at the time. Evangelism and church growth were key program components at the ABC's 1983 Biennial Convention, and new church development was highlighted at the 1985 Biennial. Academies for Growing Churches were held across the nation. Other related conferences were held on prayer, "old first churches," and "faith faces the issues." New program materials were made available to ABC churches. These conferences and resources stood in sharp contrast to what had been offered under Morikawa.

In summary, the evolution of ABC evangelism is clearly illustrated by the names given to its evangelism department: the Division of Evangelism (until 1969); the Department of Evangelism Planning (1970); the Office of Planning and Organizational Development (1972); Evangelistic Life Style (1974); Personal and Public Witness Unit (1978); and, the Division of Evangelistic Ministries (1991). In the post-war years, when churchgoing was the social norm and mainline Protestantism the cultural standard, ABC evangelism focused on visitation evangelism, as well as child and youth evangelism. With the tumult of the 1960s, evangelism became "the church in the world": strategic planning for mission to institutions and social structures, as well as social service and action. The latter half of the 1970s and the 1980s brought an attempt to balance "personal and public witness." By the start of the 1990s, evangelism emphases had seemingly come full circle to "evangelistic ministries."

Church Growth

Like other mainline denominations, ABC leaders had to contend with the impact of the "church growth movement," spawned by Donald McGavran and championed by disciples such as Win Arn and C. Peter Wagner. While one ABC executive found the movement to be "powerful, positive and practical," another described it as "glitz, theories and consultants." Most found something useful in it, but felt the need to make it more theologically "holistic." Thus, the ABC responded with Church Growth—ABC Style (Johnson, n.d.), and the "Grow by Caring" program. ABC leaders rejected two aspects of the church growth movement's "doctrine": the homogeneous unit principle and the negative view of social action in the local church. The homogeneous unit principle suggests that churches grow most effectively when believers evangelize their own kind of people (see McGavran, 1970 and Wagner, 1979). ABC leaders advocated, instead, an approach that sought social and cultural heterogeneity. According to one ABC critic, the "danger" with the homogeneous unit principle is that it works. By focusing on homogeneity, growing churches replicate modern society by fostering an enclave mentality, whereby people associate only with their own kind (Elliott, 1982:56).

To counter church growth movement doctrine, *Church Growth—ABC Style* (Johnson, n.d.:28-35) advocated a multidimensional understanding of church growth. Drawing upon the missiological work of the late Orlando Costas (1974, 1979), Johnson wrote that church growth should include numerical, organic, conceptual, and incarnational growth. Numerical growth occurs through evangelism by reaching out to uncommitted people. Organic growth involves the internal growth of the local church by deepening its faith and fellowship. Conceptual growth is "the degree of consciousness that a community of faith has with regard to its nature in mission to the world" (Johnson, n.d.:32). Incarnational growth is the growth of the church in its service to the world. Church growth, rightly conceived, should involve these four aspects. Otherwise, the church is out of balance and growing improperly.

The programmatic outcome of this church growth policy was the "Grow by Caring" emphasis, launched with great fanfare at the 1983 Biennial Convention in Cleveland (see Millar, 1989). Nine marks of the "growing, caring church" were identified and resourced: (1) personal witness, (2) social witness, (3) discipleship, (4) leadership, (5) congregational growth, (6) service, (7) stewardship, (8) [ecumenical] cooperation, and (9) [denominational] identity (Jones, 1989:165). The "Grow by Caring" program was the incarnation of the holistic approach advocated in *Church Growth—ABC Style*. "Numerical growth" is represented by Marks 1 and 5 of "Grow by Caring": personal witness and congregational growth. "Organic growth" is represented by Marks 3, 4 and 7: discipleship, leadership, and stewardship. "Conceptual growth" is represented by Marks 8 and 9: cooperation and identity. "Incarnational growth" is represented by Marks 2 and 6: social witness and service. The focus of the "Grow by Caring" program was on quantitative and qualitative growth, not just numbers alone.

In addition, "Grow by Caring" was designed for local churches, adaptable to any local context, and resourced with usable materials. Unlike other ABC emphases in years past, "Grow by Caring" was not heavily staffed with national or regional experts. Through "Academies for Growing Churches" local pastors were trained to consult with their neighboring ABC churches. As a result, more than 50% of ABC churches enrolled in the program. On the negative side, the broad emphasis of the "Grow by Caring" program had no particular cutting edge. It permitted churches to avoid the issue of numerical growth by focusing on other "growth" areas. Unlike other ABC programs, "Grow by Caring" appears to have been designed to please everyone, a feat not easily achieved by a denomination caught in the middle of theological, racial/ethnic, and regional/cultural divisions.

New Church Development

ABC new church development has followed a pattern similar to other mainline Protestant groups since World War II: significant activity from the late 1940s to the early 1960s, minimal activity from the early 1960s to the late 1970s, and a resurgence of activity in the 1980s. The ABC started 389 new churches in the 1950s, 254 in the 1960s, 168 in the 1970s, and 402 in the 1980s. Two trends in ABC new church development are noteworthy. First, the percent of nonwhite new church starts in the ABC increased from 23% in the 1950s to 67% in the 1980s. Second, 137 "new" churches, which started on their own in the 1980s (mostly ethnic and minority), came to the ABC for membership in the denomination. Only 265 new churches were started with the approval and support of the ABC's New Church Development Council in the 1980s, a total comparable to the 1960s.

The post-war years provided a feast for ABC new church development, particularly the 1950s. The "Churches for New Frontiers" program was implemented by the Home Missions Society (now the Board of National Ministries). Several million dollars were raised for new church development needs: salary support, budget support, and building construction. Churches were started in ABC regions all across the United States. Unlike more recent years in the ABC, these new churches were almost exclusively white, suburban churches. Following the feast of the "New Frontiers" era, a new church development famine ensued. From the early 1960s until the late 1970s other priorities concerned BNM staff, including the political and cultural upheaval of the nation. An additional inhibition to new church development was ABC philosophy regarding declining white, urban churches. These churches were encouraged to remain in their transitional area in order to reach the incoming population and, in some cases, to become urban Christian centers. Thus, relocation to more suitable demographic areas was discouraged and a number of church redevelopment opportunities were lost as a result.

It was not until 1981 to 1982 that the ABC began once again to move forward aggressively with new church development. With the strong endorsement of ABC national and regional executives, and the organizational efforts of the BNM New Church Development Council, the ABC's General Board affirmed new church development as a priority for the denomination. New church development was vigorously promoted, and new church development committees were established in all ABC regions. With the 1983 launch of "Grow by Caring," new church development gained increasing attention. By 1984, a new church development planner was added to the BNM staff to work with the director of new church development and the New Church Development Council.

By 1985, two significant things happened. First, the "Alive in Mission" campaign was launched at the ABC's 1985 biennial meeting in Portland, Oregon. Of the funds raised, 46% were to be set aside for new church development. As of mid-1991, $32 million in pledges had been received, exceeding the goal of $30 million. Second, the "500 More by '94" program was launched, meaning that 500 new church starts would be attempted by the ABC'S thirty-seven regions from 1985 to 1994. ABC leaders claim that the "500 More" program is different from the "Churches for New Frontiers" in several ways. First, the entire national denominational apparatus is involved. The Board of International Ministries gave a substantial cash gift to the program. The Board of Educational Ministries offered free church school materials. The Ministers and Missionaries Benefit Board offered substantial support towards pastors' pensions. The New Church Development Council developed a "structured interview process" to identify the characteristics of effective new church pastors. The hope was for a more effective program than Churches for New Frontiers. Through mid-1991, the 78% survival rate for the "500 More" new church starts was encouraging. Out of 265 new churches, 206 had survived.

The United Church of Christ

The United Church of Christ (UCC) was formed in 1957 by the union of the Evangelical and Reformed Church (E&R) and the Congregational Christian Churches (CCC), the former rooted in the Calvinist and reformed traditions of continental Europe and the latter in English Puritanism and the American restorationist movement. Reinhold Niebuhr described the E&R as a tradition of "liberal evangelicalism" while the CCC expressed a "modern liberalism shading off to Unitarianism" (as quoted by Gunnemann, 1977:23). With this heritage it is not surprising to find the UCC to be the least evangelical of the three denominations under consideration. In fact, the UCC may be one of the least evangelical of all American denominations if "evangelical" is defined by sectarian attitudes and behaviors oriented to the conversion of "non-Christians" and Christians whose beliefs and practices are considered incorrect. Ironically, evangelism is the only specific assignment given to the UCC's Board of Homeland Ministries (BHM) in its constitution.

Evangelism and Church Growth

One empirical study of forty-seven U.S. and Canadian denominations supports the notion that the UCC is among the least evangelical of denominations, given the above definition of "evangelical." In this study, UCC church leaders (laity, parish clergy, church leaders, theologians, and seminarians) scored low overall on four measures of evangelicalism: assertive individual evangelism, precedence of evangelistic goals, "born-again" Christianity, and evangelistic witness. On those measures, only Jewish and Unitarian clergy were more disinclined to evangelism. UCC laity, on the other hand, were as equally disinclined to evangelism as Disciples of Christ, Episcopalians, Orthodox, Roman Catholics, and United Church of Canada members (Schuller et al., 1980:126-27, 130-31, 172-73, 216-17). Though the Schuller study was conducted more than a decade ago, little has happened to suggest that the ethos within the UCC has changed very much. There has been considerable interest in membership growth for more than a decade in the UCC; however, such an interest does not necessarily mean a fundamental change in attitudes toward a conversionist type of evangelism.

UCC evangelism, as promoted by the BHM, has experienced "five clearly identifiable periods marked by several major turning points, or shifts," according to R. Alan Johnson. These include: the "years of consolidation" (1957–59); the "years of ferment" (1960–71); the "years of rebirth" (1972–79); a "transition period" (1979–80); and the "years of challenge and change" (1981–87). Anticipating the future, Johnson refers to the years following 1987 as "years of reintegration" (Johnson, 1987:1-2).

When the UCC was formed in 1957, the E&R and CCC each had different emphases in evangelism. The E&R Church emphasized relatively conventional evangelism programs, such as the "teaching, preaching, reaching missions" (TPRM): to teach the church, reach the unchurched, and preach the living Word (Johnson, 1977:3). In contrast, the CCCs were engaged in experimental evangelism under the leadership of Robert Spike, who was more interested in the emerging fringes of culture, such as the "beat generation," rather than the ecclesiastical status quo. The stage was set for a continuing tension within the UCC as to the substance and style of their evangelism program. Was the evangelism program of the UCC supposed to engage "the cutting edge" of American culture, however the spirit of the times may define it, or was it supposed to resource the constituent church's membership growth concerns? The latter emphasis has prevailed of late, but this tension is unresolved.

The 1960s began with the TPRM emphasis evolving into the "Mission on Renewal and Evangelism" program (MORE); nevertheless, the crises within

American society increasingly captured the attention and energy of UCC leaders. MORE became less as evangelism was more and more oriented to social action and less and less to the resourcing of local churches. While the "Local Church in God's Mission" emphasis tried to bridge the gap between social issues and local institutional concerns, the movement toward social action prevailed.

By the late 1960s, the work of the UCC evangelism division centered around personal interaction and human potential. One executive recalled that "evangelism had simply gone off into the stratosphere and was not providing the local church with any useful resources." Another recalled an alleged attitude held at the time that "you weren't being faithful to social justice if you were thinking about growing." Both the substance and style of UCC evangelism were found wanting by many at that time.

The early 1970s, or "the years of rebirth," proved to be a turning point for UCC evangelism emphases. "It was time to reform the work of evangelism by once again going to the definitional level. . . . Expectations were high for a fresh, theologically grounded, socially relevant, and biblically based understanding of evangelism" (Johnson, 1977:5). Two unrelated events in the early 1970s are noteworthy: the UCC publication of *Evangelism for a New Day* (UCBHM, 1972) and the emergence of Key '73. *Evangelism for a New Day* represented a rapprochement between evangelism as deed (i.e., social action) and word (i.e., invitation to faith) and was attempted through "action evangelism," the theological framework of which came from UCC theologian Gabriel Fackre (see Fackre, 1973, 1975). It also was more oriented to the needs of the local church for membership recruitment. Evangelism was affirmed by the UCC's 1975 General Synod, which declared that the UCC "has a Gospel to proclaim" and that "membership be strengthened in numbers and spirit" (Johnson, 1987:7).

In the meantime, the precipitous decline of UCC membership from 1965 until the late 1970s caused increasing concern. Some rationalized that the church risks numerical decline when it is "faithful to the gospel" (i.e., engaging in unpopular social action). In trying to be "an open and inclusive communion" committed to rectifying social problems, the UCC "has paid the telling but not unforeseen price" (i.e., loss of members). Others in the UCC, equally committed to social action, suggested that they had "failed to invite friends and neighbors to share with us 'the cost and joy of discipleship'" (Gunnemann, 1977:104-5). Concern for social relevance was tempered somewhat by the realities of institutional survival. Some UCC leaders were increasingly concerned about generating sustained commitment to steps necessary to reverse membership decline. By 1979, they had succeeded in making church growth a highly visible issue in the UCC. They also enlisted the services of Lyle Schaller, the most widely read church growth consultant in North America (see McKinney and Olson, 1991). Having Schaller in this capacity helped to give church growth issues even greater visibility and credibility within the UCC.

The UCC's continuing membership decline and the increased interest in church growth, pushed the denomination toward more conventional "evangelism" programs (read: membership growth). One executive claimed that "from 1980 to the present, there has been a deepening, enriching, empowering, exploding affirmation of evangelism and membership growth in this denomination that . . . is like a tidal wave. [It] is reawakening the denomination." Translated, this enthusiastic denominational "execspeak" means that a particular understanding of evangelism—obviously advocated by that executive—has received the support of many UCC people. Indeed, the changes in UCC evangelism emphases since the early 1970s have been significant. The ferment of three decades led the UCC's 17th General Synod to vote 86% in favor of making evangelism a priority from 1989 to 1993 (see United Church Board for Homeland Ministries, 1989:1). As one executive commented, this required persistence and commitment on the part of a growing number of people who recognize that if the UCC is to have a viable future and be faithful "to what the Gospel calls us to be about in word and deed . . . we must be reaching out to people whose lives have not been claimed by the Gospel. And through this persistent effort, we are today at a place where we were not 12 to 15 years ago."

New Church Development

Trends in UCC new church development are similar to other mainline Protestant denominations. Vigorous post-war church extension was followed by a drought of new church development from the early 1960s to the late 1970s. The difference from one decade to another is stark. Between 1958 and 1961, the UCC started an average of forty-four new congregations per year; between 1969 and 1971, an average of only three per year were started. From the late 1970s through the 1980s, however, the UCC has experienced a significant resurgence in new church development.

During the new church development drought there was little interest in starting new congregations. At the time, BHM money was more often used for experimental ministries than for the development of more traditional congregations. In a 1975 letter to an executive, one UCC lay leader complained that UCC new church development was too focused on "a romantic search for the new form [of congregation]," such as house churches. Not only was UCC new church development skewed in the direction of experimenting with new church forms, few saw it as a priority in the first place. For example, the UCC conference in southern California identified thirty-two mission priorities in 1973 to 1974 and new church development came out dead last. A UCC conference in one of the fastest growing areas of the U.S. was not, at that time, the least bit interested in new church development.

From 1972 to 1979, when new church development was at a low ebb in the UCC, the foundation for New Initiatives for Church Development Program (NICD) was laid. There were some "vague yearnings" to re-engage in new church development among church leaders at the time. There was no ground-swell movement pushing for it, however, the above-mentioned southern California case being an example. The impetus came from within the BHM itself, from its top executive leadership. After seven long years of study, discussion, and preparation, the NICD program was approved by the 12th General Synod of the UCC in 1979. A total of $6.4 million was received toward the campaign goal of $8 million, all of the funds raised committed to providing leadership subsidies for sixty-eight new and thirty-four "renewed" churches. Fifty-nine of the NICD projects were "Anglo" and forty-three racial/ethnic minorities (black, Hispanic, Asian/Pacific Islander, Native American). Of the 102 projects, 39 were in the Sunbelt and the remaining 63 in the Frostbelt.

Once the NICD program was completed and evaluated, a new ten-year commitment (1986–95) to new church development was proposed to the 15th General Synod in 1985 and approved. The goals: a national strategy for UCC new church development; leadership development for new churches; 150 new church starts, 50 of them being ethnic/minority; adequate funding for subsidies, site acquisitions, and construction costs; and multiple models for new church development. Six models have since been proposed: (1) new churches initiated by conferences with ministerial leadership subsidy from conference and BHM; (2) new churches started with multiple covenant partners including conference, BHM, and strong, established UCC churches; (3) new churches resulting from conference efforts and covenants; (4) churches with "renewed vision" (i.e., renewal of an established church, presumably in a state of decline); (5) newly affiliated churches (i.e., pre-existing churches that join the denomination); and (6) new churches as a result of "relocations" of established churches (United Church Board for Homeland Ministries, 1991:3-5).

As of the 18th General Synod in 1991, fifty-seven new church starts were reported out of seventy-one approved at that time. In the meantime, a ten-year national UCC strategy (1992–2001) was developed by a national new church development committee involving conference ministers—a "new kind of partnership" between the BHM and UCC conferences. In spite of all this activity in new church development, funding has been a problem. In the words of one executive, there are "more opportunities than resources available." For the current wave of new church development the BHM has provided the major funding. Other fund-raising efforts, such as the "Strengthen the Church Offering," have been disappointing: $310,776 was received between 1988 and 1990 against an expected income of $880,000. Over $2 million was projected from that same offering for 1991 through 1995. Given the offering's 1988 to 1990 track record, optimism about such income is guarded at best. "Too many hands in the pot" and "poor promotion by the Stewardship Council" were offered as reasons for the large shortfalls. There is, in addition, the politically volatile issue of having special fund-raising efforts for new church development when other national instrumentalities and conferences may want to fund projects of their own.

The United Methodist Church

Like the UCC, The United Methodist Church (UMC) is the product of mergers. The 1968 merger creating the UMC combined The Methodist Church (formed in 1939 out of three Methodist bodies) with the Evangelical United Brethren Church (formed in 1946 by a merger of the Evangelical Church with the United Brethren). (See Norwood, 1974:406-25.) This merger created the largest U.S. Protestant denomination at the time, with 11 million members and 42,000 churches located in 97% of the counties of the U.S. Since then the UMC has faced two unique challenges. First, the UMC is a national church, unlike most denominations, which tend to be more regionally concentrated. Its geographical breadth means a regional diversity that is difficult to manage. There may be "seven churches" in the UMC: the Yankee Church, the Industrial Northeastern Church, the Midwest Church, the Church South, the Southwest Church, the Frontier Church, and the Western Church (Wilson and Willimon, 1985). The exact number and boundaries may be arguable, but few doubt that regional religious cultures exist and include different understandings of what it means to be a Christian, and a church.

Second, the UMC's size and structure make it difficult to compare with most denominations. It has more than seventy annual conferences (regional judicatories), which form five large jurisdictions: Northeastern, North Central, Southeastern, South Central, and Western. Each jurisdiction could be a denomination of its own. The seventeen conferences of the Southeastern Jurisdiction, with about 13,000 churches and 2.9 million members, almost equal the combined size of the ABC and UCC. The UMC's sheer size is complicated by its decentralized bureaucracy, with national agencies located in Dayton, Evanston (Chicago), Nashville, New York, and Washington, D.C. Unlike the ABC and UCC, the UMC has no chief executive officer or any particular "corporate culture." Its general boards function autonomously under the direction of the Church's General Conference and Council of Bishops. National UMC leaders refer to their Church as a "confederation of conferences," which raises the question of how "united" the UMC really is in ideology, culture, and structure.

Given these characteristics—its geographical breadth, regional diversity, size and structure—it is difficult to generalize about evangelism, church growth, and new church development in the UMC on the national level. Granted, emphases from the general boards can and should be studied; however, United Methodism's experience of decline and response to decline varies by annual conference and regional jurisdiction.

Evangelism and Church Growth

Prior to the 1968 merger and 1972 restructuring, the Methodist Board of Evangelism had a professional staff of nearly fifty, headed for twenty-six years (1939–65) by Harry Denman, a dynamic lay preacher. The Denman era was for some the golden era of Methodist evangelism in the twentieth century: a vigorous program that promoted visitation evangelism and preaching evangelism. Since Denman's retirement, the evangelism program experienced major structural, leadership, and financial changes. In 1972 the Board of Evangelism became the Section on Evangelism of the General Board of Discipleship (GBOD), and its staff was reduced to eight people. From 1965 to 1990, eight executive secretaries served the evangelism section, the longest tenure of any being only six years. Evangelism in the UMC lost both the status and visibility of board stature within the denominational structure. UMC evangelism leaders found themselves buried within another agency and much less visible to the General Church.

Changes in board membership policy also had their impact. Before 1972, representatives on UMC general boards were allegedly appointed for their expertise. One executive doubted that the staff knew more than Board of Evangelism members did, recalling that semi-annual board meetings were "incredibly vital experiences because of the competency in evangelization that our board had." After 1972, the general boards were required to be age balanced and divided equally by clergy, laymen, and laywomen. In addition, at least 25% of a jurisdiction's membership on each general board should be racial and ethnic minority persons (Johnson and Waltz, 1987:52). One UMC executive felt that the evangelism program suffered as a result. "When [the evangelism staff] met with its section of the [GBOD] for the first time, the first thing we did was spend two days talking about evangelism and defining it because virtually every board member was a non-specialist in evangelism."

Financial changes affected evangelism as well. From 1975 to 1986, the Consumer Price Index (CPI) increased 123% while the UMC's World Service and Benevolence Funds (WSBF) increased 83%, from $52.5 to $96 million. The net result was a 40% loss of purchasing power (or $21 million) over the decade. Meanwhile, the GBOD fell further behind the CPI with expenditures increasing 60% from 1975 to 1986, from $2.5 to $4 million. To keep pace with the CPI, GBOD's 1986 expenditures should have reached $5.6 million, $1.6 million more than they expended. GBOD Evangelism Section expenditures increased by only 8% from 1975 to 1986, from $416,300 to $450,345, far below the CPI (123%) and well below the WSBF (95%) and GBOD (60%). Had expenditures for the Evangelism Section kept pace with inflation, expenditures should have been about $930,000 in 1986, more than double what was actually available (see Holsinger and Laycock, 1989:23-25).

The UMC's general boards were, like other mainline bodies, heavily involved with social concerns in the 1960s and 1970s. Traditional evangelism emphases suffered, but not because Evangelism Section leadership moved away from it. In fact, most of the eight who served as executive secretaries for evangelism from 1965 to 1990 were evangelical and predisposed to conventional forms of evangelism. One of them, George Hunter (Executive Secretary, 1977–83), was one of Donald McGavran's closest disciples in the church growth movement (see Hunter 1979, 1980, 1987; McGavran and Hunter, 1980). None of these secretaries has commanded the attention of their denomination quite like ABC and UCC evangelism/church growth executives, or has set a particular church-wide tone for evangelism. Given its large size, and the fact that the Section on Evangelism is buried within the UMC's complicated and decentralized structure, gaining the Church's attention is difficult for any evangelism executive, and none of them has stayed long enough to do so.

In spite of the many structural, leadership, and financial changes endured by the Board of Evangelism and GBOD Section on Evangelism, the type of evangelism it advocated remained rather consistent over time. The Council on Evangelism, an auxiliary organization since the Denman era, has continued to conduct biennial congresses on evangelism, although attendance has dropped in recent years. During George Hunter's tenure as evangelism secretary, the Foundation for Evangelism was revitalized to advocate and fund UMC evangelism. One project involved helping UMC seminaries endow chairs in evangelism for their faculties, some named for the Methodist missionary, E. Stanley Jones. As of 1990, six UMC seminaries had either established or nearly established these evangelism faculty positions. In addition, evangelism and church growth programs were offered consistently. Recent examples include: "Offer Them Christ," "Growth Plus," consultations with large church pastors, church school growth, a telephone hotline to help retain relocating UMC families, special emphases on baby boomers, Hispanics, and Asians.

Though evangelism emphases were fairly consistent since the 1960s, it was during the 1984–88 quadrennium that the UMC's membership decline gained church-wide attention. It began, at least symbolically, with the eleventh hour resolution at the 1984 General Conference to double membership to 20 million by 1992. Though some viewed the resolution as well intended but unrealistic, the ferment that it spawned was quite real.

Following the 1984 General Conference, a membership growth committee was formed by the Council of Bishops and chaired by Bishop Richard B. Wilke of Arkansas. Soon thereafter, a spate of books appeared on the theme of "what's wrong with the UMC and how to fix it." Beginning with Bishop Wilke's book, *And Are We Yet Alive,* six books on that theme appeared between 1986 and 1989 (Wilke, 1986; Hunt, 1987; Johnson and Waltz, 1987; Willimon and Wilson, 1987; Heidinger, 1988; Holsinger and Laycock, 1989). Prior studies of UMC decline, such as Hartman's study (1976) of UMC membership trends from 1949 to 1975, simply did not get the attention of the general church quite like Bishop Wilke. From 1968 until 1984, the General Conference and general boards were too busy getting organized, battling social ills, and celebrating the Methodist bicentennial in 1984 to deal with decline.

New Church Development

The responsibility for new UMC churches lies with the annual conferences. The function of the general boards in the area of new church development is primarily advocacy, resourcing (financial and training), and consultation. Traditionally, the UMC's National Division of the Board of Global Ministries (BGM) had the primary national responsibility for resourcing new church development. Prior to 1970, a staff of six served the church extension department in that board. Their job was to resource conferences at every stage of developing new churches, including providing loans for buildings. After 1970, the church extension department was shut down and new church development resourcing subsumed under other work areas. In 1983, the GBOD added a staff position in new church development to augment the remaining services available through the BGM. For a denomination as large as the UMC, there are remarkably few general board staff working in new church development in 1990.

Like other mainline denominations, UMC church extension efforts declined after the 1950s. Between 1958 and 1961, The Methodist Church started an average of 124 new churches per year (Johnson and Waltz, 1987:39-40). Between 1966 and 1969, this average dropped to 49 new churches per year; and between 1970 and 1974, it dropped even further to just under 20 per year. In 1975 to 1979 the number of new church starts was up to about 34 per year; and between 1980 and 1984, reached almost 66 per year (Johnson, 1986:2). From 1985 to 1987, the UMC averaged just under 60 new churches per year.

When studied by jurisdiction, clearer patterns emerge. All UMC jurisdictions have followed the overall pattern of more new churches in the 1960s, fewer in the 1970s, and more again in the 1980s. Of the five UMC jurisdictions, the Southeastern and South Central jurisdictions have started the most churches. With the exception of Kansas, Missouri, and Nebraska, they consist of Sunbelt states, from Virginia to New Mexico. Of the five jurisdictions, these two have not declined in membership like the other three jurisdictions and mainline Protestantism in general. With the exception of 1975 to 1979, they have started the greatest percentage of new churches: 1966–69, 129 of 196 (66%); 1970–74, 67 of 98 (68%); 1975–79, 81 of 171 (47%); 1980–84, 161 of 328 (49%); 1985–87, 105 of 179 (59%).

The percentage of new racial/ethnic, minority UMC churches has changed over time as well. In the 1966–69 period, 7% of all new UMC churches were ethnic. By the 1980–84 period, 43% of all UMC new church starts were ethnic. Of all new ethnic UMC churches started between 1966 and 1984, 65% were Asian, 22% Hispanic, 10% black, and 3% Native American (Johnson, 1986:7). From 1984 to 1987, the percentage of ethnic new church starts dropped to 28% (65 of 232), but this was due to an increase in Anglo new churches rather than a decrease in the ethnic new church starts. The highest percentage of ethnic new church starts have been in Northeastern, North Central, and Western jurisdictions. From 1980 to 1984, for example, 45 of the 54 new churches (83%) started in the Northeastern jurisdiction were ethnic, versus 14 of 80 new churches (17%) in the Southeastern jurisdiction (Johnson, 1986:8).

By 1990, the UMC had neither a national program nor a strategy for new church development. At one time both the ABC and UCC were similar to the UMC in this regard: the primary initiative for new church development rested with the regional judicatory. By 1990, however, both the ABC and UCC had moved toward a coordinated national strategy for planning and funding new churches. The UMC, on the other hand, continued its long-standing policy of initiating new churches at the conference level. The result is that the UMC continues to experience a wide variation in new church development activity from conference to conference. Availability of funding for new church development also varies widely, from conferences like Virginia, which sought to raise $20 million in the mid-1980s for new church development, to others that had set aside very little.

Steadily declining membership had worried some national executives and bishops, and some conference level leaders as early as the late 1960s; yet, only since 1984 has the matter garnered much church-wide attention. As of 1990, the UMC still did not have any national strategy for evangelism, church growth, or new church development. At the conference level, however, some ambitious emphases have emerged. The annual conferences most active with evangelism, church growth, and new church development have been, for the most part, in the Sunbelt, where an evangelical tradition remains strong. Only recently have some northern conferences engaged in more concerted efforts in these areas. In addition, because of the structure of the UMC, the denomination's general boards have engaged mostly in advocating and resourcing their particular areas of expertise. Given the UMC's susceptibility to regional religious cultures and lack of theological consensus, its decentralized structure and lack of focused national goals, it is no surprise to find that the dream of the 1984 General Conference resolution to have 20 million United Methodists by 1992 remains unfulfilled.

Excursus: The Presbyterian Church (U.S.A.)

Before offering any conclusions from the ABC, UCC, and UMC, perhaps questions should first be asked about the uniqueness of their experience with evangelism, church growth, and new church development. Were the changes they experienced from 1965 to 1990 unique among mainline Protestants? Were the similarities between them coincidental or indicative of transdenominational patterns? Two recent histories of Presbyterian evangelism provide an insightful comparison (Walter, 1991; Bullock, 1991). They suggest that the patterns were pervasive across mainline Protestantism. ABC-UCC-UMC experience was not unique or coincidental.

Formed in 1983, the 2.9 million member PCUSA consists of two predecessor denominations: the United Presbyterian Church in the U.S.A. (formed by a 1958 merger of two Presbyterian bodies) and the Presbyterian Church in the U.S. An overlay of their evangelism and new church development emphases over time onto those of the ABC, UCC, and UMC shows a strikingly similar pattern (see Coalter, 1991; also, Bullock, 1991). Historically, one long-standing Calvinist controversy has been whether one should "await" or "awaken" the divine election of sinners (Coalter, 1991:33-34). Mainline Presbyterians have chosen to do the latter. Following their Arminian counterparts, they have hedged their bets on evangelism to mitigate the harshness of predestination. In addition, the "personal" versus "social" gospel debate has plagued Presbyterians for many years.

In this century, Presbyterians have moved from mass evangelism early on to more interpersonal forms by mid-century. By the 1960s, these methods were subordinated to "social transformation or action evangelism," a difficult shift that "illuminates a serious and debilitating division of Presbyterian evangelical impulses by the late 1980s. The Presbyterian tradition had long-standing parallel allegiances to the salvation of individuals while simultaneously promoting a redemptive transformation of American culture. Events within and without the church have led Presbyterians in the last three decades, however, to view these parallel thrusts as, at best, sequential rather than concurrent means, and frequently even conflicting options, for spreading the evangel" (Coalter, 1991:35). These "dual allegiances" have also created a dilemma within the ABC, UCC, and UMC. Evangelism emphases have tended to be sequential rather than concurrent. Along with their mainline Presbyterian counterparts, they have come to view evangelism as primarily "membership recruitment" rather than Christian witness meant to convert souls and transform society.

Presbyterian new church development has been no different from that of the ABC, UCC, and UMC. At the turn of the century, at the height of the "social gospel" era, Presbyterians engaged in urban mission because of increasing industrialization, urbanization, and immigration. By mid-century, the suburbanization of America prompted a shift in church extension efforts away from the inner cities to the burgeoning suburbs (Bullock, 1991:56-57). It was these mid-century new church development efforts that had waned by the mid-1960s among mainline denominations, including the Presbyterians. After a time of reduced activity, especially in "less promising fields" (i.e., inner city, town and country, experimental), mainline Presbyterians renewed their interest in "conventional" and more promising new church development (i.e., "high potential, self-supporting churches") by the late 1970s (Bullock, 1991:60-61). Spiraling costs, however, have made it difficult for mainline Presbyterians to start new churches at the same rate as mid-century (Bullock, 1991:81).

Future Strategies

The Presbyterian parallels with the ABC, UCC, and UMC are striking. The experiences of these denominations are not unique among the Protestant mainline, and are not coincidental. From the 1940s to the 1960s, they each engaged in conventional evangelism and new church development in an era when birthrates and participation in traditional religious institutions were at an all-time high, when their niche in a tripartite (Protestant-Catholic-Jewish) religious marketplace was *assumed* to be secure. From the early 1960s to the mid-1970s, each of these denominations sought to bear Christian witness to the social issues of the day while watching their memberships peak, then decline at a rapid pace. From the late 1970s to 1990, each denomination sought to counter membership decline by returning to more conventional personal evangelism and new church development programs, as well as by adding and adapting church growth techniques. Clearly, they have shared similar experiences and challenges: contextual changes, theological dilemmas, ideological battles, identity crises, membership losses, aging constituencies, shrinking financial support, spiraling costs and bureaucracies weighed down by diversified programs, and frequent restructuring.

Looking, therefore, at a period somewhat broader than 1965 to 1990 and delving a bit deeper than "who did what when" in which denomination, the questions are these: How shall changes in evangelism, church growth, and new church development in the ABC, UCC, and UMC be understood? Were their programmatic responses effective? What do these changes reveal about the dilemmas and challenges these denominations face today? Has the ambivalence toward evangelism in these three denominations subsided?

The Context of the Future

Before offering specific observations on evangelism, church growth, and new church development in the ABC, UCC, and UMC, four general observations are important. First, historic theological differences have caused tension and disagreement over denominational priorities in all three denominations in recent years. Evangelical caucuses advocate "historic Christianity," meaning more orthodox theology, a conversionist approach to evangelism and mission, and usually a more conservative orientation on social and political issues. Theological breadth, and conflict, especially within the ABC and UMC, has made programming for evangelism, church growth, and new church development particularly challenging and, at times, politically volatile (see Nash, 1987; Tricules, 1987; Sanders, 1987; and Heidinger, 1987).

Second, denominational programs have, in general, broadened since the 1960s. Until then, denominational boards focused mostly on domestic and foreign mission, evangelism and church extension, Christian education and publication. Since then, staff and funding were added to focus on peace and justice, feminism, minority group concerns, and the environment, among other things. The result is national boards that are larger in scope and scale. In an era of retrenchment, many more programs of considerable merit, from ecology to evangelism, have been forced to compete for a shrinking pool of funds.

Third, the quota system for appointment to national denominational boards has meant, in many instances, a trade-off of competence for inclusiveness. Though affirming inclusiveness in principle, many denominational executives interviewed for this study felt strongly that the cost outweighs the benefit. However controversial or politically incorrect it may be to suggest that such inclusiveness has its disadvantages, the impact of the practice on national denominational programs such as evangelism cannot be ignored.

Fourth, the importance of regional judicatory executives—executive or conference ministers in the ABC and UCC, bishops and district superintendents in the UMC—cannot be ignored. They can enhance or inhibit, make or break, national denominational emphases. Though ABC and UCC regional executives are not called bishops, they should be for the power they wield (Paul Harrison's [1959] classic analysis of authority and power in the free church tradition still rings true). They know what churches in their regions will tolerate, perhaps even use, and offer resistance when a national program doesn't suit them.

Ideology and Theology in Evangelism and Church Growth

Evangelism is an ideological battleground. Knowing who the critics were at any given time reveals which form of evangelism (i.e., ideology) prevailed. When social action dominated, the critics were alienated evangelicals. Viewed in that context, Key '73 could be seen as a conservative protest movement within mainline Protestantism. Though a disappointment as an evangelism effort, if not an outright failure, Key '73 served as a harbinger for mainline Protestant evangelism. Indeed, since the late 1970s, pietism and personal evangelism have been on the upswing.

With the exception of the UMC, evangelism staffing and funding did not decline from 1965 to 1990. The question therefore, is not how much money was spent on evangelism or how much staff there was from time to time, but how that staff was used and how that money was spent. Those who champion personal evangelism refer to the 1960s to mid-1970s as evangelism's darkest days; whereas, those who champion social action evangelism see the return to more pietistic, personal evangelism as regressive.

Within all three denominations the perennial sociological and theological dilemma persists. What is the church's evangelistic priority? Is it changing social structures in order to redeem all of society, or "saving" souls in order to redeem individuals? How is evangelism defined: Is it everything that the church does, or is it the specific activity of presenting the claims of Christ to individuals for the purpose of their conversion? The century-old battle of "social" gospel versus "personal" gospel rages on.

Differences in regional religious cultures are significant in these denominations, especially the UMC. What works in Waco may not work at all in Worcester. Mainline Protestants located in the evangelical South are much more likely to espouse and practice conventional evangelism than those located in Catholic/Congregational New England, where the evangelical tradition has always been marginal. Overcoming these regional differences is no easy task for any denominational evangelism program.

Many laity and clergy in these denominations are not evangelical at all, even in the broadest sense. Inviting people to follow Christ is not the driving motivation for evangelism for many others. The more common motivation for "evangelism" is membership recruitment: getting "more new members for our church." Many laity and clergy live out their faith and church life in a "nurturing" church that does not emphasize conversion. People are Christians by birth, or by "joining" a local church, and not because of any particular spiritual qualifications.

Evangelism programs in these denominations, no matter how brilliantly conceived or assiduously promoted, often face the challenge of having to convert their own people first as to the theological propriety and sociological necessity of evangelism. American mainline Protestants are imbedded in a secular, pluralistic society. The values of religious tolerance and civility are deeply ingrained within the ABC, UCC, and UMC. Therefore, "introducing Christ" to someone or "inviting them to church" must be weighed against whether or not that introduction or invitation would be offensive.

The significance of the church growth movement since the early 1970s cannot be underestimated. All of the executives interviewed were well aware of it. All had an opinion, from positive to negative. Many felt the need to respond to it, sometimes with creative results. If the church growth movement has done any service to mainline denominations at all, it has goaded them into self-examination. The ABC, UCC, and UMC all responded in one way or another to the church growth movement and used it, even if as a counterpoint, to shape their own approach.

Beneath the rhetoric of pious purposes, efforts in church growth (and new church development) could be construed as strategies for institutional survival. Denominations need a constituency of local churches to survive; the more that are growing the better. The church growth movement emerged at a propitious time in the 1970s, when mainline decline was at its worst. That mainline denominations became interested in evangelism and church growth at the very time their membership losses were the greatest should come as no surprise.

Future Challenges for New Church Development

Without a doubt, the 1970s were pivotal years for new church development in the ABC, UCC, and UMC. Ezra Earl Jones's book, *Strategies for New Churches* (1976), marked the watershed between the paucity of new church development from the early 1960s to the mid-1970s and the resurgence of it thereafter. In the meantime, a new church development movement swept North America—due in part to the impact of the church growth movement. The challenges facing new church development are similar in all three denominations.

First, there is a dearth of qualified pastoral leadership. Many pastors have little exposure to evangelism, church growth, and new church development and were not raised in growing churches. In addition, many use models of ministry that are usually inappropriate for new church development: the manager, the enabler, the pastoral caregiver/counselor, and the social activist.

Second, more conventional models of mainline Protestant new church development are expensive and increasingly so. The costs for pastoral leadership, congregational subsidies, site purchase, and facility construction have increased substantially.

Third, funding new church development has been a problem. Competition for the denominational dollar is intense. In 1990, for example, eighteen of thirty-nine UCC conferences were involved in some type of major fund-raising drive. In each denomination, there are more new church opportunities than resources available. Special offerings and fund drives have had mixed success.

Fourth, American culture has changed. Starting new churches in the 1980s and 1990s is much different than in the mid-century "boom" years. The "religious marketplace" has changed. The pervasive "church-going culture" of the post-war years is long gone. New churches, as well as established ones, must now "know their market" and establish visibility. With the "declining significance of denominationalism" (Wuthnow, 1988:71ff.), the ABC, UCC, and UMC, along with other mainline bodies, can no longer rely on "brand name" alone to attract people to their churches.

Fifth, on the negative side of recent new church development efforts, it appears that each denomination has been on their own, reinventing the proverbial wheel. There seems to have been little opportunity or interest for new church development leaders "to talk shop" with their counterparts in other denominations. Given the creativity that has recently emerged in new church development and church extension, that is indeed unfortunate.

The resurgence of new church development since the mid-1970s seems to be a positive development in all three denominations. The numbers of new churches started by the ABC, UCC, and UMC since 1980 have increased. The ABC and UCC have been in the process of developing national strategies for new church development; yet, as of 1990, the UMC had none at all. Each has developed national training conferences for their new church pastors. New church pastors and lay leaders enjoy a variety of resources that did not exist a decade ago. In addition, new models of church extension have been developed or explored. A good example is the UCC strategy for the next ten years (1992–2001), which speaks of six "church development models" (see United Church Board for Homeland Ministries, 1991).

The Battle of the "E" Word

We do not yet know what impact the evangelism, church growth, and new church development emphases of the 1980s will have on these three denominations. Yet, the "E word" (evangelism), an anathema for some people in these three traditions, has undeniably found its way to center stage. People at every level of these denominations are talking and learning about a concept and practice that was for many years left to evangelicals and fundamentalists. The word is being reclaimed for mainline Protestant parlance, and the concept is being reconsidered for mainline Protestant praxis. This could not have happened had there not been a concerted effort over the past fifteen years to reclaim personal evangelism, reaffirm new church development, and introduce church growth methodologies. If the three denominations under consideration have done anything at all to "turn things around," their leaders have seemingly raised the awareness of their constituents. One evangelism consultant has identified thirty-four factors that indicate that mainline Protestant attitudes toward evangelism have indeed changed and "that their now legendary decline can stop." Among them are (1) willingness of denominational leaders to deal with decline, (2) proactive leadership in mid-judicatories, (3) seminaries interested in evangelism, (4) willingness by denominations to fund evangelism, (5) pressure from "loyal" evangelical caucuses in denominations, (6) determination to plant new churches, (7) more pastors interested in evangelism skills, (8) more lay interest in evangelism and attendance at evangelism workshops, (9) recognition that service and proclamation are equally important, (10) recognition that denominational loyalty has waned and "passive" evangelism does not work, (11) availability of excellent evangelism resources and the willingness to use them, and (12) movement away from the "church growth fad" and evangelism "gimmickry." These indicators show that mainline Protestant attitudes toward evangelism are changing sufficiently enough to see a "cloud of hope building on the horizon" (Miller, 1989).

Herb Miller's encouraging observations indicating changing attitudes toward evangelism are based upon a particular view of evangelism. He is hopeful because the pendulum is swinging toward a more conventional form of evangelism. This study's findings on evangelism, church growth, and new church development in the ABC, UCC, and UMC support Miller's observations, even his hope, to a degree. On the other hand, Miller is silent about the fundamental ambivalence toward evangelism that confuses and occasionally divides the saints in mainline Protestantism. Milton Coalter makes the point well.

> One observation about Presbyterian and mainstream Protestant evangelical impulses can be ventured. The tensions between advocates of social action evangelism and verbal [i.e., personal] evangelism have yet to be resolved. In part, this is because neither can be dissolved adequately into the other. The two options are, in fact, not options in the Reformed tradition or, more broadly, in Christianity. They are instead the twin outgrowths of the *euangelion* proclaimed by Christ, who came to save sinners and to teach them a redemptive transformation of relationships that unavoidably involves Christians in reforming cultures (Coalter, 1991:53).

Advocacy for social action on the one hand, and personal evangelism on the other, remains strong in the ABC, UCC, and UMC, as well as the PCUSA, and the debate they cause remains unresolved. Neither side "has captured the imagination of the . . . mainstream Protestant masses who exhibit in varying degrees significant ambivalence, apathy, and/or discomfort with the topic of evangelism" (Coalter, 1991:54). That evangelism should have to be *voted* a "priority" by the UCC, let alone by any Christian denomination, is clear evidence of "ambivalence, apathy and/or discomfort" with evangelism. Even more, it is evidence of deep-seated confusion as to what the church's most basic tasks are in the first place. Significant changes toward more conventional evangelism, and greater interest in church growth and new church development have indeed occurred in mainline Protestantism since the late 1970s. Yet, without any rapprochement between those whose great commission is Luke 4:18-19, those whose great commission is Matthew 28:18-20, and all those in between, the evangelism dilemma will continue to nag the mainline denominations for years to come. For the time being, however, while creative energies and greater resources are focused on more conventional evangelism, church growth, and new church development, slowing down the membership slippage does seem to be within the realm of possibility.

C h a p t e r   F o u r

Growth and Decline in an Inclusive Denomination:

The ABC Experience

Norman M. Green and Paul W. Light

N
o other Protestant denomination in the United States has as much racial/ethnic diversity as the American Baptist Churches in the USA.[1] Major shifts in the absolute and relative size of the racial/ethnic groups in the ABC have taken place in the past thirty years, resulting in a decline in the white majority and an increase in the nonwhite minority. This chapter describes these changes and analyzes their institutional and contextual sources.

A description and analysis of the overall pattern of decline in the ABC must include the differing patterns of decline and growth among racial/ethnic groups in the denomination. Changing patterns of denominational mission support are also important in order to understand the current state of the ABC.

This case study is instructive for denominations other than the ABC. Many denominations share the intent of the ABC of becoming more inclusive and of ministering to racial/ethnic populations. Many denominations also share with the ABC the recent patterns of decline in the numbers of white churches and white members.[2]

Trends in the Number of Churches

There has been a steady decline in the number of churches in the ABC over the past twenty-five years.[3] In 1967 the denomination contained 6,001 churches. In 1990 the number of churches had dropped to 5,737 churches— a 4% decline. This trend masks very different patterns for the racial/ethnic constituent churches in the ABC. During this period the number of white churches declined by 17.5%, whereas the number of African-American churches increased by 112.6% and the number of other churches (Hispanic, Asian, Native American, Haitian) increased by 52%. The numbers of churches at the beginning and end of this period are shown in Table 4.1.

TABLE 4.1
Number of Churches in ABC/USA

	1967	1990	change	% change
Total	6,001	5,737	−264	−4.4
White	5,295	4,370	−925	−17.5
African-American	485	1,031	+546	+112.6
Other	221	336	+115	+52.0

The trend lines in the number of churches for the entire ABC, and for sub-groups are smooth and consistent from 1967 to 1990. These lines are graphed in Figure 4.1. White churches decreased steadily, whereas black churches and "other" churches increased in number throughout the period of study.

FIGURE 4.1
Number of Churches—ABC/USA
1967–1990

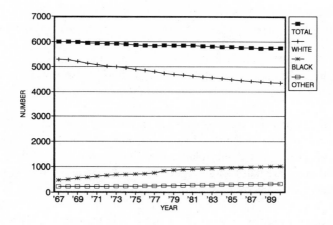

It is clear from Table 4.1 that the greatest absolute change in the number of ABC churches from 1967 to 1990 is the loss of 925 white churches. That represents a net average loss of more than 44 churches a year for twenty-three years. Since new white ABC churches were started throughout that time period, the real number of white church loss is closer to an average of 52 churches per year.

Churches are lost to the ABC by (1) disaffiliation from the denomination, (2) church closings due to insufficient membership base, and (3) church mergers. In the ten-year period from 1980 to 1990, 659 churches withdrew from the ABC, closed, or merged. Of that number, 65% withdrew, 31% closed, and 4% merged into another church.

White ABC churches that disaffiliate usually do so in protest of ABC ecumenical relationships (such as participation in the National or World Council of Churches) or in protest of policy statements or resolutions from the ABC. Some churches leave the denomination because they see the ABC as changing. It doesn't "feel" like it did in the past. The increasing racial/ethnic diversity (along with different styles of mission, leadership, and relationships) is not seen as a positive change by all churches. The continuing theological and evangelical/mission diversity is also hard for some to accept. As a result, independence is attractive to some congregations.

ABC churches that close are predominately white and are usually located in small towns and rural areas of the Northeast, Mid-Atlantic, and North Central regions. Baptists, along with Methodists in the nineteenth century, were active in establishing churches on the frontier as the population moved west. These areas, from the Hudson River to the Great Plains, north of the Mason-Dixon line, have experienced demographic shifts during the past two decades that have played important roles in the closing and merging of many white ABC churches.

The decline in the number of white churches is due in part to contextual factors, such as demographic shifts. The decline is also due to internal or institutional factors, such as diversity of theological stands and membership diversity.

Much of the African-American growth in the late 1960s and 1970s can be attributed to the influence of key black leaders and to the prominence of civil rights issues in the ABC. The relationship that Martin Luther King, Jr. and other Southern Christian Leadership Conference organizers had with American Baptists was a major reason for African-American churches becoming related to the ABC. The Ebenezer Baptist Church of Atlanta, pastored by Martin Luther King, Sr., joined the ABC in 1960. Martin Luther King, Jr. was a graduate of Crozer Theological Seminary, an ABC institution.

There are many educational factors behind the increase in African-American participation in the ABC. The roots of this influence stem from the denomination's commitment to black education following the Civil War. Northern Baptists were prominent in founding and funding colleges and seminaries in the South. Later, Baptist seminaries in the North were important in training black church leaders who became influential in the ABC.

Parallel to the educational factors that influenced black participation in the ABC were denominational concerns for human and civil rights. From its early stands for abolition and education, the ABC contributed to the growing movement for social justice through policy statements, resolutions, political action, and by civil protests. In the mid-1970s, an ABC program called Fund of Renewal sought to raise $7.5 million for minority education and inclusion in the denomination. While the financial goal was not realized, this program of breaking down racial barriers in regions, associations, and between churches contributed to minority growth in the ABC.

It could be noted that the Congregational/UCC tradition can recall a similar history of involvement in black education and civil rights concerns. The difference between African-American attraction to the UCC and the ABC is due in large part to two factors. The first is polity. Both the ABC and UCC maintain the autonomy of the local church as a manifestation of the Body of Christ, empowered to act in all matters of life and faith. There are, however, differences such as: definitions of what defines a cooperating church; how standards are enforced; per capita support expectations; and the denomination's role in pastor selection. It may be a question of "freedom" or it may be a question of "laxity," but African-American churches have more autonomy in the ABC and African-American Baptist denominations than they would have in the UCC.

The second factor is the ease with which an African-American Baptist church can add an ABC affiliation without a name change and without disaffiliating from another denomination.[4] In various regions of the ABC, the increases in the number of African-American ABC churches can be traced to the regional leadership's openness to accept, and even to recruit, black congregations. In the 1960s and 1970s, ABC agencies actively recruited African-American churches and pastors in the South to affiliate with the ABC. The number of black ABC churches in the South doubled between 1967 and 1973 (from 70 to 144 churches) and grew another 150% by 1978.

Another reason for the increase in the numbers of African-American churches in the ABC is economic. Because of the growing endowment in the ABC retirement plan and an excellent record of management of funds by the Ministers and Missionaries Benefit Board, the ABC retirement plan (and the related health plan) has become a major economic benefit for ABC pastors, lay workers, and ABC churches. Black pastors and churches were actively recruited by the Ministers and Missionaries Benefit Board, out of a concern to help churches provide a financial support for pastors. Since none of the Baptist denominations that are primarily African-American have such a plan, this economic benefit has been attractive for African-American pastors and congregations.[5]

Thus, the important institutional factors that have contributed to the increase in the number of African-American churches in the ABC are:

1. The leadership and influence of key black leaders in the denomination
2. The historic mission of the ABC in minority education and civil rights
3. The name and polity of the ABC, which allows for confederation
4. The active recruitment of African-American leaders and churches by key white leaders
5. The economic benefits of a well-managed retirement plan

The two contextual factors that affected the increase in the number of African-American ABC churches were the broader civil rights movement in the nation, and demographic changes among the black population. Black population growth in the South and the West, as well as in the urban centers of the Mid-Atlantic, coincided with the location of growth of African-American churches in the ABC.

In 1967, the 485 black churches in the ABC were 8% of its 6,001 churches. In 1990, the 1,031 black churches made up 18% of its 5,737 churches.

In the past ten years, the number of ABC Hispanic churches has increased from 203 churches to 228 churches—a 12% increase. At the same time, Hispanic population growth for the nation was 53%. Although much of this population increase was in areas where the ABC has not had a strong presence, this contextual factor has been important in the growth of Hispanic churches in the ABC.

The growth in the number of Hispanic ABC churches was also influenced by institutional factors. Mission work by the denomination in Mexico and Cuba dates from the 1860s; in Puerto Rico, from the 1890s. Today, only the churches in Puerto Rico are counted as churches of the ABC/USA, but this early mission activity has influenced Hispanic church growth in mainland USA. ABC refugee programs for waves of Cuban and Central Americans have also contributed to Hispanic church growth within the ABC.

While the number of Asian-American ABC churches was small in 1980, the growth rate for the decade ending in 1990 was larger than for Hispanic churches. The number of Asian churches grew from twenty-two in 1980 to forty-seven in 1990—an increase of 114%. In the general population, Asian and Pacific Islanders experienced a growth rate of 108%.

The denomination's investment in Asian missions began in 1813 in Burma and spread to Siam, China, and India by 1835. Baptist work in Japan was established in 1872 and in the Philippines in 1901. Refugee resettlement of South-east Asians also has contributed to an increase in the numbers of Asian-American churches in the ABC. New church development has involved Hmong, Cambodian, Indonesian, and Korean segments of the population.

There also is substantial regional variation in ABC rates of growth and decline. In the Western and Southern areas of the U.S., the number of ABC churches has increased slightly since 1967, while the greatest decline has been in the North Central region of the nation.[6] Over the past twenty-three years in the ABC: (1) the number of white churches declined in all sections of the U.S., (2) the number of African-American churches increased in all sections, doubling in the West and tripling in the South, (3) the number of "other" churches increased in all sections except for the North Central region, where the decline was slight.

Trends in Resident Membership

Total resident membership in the ABC declined by 10% since 1967—as compared to a 4.4% decline in the number of churches.[7] Thus, ABC membership losses due to fewer churches are exacerbated by membership losses from declining congregations. This membership decline is due to a steep decline in the number of white members. For every three members of white ABC churches counted in 1967, only two could be counted in 1990. In this period, the membership of African-American ABC churches almost doubled. Other ethnic churches experienced a 69% growth in membership. Table 4.2 shows the absolute and percent changes in resident members.

TABLE 4.2
Resident Membership in the ABC/USA

	1967	1990	change	% change
Total	1,335,342	1,201,741	− 133,601	− 10.0
White	1,077,388	693,701	− 383,687	− 35.6
African-American	234,894	469,101	+234,207	+99.7
Other	23,060	38,939	+15,879	+68.9

The patterns of change in resident membership as shown in Figure 4.2 reveal that slight increases were recorded in 1970, 1971, and 1972 as the African-American membership rose more than the white membership decreased. A similar situation occurred in 1980.

FIGURE 4.2
Resident Membership—ABC/USA
1967–1990

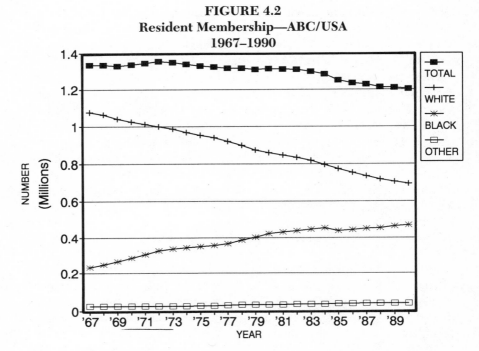

Only the South recorded an increase in resident members over the twenty-three-year period. In this region African-American membership grew faster than white membership declined. The increase in the number of Hispanic ABC churches in Puerto Rico also contributed to the growth rate in the South.

The growth of the "other" churches is important, although the white decline and African-American increase is the more significant story. This "other" category is made up of Hispanic, Asian, Native American, Haitian, and European ethnic constituents. Each deserves a description and analysis in its own right, but cannot be dealt with in appropriate detail here. Hispanic and Asian constituencies have been growing, while Haitian churches in the ABC are relatively new. The size of the Native American constituency has not changed much in recent years, whereas the number of distinctly European churches has declined.

In terms of resident members, the "other" category constituency of the ABC has grown from 1.7% of the ABC in 1967 to 3.4% in 1990. At the same time the African-American constituency has grown from 17.6% to 38.6% of the ABC, and the white constituency has declined from 80.7% to 58.1% of the denomination.

Another way of seeing membership growth and decline is pictured in Figure 4.3. This chart shows resident membership change over a five-year period from 1984 to 1989. Churches that increased resident membership by 10% or more in that time span were placed in a "grow" category, those that declined by at least 10% were placed in a "decline" category, and the rest were called "stable."

FIGURE 4.3
Growth Status by Race/Ethnicity—ABC/USA
1984–1989

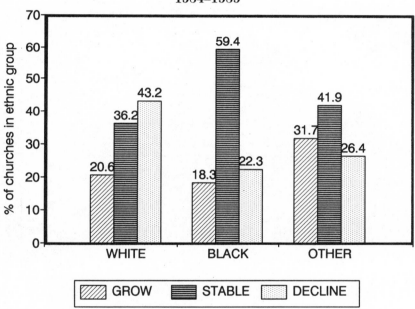

It is clear that some white churches are growing (about one in five). It is also clear that some African-American churches are declining (about one in five). It is important to note that the proportion of white declining churches is approximately twice that of the other groups.[8]

Trends in Worship Attendance

Worship attendance from 1977 to 1990 shows a pattern of change that differs somewhat from the graphs seen earlier.[9] From 1977 to 1990, worship attendance rose until 1982, fell until 1989, and rose again in 1990. That overall pattern, as well as attendance for white, African-American, and other churches is graphed in Figure 4.4.

FIGURE 4.4
Worship Attendance—ABC/USA
1977–1990

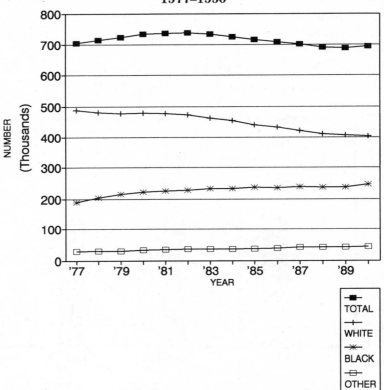

Increases in the total ABC are due to the fact that African-American and "other" gains are greater than white losses. Also, the decline in white worship attendance since 1977 has not been as sharp as the decline in white resident membership. The white worship attendance decline was slight prior to 1983, greater until 1988, and shows signs of moderation since 1988. White worship attendance even increased in the North Central section in 1990, the region of greatest white membership decline over the past twenty-three years.

Table 4.3 shows the changes in worship attendance and membership from 1977 to 1990. The largest percentage gains are for worship attendance and resident members for "others." These gains are primarily for Hispanic and Asian churches within the "other" category. Worship attendance for these groups grew by 56%.

TABLE 4.3
Worship Attendance and Resident Membership in the ABC/USA: 1977 and 1990

	1977	1990	change	% change
Total				
Worship Attendance	704,587	694,385	− 10,202	− 1.5
Resident Members	1,318,070	1,201,741	− 116,329	− 8.8
White				
Worship Attendance	487,997	404,190	− 83,807	− 17.2
Resident Members	919,821	693,701	− 226,120	− 24.6
African-American				
Worship Attendance	188,728	246,832	+58,104	+30.8
Resident Members	368,075	469,101	+101,026	+27.4
Other				
Worship Attendance	27,862	43,363	+15,501	+55.6
Resident Members	30,174	38,939	+8,765	+29.0

For "others" the number of worship attenders was greater than the number of resident members in 1990. Figures 4.5 and 4.6 show the result of this effect on 1990 membership and worship totals.

FIGURE 4.5
1990 Resident Membership ABC/USA

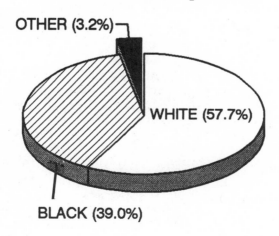

OTHER (3.2%)
WHITE (57.7%)
BLACK (39.0%)

FIGURE 4.6
1990 Worship Attendance ABC/USA

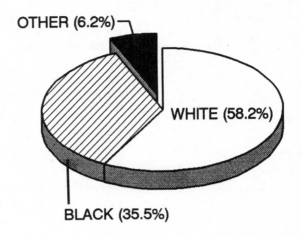

Trends in ABC Mission Support

Although the ABC has reported increased amounts of giving for the denomination's mission program, the rate of increase has not kept pace with inflation. This analysis of trends in American Baptist Mission Support (ABMS) is based upon the value of money given in 1977 (constant) dollars. The decline of mission support in constant dollars helps explain the decrease in the number of denominational staff.

Table 4.4 shows that the value of ABMS has declined about $4.5 million in a thirteen-year period, with white ABMS falling $4.6 million in value from 1977 to 1990.

TABLE 4.4
American Baptist Mission Support (ABMS)
in Constant 1977 Dollars for 1977 and 1990

	1977	*1990*	*change*	*% change*
Total	$21,867,826	$17,411,467	−$4,456,359	−20.38
White	21,171,740	16,539,074	−4,632,666	−21.88
African-American	392,986	537,058	+144,072	+36.66
Other	303,100	335,335	+32,235	+10.64

FIGURE 4.7
American Baptist Mission Support—ABC/USA
1977–1990 (Log Scale)

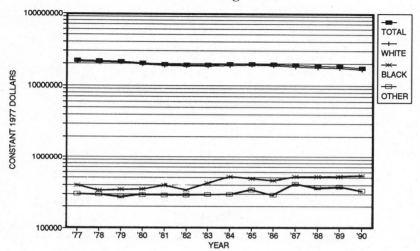

Not surprisingly, the decline in ABMS has been the greatest where the decline has been the greatest in white churches and white resident membership, i.e., the North Central and Mid-Atlantic regions. African-American ABMS support increased in the sections of the nation where the greatest increases in African-American ABC churches and resident members were recorded, i.e., the South and the West.

Trends in ABMS support are shown in Figure 4.7, plotted on a logarithmic scale. This graph shows that year-to-year fluctuations were not large. It also shows how much white contributions controlled the total. In 1990, white ABMS giving was 95% of the total ABMS giving, while African-Americans contributed 3.1%, and Hispanics contributed 1.4%.

In any given year between 1977 and 1986, from 86% to 90% of all ABC churches gave to ABMS. The percentage of white churches giving varied from 94% to 95%, while for African-American churches it was 58% to 63%. For Hispanic churches, it varied from 73% to 84%, and for Asian churches, it was as high as 77%.

When comparing American Baptist Mission Support from African-American churches to white churches, several differences must be considered. In the first place, a higher percentage of African-American churches are aligned with more than one denomination than are white churches. In the second place, African-American churches have traditionally committed a higher percentage of their mission dollars to local church mission projects in health, housing, education, and so on, than to denominational projects and programs.

For the "other" churches, lower economic circumstances of refugees and other immigrants, along with start-up costs associated with newly formed churches, are major factors in this mission support phenomenon.

Another way to understand the changes in the denomination's mission support is to analyze per capita (by worship attendance) giving to ABMS. For all ABC worship attenders, per capita ABMS giving dropped from $31 per attender in 1977 to $25 per attender in 1990. African-American per capita ABMS increased slightly, while white and other per capita mission giving declined. The trends line for all groups in Figure 4.8 shows an up-and-down pattern of change.

FIGURE 4.8
ABMS Per Capita (Worship Attendance)—ABC/USA
1977–1990

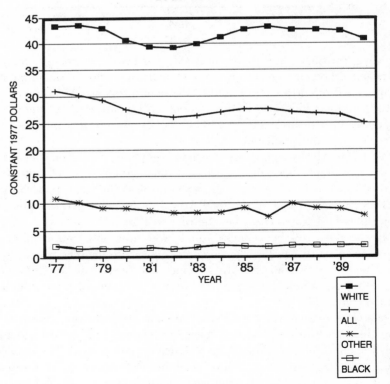

Implications

What are the implications of this study for the future of the ABC, and what is the environment for dealing with the implications? Planners and decision makers must resist the temptation to key on limited data and assert, "We have bottomed out," or "Our worship attendance is increasing." It takes more than two data points to define a trend, and it takes broad analysis to forecast the future. This study focused only on racial/ethnic groups, and ignored age of congregations and members, as well as types of church locations. Though other studies are needed at regional and national levels, it is possible from this study to offer some hypothesis for future development.

The trends in this study indicate that further erosion of white membership is to be expected, that further erosion of mission support of ABMS is to be expected, and that gains in black, Hispanic, and Asian members will not offset white decline. Institutional factors such as a slower decline in white worship attendance in the last two years may produce positive changes. Contextual factors such as the hoped-for return of the baby boom generation to church participation also may affect the future of the ABC. Planners, however, must take account of the past if favorable scenarios are to be realized in the future.

Unless mission giving patterns increase sufficiently to overcome the effects of inflation, cuts in denomination staffing and programming will continue. The ABC experienced cutbacks in many regional and national programs. Regional and national boards must face the probability that the retrenchment is not over. If retrenchment continues it will cause major tensions in the ABC over mission priorities, the kinds of services and programs offered, and the future mission orientation of the denomination. Cuts will not be uniform in all areas and endeavors. Since there are differences in mission goals, priorities, and funding between ABC racial/ethnic cohorts, arguments are certain to divide along racial/ethnic lines on some issues.

If trends continue, it is reasonable to expect that in the next twelve to fifteen years the traditional white majority will become the white minority. If that possibility casts fear in the hearts of many American Baptists, the denomination will face a stormy future. Changes in racial/ethnic participation in the last two decades have raised issues with which the denomination is now struggling. Justice and fairness issues about affirmative action within the denomination have been resolved at the policy level, but changing practices in recruiting and hiring has been slow. Questions of power and responsibility will continue to be crucial in the ABC.

As ABC leadership continues to affirm pluralism and inclusiveness in its public life, and as the nonwhite membership approaches white membership in size, it remains to be seen if white disaffiliation will increase. There is no model upon which to pose a prediction. Disaffiliation from white churches because of racial/ethnic diversity was a minor factor in the past, however.

If inclusion is to be realized in the ABC, it must work at all levels from the General Board to national and regional boards, and to the local churches. Inclusion requires that the wants, goals, needs, and values of all members and all local churches be considered in designing the mission goals of the denomination in the future.

The challenge before the ABC leadership at all levels is to bring about inclusion at the very time it must wrestle with diminishing resources.

Part Two

THE GROWTH AND DECLINE OF CONGREGATIONS

C. Kirk Hadaway and David A. Roozen

Why do some churches grow and others decline? That is the central question addressed by the chapters in this section. Our concern also is with the link between congregational and denominational growth. By understanding why congregations grow, it is possible to identify potential sources of denominational growth.

In this section, we find that evangelism is a major source of congregational growth. It follows that denominations with more evangelistic churches see more growth at an aggregate level. In addition, we find that newer churches grow faster than older churches. It also follows that younger denominations and denominations that start more new churches will have an advantage over denominations that start few new congregations. Growing denominations, however, are not growing simply because they start more new churches, and declining denominations are not declining because they lose more churches than they "plant." Growing denominations are expanding in membership because they have proportionately more growing congregations than they have declining congregations (see Marler and Hadaway, chapter 2). Factors that encourage local church growth are critical to understanding *denominational* growth.

This section has three major components: (1) an introduction to church growth perspectives, (2) tests of church growth strategies, and (3) analyses of the factors associated with growth and decline in congregations. The first chapter, by Inskeep, introduces the divergent research concerns of the "church growth school" and social scientists. The next two chapters test the effectiveness of church growth strategies. Do programs designed to produce growth actually do so? The final four chapters address the relative influence of a number of factors related to church growth and decline. Hadaway looks at the role of evangelism in producing church growth among Southern Baptist congregations. Thompson, Carroll, and Hoge consider factors associated with the growth or decline of Presbyterian churches. The same general approach is taken by Olson and Donahue and Benson with data from several denominations.

In order to understand why some churches grow and others decline, it is necessary to understand the way social forces influence church membership change. Hoge and Roozen (1979) argue that the growth of a local congregation is affected by its environment and by its own actions. They also argue that these factors—the context and the institution—operate at the local and national levels. Thus, Hoge and Roozen conclude that the church responds to social forces at four primary levels: national institutional, national contextual, local institutional, and local contextual.

This approach proved useful. The following chapters suggest helpful modifications to the Hoge and Roozen scheme, however. Two studies (Hadaway, chapter 8 and Thompson, Carroll, and Hoge, chapter 9) show that the institutional dimension can be subdivided meaningfully into what an institution *is* and what an institution *does*. In addition, it is difficult to study the effect of national institutional and national contextual factors on the fortunes of local churches. We are then left with three primary influences at the congregational level: the local context, institutional character, and institutional actions.

Social-scientific studies of church growth and decline underscore the importance of the local context. By contrast, members of the "church growth school," church growth consultants, and other advocates of "practice wisdom" emphasize the importance of institutional factors—what the local church is able to do in order to grow. Although these groups or observers generally talk past one another, Ken Inskeep suggests that the issue is one of balance rather than neglect. Further, the differences in emphasis between the two groups are highly related to their goals. Church growth writers are interested in reaching more people for Christ. Their focus, naturally, is on what churches as institutions can do to grow, and thereby achieve their evangelistic aims. The context is viewed by church growth writers as either a help in this process or a hindrance. While contextual factors are not ignored, they are not the primary focus. Conversely, social scientists are often accused of "environmental determinism." But as Inskeep notes, this label is unfair because social scientists never suggest that the local context determines whether a church grows or declines. They tend to emphasize the local context for two reasons. First, almost everyone agrees that the local church is affected by its immediate context. And second, the availability (and accuracy) of census data makes it relatively easy to measure local contextual change.

The chapters that follow consider the context of church growth, but they also look very closely at the power of the church as an institution. These are the most balanced studies to date on church growth and decline. What factors are related to growth or decline at the local level? We have identified eight areas for comment. Not all are major sources of growth (or decline), but all address serious church growth concerns. This list may be used as a guide when reading the chapters that follow.

> **1. Members of growing churches exhibit greater institutional commitment and greater desire for growth than members of plateaued and declining churches.**

According to the studies by Hadaway and Donahue and Benson, members of growing churches are more active, on average, than members of nongrowing churches. Commitment and interest levels are higher. Growing churches "feel" different from nongrowing churches—and this climate difference is as much a result of growth as it is a cause. Still, in growing churches, there is a sense that this is "the place to be." Members don't want to miss out if they are in town, so they attend more regularly.

Further, the chapter on evangelism by Hadaway and the chapter by Royle show that the "desire" for growth is related to both increased membership and additions. Desire for growth leads to institutional actions designed to produce growth. The fact that members want to grow also helps churches in other ways. Churches that desire growth seem friendlier and more welcoming to newcomers. Such churches exude a different "spirit" that visitors find attractive.

> **2. Growing churches emphasize outreach and (or) evangelism.**

Outreach seems to be the single most important action a church can take if it wants to grow. Even though some authors have minimized the effects of evangelism in reaching the unchurched (see Inskeep, chapter 5), the empirical evidence suggests that outreach is important to church growth. The effects of outreach and evangelism are reported in the chapters by Royle, Hadaway, Olson, and Thompson, Carroll, and Hoge. In fact, this is the most consistent finding in the section.

The chapters in this section employ a broader definition of evangelism than door-to-door witnessing or street-corner preaching. The relationship is between recruitment efforts (including evangelism) and growth. As Olson puts it, the key is an "outward orientation." Churches that are primarily concerned with their own needs are unlikely to grow.

The importance of outreach, evangelism, and recruitment cannot be overemphasized. Indeed, evangelistic activity is the only program variable that retains a strong relationship to growth when statistical controls are in effect. Quality worship, Christian education, and many other programmatic variables are related to growth, but most have little independent effect. By contrast, the independent effect of evangelistic activity is quite strong.

3. Growing churches are newer and younger.

Older churches and churches dominated by older persons are less likely to grow than newer churches and churches with a large proportion of younger adults. The presence of school-age children also seems to help.

Newer churches tend to grow faster than older churches. This is another consistent finding in the section. Even when other factors are controlled, the age of a church is strongly related to church membership change in Hadaway's evangelism chapter and in the chapter by Donahue and Benson. Also, in the previous denominational section, the chapter by Marler and Hadaway shows that church age is strongly related to church growth in very different denominations. It is not so much that old age hurts; it is that younger age helps.

New churches have a "window of opportunity" for growth. After about fifteen years, however, the likelihood for growth drops greatly. To a certain extent, the growth of young churches reflects their location. Many are in growing suburbs (see Marler and Hadaway). But even when we control for population growth, the influence of (young) age remains. As Olson suggests elsewhere (Olson, 1989), the members of newer churches have fewer close friendship ties in the church, and most persons desire more friends. Newer churches can integrate newcomers more easily than older churches where friendship cliques are well defined and difficult to join.

Younger church members also help congregations grow. This is evident in chapters by Hadaway, Donahue, and Benson, and Thompson, Carroll, and Hoge. Churches that are dominated by older members present a number of barriers to growth. These churches tend to be located in older residential neighborhoods near inner cities. Their programs and worship styles do not fit the needs and interests of young families and single adults. For many reasons, then, churches with disproportionate numbers of older members are less attractive to younger prospects.

As a church ages the situation grows worse. Members die or move away, and they are not replaced. The concentration of older persons increases and the church becomes progressively less likely to attract young adults. By contrast, churches that are dominated by young families do tend to grow. Such churches tap into the largest population cohort. Again, some of this success is a result of sheer demographics. For example, churches located in growing suburbs have a "ready supply" of young families. Churches in older neighborhoods, however, have proportionately fewer young families. Of course, demographics are not the whole story. Young adults are a hard-to-reach population. Churches that are able to reach this group are doing something programmatically beyond business as usual. They are offering programs and activities that no one else is offering, or they are offering a superior product (program). Baby boomers, after all, are church shoppers who make the "church choice" only after careful deliberation.

4. The influence of demographic variables has decreased, but it remains important.

Population growth, particularly as evidenced by new housing construction, remains a major source of church growth. Churches in growing areas grow faster, on average, than churches located in areas of population stagnation and decline. This is true for all churches, white or black (see Marler and Hadaway in this volume). This is hardly a surprise. Most clergy know from experience that churches in growing suburbs are more likely to grow than churches in older neighborhoods. As Olson suggests, however, the slowing rate of population change in urban America (due to population growth, population decline, racial transition, and white flight) means that the influence of demographic factors is reduced. Fewer churches are surrounded by booming suburban neighborhoods, and fewer churches experience rapid neighborhood transition. The growth of "programmatically poor" churches in suburban neighborhoods is less likely—as is the decline of "programmatically rich" churches in racially changing communities. The result is a lower correlation between population change and church growth. The potential influence remains, but when population change slows, the influence of the context decreases.

Yet the context of the church cannot be ignored because all churches are affected by their settings. *The character of the context makes it that much easier or that much harder for a church to grow.* Population growth in the form of newer housing helps churches grow, as does a large proportion of baby boomer families. Racial transition and large percentages of older persons lessen the chances for growth.

5. The influence of congregational conservatism has never been strong and may have diminished.

Earlier studies of United Presbyterian and Southern Baptist congregations showed a modest relationship between conservatism and church growth. Current research shows no increase between the two. In fact, conservatism remains a minor correlate of growth among Southern Baptist churches. And by contrast, Thompson, Carroll, and Hoge find that there is a small association between growth and *liberalism* among Presbyterian churches.

A connection between conservatism and growth is implied in the work of Dean Kelley (*Why Conservative Churches Are Growing*). Kelley's major point, of course, has nothing to do with conservatism per se. His primary thesis is that "strict churches are strong." "Social strength" tends to be accompanied by growth; and strict churches tend to be conservative. The connection is not direct, but it follows that conservative churches should be growing. They are, or at least they were, but the reasons for this growth have little to do with strictness. There is no clear relationship between strictness at the local congregational level and church growth.

6. Correlates of growth vary by location and church type.

Among other factors, congregation type and location affect growth. Smaller churches and churches in rural areas are less affected by their contexts and by institutional change. This finding is consistent with past research on church growth. In rural areas and small towns, rapid growth is difficult. At the same time, rapid decline is very unlikely. This tendency toward stability results in part from demographic factors. Rural areas and small towns experience less dramatic changes in population than metropolitan neighborhoods. There is no suburbanization, no urban decay, no white flight, no racial transition, no rapid population growth, and no rapid population decline in most rural areas. Institutional factors also are at work. Rural churches and small town churches are slow to change. These congregations are often dominated by longtime members who prefer that things be done "like they've always been done." For contextual and institutional reasons, therefore, very little seems to impact the growth of churches in small towns and rural areas.

For churches in metropolitan areas, the situation is entirely different. Great demographic possibilities exist for growth and decline. In addition, urban churches appear to be more open to change than rural churches.

Region is also an important factor in relation to growth. Church growth is more likely in certain parts of the nation—particularly in the South—than it is elsewhere. In general, the subculture of the South supports churches. In some declining mainline denominations, growth is rare outside the South. Regional factors, then, do encourage growth. As shown by Thompson, Carroll, and Hoge, correlates of growth are stronger in the South among Presbyterians. Programmatic growth strategies work in this region. In the Northeast, by contrast, growth is difficult regardless of what a pastor and a church try to do.

7. Denominational affiliation is a significant correlate of growth, over and above the actions taken by a local church.

A culture of growth is not limited to a region, however. As discrete subcultures themselves, religious denominations either encourage or discourage growth (see Marler and Roozen, chapter 12). The liberal/mainline subculture, for example, is not particularly friendly to church growth. Even when researchers control for evangelism, commitment, location, and other factors, the churches in conservative denominations do better than the churches in more liberal denominations. This is seen in the chapter by Olson and in the earlier chapter by Marler and Hadaway. In liberal/mainline denominations, growing churches are suspect. The pastor of a large, growing United Church of Christ congregation in Connecticut even suggested that other mainline pastors think that the pastor of a growing church must have "sold out" in order to grow—resorting to questionable marketing techniques and other "gimmicks."

In some denominations, an ethos exists that encourages growth-related activities and insulates the denomination from social change. Evangelical churches, apparently, are less affected by their social contexts. Their aggregate rates of growth may parallel the trends seen in mainline denominations, but evangelical churches tend to fare better in both "good" times and "bad."

8. Programmatic efforts to achieve growth often result in more activity than sustained growth.

The "activity effect" is seen clearly in the two program evaluation chapters (Royle, chapter 7 and Hadaway, chapter 6). Growth consultations and programmed growth campaigns often produce a flurry of activity in a local church. The activity may produce short-term growth if the level of excitement in the congregation grows, and if that excitement is channeled into activities designed to attract and incorporate visitors. But such growth rarely lasts very long.

This finding is a little distressing because one of the major reasons for studying growth and decline is to determine what changes must be made in order to transform nongrowing churches into growing churches. Clearly, doing so is a difficult process. Why? Because in order to grow substantially and to continue to grow, lasting changes must be made in the structure and character of nongrowing churches. Church growth writers contend that we now know what churches must do in order to grow. The problem is getting churches to be what they ought to be and do what they ought to do. This is a tall order because actions flow from identity—they cannot simply be applied like a thin veneer to the surface of a church. The change must be deeper.

Efforts to change the orientation of nongrowing churches often result in actions that produce short-term growth. The activity and new directions provided by a church growth plan, for example, often produce a sense of excitement and heightened commitment. Visitors are attracted to the church, and members tell their friends about it. More growth results, but the growth will not last unless growth-producing actions are: (a) clearly connected to a congregation's sense of overall purpose and direction, and (b) intentionally structured into the daily organizational life of the church. Unfortunately, this does not happen in many cases. After a year of growth, most churches that participate in programmed evangelistic or church growth efforts settle back into previous patterns of stability or decline (see Hadaway, chapter 6).

The distinction between "what is" and "what can be" is a major sticking point for social researchers and advocates of the church growth movement. The empirical analysis of social researchers focuses on "what is." "What can be" only follows by projection: Findings may lead to programmatic implications. But by and large, social scientists avoid saying "do this and it will help your church grow" or "don't do this because it tends to lead to decline." Without clearly stated implications, it is difficult for denominational program leaders or local church pastors to use social research on church growth.

By contrast, church growth writers are very practical. They tell church leaders what to do and how to do it. They are less concerned with "what is" and more concerned with "what can be." This future orientation breeds a tendency to move rapidly from casual observations of exemplar growing churches to general prescriptions for action. Most church growth writers depend upon case studies of large, growing congregations rather than careful analysis of the factors associated with growth and decline across a sample of congregations. The implication of this method is that nongrowing churches can grow by emulating the activities of a few "successful" growing congregations. "What worked for one church will work for another" is the guiding principle behind this approach. And while the maxim may prove true in some cases, it is still important that such strategies be tested to see how likely they are to produce the desired change across congregations.

More research is needed on church growth and decline, and the chapters included here fill part of that need. We now know much more about the characteristics associated with growth. In addition, we know more about the probable success (or failure) of specific programmatic actions. The next step is to integrate these findings with the existing literature and to create an ongoing process in which research leads to action—and in turn—to more evaluation. The process should continue, but first it must begin.

Chapter Five

A Short History of Church Growth Research

Kenneth W. Inskeep

The contemporary literature on church growth develops in two very different cultural worlds and under very different circumstances. Studies of mainline denominations are undertaken by professional social scientists working within academic communities. Their goal is to develop theoretical models that are useful in describing or explaining the membership declines suffered by mainline denominations since the 1960s. "Church growth" researchers, on the other hand, are largely conservative Protestant church professionals who began studying church growth out of the perceived need to "save as many souls" as possible. Their goal is to develop practical and successful techniques for bringing people to church.

As one would expect, given the different purposes and experiences of these two groups of researchers, the problem of church growth is approached from different points of view and out of dissimilar biases. The social scientist tends to show more awareness of the social context of church growth by explicitly considering "contextual factors."[1] Contextual factors are those forces external to the denomination or congregation that shaped its future—such as demographic changes in neighborhoods and falling or rising birth rates among different populations. At the same time, though with less emphasis and a certain reluctance on the part of some, the social scientists also considered "institutional factors" of church growth. Institutional factors are forces within denominations or congregations. They include patterns of organization and structure, the strictness of a group's religious beliefs, church programs, and other characteristics and orientations. Those in the church growth movement emphasize institutional factors of church growth almost exclusively. Their case studies, or case examples, lead them to concentrate on the internal dynamics of congregations rather than the social context. The following summary of the relationship between contextual and institutional factors provides a useful framework for considering the history of church growth research.

Social Scientific Research

The Kelley Thesis: An Institutional Account of Mainline Membership Decline

The tendency of most social scientists to emphasize contextual explanations of church growth and decline can be understood, at least in part, as a reaction to the first account of membership decline in mainline denominations by Kelley.[2] In 1972, Kelley argued that the growth of membership in conservative churches and the decline of membership in mainline churches was directly related to different types of religious commitment and organizational structure. Kelley never framed his thesis in institutional or contextual terms, but he clearly argued that the problem of membership decline in mainline churches was a result of their institutional inability to advance a belief system or an organizational ethos that would foster ardent membership commitment. Kelley, in a chapter titled "Traits of a Strong Religion," noted:

> Those who are accustomed to the placid and circumspect ways of the mainline Protestant denominations in America today may not think of religion as a strenuous and fateful adventure, catching up men's lives in a surge of significance and purpose, changing the very definition of what it is to be a man worthy of respect, and thus shifting upward a whole society's expectation of human behavior. But religion has often been this kind of movement in the past and will be in the future. (Kelley, 1972:56)

Kelley then set about developing a model of a "strong" religion, which he defined as one for which its members would be willing "to suffer persecution, to sacrifice status, possessions, safety, and life itself for the organization, its convictions, its goals" (1972:57). A strong religion demanded commitment, disciplined control, and missionary zeal (1972:58). Kelley argued that ecumenism and religious strength were incompatible and mutually exclusive. Strong religions were absolutist about beliefs, fanatic in their commitment, and demanding of strict conformity (1972:78). Weak religions were relativistic, accepting of diversity and dialogue, "lukewarm" about "truth," individualistic, and reserved. If a group was to grow, the community must be everything and the individual nothing. As Kelley put it:

> The appreciation of individual worth and freedom is one of the highest achievements of modern man, but it does not do much for social strength. If each member is unwilling to give unquestioning obedience (or even much questioning

obedience) to a leader or group, it makes for an atomistic aggregation of individuals rather than a cohesive, deployable organization. (Kelley, 1972:85)

Conservative Religious Belief and Its Relationship to Growth

Kelley's description of weak and strong religions as an explanation for the decline of mainline denominations provoked considerable controversy and generated a whole host of possible hypotheses for social scientists to test. Perhaps because of the title of Kelley's book—*Why Conservative Churches Are Growing*—much of the debate over his thesis focused on conservative versus liberal theological approaches to religion, rather than strict versus more relativistic religious beliefs and organizations. Bibby (1978) was one of the first of the social scientists to dispute the conservative versus liberal hypothesis. Based on his analysis of church membership data from a Canadian national survey, Bibby argued that if births could account for the growth in conservative evangelical congregations, rather than proselytism, then conservative theology per se could not be named as the church growth catalyst. Or, to put it another way, Bibby intended to show that contextual factors (birthrates) were more important to church growth than institutional factors (conservative theology) in explaining church growth. Bibby concluded that "neither the Conservatives nor the Mainliners were very successful in recruiting active followers from outside of the Christian community" (1978:136). Instead, higher birthrates and the willingness of conservative evangelicals to expose their children to more formal and informal religious socialization were the major sources of growth for conservative religious groups.

Bibby may have felt that he successfully disproved Kelley's thesis, but he was not as successful in demonstrating the unimportance of institutional factors in explaining church growth. He pointed directly to the institutional role of religious socialization. Bibby showed that conservative evangelicals were more likely to keep their children from leaving the church through their more effective efforts at socialization. He noted that 65% of the mainline affiliates were exposed regularly to Christian education in childhood, but less than 30% of mainline affiliates with children were "seeing to it that their children had a similar experience" (1978:136).

A similar study by Bouma (1979) compared the membership trends of the Christian Reformed Church (CRC) and the Reformed Church in America (RCA). He showed that the CRC absorbed the bulk of post-World War II Dutch Reformed immigrants to North America, and it was this immigration, not strong evangelistic efforts, that led to growth. At the same time, Bouma also argued, like Bibby, that the CRC lost fewer of the children it baptized.

As Bouma put it: "The secret of growth of the CRC is to be found not in evangelism, nor in attracting members from other denominations, but in the successful socialization of its young people" (1979:134).

Bouma's finding seems to confirm as much of Kelley's thesis as it disputes. The strict institutional demands of the CRC resulted in fending off losses, if not in producing gains. Bouma argued explicitly that the CRC was very demanding of its young members, strongly encouraging them to attend Christian day schools and church schools and to participate in youth groups and other mechanisms of "theological indoctrination." The result was higher retention of the children it baptized. Perhaps because Kelley's thesis was understood in terms of gains rather than fending off losses, or perhaps because Bouma misunderstood the institutional implications of his own findings on socialization, he concluded that Kelley's thesis was wrong and had, if fact, done great harm. "Policy makers in the church have been very much astir since the publication of Kelley's causal conjecture. It is unfortunate that such a rather shallow piece of social science has been used as a basis for policy decisions" (Bouma, 1979:135).

Hoge and Roozen: Institutional Factors Versus Contextual Factors

In 1979, Dean Hoge and David Roozen edited a volume called *Understanding Church Growth and Decline: 1950–1978*. The book was an attempt to pull together a series of social scientific articles on growth and decline. The majority of material concerned the decline of mainline denominations and factors that accounted for the decline. Hoge and Roozen, in pointing to the importance of contextual and institutional factors, were the first to explicitly provide a conceptual framework for understanding church growth and decline.

One of the significant studies of the volume was conducted by Wade Clark Roof and several others (Roof et al., 1979) on church membership change among United Presbyterian congregations. The study was based upon a sample of Presbyterian churches that were declining (30% or more total over a six-year period), those that were "typical" (not more than a 21% loss), and those that were growing the fastest (a 5% or greater gain). A set of questionnaires was distributed to the congregations to be completed by the pastor and a sample of church members.

Hypotheses derived directly from Kelley's thesis pervaded the study. The research also addressed difficult questions that were provoked by Kelley's book. For example, some Presbyterian theologians had begun to argue that church growth was "not the point" (Hudnut, 1975), and that an emphasis on growth might actually stand in the way of achieving other congregational goals. At best, growth was one goal among many. Clark Roof and his associates dealt with the question through the following hypothesis: "Considering five church goals—numerical growth, level of individuals' religious commitment, level of members' satisfaction and enthusiasm, level of love and care within the membership, and effectiveness of social witness—they are not mutually exclusive, and they do not form a fixed-sum system" (Roof et al., 1979:201).

Alongside the question of whether or not church growth was possible without the sacrifice of other important congregational goals, the Roof study (Roof et al., 1979) also raised the question of the relative explanatory power of contextual versus institutional factors. The author's partiality to context was quite evident in the way the hypotheses were proposed. For example, hypotheses having to do with context were stated outright: "Congregations will tend to grow if the community in which they are located is affluent." The institutional hypotheses, however, all began with the qualifying phrase: "If contextual factors are equal . . . congregations will tend to grow if they have internal harmony and cooperation." Three of the institutional hypotheses reflected Kelley's thesis and were stated conditionally. For example, "If contextual factors are equal, congregations will tend to grow if they maintain a clear sense of doctrinal truth, a clear system of meaning and value, intolerance of inner pluralism or dissent, and a high level of demand on members" (Roof et al., 1979:203).

Despite the contextual qualifications proposed for the institutional hypotheses, both contextual and institutional factors emerged as important. Affluence of the community surrounding the congregation and favorable demographic shifts were named as the two most important contextual factors. It was clear that growing Presbyterian congregations were most successful in communities of affluent, young, middle-class, largely white families. Satisfaction with church worship and program, and congregational cooperation and harmony among members were among the most important institutional factors. The role of the pastor was not directly important unless he or she was a factor in congregational conflict or stood in the way of congregational satisfaction with worship (Roof et al., 1979:222). According to Wade Clark Roof and associates: "Churches that grow are those able to generate high levels of membership satisfaction" (Roof et al., 1979:213).

The hypotheses related to Kelley's thesis were generally dismissed. As Roof put it: "Our data offers only weak support for his argument" (Roof et al., 1979:216). However, the same paragraph states, "we see that demands on members and conservative theology relate positively to growth to a noteworthy degree." In any case, it was clear that both institutional and contextual factors were important in understanding church growth. "In this study of Presbyterian congregations, we find that the two sets of factors are roughly equal in strength" (Roof et al., 1979:222).

After Hoge and Roozen: The Central Role of Context

Throughout the early 1980s the debate over the most appropriate explanation of church growth and decline continued to react to Kelley's initial work. Several studies contributed to the dialogue, sometimes only considering contextual factors and at other times carving out a more central role for the social context. Perry and Hoge (1981) use data gathered from 204 Presbyterian congregations to argue that Kelley's thesis was weak and unsubstantiated. As they put it: "Apparently the arguments about strictness, conservative theology, and evangelism made by Kelley and the Church Growth Movement writers are unimportant. Only their arguments about social action have a bit of relevance for understanding Presbyterian congregations" (1981:231). They continued: "theological tendencies, priority given to evangelism, desire for growth, and compatibility of pastor and laity are not important causes" (1981:231).

In studying the mainline and conservative churches of four SMSAs in the United States, Hadaway (1981:88) emphasized "the predominant impact of population change on church membership" for the growth and decline of mainline churches. In another study of churches in Memphis, Hadaway stated:

> Using Memphis as an example, we showed that church growth is quite unlikely in the downtown, inner city, and even in older established neighborhoods. However, as we move outward from the city to the suburbs and to areas where new housing is currently being constructed, membership growth becomes progressively more likely. These finding underscore the tremendous impact of urban location on the church, an impact that cannot be ignored if church planning is to be realistic. (Hadaway, 1982:384)

Both of these studies were concerned with only contextual factors.

In 1983, McKinney and Hoge tried explicitly to pin down the relative influence of contextual and institutional factors. In a study of United Church of Christ congregations, they found that congregations grew when they were in affluent, middle-class, largely white residential neighborhoods with a high percentage of home ownership and few other Protestant churches as competitors. Within the congregations, congregational harmony and cooperation and general laity satisfaction with worship and program were very important. The context, McKinney and Hoge argued, accounted for 50% to 70% of the explained variance in growth, while the institutional variables accounted for 30% to 50% of the variance (1983:64).

Bibby with Brinkerhoff (1983) took on the popularized Kelley's thesis once again in a return trip to twenty Canadian conservative evangelical congregations first studied in 1971. They classified each of the new members of the congregations as: reaffiliates—those transferring from other churches; off-spring—those who had joined the church prior to age ten and had at least one parent who was a member of the congregation; and proselytes—those who had come to the congregations from outside of the conservative evangelical community. Significantly, sixteen of the congregations still existed in 1981, but of the sixteen, five had relocated. As Bibby and Brinkerhoff described it:

> All five of the congregations that had moved had originally been in neighborhood locations, nestled in residential communities and in all but one case removed from major roadways. They now, without exception, are located permanently or temporarily in facilities serviced by major arteries, with minimal explicit neighborhood identification. Five of the eleven churches that did not move were either major regional congregations or single denominational churches (i.e., with no city branches). The remaining six are all denominational branch churches bearing neighborhood names. They are also essentially the smallest and probably the most fragile six churches in the sample. (Bibby and Brinkerhoff, 1983:256)

Bibby and Brinkerhoff argued that "the additions to theologically conservative, Protestant churches were primarily geographically mobile evangelicals and members' children" (1983:259). About 10% to 15% came from outside the evangelical community. At the same time, and as Bibby had argued earlier, it was clear that evangelical congregations held on to their members with considerably more efficiency than did mainline churches. As Bibby and Brinkerhoff then put it, reconsidering Bibby's earlier thesis and offering some credit to Kelley, "Kelley's thesis thus appears to have explanatory value in accounting for members and offspring retention, rather than being required to account for a striking level of outreach" (1983:259).

The congregation's location was clearly, however, another factor in the retention phenomenon. Not all the conservative evangelical congregations were doing well. Those congregations that drew their membership from a wider regional basis were doing better than those congregations with ties to working-class neighborhoods. Those congregations that had moved near major transportation arteries were better off than those that had not. Bibby and Brinkerhoff noted: "It is interesting to observe that the four conservative churches which ceased operations in the 1970s came from the two most vulnerable categories—three were neighborhood Nazarene, Baptist, and Missionary branch congregations, while the fourth is a new independent, single denominational Baptist group" (1983:260).

The Church Growth Movement

Donald McGavran

There is considerable apprehension about the church growth movement among social scientists. More than a small part of this apprehension is due to differences in perspective and levels of methodological sophistication. There is little doubt that McGavran, who is credited with founding the church growth movement, was primarily interested in church growth, not for scientific reasons, but because he sought converts to the Christian faith. Methodologically, church growth proponents typically embrace anecdotal case examples rather than larger, theoretically based empirical surveys of groups of congregations. But even though the church growth movement heavily stressed institutional factors, McGavran's work, in particular, acknowledged the power of the social context.

The contextual question was obvious in McGavran's examinations of missionary efforts around the world (*Understanding Church Growth*). As McGavran put it: "The churchman who would understand the ways in which the Holy Spirit, through establishing thousands of new communities of the redeemed, is spreading abroad the 'sweet savor of Christ,' must ask why evangelism issues in conversions in some populations and not in others" (1970:123).

McGavran's answer to this question was a complicated one. He first dismissed explanations for church growth that he considered "rationalizations" or simple excuses for giving up (1970:136). He attacked the Presbyterian and Congregational missionaries in Japan in the late nineteenth century for defensive thinking, even though he recognized the obstacles they faced. He belittled what he defined as the shared "rationalization" of the time—that the church had "gained a more realistic conception of the task and . . . had entered a more mature stage of its existence." But, on the other hand, and perhaps more significantly, McGavran also dismissed single-minded theological explanations for church growth as one-sided and naive. He quoted a Pentecostal missionary who argued that "joyous abandonment to the Lord and unquestioning obedience to the Bible" were the reasons so many had accepted the Pentecostal faith and added: "one may rejoice that these Christian graces have been found in considerable measure among Pentecostal Christians and yet observe that many environmental factors have played significant roles in their church advance" (1970:137).

McGavran's focus, nevertheless, was itself single-minded. It was church growth. He noted: "the student of church growth cares little about whether a church is credible; he asks how much it has grown. He rates performance higher than promise" (1970:137). The "salvation of souls" and nothing else gave a church credibility and, therefore, almost any approach that brought converts was good—including the application of the findings of more secular disciplines and studies to the task of saving souls. Once this was understood, the use of case examples to develop techniques for the purposes of evangelism took on its own legitimacy and immediacy; McGavran wrote freely about "indoctrination" as an effective church growth technique. As McGavran (1970:141) put it, referring to the Seventh Day Adventist Church in Peru, "the Church and mission gave prolonged postbaptismal training to Christians and to their children and grandchildren. . . . Dr. Money credits Adventist effectiveness to *systematic postbaptismal indoctrination*" (emphasis added).

Based on a variety of case examples, McGavran outlined twelve "reasons for growth." Many of the twelve reasons emphasized the context of mission work. Conversions, he argued, were the result of the right message being in the right place at the right time, as well as the willingness to abandon old techniques and experiment with new. McGavran listed several "common reasons why churches do or do not grow" (1970:140).

1. Environmental and church factors favorable to church growth appeared at the same time.
2. The gospel was preached to some clearly receptive part of the mosaic.
3. Someone had a particular plan for multiplying churches that fitted his special population.
4. Leaders were chained to existent nonproductive work. Or, church and mission were devoted to a nonproductive pattern, once needed but long since outmoded.
5. Church and mission allowed themselves to remain stuck in an area of low potential.

Finally, McGavran gave credit to the Spirit of God when he referred to "praying Christians filled with the Holy Spirit" as the reason for a revival in Chile.

McGavran was quite convinced that the contextual factors were important to church growth. At the same time he was equally confident that institutions were not, or should not be, victims of their contexts even if this meant abandoning unproductive social environments for new ones. It was this intense desire for expansion, in spite of all circumstances, that set the church growth movement apart.

A More Recent Example of the Church Growth Movement Approach

Because of the vast number of church growth works, it is impossible to adequately review them in detail. A recent work, however, called *To Spread the Power* (Hunter, 1987), serves as an example of the kind of material that is typical of the church growth movement in the United States. As noted earlier, the body of works for the church growth movement is largely based on case examples of congregations. Out of these examples came a collection of techniques aimed exclusively at achieving congregational growth. While most of the techniques focus on the congregation as an institution, the techniques themselves are often designed to encourage congregations to better understand and address the realities of the social context within which they are trying to do ministry.

Hunter argues that one of the most successful strategies for achieving church growth was to use the existing social networks. He (1978:96) referred to these networks as the "bridges of God" (a term borrowed from McGavran). Most people become members of congregations through their personal contacts with other people who were already members. The key, according to Hunter, is to consciously and systematically harvest these social networks. To do this, Hunter offered a number of guidelines (1978:96):

1. Secure the names of all undiscipled persons with the social webs of your active credible Christians. Have some member of your evangelism committee visit, along with each active member, the undiscipled persons he or she has listed.
2. As you win some of those target persons, secure the names of their undiscipled relatives and friends. Have an evangelism committee member visit with them.
3. Survey each member each season to get the names of new undiscipled prospects. This will continually reveal a fertile harvest field for your church—undiscipled persons who are already linked to one or more persons in your congregation.

Once this population of prospects was defined, Hunter encouraged his readers to tailor their message to the needs of the context—to research, market, and promote the church. To do this effectively the old view of personal evangelism, which Hunter described as "a rehearsed authoritarian presentation that claims to be the only way to see things" (1987:101), had to be abandoned. Instead, Hunter insisted on "evangelists" who based their work on six principles:

1. Effective faith sharing is more relational than verbal.
2. The evangelist does much more listening than talking.
3. The evangelist vocalizes suggestions more than propositions.
4. Christianity is more caught than taught.
5. Conversion is almost never instant, but takes some weeks or months from insemination to new birth.
6. The occasions for evangelistic conversations usually arise situationally. The message is seldom a rehearsed theological formula out of a book or a packaged evangelistic program. It is usually specific, tailored to the recipient's felt need, point of openness, search, or pain, and presents the facet of the gospel that is most immediately relevant.

Conservative congregations were urged to give their people what they wanted. Often the best strategy for doing so was to provide a variety of settings for the proclamation of the message—so that almost anyone could find something to their liking. This consumer-oriented approach was related to McGavran's "homogeneous unit" principle. The point was not, at least according to the proponents of church growth, to keep certain kinds of people out, but to provide different types of congregations and/or settings where people could find people like themselves. More units provided members with more options, and as Hunter put it: "as we multiply options for people we are able to include and involve more people" (1987:118).

Finally, Hunter, like many other church growth advocates, referred to building a growing congregation as an "entrepreneurial task" (1987:128). His use of business and marketing language was no accident, and the church growth movement did not apologize for it. They were consciously applying marketing principles to evangelism. Once again, Hunter offered these "nine simple steps to starting new groups in your church" (1987:128):

1. Define the target group of people to minister to.
2. Research the target audience and the kind of ministry that would possibly respond to their particular needs.
3. Find a committed lay person(s) willing to be involved in starting such a new group. The person should be similar to the target group.
4. Train this person in the logistics of starting a new group.
5. Begin the recruiting process prior to the first group session.
6. Find an appropriate meeting place.
7. Stress the importance of the first several months. They are critical to the success of the group.

8. Keep accurate records of the experience for reference in starting later groups.
9. Build in monitoring and evaluation procedures for the first nine months.

Schaller: Church Growth for Everyone

Part of the popularity of the church growth movement literature is clearly due to its practicality. The literature offers clear suggestions to any pastor or church leader who is willing to listen. It does more than imply that even the most difficult of contextual circumstances could be overcome and churches could grow simply by rethinking and reorganizing themselves. The process of rethinking and reorganizing might be difficult, but techniques for doing so were in no short supply. One of the authors who has been most successful at helping pastors and lay members of congregations rethink and reorganize themselves without regard for theological perspectives has been Lyle E. Schaller.

Schaller, a former urban planner, is an engaging writer who has written extensively, with over forty books since 1964. He offers his insights into church growth and strategic planning by telling illustrative stories (about the experiences of a wide variety of pastors) developed from his extensive interviews. Schaller is a proponent of growth as a means through which congregations can "fulfill" their places "in God's plan" (Schaller, 1981:13).

For Schaller, a focus on growth serves several very important functions in the life of a congregation. For example, he argues that growth keeps the goals of a congregation focused by encouraging the congregation to look beyond taking care of the "in" group members to reaching out and serving the needs of the community (1991a:159). This reaching out is so important because it demands that congregations innovate and offer more and more choices. This is the only way to attract "new generations of churchgoers." At the same time, the drive to innovate, more often than not, improves the overall quality of the mission and ministry of the church for all of its current members. In other words, the growing church is driven by the needs of unchurched people rather than the needs of its own members. The growing church is driven by the need to perpetually question the old and bring on the new. Schaller, in characteristic style, asks pastors:

Do you expect new people to come to your church to fill your empty pews, to help support your budget, to contribute to those annual payments on the mortgage, to staff your Sunday school and to accept without question your priorities, policies, traditions and schedules? Or are your leaders willing to change the shape of the vessel that carries the Good News that Jesus Christ is Lord and Savior? (1991*b*:132)

Discussion and Conclusions

Despite the very different circumstances under which studies of church growth have taken place, there are significant and similar conclusions that can be drawn from this material. Even though social scientists studying church growth may have reacted against Kelley's institutional thesis of mainline decline, they never totally dismiss the importance of institutional factors. In fact, in many cases they affirm the power of these influences. On the other hand, those in the church growth movement who focus almost exclusively on the institutional factors paid repeated homage to the context. From the beginning of the church growth movement, McGavran pointed to the necessity of taking into account the social context, and those who follow him do so every time they talk about the need to adequately understand the social context where congregations operate.

The role of contextual factors in church growth and decline can never be ignored, but "negative" contextual factors cannot, in and of themselves, deal fatal blows to either congregations or denominations. Contextual factors are fatal only if change is resisted. It is clear that congregations cannot control their contexts, but they can control their relationship to their contexts. This is the point that those in the church growth movement make when they argue that a failing congregation has only two choices—to move to a setting where it can be more successful, or to rethink and reshape itself with regard to its existing context. This conclusion is not very different from the conclusions drawn by social scientists like Walrath and Hadaway. In the Hoge and Roozen volume, Walrath noted: "congregations that thrive amid change generally are those that are able to relate effectively to their contexts, maximizing the positive factors, minimizing the negative factors, programming toward the context's future rather than hanging on to a past that sooner or later is bound to vanish" (1979:269). Hadaway, in a 1982 study concluded: "radical change in the identity of the church and new avenues of entry for newcomers are essential if a decline is ever to be halted. Yet most churches do not react in time; they dwindle and die or simply move to new neighborhoods where racial transition is not yet a problem" (1982:374).

The problem for mainline pastors and church leaders is the slow "reaction time" of their congregations. In part, ironically enough, this results from the fact that these congregations are institutionally, if not theologically, conservative. Hadaway argues that congregations in general are conservative: "the church is a conservative, neighborhood-based organization composed of entrenched social groups" (1982:374). This is rarely the case in new congregations, or in congregations that focus first on growth. These congregations may be theologically conservative, but they are institutionally "liberal" enough to make the inevitable changes that their context demands—and they grow as a result.

Chapter   Six

Do Church Growth Consultations Really Work?

C. Kirk Hadaway

For many pastors, the "mainline membership decline" is old news. Even if their own church is not declining, they know scores that are. Pastors are well aware that most mainline denominations peaked in the mid-1960s and have continued to decline into the 1990s. They also have been to conferences dealing with the decline and heard innumerable explanations for the losses. Most have heard enough. In fact, at a recent interdenominational meeting to plan a conference on the future of the church, a pastor remarked, "One more conference on the decline of the mainline church, I do not need." What this pastor wanted was not more analysis of the problem, but some solutions.

The majority of churches in the United States are either plateaued or declining in membership. And while this problem is more serious among mainline churches, Marler and Hadaway (1992:61) show that this generalization also holds for churches in growing denominations such as the Southern Baptist Convention and the Assemblies of God. One response to this situation was the "church growth movement," which has produced many books designed to help churches grow (Benjamin, 1972; Wagner, 1976; Werning, 1977; McGavran and Hunter, 1980; Gibbs, 1982; Miles, 1981; Reeves and Jenson, 1984; Wagner, Arn, and Towns, 1986). Other responses have included a literature on congregational planning (Schaller, 1971, 1979; Walrath, 1979; Dale, 1981), a series of "church growth" books written outside the confines of the church growth movement (Schaller, 1981, 1983; Callahan, 1983; Miller, 1987; Johnson, 1989; Hadaway, 1991), training conferences and workshops on church growth and evangelism, and on-site evangelism/church growth/congregational planning consultations.

The effectiveness of the last of the above responses—evangelism/church growth consultations—is the focus of this analysis. Do they work, in the sense that they help churches grow?

Church growth consultations come in all shapes and sizes, but most involve one of two strategies. The first is for the consultant to visit a congregation as part of a prepackaged evangelism/growth program. According to

Herb Miller (1989), the goals of a congregational visit are inspiration, motivation, attitude change, and education. The consultant attempts to convince members that evangelism is important, to motivate them to be involved in evangelism, to show them that they can reach people for Christ, and to present a program that will give them the necessary skills in evangelism. The second general type of consultation does not sell a prepackaged program. Instead, the consultant helps the church to develop a strategy of its own. The purpose of the consultant's visit in this case is to gather information and to give counsel to church leaders or a planning task force. The consultant does not motivate the congregation around a strategy, because the strategy does not yet exist. The consultant helps the church create a strategy by (1) telling them what they need to do, or (2) helping them reach their own conclusions.

Whatever style is employed, church growth consultants have not systematically evaluated the effectiveness of their consultations. When asked, "does it work" they can give examples of churches where it worked well, but they can give no figures on the percentage of churches that grew as a result of the program or the average number of new members gained by participating churches. This study is an effort to determine whether or not consultations have an effect on the membership, Sunday school, and worship participation among 208 Disciples of Christ congregations.

Methods

In order to test the effectiveness of church growth consultations it was necessary to obtain a list of participating churches and examine their membership records. Such a list was provided by the National Evangelistic Association for Christian Churches (Disciples of Christ). The list included churches that had participated in one of six NEA evangelism consultation programs from 1981 to 1988.

Four of the NEA consultation models are prepackaged evangelism/church growth programs. Of these four, three involve a one-day, on-site consultation, while the fourth is a half-day consultation. The two nonpackaged models allow the church to create their own strategy plan with the help of the consultant. One is a single-day event that is designed to help a church develop a tailor-made evangelistic program. The final model is an open-ended planning consultation, called a "parish enrichment conference." The programmatic outcome of this consultation depends on the needs and orientation of the church, rather than on a predetermined agenda to promote evangelism.

Various measures of "effect" were possible. However, because the focus of this book is church growth, the effect of the consultation was measured in terms of gains in membership, enrollment, and participation. Thankfully, yearbooks for the Christian Church (Disciples of Christ) contain consistent records from 1981 through 1988. The variables chosen to test the effectiveness of the consultations included total membership, participating membership, average worship attendance, and church school enrollment. Change in each of these areas was measured on a yearly basis.

The initial list of 307 participating churches was reduced to 208 churches that had participated in consultations from 1983 to 1986. This reduction allowed measurement of change during the year prior to the consultation, the "treatment year" in which the consultation took place, and for the two years following the consultation. Due to the relatively small number of churches in this test, it was not possible to separate the effects of each consultation model.

Three types of analysis were performed to compute: (1) the average effect on churches participating in the consultations, (2) the aggregate (cumulative) effect of the consultations, and (3) the percentage of churches that were "revitalized," as measured by average worship attendance.

Findings

In Figure 6.1, the average percent change for the four test variables (membership, participating membership, average worship attendance, and church school enrollment) are compared for the year prior to the consultation, the consultation year, and for the two years following the consultation. As can be seen, the average church that was involved in a consultation declined by 1.0% in participating membership in the year prior to the consultation. In the year of the consultation the average church grew by 1.7% in participating membership. However, the positive effect of the consultations did not continue, as the average church lost participating members in the two years following the consultation.

The same basic pattern exists for all of the measures. Growth (or a very low level of decline) is evident during the year of the consultation. Only in the area of total membership does the positive effect continue thereafter.

Figure 6.2 looks remarkably similar to Figure 6.1. Here the data for all churches are added together to form an aggregate total. It can be seen that the churches lost (cumulatively) 3% of their participating members and 1.2% of their worship attendees in the year prior to the consultation. On the other hand, during the year of the consultation the churches cumulatively grew 1.3% in participating membership and 0.5% in worship attendance. As was seen in Figure 6.1, performance declined in all areas in the year following the consultation—except for total membership.

FIGURE 6.1
The Impact of Intervention:
Average Percent Change for Participating Churches

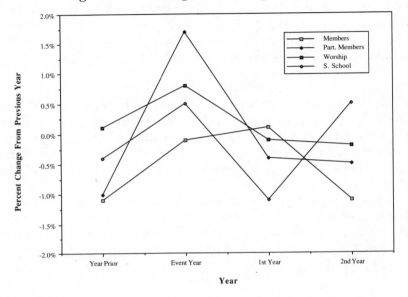

FIGURE 6.2
The Impact of Intervention:
Aggregate Change for Participating Churches

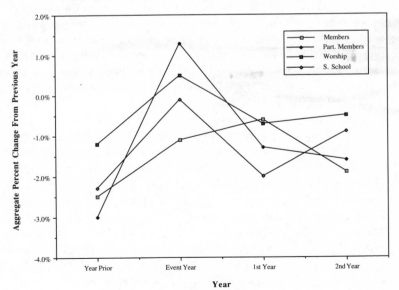

The results of this analysis clearly show that the consultations tend to have a positive effect on participating churches. However, the positive effect does not last very long—at least for most churches. This is consistent with the expectations of Herb Miller, who directs the National Evangelistic Association, now called The Net Results Resource Center. According to Miller, participating churches tend to have a surge in membership additions, but the surge typically does not last beyond the first year of the program. After the first year, various events conspire to reduce the long-term effect of the program. Pastors move, priorities change, and enthusiasm that was high in the months surrounding the consultation event begins to lag. As a result, churches tend to settle back into old patterns that were dominant prior to the consultation. The church added some new members, however, and because all churches do not regularly clean their memberships rolls, growth in total membership continues for an additional year.

As a final test of the "impact of intervention," the percentage of participating churches with some growth during the consultation year was measured, along with the percentage of these churches that continued to grow during the subsequent two years. This was an effort to determine the likelihood that a church selecting one of the six options would see some long-term results.

In the year prior to the consultation, 44% of the churches grew by at least one person in average worship attendance. During the year of the consultation, this percentage increased to 50%. Very few churches (only 12%) grew during the consultation year and during the two subsequent years. Two years after the consultation, however, 43% of the churches had average worship attendance that was higher than they had during the year of the consultation.

These trends suggest that few churches are thoroughly revitalized through consultations. The consultations and the programs they promote do have a measurable effect on church growth, however.

Concluding Remarks

Are these results good news or bad news for church consultants? And what do they say to churches that are considering investing in a consultation?

The answers to these questions depend upon one's perspective. In a very real sense the results are good news for church consultants, or at least for "The Net Results Resource Center" church consultations. They can say that, on average, their consultations do have a positive effect on the membership, worship attendance, and church school enrollment of the average participating church. This is true even though the consultations are of short duration, and in spite of the fact that many churches do not follow through with the programs launched through the consultations.

Yet there also is a warning implied in the data. Few churches see long-term growth as a result of the interventions. The surge in growth typically is for one year, a fact that suggests that church growth consultations are often the "mainline equivalent of a revival" (or at least the type of revival that produces measurable results). The consultation generates enthusiasm and activity. Members tell their friends about what is happening at the church. For a time, the church seems "vital" to members and visitors. As a result, worship attendance increases and more persons than usual join the church. Growth happens.

Unfortunately, it is easy for enthusiasm and activity to wane. When this occurs, the church returns to the old ways of doing things. Excitement drops and the church no longer seems as vital to newcomers. Further, programmatic changes that encourage outreach and evangelism tend to break down because the pastor and church leaders no longer give these areas priority.

Clearly, enthusiasm among members and programmatic changes that encourage outreach will produce a temporary surge of growth in most churches. Consultations help in this process by providing motivation and concrete strategies for evangelism. In order for a church to see long-term benefits from a consultation, however, profound changes must be made in the identity and structure of a congregation. Most consultants know this and offer strategies to make the long-range changes. This is a long process that begins with the self-defined purpose or identity of the congregation. Until a church's identity supports outreach or active membership recruitment, and until outreach is built into the goals and structure of the church, these efforts are unlikely to last very long. Further, unless a church "has the goods" that meet people's needs, members are unlikely to invite friends and co-workers to the church, regardless of an identity that supports outreach. The challenge to church consultants is to create planning models that recognize these realities and that assist churches in the process of becoming vital, accepting institutions that reach out to the communities that surround them.

Chapter Seven

The Effect of a Church Growth Strategy on United Church of Christ Congregations

Marjorie H. Royle

One response to the continued decline of old-line Protestant denominations has been a growth industry in church growth books, workshops, and consultation services. Everyone, it seems, has ideas about what to do in order to grow—from adding parking spaces, to follow-up calling on visitors the same day they visit, to slick advertising. Communications, marketing, and organizational theory all have contributed ideas, along with theology and sociology. In most cases, however, the ideas and particular techniques advocated are based on individual experience rather than empirical research. Thus, a practical question about such techniques is, "Do they work?"

A second question about such techniques is "*Where* do they work?" Studies of church growth included in *Understanding Church Growth and Decline: 1950–1978* (Hoge and Roozen, 1979) underscore the importance of community context and the interaction of contextual and institutional factors in understanding church growth. For example, in both Presbyterian (Roof et al., 1979) and United Church of Christ (McKinney, 1979) congregations, different institutional factors were related to congregational effectiveness in urban, suburban, and rural churches. The Presbyterian study also found that different factors were related to church growth in growing and stable communities. If institutional correlates of growth vary by community context, techniques to promote church growth may be differentially effective as well. In addition, because congregational size is important in understanding church dynamics (Dudley, 1983; Rothauge, n.d.; Schaller, 1982), church growth techniques may not be equally effective in churches of different sizes.

A Church Growth Intervention Program

The United Church of Christ, like other Protestant denominations, continued to experience small annual membership declines throughout the 1980s.

One denominational response to this continued decline was the development of a series of church growth workshops held throughout the United States from 1984 to 1987. The workshops were designed to create positive attitudes about evangelism and church growth, to provide practical ideas for growth-producing activities, and to motivate participants to persevere in their efforts. Participating churches agreed to send their pastor and a team of lay people to a series of three workshops over a two-year period. They also agreed to work in their local congregations between workshops and to report their progress. People from over 1,325 congregations, nearly one quarter of the denomination, attended at least one phase of the program.

The program was modeled on the writings of Lyle E. Schaller and led by two members of the national evangelism staff (see Schaller, 1983). Several hypotheses about church growth were implicit in the program. Workshop leaders taught that, in order for a church to grow, church members must:

1. Have positive attitudes about growth.
2. Work intentionally on evangelism and growth.
3. Improve the marketing of the church and create a higher community profile.
4. Welcome newcomers actively.
5. Work to assimilate newcomers into church life.
6. Provide a compelling product that helps members grow in their faith.
7. Be active in meeting community needs.

Concepts were taught and practical suggestions presented in each of the seven areas. The program evolved over the years, although elements from all areas were present in some form in most of the presentations. Particularly in the second and third phases, participants shared with one another their past successes and failures and future plans.

As the intervention program came to a close, an evaluation was performed to learn how valuable it was in spurring growth in the participating churches, and how it might be redesigned to be more effective. Because churches implemented the program differently, the evaluation also provided an opportunity to determine how useful particular interventions were in producing growth.

Because participation was voluntary, however, participating and non-participating churches were not equivalent in ways that may limit attempts to generalize the results. Churches that chose to participate were larger than nonparticipating churches. Participating churches also were more likely to have declined in membership and to have a lower proportion of members attending worship. These patterns suggest that participating churches also had more inactive members than did nonparticipating churches. Although not a random sample of all UCC congregations, the group of participating churches represents an appropriate collection of the kinds of churches that would be candidates for growth programs. Although these findings may not be applicable to all churches (for instance, the dynamics of growth in new churches may be quite different), they are applicable to the typical old-line church that wants to pursue church growth.

The Evaluation

The Survey Sample

Six hundred congregations were randomly selected to participate in the evaluation study. Each was sent a packet of four surveys in June, 1987. By that time, all congregations had completed at least two phases of the program, and many had completed all three. The pastor was asked to complete an eighty-four-item survey that included questions about whether the church had organized for evangelism and church growth, whether it had implemented specific program suggestions, whether attitudes about growth had changed, and whether other changes had taken place since the workshop.

In addition, the pastor was asked to give copies of a shorter, forty-six-item survey to up to three lay persons who had been part of the team attending the workshops. These surveys contained some of the same questions that were included in the pastor's questionnaire concerning changes in attitudes and programming in the church.

At least one survey was returned from 259 congregations for a return rate of 43.2%. Of these, responses from 213 churches, 35.5% of the original sample, were complete enough to be used in the analysis.[1]

Two other types of information were added to the records for these churches. First, several measures of church membership from denominational records were added. Total membership, average worship attendance, numbers and types of gains and losses for 1985 through 1987, and church size in 1983 (before the program began) were all included. Second, the percent population change in the area defined by the church as its parish was added.[2]

The number of new members received into the church from 1985 to 1987 was used to measure church "growth."[3] To determine the effects of program activities, a partial correlation was calculated between new additions and each measure of program or attitudinal change. The partial correlation was used to remove the possible effects of two factors that also might explain the number of new members received: church size (measured in 1983 before the program began) and population change (since 1980).

To address the question of where the program works best, churches were categorized in two different ways. By using census information, three groups of churches were identified: (1) those in communities of decline or no growth, (2) those in communities with slow growth of less than 10% between 1980 and 1986, and (3) those in communities with growth of 10% or more. Churches also were divided into three size categories: (1) up to 150 members, (2) 151 to 300 members, and (3) 301 or more members.

Then, partial correlations were calculated between program measures and the new member measure separately for each subgroup.[4]

All Churches

National denominational records for all churches (not just the 213 for which survey results were available) were analyzed to estimate the effect of the entire program, nationwide. All 4,184 participating and nonparticipating churches were identified in areas where the program was offered. Then, partial correlations were calculated between participation in the program and (1) the number of new members received in 1987, and (2) the total number received from 1985 to 1987. As in the survey sample, the use of partial correlations removed the effects of church size in 1983 and community population change—partially compensating for the fact that participating and nonparticipating churches were not equal in size.

This analysis probably underestimates the effect of the program for three reasons. First, the participating churches were counted as those having had one person attend one workshop (rather than a team attending all three phases of the program). Second, even when church teams participated fully in the program, they were not always able to implement changes when they returned to their local churches. Finally, participating churches were self-selected. Although they may have had more interest in church growth, they also probably were in greater need of it, as reflected in their greater decline in membership prior to the workshops.

To determine where the programs might have been most effective, the 4,184 churches were divided into groups by community growth or decline, church size, and the church's prior record of growth or decline. Because of the larger numbers of churches, more categories of church size and community growth or decline were used for these analyses. Partial correlations were calculated within these groups.

Results

The Survey Sample

Activities suggested by each implicit hypothesis about church growth (see seven hypotheses at the beginning of the chapter) were significantly related to increased numbers of new members, at least among some types of churches. Table 7.1 summarizes the results of analysis for the entire sample. It also shows variation in the relationship with church growth among churches in communities experiencing different rates of population change. The specific correlations are given in Table A7.1 (Supplemental Appendix).

Attitude changes. Changing the attitudes of church members about growth so that they want their church to grow and believe that growth is possible was related to church growth, but only for churches in communities with no growth. These churches may have been the ones with members who were the most discouraged about the possibility of growth before the workshops, so they may have had the most room for positive attitude change. Although the attitudes of those people attending the workshops were more likely to have changed than those of the congregation at large, attitude change among the larger congregation was more strongly related to increased numbers of new members.

TABLE 7.1
Relationships Between Local Church Efforts and
Total New Members in 1985–1987

Measure	Total Sample (N=213)	Type of Community		
		No Growth (N=70)	Small Growth (N=91)	Growth (N=52)
	Attitude Change			
Members want growth		Some		
Growth is possible		Some		
Increased energy level		Strong		
Positive attitude about growth:				
pastor		Some		
committee		Some		
church members		Strong		

Measure	Total Sample (N=213)	Type of Community		
		No Growth (N=70)	Small Growth (N=91)	Growth (N=52)
Intentional Efforts				
Size of Committee	Strong	Strong		
Numeric goals		Some		
Members have ideas re how-to		Some		
Ability to generate new ideas	Slight	Strong		
Increased involvement of all church committees		Slight		
Congregation was involved	Slight	Some		
Amount of budget for growth	Some		Strong	Strong
Money spent for projects	Slight			Some
Resources were available		Some		
Number attending workshops	Slight			
Number of activities	Some	Some		Strong
Marketing Activities				
Special Sundays	Slight			
Visitor Sundays				Strong
Money spent on media ads				Some
Clergy/lay calling teams				Some
Efforts to Welcome Newcomers				
Name tags	Strong	Strong	Some	Strong
Money spent for name tags	Slight			Some
Usher training	Slight			
Membership Sundays	Slight			
Non-traditional follow-up	Some	Strong	Some	
Efforts to Assimilate Newcomers				
Number of new groups formed	Strong	Strong	Strong	Strong
Increased fellowship groups	Some		Some	Some
More newcomers in groups	Some	Strong	Some	
Efforts to Improve the Product				
Quality of music		Some		
Lay involvement in worship		Some		
Opportunities to share faith		Some		
Retreats		Some		

Measure	Total Sample (N=213)	Type of Community		
		No Growth (N=70)	Small Growth (N=91)	Growth (N=52)
Efforts to Meet Community Needs				
Facilities used by community	Slight			
Users invited to church		Some		
New or strengthened social service ministries	Some		Slight	Some
Ministries chosen by study	Slight	Some		
Ministries chosen as evangelism tool	Some	Strong		Some

Note: All correlations were partial correlations, with the effect of church size in 1983 removed. Correlations for the total sample also partial out the effect of community growth or decline.

Slight = statistically significant correlation in .10–.19 range
Some = statistically significant correlation in .20–.29 range
Strong = statistically significant correlation of .30 or greater

Intentional efforts. Organizing and working for church growth were also related to adding new members under all conditions of community growth. More resources invested, whether people on the committee, attendance at the workshops, money in the budget, or number of activities undertaken, all seemed to produce more new members. Particular details of organization, such as starting a new team and holding regular meetings over a long period of time, were not significantly related to the outcome, appearing to matter less than the amount of resources put into the effort. Setting numeric goals seemed more helpful than setting either program or general goals.

In general, effects were strongest in conditions of no community growth. In these churches, particularly, involvement of the whole church seemed important, as did the church's access to ideas about how to grow.

Marketing activities. Although pastors reported that they had increased efforts in many activities related to attracting people to church, only a few of these activities were significantly correlated with increased numbers of new members. For these activities, the relationships were strongest in growing communities. This finding suggests that promotional activities may have their greatest value in situations where the church must inform newcomers of its existence. Such efforts may not be effective in communities where the church is already a familiar presence.

Although several activities for creating increased visibility, such as special events, media expenditures, and calling in the community, were related to attracting new members, others were not. Newspaper advertisements or stories about the church, and efforts spent in developing a church brochure were unrelated to numbers of new members received. Although one of the most common activities that congregations undertook after attending the workshops was improving their signs, such improvement was not significantly correlated with attracting new members. The use of radio, television, and cable television programming also was not significantly related to bringing in new members, although the few congregations that increased their use of the media experienced an increase in church attendance.

Efforts to welcome newcomers. The results summarized in Table 7.1 support the claims of many church growth programs that congregations need to work hard at welcoming newcomers. Although many members do not like wearing name tags, they were significantly related to increased new members under all conditions of community growth. In addition to being useful in themselves, name tags may be an indication of a congregation's willingness to put personal anonymity aside in order to welcome others.

Several activities in this area were not significantly related to numbers of new members, however. Although workshop leaders stressed the importance of the coffee hour in welcoming guests and the use of print media, such as the church bulletin and newsletter in creating an attractive and welcoming impression, improvements in these areas were not related to receiving new members.

Church growth advocates stress the importance of immediate follow-up calls on visitors. Little connection was found, however, between follow-up practices and the number of new members received. Correlations generally were positive, but the only statistically significant relationship was with follow-up by some unusual means, such as church members bringing a loaf of "Friendship Bread" to visitors. Average time to follow-up, the percentage of visitors receiving any follow-up call, and whether a visit was followed up by letter, telephone, or in person were not significantly correlated to numbers of new members.

Efforts to assimilate newcomers. Clearly, as church growth experts advocate, involvement of newcomers in groups is a crucial activity in building membership. Congregations that formed new groups and were successful in getting newcomers involved in groups had more new members than other congregations. These partial correlations were among the largest and the most consistently positive across community growth levels of any in the study.[5]

Efforts to improve the product. Efforts to improve the church program, including revitalizing worship life and providing spiritual development opportunities were significantly related to the number of new members received, but only for churches in communities that were not growing. Where competition among churches for members is strong, that is, in communities with a stable or shrinking population, the quality of the product may be more important than in churches in communities with less competition.

Efforts to meet community needs. Involvement in social service ministries and community outreach activities was positively related to receiving new members for churches, regardless of the community setting.[6] Developing social service ministries as a result of church growth-related community study or as a part of a total evangelism strategy appears to have been particularly effective.

Differences by church size. When analyses were performed separately on churches of different sizes, activities were found to be effective for some churches, but not for others (see Table 7.2 below and Table A7.2 in the Supplemental Appendix). Differences in church growth effectiveness were not as clear by size as they were by community growth, however. Many activities, such as those measuring the amount of intentional effort, celebrating special or Visitor Sundays, using name tags, involvement of new members in group activities, and new or strengthened social service ministries, were significantly related to the number of new members regardless of church size.

Some measures were significantly related to receiving new members for churches of less than 300 members, but not for the larger churches. These measures included setting numerical goals, involving the whole congregation, holding Visitor Sundays, usher training, and following up visitors by personal visits.

For the smallest churches, those of 150 or fewer members, newspaper ads, money spent for name tags (perhaps so people would wear them), and Membership Sundays were related to receiving new members. The presence of community service ministries among these churches was negatively related to the number of new members received. Perhaps very small congregations, often without full-time staff, have little energy left for nurturing newcomers if they also support significant community ministries.

Other measures were significantly related to the number of new members, but only for churches of over 300 members. They included the ability to generate new ideas, celebrating special Sundays (like Homecoming Sunday), new or improved coffee hours, nontraditional ways of following up visitors, providing opportunities for the pastor's own spiritual growth, and choosing community ministries as an evangelism tool.

TABLE 7.2
Relationships Between Local Church Efforts and
Total New Members in 1985–1987 for Different Size Churches

Measure	Total Sample (N=213)	150 or less (N=39)	151–300 (N=70)	Over 300 (N=104)
Intentional Efforts				
Church started a new team			Some	
Size of committee	Strong	Strong	Strong	Strong
Numeric goals		Strong	Some	
Ability to generate new ideas	Slight			Some
Congregation was involved	Slight	Some	Some	
Committee had a budget			Slight	
Amount of budget for growth	Some	Strong	Strong	Some
Money spent for projects	Slight	Strong	Some	
Number attending workshops	Slight		Strong	
Number of activities	Some	Strong		Some
Marketing Activities				
Special Sundays	Slight			Slight
Visitor Sundays		Strong	Some	
Newspaper ads		Strong		
Money spent on media ads			Some	
Clergy/lay calling teams			Strong	
Efforts to Welcome Newcomers				
Name tags	Strong		Strong	Strong
Money spent for name tags	Slight	Strong		
Usher training	Slight		Some	
Coffee hour				Slight
Membership Sundays	Slight	Strong		
Follow-up by personal visit		Some	Some	
Non-traditional follow-up	Some			Strong
Efforts to Assimilate Newcomers				
Number of new groups formed	Strong		Strong	Strong
Increased fellowship groups	Some	Some	Some	Slight
More newcomers in groups	Some		Some	Some

Measure	Total Sample (N=213)	Size of Church 150 or less (N=39)	151–300 (N=70)	Over 300 (N=104)
Efforts to Improve the Product				
Opportunities for pastor's growth				Slight
Efforts to Meet Community Needs				
Facilities used by community	Slight		Some	
Church has social service ministries in community		Strong		
New or strengthened social service ministries	Some		Some	Some
Ministries chosen by study	Slight		Some	Some
Ministries chosen as evangelism tool	Some			Strong

Note: All correlations were partial correlations, with the effect of church size in 1983 and community growth or decline removed. Measures were omitted from the table if no partial correlation was significant.

Slight = statistically significant correlation in .10–.19 range
Some = statistically significant correlation in .20–.29 range
Strong = statistically significant correlation of .30 or greater

Finally, a few measures were significantly related to new members, but only for churches of between 151 and 300 members. These included financial commitment: having an evangelism budget, and spending money on media ads. Two other significant measures were institutional support: starting a new team or committee for church growth and sending a larger number of members to the workshops. A final item that was undertaken by only a small number of churches—the use of clergy/lay calling teams in the community—also is a measure of the seriousness with which the congregation takes the church growth program. Perhaps congregations that support a full-time pastor and try to provide a full range of programming without the resources of larger churches, must make evangelism a top priority in order to grow.

Total program effects. Survey results demonstrated that the program was effective in causing a considerable amount of activity and change in the congregations. On the surveys, the majority of clergy and laity reported many new or changed activities and improved attitudes about growth. Things happened as a result of the program, although short-term, limited activities such as developing a brochure were more likely to happen than longer-term commitments such as developing clergy/lay calling teams. However, things did not happen in every church. Pastors in nearly a third of the congregations (31%) reported that they were not successful (or not yet successful) in getting organized. Those in this category very often reported a change in key clergy or lay leadership or some other major internal upheaval.

All Churches

When new member statistics were examined for all 4,184 congregations, participation in the church growth program was related to increased numbers of new members, but only in some types of churches or communities. For the total group of churches in areas in which the program was offered, when church size and community change were taken into account, churches that participated in the program were no more likely to have gained new members than those that did not participate. The partial correlations, controlling for prior membership and community growth, are displayed in Table 7.3.

The program was effective in communities with slow or moderate growth, but not in stable or declining communities or those experiencing rapid growth. The finding that the program had little effect in rapidly growing communities is not surprising, and may indicate that the need is less there. The lack of effect in stable or declining communities is surprising, however, because in these communities churches that implemented various parts of the program were successful in recruiting new members, according to the findings from the sample survey. One possible explanation might be that the program was less successful in motivating congregations in these communities to implement the program, but those that did so gained members. Another might be that, in such communities, the more successful congregations were more likely to have returned the surveys.

The program also was successful in the smallest churches and in those with between 250 and 500 members. Many ideas presented in the workshops may have been implemented already in the largest churches, leaving little room for improvement. In fact, on the survey, the largest churches indicated that they had been doing many of the recommended activities prior to the workshops.

Finally, churches that had been relatively stable in size before the program appeared to benefit the most from it. Previously growing churches may not have needed it, while it may have come too late for declining churches.

TABLE 7.3
Partial Correlations Between Participation in
Church Growth Program and Number of New Members Received

Church or Community Type	Number of Churches	Number of New Members Received	
		In 1987	In 1985–1987
Total Group	4,184	.03	.00
Communities of:			
No growth	1,476	.00	−.03
Slow growth	1,881	.07°	.00
Some growth	625	.11°	.07
Rapid growth	145	−.04	−.07
Size of church:			
Less than 100	898	.11°°	.17°°
100–250	1,464	.03	.03
251–500	1,074	.06	.12°°
More than 500	664	.03	−.04
Church history of:			
Decline	1,345	.02	.00
Stable size	1,692	.10°°	.12°°
Growth	988	.04	−.03

Note: Only church size was partialed out for different levels of community growth or decline.
°p < .01
°°p < .001

It Works for Some Churches

Several conclusions can be drawn from the evaluation of this church growth program. First, a multiple-phase program that provided information, trained leaders, and brought participants back together to report their progress was successful in generating a considerable amount of activity in the churches. That activity, in some cases, resulted in increased numbers of new members.

Second, activities designed to attract, welcome, and include prospective members were related to growth, particularly when the congregation at large was involved. More efforts did produce more growth. Some support was obtained for the hypotheses that positive attitudes about growth, intentionality, marketing, efforts to include newcomers, improvement of the product through worship and spiritual development, and involvement in outreach activities are important in helping churches gain new members, at least for some types of churches.

Third, the effects of the program were much stronger in some types of churches than in others. Two factors seemed to be important in determining where it was most effective. First, the churches needed some resources (people, funds, time, and so on) at their disposal. Declining churches may not have had these. Second, these churches must not already have been involved in many of the suggested activities for the program to be effective. Growing or larger churches may have already been too involved for much change to occur.

Finally, community context is an important factor in understanding church growth. Different activities were effective under different community growth conditions. For example, churches in communities with no growth need to work harder in providing high quality programming and seeking out and integrating new members, while churches in rapidly growing communities must work harder at letting the community know they are there. Understanding the local context and its interaction with church climate and programming is crucial to understanding the dynamics of church growth and decline.

Chapter Eight

Is Evangelistic Activity Related to Church Growth?

C. Kirk Hadaway

The goal of membership growth at the individual congregational level, while not universally accepted as desirable, is quite pervasive among Protestant religious denominations in the United States. Indeed, in many denominations, where adherents call themselves "evangelical," growth (or lack of growth) is a dominant indicator of success (or failure). Growing churches are perceived to be effective in "winning the lost" and are thus contributing toward the fulfillment of Christ's great commission. Stable and declining churches, on the other hand, may not be seen as necessarily failing in their efforts to reach people for Christ, but they are often viewed less positively than are growing churches.

The perceived link between church growth and evangelistic success suggests a hypothesis: higher levels of evangelistic activity are associated with higher rates of membership growth at the congregational level. This hypothesis, while frequently voiced by members of the "church growth movement" has not been tested in any systematic way. That is the purpose of this chapter.

Research on Evangelistic Activity and Church Growth

Research into the influence of evangelistic activity on church growth has been rare. Studies by Bibby and Brinkerhoff (1973, 1983) and Bouma (1979) have shown that evangelizing secularized "outsiders" has been a minor source of growth for conservative churches when compared to the influence of higher birth rates and more successful retention of geographically mobile members. On the other hand, Hadaway (1978), Hadaway and Roof (1979), and Nelson and Bromley (1988) have shown that smaller conservative denominations and sects grow primarily through attracting members from outside their ranks, though not necessarily from proselytizing "nones." Clearly, a distinction must be made between evangelizing the small percentage of Americans who say they have no religion and broader efforts to attract inactive Christians, members of other denominations, and persons who have moved. Because such a small proportion of the population say they are "nones" (about 8%), few churches can be expected to see much growth through evangelizing this population. However, more general efforts at evangelizing the "unchurched" and outreach efforts to attract church shoppers hold greater chance for success.

The first direct test of the relationship between evangelistic activity and church growth was provided by a major study of church membership trends conducted by the United Presbyterian Church in the U.S.A. in 1976. The results of this study were reported by the General Assembly Mission Council (1976) and by Roof, Hoge, Dyble, and Hadaway (1979). In general, the Presbyterian membership trends study found positive, but rather weak, relationships between indicators of recruitment activity and church growth. The strongest correlate asked, "Overall, to what extent are members of your congregation involved in recruiting new members?" This item produced a correlation of .17 with percent membership change—significant, but not very strong. Other questions, such as contacting new residents in the community, following up worship service visitors with personal contacts, and the presence of an organized program for recruitment produced even weaker correlations with growth, on the order of .05 to .06. Further, a yes/no question dealing with the training of members in evangelism was not related to growth and a question on recruitment of church school pupils actually produced a negative correlation with growth. Given these findings, it was no surprise that recruitment activities added very little to the explained variance in church growth when statistical controls were in effect.

Finally, a study that compared churches on membership plateaus with churches that had experienced rapid growth after years of stability showed that evangelistic activity was a major predictor of "breakout growth" (Hadaway, 1991). This study was an effort to determine the major predictors of congregational revitalization (measured by membership and attendance change). Particular attention was given to the development of sensitive measures of growth-related institutional characteristics. Results suggested that previous studies may have underestimated the impact of institutional factors on church growth.

Methods of Research

In order to examine the relationship between evangelistic activity and church growth, a lengthy questionnaire was created and distributed to roughly equal sets of growing, plateaued, and declining Southern Baptist churches in early 1988. The survey contained 102 closed-ended questions. Its purpose was to test a variety of church growth assumptions and hypotheses among metropolitan Southern Baptist churches. A total of thirty-four questions dealt with evangelism, outreach, and recruitment.

Sample selection procedures were similar to those used in the earlier United Presbyterian study. Rather than a simple random sample of churches from the entire Southern Baptist Convention, random samples were taken from sets of growing, plateaued, and declining churches. This strategy was employed in order to reduce the substantial error component that plagues church growth studies. Periodic roll cleaning, sloppy record keeping, and the tendency of most churches to have inflated membership rolls reduces the value of a membership change variable when taken in a general sample.

In order to reduce error variation selection criteria were used to ensure that the churches that were called growing were really growing, and that the churches that were called declining were really declining. Growing churches were defined as congregations that experienced increases of 15% or more in total membership and increases of 10% or more in Sunday school average attendance from 1981 to 1986. Further, to be called growing a church must have experienced a net increase of at least one member in four out of five years over the same period. Plateaued churches were defined as congregations that experienced increases or declines of 5% or less in total membership and Sunday school average attendance from 1981 to 1986. In addition, no church could be included in the plateaued population that had growth or decline greater than 5% during any one year. Declining churches were defined as congregations that experienced losses of 15% or more in both total membership and Sunday school average attendance. Declining churches also lost at least one member in four out of the five years from 1981 to 1986.

Although restrictive, the above criteria prevented labeling churches as declining when they had only cleaned their rolls, or labeling a declining church as growing because of a reporting error in a single year, or because they were padding their membership rolls. The scheme was not foolproof, of course, but it was much better than simply categorizing churches based on membership change from time one to time two.

Questionnaires were sent to the pastors of 990 metropolitan Southern Baptist churches. Of these, 113 were found to have no pastor and were removed from the sample. Of the remaining 877 churches, 543 returned usable survey forms, for an effective response rate of 61.9%. This rate of response was judged to be good for a mail questionnaire of eight pages. To check for possible response bias, nonresponding churches were compared to responding churches on a wide variety of items taken from the Uniform Church Letter—a lengthy form that is filled out by nearly all Southern Baptist churches on an annual basis. No significant differences were found between responding and nonresponding churches in size, location, baptisms, and a number of other variables.

After data from the responding churches were received, coded, and checked for errors, the data set was merged with Uniform Church Letter data for 1981 to 1987. In this way additional independent variables were added.

Southern Baptist Versus Presbyterian Data

The purpose of the survey used in this project was to examine many potential correlates of church growth, not to replicate previous surveys. Although similar in some respects, there were major differences between the *Membership Trends* study conducted by the United Presbyterians and the present study of Southern Baptist churches. Still, comparing the results of the two surveys on the one item they share may be instructive.

Most of the items relating to recruitment in the Presbyterian study were judged to be inappropriate for inclusion in this project. In some cases the language used did not communicate well to Southern Baptists, while in other cases a "list format" was used in the question design that typically reduces response and lowers correlations with the dependent variable. One question was repeated, however. It asked, "Overall, to what extent are members of your congregation involved in recruiting new members." Response categories were: (1) extensively, (2) moderately, (3) minimally, and (4) not at all. This item showed the strongest correlation with growth of any recruitment item on the Presbyterian survey.

Before comparing responses, it should be noted that the growing church category for the Presbyterian churches was 5% or greater growth over a six-year period (1968-74). Their plateaued category or "typical" church declined by 21% or less, and their declining category lost 30% or more of their members during the same six years. The Southern Baptist growing church category has a higher cutoff level, the plateaued category of Southern Baptist churches is more restricted than is the middle category of Presbyterians (and contains some churches with modest growth), and the rapidly declining category of Presbyterian churches is restricted to churches declining at a more rapid pace than was true for Southern Baptists (but Presbyterian churches had an extra year to log the decline). Further, the Southern Baptist churches were 100% metropolitan, whereas the Presbyterian churches should be around 60% metropolitan, if their reporting churches were representative of the larger denomination (see Hadaway, 1988).

Table 8.1 compares the Presbyterian data to the Southern Baptist data. As can be seen, Southern Baptist churches in each of the three growth/decline categories are more likely to report extensive or moderate involvement of their members in recruitment. The difference is relatively small among declining churches (only 6 percentage points when the extensively and moderately categories are combined), but it increases among plateaued and growing churches. For growing churches the difference is 24 percentage points. It also can be seen that the relationship between congregational involvement in recruitment and church growth is much stronger among Baptist churches than it is among Presbyterian churches. For Presbyterian churches the correlation (Pearson's r) was .17, while for Southern Baptist churches the value was .28.

TABLE 8.1
Involvement in Recruitment by Church Growth Among United Presbyterian and Southern Baptist Churches

Involvement in Recruitment	United Presbyterians			Southern Baptists		
	Growing (N=190)	Plateaued (N=203)	Declining (N=221)	Growing (N=194)	Plateaued (N=186)	Declining (N=160)
Extensively	5%	1%	3%	14%	3%	4%
Moderately	40	26	29	55	38	34
Minimally	53	67	63	29	56	56
Not at all	2	6	5	1	3	5
	Pearson's r = .17			Pearson's r = .28		

From these data it is not possible to determine whether the differences observed reflect differences between Presbyterian churches and Southern Baptist churches or were due to methodology that more efficiently separated the three groups, and thus made prediction easier. The answer is probably, "a little of both."

Southern Baptist churches have much more of an evangelistic reputation than do Presbyterian churches, and there is also probably a wider range of outreach activity among Baptist churches than there is among Presbyterian churches. Both denominations have churches that are doing nothing in this area, but the activities of the most outreach-oriented Southern Baptist churches are probably far beyond the comfort level of most Presbyterian churches that also emphasize recruitment. On the other hand, the more restrictive definition of growth used in the Southern Baptist survey is also likely to have produced some of the differences shown in Table 8.1. The Presbyterian survey categorized many churches as growing that actually showed little gain. For a church of 100 members to grow by one member per year does not seem like much growth, but such a church would fall into the

Presbyterians' growth category. Restricting growth to 15% or more in the Southern Baptist survey seems somewhat more appropriate because it excludes churches that are on statistical plateaus. It is possible that levels of evangelistic activity and recruitment provide a way of discriminating primarily between growing churches and churches that are not growing, rather than between plateaued and declining churches. If this is the case, restricting the growing church category to churches that show substantial growth may work to increase the size of the association produced between recruitment and church growth.

Basic Relationships

Thirty-four questions on the Southern Baptist church growth survey dealt with some aspect of evangelistic emphasis, evangelistic activity, outreach, and recruitment. Of these items all except one were associated with church growth in the expected manner. That is, growing churches tended to score higher on measures of evangelistic emphasis and activity than did plateaued or declining churches.

The one item that was related to growth in a reverse manner asked, "Has your church targeted any specific groups for intensive outreach, or are you simply trying to reach anyone who will respond?" Even though the association was negative, its magnitude was essentially zero (gamma = −.0006). This question appears to be a limited test of Wagner's (1976) and McGavran's (1970) homogeneous unit principle, which suggests that a church should try to reach "our kind of people" if they want to achieve rapid growth. The true source of the question, however, is Lyle Schaller's (1983) book, *Growing Plans.* In a chapter on the middle-sized church, Schaller indicates that churches that answer the question, "Who are the folks you are making a special effort to reach?" with the response, "No special group, we're open to serving everyone who comes here" are typically passive congregations that are declining in numbers (Schaller, 1983:69-70). However, results from this survey of Southern Baptist churches indicate essentially no difference between growing and declining churches in response to the question employed. Interestingly, plateaued churches were least likely to be "trying to reach several key target groups."

Four other questions on the survey were related to church growth in the expected manner, but the relationship was insignificant at the .05 level. These questions asked (1) is personal evangelism the most important aspect of a pastor's work? (2) does the pastor regularly take laypersons on witnessing visits? (3) is the pastor personally involved in training laypersons for evangelistic outreach? and (4) does the church have greeters to meet people as they come to the church on Sunday morning, and if so, do they record the names of new-comers so they can be visited later? This last question, which was asked in two parts, was also drawn from Schaller's *Growing Plans* (page 74). Having greeters was significantly related to growth (gamma = .25), but the combined question, while related to growth, dropped in magnitude to insignificance.

Despite the few items that produced small relationships with growth, the large majority of the evangelism/recruitment questions produced relatively strong, significant relationships. Gamma values for these significant items ranged from .09 for a question asking pastors to rate the "concern for the lost" in their congregation, to .46 for an item asking pastors to rate their church on "winning the lost, evangelism." Pearson's r coefficients ranged from .08 to .35.

Table 8.2 shows the relationships for nine questions that were associated with growth at a fairly substantial level.

TABLE 8.2
Evangelism Indicators by Church Growth

	Growing (N=194)	Plateaued (N=187)	Declining (N=162)	(Gamma)
1. Rate your church: Winning the lost, evangelism (% exceptional or good)	51.3%	17.4%	16.1%	.46
2. Regular program for evangelism training? (% yes)	58.0	34.9	25.6	.44
3. Evangelism campaign in past 3 years? (% yes)	66.8	35.7	35.0	.42
4. Does the church have an effective Sunday school outreach program? (% yes)	53.1	34.3	22.4	.43
5. Involvement of members in recruitment (% extensively or moderately)	69.6	40.9	38.8	.40
6. How often is the visitation program conducted? (% weekly or more than weekly)	75.8	50.8	43.7	.35
7. Concerted effort to enroll as many as possible in Sunday school to increase attendance? (% yes)	61.3	40.0	35.2	.35

	Growing (N=194)	Plateaued (N=187)	Declining (N=162)	(Gamma)
8. Does Sunday school have a regularly scheduled time for visiting prospects? (% yes)	74.1	53.8	49.4	.34
9. Do members receive field training in how to visit and win the lost? (% yes)	81.9	65.8	60.4	.34

The first line of Table 8.2 shows the relationship of church growth to the question asking pastors to rate their church in "winning the lost, evangelism" as either "exceptional," "good," "average," or "below average." The gamma value is based on the full range of responses, but the percentages shown in the table combine the exceptional and good categories. As can be seen, 51.3% of the 194 pastors of growing churches rated their churches as exceptional or good in evangelism, as compared to only 17.4% of plateaued churches and 16.1% of the declining churches. Obviously, the pastors of growing churches are much more likely to rate their churches as effective in evangelism than are plateaued or declining churches. The relationship is strong and dramatic. It also shows that this variable, like many other evangelism and outreach items, provides better discrimination between growing churches and the other two types than it does between plateaued and declining churches. Apparently, certain types of evangelistic activity may help explain why some churches are able to grow rapidly, but they do not help much in explaining why some churches remain on the plateau, rather than decline.

The second item in Table 8.2 deals with evangelism training and produces a stronger, more linear relationship with church growth. Evangelism training *does* help discriminate between plateaued and declining churches. The last item in the table also deals with evangelism training and produces a similar relationship. Apparently, however, many more churches in all three growth/decline categories use evangelistic field training than have regular programs for evangelism training. Some churches must train their members in evangelism as the need arises, or occasionally, rather than as an ongoing emphasis of the church.

The third item in Table 8.2 dealt with whether the church had participated in any sort of programmed growth or evangelistic campaign during the past three years. Six currently available types were given as examples and pastors responded either "yes" or "no." The results indicated that 66% of growing churches had used such campaigns, as compared to only 35% of plateaued and declining churches.

Questions 4, 7, and 8 all dealt with Sunday school outreach and visitation. The strongest association with growth was shown in a question that asked pastors if their church had an effective Sunday school outreach program. This question was essentially a Sunday school recruitment item rather than a true evangelism measure. Question 7 dealt with a particular Sunday school growth strategy that is promoted by certain agencies of the Southern Baptist Convention. Churches are encouraged to enroll as many persons as possible in their Sunday school, whether these persons are Christians, current attenders, or not. By having these persons on the roll, they will be contacted continuously, invited to functions, and so forth, just like active Sunday school members. As a result, many who are enrolled will begin to attend, thus eventually increasing average Sunday school attendance. Apparently, this strategy is related to growth. In question 8 it can be seen that regular Sunday school visitation of prospects is quite widespread among Southern Baptist churches. Of growing churches, 74% have such a visitation time, as compared to only around half of plateaued and declining churches.

Involvement of members in recruitment (item 5) was discussed in the previous section in comparison to the Presbyterian survey. As noted earlier, it produces a fairly substantial relationship with growth.

Finally, in item 6 pastors were asked if their church had a definite, regular visitation program, and if so, how often was it conducted. These two questions were combined to form a single variable with response categories that ranged from "more than once a week" to "no regular visitation program." This item produced a gamma of .35 and a Pearson's r coefficient of .26 with the three-category church growth variable. As can be seen, over three-quarters of growing churches conduct visitation at least once a week, as compared to half of plateaued churches and 43.7% of declining churches.

The relationships shown in Table 8.2 clearly demonstrate that evangelistic emphasis and training, evangelistic activity, outreach, prospect visitation, and general recruitment efforts are all related to church growth, and in most cases the relationship appears to be quite substantial. Such findings appear to indicate that previous research efforts may have underestimated the relationship between evangelism/recruitment and growth, or that the relationship is simply much stronger in conservative Protestant denominations like the Southern Baptist Convention.

An Evangelism/Outreach Scale

In order to estimate the overall impact of evangelistic activity and emphasis on church growth, it is useful to create an evangelism/outreach scale. Once created, this scale is employed with statistical controls to estimate the total amount of variance explained in church growth.

The first step in creating the evangelism/outreach scale is to examine the structure of the items to be employed. In order to do this, the twenty-four evangelism/outreach items that are significantly related to growth are subjected to factor analysis.[1] This procedure suggested six factors, which were treated as subscales of evangelism/outreach.

For each individual factor, the survey questions that were most central to the factor were combined, and the resulting six variables compared to the church growth measure.[2] Each subscale was refined by alternatively adding or deleting items and determining the effect on the subscale's correlation with church growth. After the scales have been refined they are combined into an overall evangelism/outreach scale.[3] The resulting scale is composed of fourteen of the original twenty-four evangelism/outreach items.

Among the churches included in this survey, scores on the scale range from 24 (high evangelism) to 70 (low evangelism). The scale produced a Pearson's r correlation of .46 with church growth. This was a substantial increase over the correlation of the strongest member of the scale with growth, which produced a Pearson's r of .35. A correlation of this size (.46) indicates a very strong relationship with growth, especially given the nature of data used.

The scale also appears to be reliable. The fourteen items produce a standardized alpha coefficient of .83. The items used in the scale are listed in Table 8.3.

By squaring the Pearson's r coefficient it can be determined that the evangelism/outreach scale accounts for approximately 21% of the variance in the three-category measure of church growth and decline. For an institutional variable, this is a surprisingly large amount of variance explained given the results of previous studies. It indicates that evangelistic/outreach activity and emphasis are quite important to church growth.

In order to examine the relationship of evangelism and church growth more fully, the evangelism/outreach scale was divided into five roughly equal categories (from high to low) and crossed against the church growth measure. The results can be seen in Table 8.4 and are quite dramatic.

Of the growing churches, 42% scored high on the evangelism/outreach scale as compared to only 11% of the plateaued churches and about 6% of the declining churches. Further, when the top two categories of evangelism/outreach are combined, the percentage of growing churches soars to a full 74%, as compared to just under 23% of declining churches. This represents a difference of 51 percentage points, and produces a very strong gamma coefficient of .52.

TABLE 8.3

Items Included in the Evangelism/Outreach Scale

	Pearson's r with growth
1. Rate your church: winning the lost, evangelism	.35
2. Participation in programmed growth or evangelistic campaign?	.27
3. Involvement of members in recruitment?	.28
4. Does the church have a regular program for training members in evangelism?	.27
5. How often is the visitation program conducted?	.26
6. Does the church have an effective Sunday school outreach program?	.26
7. Rating of church: evangelistic to unevangelistic	.23
8. Concerted effort to enroll as many as possible in Sunday school to increase attendance?	.22
9. Does Sunday school have a regularly scheduled time for visiting prospects?	.21
10. Number of visits made by church staff (adjusted for church size)	.20
11. Do members receive field training in how to visit and win the lost?	.19
12. Has church sent out a brochure or other mass mail-out to community residents?	.17
13. Do people who visit your worship service and make themselves known receive a visit?	.14
14. Most SBC pastors place too much emphasis upon soul winning (coded in reverse)	.12

TABLE 8.4
Evangelism Scale by Church Growth

Evangelism/ Outreach Scale		Growing (N=166)	Plateaued (N=155)	Declining (N=136)
High 1		42.2%	11.0%	5.9%
2		31.9	18.7	16.9
3		12.0	21.9	19.1
4		10.2	23.2	31.6
Low 5		3.6	25.2	26.5
	Gamma = .52	Pearson's r = .46	p < .0001	

Once again, however, we see that the relationship is not linear. Whereas growing churches are much more likely to score high on the evangelism/outreach scale than are plateaued and declining churches, there is not much difference between plateaued and declining churches. Apparently, evangelism explains growth, but is of little value in explaining decline.

The Impact of Evangelism in a Multivariate Context

The next step was to examine the impact of evangelism/outreach on church growth in a multivariate context. Does the strong relationship hold even when controlling for other institutional variables and for the social context of the church? The tables that follow help answer this question.

For this line of investigation all items included on the survey were examined, along with a number of questions from the Uniform Church Letter.[4] Further, demographic information for the zip code surrounding each church was added to the "record" and correlated with church growth. Demographic data were supplied by CACI and are based on the 1980 United States Census with 1989 estimates.

Various items from all three sources were significantly related to church growth. These predictors were divided into three broad categories: (1) contextual variables, (2) congregational characteristics, and (3) institutional (programmatic) variables.[5]

The first group of items concerned the social context of the church. This set included variables such as population growth, racial transition, the proximity of other Southern Baptist churches, the age and condition of the houses and businesses in the area, the buying power of community residents, and many other items. The second set of variables were "structural," rather than programmatic. They tapped characteristics of the church itself and of its members, rather than its location or its activities. One such characteristic concerned the age distribution of members. What proportion are elderly or are in the prime "baby boomer" cohort? Several questions were combined to form a scale that tapped this characteristic. Other variables in this set dealt with the congregation's date of organization, the age of its sanctuary, the length of the current pastor's tenure, the proportion of adult members in professional or managerial occupations, and so forth.

The final set of items included programmatic variables as well as institutional measures designed to tap nonprogrammatic actions and orientations of members. Even though some of these measures *could* be considered congregational characteristics, they were included in this section because they may be altered through education and exhortation. One such item is the degree to which church members favor innovation over tradition.

Multiple regression analysis was conducted within subsets of items to determine those variables which best predicted church growth in a multivariate context.[6] Variables that contributed to the total explained variance at the .05 significance level were selected for further analysis. Eventually the list of variables in each set was reduced to five contextual variables, five items measuring congregational characteristics and seven institutional variables.

In the top third of Table 8.5 it can be seen that contextual variables explain 22% of the variance in church growth. In other words, at least 22% of church membership change can be explained by the social setting of a church. One variable dominates this set in terms of predictive power: the percentage of housing that was built from 1975 to 1980. Churches that are in areas with a large proportion of new housing are more likely to grow than are churches where the housing stock is older. Other significant items included the pastor's perception of growth in the community (as reported in 1983 on the Uniform Church Letter), racial transition in the community (a negative relationship), the condition of nearby residences and businesses, and the distance to the nearest SBC church. Southern Baptist churches are more likely to grow in areas that are growing in population, where racial transition is minimal, where nearby residences and businesses are in good repair, and where other SBC churches are not in close proximity.

The second set of variables was much more predictive of church growth than was the social context. Variables measuring congregational characteristics accounted for 34% of the variance in church growth. Again, one variable dominates. In this case it is the age structure of the church. Churches with a smaller proportion of elderly members, with a smaller proportion of Sunday school classes for the elderly, and with a larger proportion of members in the thirty to forty-four age group (in 1988) were much more likely to grow. In addition, congregations that have a larger proportion of adult members who are professionals and managers were more likely to grow, as were younger churches (both in terms of date of organization and in age of the current sanctuary). Finally, churches that Schaller (1975) has labeled "ex-neighborhood churches" (churches where most of the active members once lived nearby, but have since moved away and drive back to worship) were less likely to grow than were churches that were not of this type.

TABLE 8.5
Multiple Regression:
Three Sets of Church Growth Predictors

	Pearson's r	Beta
Contextual Variables		
1. % of Housing Built 1975–1980	.33	.26
2. Pastor's Perception of Population Change (1983)	.30	.14
3. Racial Transition (Increase in % Black)	−.14	−.14
4. Condition of Nearby Houses and Businesses	.21	.13
5. Distance to Nearest SBC Church	.19	.11
Adjusted R² = .22		
Congregational Characteristics		
1. Age Structure	−.47	−.32
2. % of Adult Members Professionals or Management	.33	.19
3. Year Congregation Organized	.22	.13
4. Age of Sanctuary	−.35	−.12
5. Church Is "Ex-Neighborhood" (Members Drive Back)	−.21	−.08
Adjusted R² = .33	R² Set 1+Set 2 = .34	
Institutional Variables		
1. Envangelism/Outreach Scale	.46	.26
2. % of Members Attending Worship	.23	.15
3. Ratio: Sunday School Enrollment to Membership	.29	.13
4. Hours Pastor Spends Counseling Members	.27	.12
5. Live in Past/Dream About Future Continuum	−.35	−.11
6. Innovation/Tradition Continuum	.35	.11
7. Loving/Cold to Visitors Continuum	.23	.09
Adjusted R² = .35	R² Set 1+Set 2+Set 3 = .43	

In the bottom third of Table 8.5 it can be seen that of the seven institutional variables that emerged from the subset regression analysis, the most powerful predictor (by far) was the evangelism/outreach scale.[7] Also fairly important was the percentage of members attending worship on an average fall Sunday. Other variables significantly related to church growth when statistical controls were in effect included the ratio of Sunday school enrollment to resident membership,[8] hours the pastor spends counseling members, the tendency of church members to "live in the past," the tendency of church members to favor innovation over tradition, and the extent to which members are nurturing to visitors. Churches with a high ratio of Sunday school enrollment to resident membership, where a larger percentage of members attend worship on an average Sunday, where the pastor spends a large amount of time counseling members, where members are future oriented, where members tend to value innovation over tradition, and where members are loving to visitors are more likely to grow than are churches that lack these characteristics. This set of seven variables explained 35% of the variance in church membership change—the most of any set.

It can be argued that the three sets of variables have a natural order in terms of causation. That is, the context is causally prior to the other two sets of variables, because the church rarely has any control over its setting. Congregational characteristics may be influenced by the context (for example, a church may be composed of older persons because there are only older persons in the neighborhood), but congregational characteristics are not likely to have a direct influence on the context. Similarly, institutional variables have no effect on the context. Using this logic, it can be stated that 22% of the variance in church growth can be explained by the demographic setting alone. To determine the value of the other two sets in predicting church growth, it is necessary to see how much additional variance they explain beyond the 22% attributed to the context.

It also can be argued that congregational characteristics are causally prior to the institutional variables. The characteristics of the church and its members probably constrain institutional activity and orientation more than the reverse. This is clearly true for the date of organization, the age of the sanctuary, and the status of the church as "ex-neighborhood." However, it is likely that the age structure of a church is determined, at least to a certain degree, by the activities and orientation of members. Likewise, the presence of professionals and managers results, in part, from the type of programming, the leadership style of the pastor and other institutional variables. Nevertheless, it seems more appropriate to place institutional variables *after* congregational characteristics.

As can be seen in Table 8.5, adding congregational characteristics to the contextual set increased the explained variance from 22% to 34%—a gain of 12 percentage points in our ability to predict church growth. Adding institutional variables adds another 9 percentage points, resulting in a total explained variance of 43%. In other words, these seventeen variables explain almost half of the total variation in church growth.

In Table 8.6 all seventeen items were entered into a regression equation in stepwise fashion. Seven were found to be statistically significant.[9] Decreasing the number of variables from seventeen to seven does not reduce the variance explained in church growth. In fact, the adjusted R^2 increases slightly. The seven variables explained 44% of the variance in church growth. The beta coefficients on the right side of the table indicate that *the evangelism scale is the most important predictor of church growth.* However, the age structure of the congregation rivals evangelism in magnitude. Both variables are extremely important predictors of church growth and dwarf the other variables in terms of impact.

Another significant predictor of growth was the proportion of housing built since 1975. Growth is easier in areas with newer housing. This is an influence that overshadows the effect of sheer population growth in the community. SBC churches also tend to experience more growth when they are not too close to other churches of the same denomination. In addition, younger churches are more likely to grow than are older congregations. Churches that have a large proportion of their members who attend on a regular basis are more likely to grow, as are churches that maintain a high ratio of Sunday school enrollment to resident members.

TABLE 8.6
Multiple Regression: Variables Combined

Independent Variables	Pearson's r	Beta
1. Evangelism/Outreach Scale	.46	.29
2. Age Structure	−.47	−.22
3. % of Housing Built 1975–1980	.33	.14
4. Distance to Nearest SBC Church	.19	.13
5. Year Congregation Organized	.22	.12
6. % of Members Attending Worship	.23	.11
7. Ratio: Sunday School Enrollment to Membership Adjusted R^2 = .44	.29	.10

Institutional Factors Are Important

This chapter examines the possible relationship between evangelism and church growth. Previous studies had shown that a relationship existed, but that it was weak and was of relatively little importance when compared to other predictors—especially those dealing with the context of the local church. There seemed to be some question, however, whether the questions employed to measure evangelistic effort and emphasis were adequate to make a generalization to all Protestant denominations in the United States. Further, subjective evidence suggested that evangelism might be more important than had been previously shown.

In order to test the relationship between evangelism and church growth more adequately, a wide variety of evangelism/outreach questions were included on a church growth survey; and to reduce the inevitable error component when dealing with church statistics, very rigorous definitions of growth, plateau, and decline were developed. The results showed that, indeed, various measures of evangelistic activity, evangelistic emphasis, simple outreach, and evangelistic training were related to church growth in a substantial way. Further, the various measures of evangelism worked together, so that an evangelism/outreach scale produced a stronger relationship with growth than did any single evangelism measure.

Another major finding was that evangelism is of value in discriminating between growing and nongrowing churches, but not between plateaued and declining churches. The vast majority of rapidly growing churches score high in evangelistic emphasis, while plateaued and declining churches tend to score a great deal lower. However, declining churches do not tend to score much lower than do plateaued churches on the evangelism scale. This makes a certain amount of sense. Plateaued churches are not very evangelistic. If they were, perhaps they would be growing. Declining churches are also not very evangelistic. If they were, perhaps they would be growing as well. The two nongrowing groups (plateaued and declining churches) share low levels of evangelism.

Multiple regression analysis reveals that the impact of evangelism and outreach remains, even when controlling for the influence of the context, age, and location of a church. In fact, *evangelism appears to be the only programmatic activity that retains a meaningful relationship with church growth when statistical controls are in effect.* Other institutional correlates are important, to be sure, but most are things that are hard for a congregation to control.

It would be difficult, for instance, for a church to change the age structure of its membership, even though a younger age structure seems essential to church growth for most congregations. Churches that are successful in reaching the large "baby boom" cohort and their children are more likely to grow than churches that are dominated by the elderly. This is not surprising but it also is not easy to change. Most churches would love to reach the boomer generation, but have been unable to do so.

Church location is even more of a "given." Churches exist in social settings. New housing nearby helps churches grow. Why? Because new housing implies population growth of a particular type: suburban growth. SBC churches do better in areas where the population is increasing through the addition of new, single-family housing. SBC churches also do better in areas where their competition is limited. Growth among SBC churches is best on average outside the South and in growing areas that have yet to become "overchurched." Growth is very difficult in older urban and suburban neighborhoods where past population growth fueled the development of too many churches. Now these churches must compete for a dwindling supply of new residents.

The age of a congregation also is a "given." New churches are more likely to grow than are older congregations. This holds even when controlling for the context. New churches, like all new organizations, are more permeable and accepting because friendship networks have not yet solidified (Olson, 1989). Thus, assimilation of new members is easier.

A high percentage of members who attend on an average Sunday implies commitment and perhaps a congregation that has some elements of a social movement. When members are in town, they will attend. This is important for a church that wishes to grow, but it also is difficult to create. How does a church induce commitment among its members or transform itself into a social movement? The answer is not clear, especially from a programmatic perspective.

The weakest significant predictor of church growth is the ratio of Sunday school enrollment to resident membership. To a certain extent this variable reflects action on the part of the church, but there also is a component that is hard to control. A high ratio means that the Sunday school enrollment is close in magnitude to the resident membership of a church (and in some cases, the enrollment is larger than the membership). Churches that make a concerted effort to expand their enrollment through growth campaigns tend to have a high ratio. A high ratio is expected to enhance growth because it implies that a large number of those on the Sunday school roll will be prospects. Members can then "work" this list and draw these marginal Sunday school members into the church. Many churches try this, but apparently it is only those congregations that are successful in adding many persons to the Sunday school roll that achieve growth. So the effort is not enough—what is important is success at the effort.

The major questions suggested by this research concern the source of the differences between these findings and previous efforts to measure the influence of evangelism/outreach on church growth. Are these differences due to the fact that earlier studies looked at denominations that were relatively unevangelistic and that contained much smaller proportions of rapidly growing churches? Are the differences due primarily to differing methodology, or have the times simply changed? It is likely that all three possibilities contributed to the effect seen in Table 8.6. Denominations that have very small numbers of rapidly growing churches and where evangelism is not emphasized would necessarily produce smaller relationships with growth. Similarly, methodology that mingles plateaued churches with growing congregations would also tend to reduce the correlation between evangelism and church growth. And finally, all of the studies in this section on congregational growth suggest that the impact of institutional factors on church growth seems stronger in the late 1980s than it was a decade ago.

Evangelism is an important influence on church growth—at least among Southern Baptist churches. Its importance within mainline denominations seems clear, as well. It would appear that the relationship is stronger than was previously estimated. Evangelism may be the most important one thing church leaders can do if they want their church to grow.

Chapter Nine

Growth or Decline in Presbyterian Congregations

Wayne L. Thompson, Jackson W. Carroll, and Dean R. Hoge

Mainline Protestant denominations in the U.S. have had membership declines from the middle 1960s until today, and the declines have evoked a vigorous debate about the cause. Why are so many congregations declining? What is the role of congregational leadership and priorities, the role of community changes impacting churches, the role of national leadership, and so on? The Presbyterian Church (U.S.A.), the subject of this chapter, has also experienced a polarization of theological views that has compounded the debate. Each faction has its own ideas about what is ailing the denomination.

Sociological research on Presbyterian congregational growth or decline was at its greatest intensity in the 1970s. Several studies were completed, most notably a nationwide study by a task force commissioned by the United Presbyterian Church U.S.A. General Assembly in 1974. It serves as a background for the present effort.

The task force gathered empirical data on 681 congregations. Nationwide random samples were made from three categories of local churches in the denomination—the 10% fastest growing between 1968 and 1974, the 10% fastest declining during that period, and those experiencing typical loss, but less than 20% (the typical membership loss was 15.4%). Between 200 and 300 churches in each category agreed to participate, and each was sent a "church questionnaire" asking about the church and community, to be filled out by a knowledgeable person, and sets of "member questionnaires" for designated types of active members. The task force made a report in 1976. In 1976 to 1978 a team of sociologists analyzed the total set of data, producing an article in the 1979 book, *Understanding Church Growth and Decline 1950–1978*; the authors were W. Clark Roof, Dean Hoge, John Dyble, and Kirk Hadaway.

The research team assessed the importance of nearly 500 factors for congregational growth or decline, using the data from all 681 congregations. All the variables were classified as contextual (describing the community context where the church was located) or institutional (describing the church's program, leadership, recent history, and so on). (For details see the excursus at the end of the chapter.) The researchers computed a membership change measure (1968–74), by dividing the 1974 membership figure by the 1968 figure. Then they measured the impact of the numerous factors on membership change. The overall variance explained in membership change was 26%; 14.6% was explained by contextual variables, which were entered first into the analysis, and 11.4% more by institutional factors.

Other studies done in the 1970s and 1980s came to similar conclusions. Contextual factors turned out to be stronger than institutional factors, yet *both* were important (see McKinney, 1979; McKinney and Hoge, 1983). The present study is a partial replication and expansion of the 1975 study, using more recent data.

Data and Methods

Shortly after the merger between the United Presbyterian Church in the U.S.A. (North) and the Presbyterian Church in the U.S. (South) in 1983, the denominational Research Unit asked Hartford Seminary's Center for Social and Religious Research to assist it in carrying out the Presbyterian Congregational Profile Study. The purpose was to help identify needs of the congregations and to serve as a baseline for future research. In 1985 the research team drew a sample of 1,000 congregations stratified by region and size. The sample was random geographically, but larger congregations were slightly oversampled and smaller congregations slightly undersampled for two reasons. One reason was to include enough congregations of each size, since the predominant number of congregations was small. The second reason was to report more accurately the denomination's membership within regions. While the majority of congregations are small, the majority of members are in the larger congregations.

The Presbyterian Church (U.S.A.) has Korean-language congregations in many areas, but the research team decided not to include them in the study due to language difficulties.

Letters were sent to the pastors in the sample to request participation. A total of 707 said yes, and they were sent two kinds of questionnaires. The first was a Fact Sheet asking about congregational characteristics and programs, to be filled out by the pastor or session clerk (the "session" is the highest elected lay committee in a Presbyterian congregation). The second questionnaire was for all members of the session, asking them to report about their congregation's life. A total of 6,362 of the session questionnaires was filled out from 615 congregations, and Fact Sheets were returned by 593 churches. All analysis was done on these 593, and the unit of analysis was the congregation. During the analysis we found ten cases with incomplete or erratic membership data, and we removed them, leaving 583 congregations.

The session questionnaire data were aggregated into mean scores or percentages and added to the Fact Sheet data from each congregation. We added denominational yearbook data (membership and financial data from 1970, 1980, and 1985) and U.S. Census data from the zip code area in which the congregation is located. The census data measured the population and economic characteristics of the zip code area in 1970 and 1980, with some projections for 1985 made by the National Planning Data Corporation. The result of these efforts was a rich set of data on these congregations, including objective information on zip code areas. (Two earlier articles based on this data provide more information about the study and sample—Roozen and Carroll, 1989; and Carroll and Roozen, 1990.)

The churches in the sample were quite typical. In 1985 the median size of the congregations in the sample was 142 members, and the mean was 210. Sunday worship attendance averaged 108. The average year of the congregation's founding was 1890, and the average year of beginning worship at its present location was 1923.

The present study differs from the earlier one in four important ways. First, it contains objective data on the community—not just descriptions of the community by pastors or session leaders. The new data include census information on the zip code area in which the church is located, while the earlier study had to rely on ratings of the "neighborhood within a half mile of your church building" made by knowledgeable persons in each church. The zip code area is typically larger than a half-mile radius. Second, the new study gathered different kinds of institutional variables. Since the overall project had a broader agenda than just growth or decline, some topics were studied more thoroughly than in 1975, others less. Third, the new study includes both former denominations. Whereas the 1975 study looked at UPCUSA (northern) churches only, the 1985 data include both northern and southern churches.

The fourth difference requires a word of clarification. The 1975 task force decided to study trends over a six-year period, since this seemed long enough that short-range fluctuations or chance occurrences would have little impact, yet short enough that the influence of particular pastoral leadership styles and programs could be isolated. If a longer period of time had been studied, more pastorates would have been involved, and the effect of pastoral leadership might have been obscured. In the new study we extended the span to eight years, 1980 to 1988, for two reasons. First, the institutional data were from 1985, and we wanted to include as recent membership information as possible. We had 1980 membership data, and we stretched the study period to eight years, thus moving 1985 nearer the middle of the time span under study and improving the time sequence of the variables (since explanatory variables should be measured as early as possible). Second, membership decline among Presbyterian churches had by now continued unabated for more than two decades, making us less convinced that individual pastorates or programs were decisive. By 1988 it no longer seemed so important to be able to isolate leadership of individual pastors, and a longer time span seemed useful.[1]

The new study thus has a technical improvement over the earlier one: the measurement of the institutional variables was during the time period under study. These variables were measured in 1985, near the middle of the 1980–88 period. In the 1975 study this was not possible, and the task force had to rely on 1975 questionnaire information attempting to describe the state of the congregation about five years earlier to use it to help explain trends from 1968 to 1974.

Data Analysis

Because of the numerous variables available, we began exploratory analysis by correlating the many predictor variables with church growth or decline from 1980–88 and also from 1985–88. For the 1985–88 time span, we found only weak and ambiguous results, thus we dropped it from consideration. Apparently three years is too short a span for a clear analysis.

Most of the congregations in our sample experienced membership decline from 1980 to 1988. Fifty-four percent lost 10% or more of their membership; 26% were within 10%, up or down, of their 1980 figure, and 20% gained 10% or more. The median membership change was a 12% loss. Losses were greater among the congregations formerly belonging to the United Presbyterian Church U.S.A. (northern branch), but the proportion is unclear, partly because by 1980 many congregations and their presbyteries in the border states were aligned with both denominations in union presbyteries.

Part of this pattern is attributable to population shifts in the U.S. in the 1980s. While the areas of greatest membership in the UPCUSA (from the Great Lakes eastward through New York) experienced population losses, the areas of strength for the PCUSA (Virginia, the Carolinas, and Florida) were more stable and, in some cases, growing. Thus one underlying factor explaining growth or decline of individual congregations is overall population movement within the U.S. The regions with least membership decline in the Presbyterian Church (U.S.A.) in the 1980s were the South and South Central regions.

In accordance with past research, we categorized factors affecting growth or decline into local contextual and local institutional factors. This categorization was first set forth by Roozen and Carroll (1979) and later used by other researchers (Roof et al., 1979; Warner, 1988; Wuthnow, 1989). We lacked information on nationwide factors, so our analysis was solely at the local level. A third category was added in the present study—"congregational demography." It encompasses the level of affluence in the congregation, age of members, and rate of member turnover. Such variables cannot be conceptualized as part of the environment in which a church organization operates, since members are critical resources of congregations. And these variables cannot easily be classified as institutional factors, which include programs, policies, leadership, and cultural factors in church life. Unlike institutional factors, they cannot be easily changed through intentional action. Thus we have kept them in a distinct third category. In the 1975 study the researchers did not include these factors because of uncertainty about how to interpret them.

Findings

Over 200 predictor variables were available for the analysis. We correlated all of them with the membership change measure and retained only those having correlations significant at or near the .10 significance level. This is a very weak requirement, chosen to avoid deleting any variables that could possibly be important in later subgroup analyses or that could be interesting but not perfectly measured here.

A total of thirty-two variables were retained; all the others had very weak correlations with membership growth or decline. Of course, some of the variables we abandoned may be important in specific settings but not in the overall national sample. For example, the level of affluence of the neighborhood may be predictive of church growth in big cities but not in the overall sample. We could not follow up all these possibilities. Rather, we selected the thirty-two variables with the most overall importance empirically and limited analysis to them. They formed fifteen categories or "clusters," each measured by one, two, three, or four variables:

I. Community Context
   (A) Change in Affluence
   (B) Population Change
   (C) Age
   (D) Educational Attainment
   (E) Women's Labor Force Participation
   (F) Housing and Residential Mobility
   (G) Community Type

II. Congregational Demography
   (H) Membership Composition and Change
III. Institutional Factors
   (I) Christian Education Program
   (J) New Member Recruitment and Integration
   (K) Theology
   (L) Relations to Other Churches
   (M) Facilities
   (N) Influence in Decision Making
   (O) Congregational Climate

The clusters are listed roughly in order of causal precedence, with the community context variables first, then the congregational demography variables, then the institutional factors.

Table 9.1 shows the associations of these thirty-two variables with growth or decline from 1980 to 1988. The zero-order correlations are shown in the first column. The middle column gives standardized regression coefficients (betas) for variables in each cluster, controlling for other variables in that cluster. The right-hand column shows variance explained by each cluster.

TABLE 9.1
Variables in Final Analysis: Zero-order Correlations[1], Regression Coefficients Within Clusters (Betas)[2], and Explained Variance for Clusters

	Zero-order Correlation	Beta	R^2 for Cluster[3]
I. Community Context			
A. Change in Affluence			
Per capita income, percent change 1969–79	.13	.13*	.02
B. Population Change			
Percent change 1970–80	.31	.20*	
Percent change 1980–85	.30	.15*	.11
C. Age			
Percent 35 to 44, change 1980–85	−.04	−.01	
Percent 45 to 64, change 1980–85	.26	.23*	
Percent 65 and up, change 1980–85	.14	.09	

	Zero-order Correlation	Beta	R^2 for Cluster[3]
Ratio of widowed persons to persons age 18 or older	−.19	−.04	.07
D. Education Attainment			
Some college or more	.20	.20*	.04
E. Women's Labor Force Participation			
Proportion of mothers who work full-time outside the home	−.11	−.11*	.01
F. Housing and Residential Mobility			
Proportion of dwellings built after 1970	.28	.20*	
Ratio of persons over 18 living in same house entire life to all persons over age 18, 1980	−.26	−.11	.08
G. Community Type (reported by pastor)			
Urban south versus others	.00	.02	
Suburban south versus others	.22	.22*	.04

II. Congregational Demography

H. Membership Composition and Change			
Percent of members with over $35,000 household income	.08	.05	
Percent of members age 35 to 54	.10	.03	
Percent of members age 55 and older	−.13	−.07	
Percent of members in two-parent households with school-age children	.13	.08*	.02

III. Institutional Factors

I. Christian Education Program			
Session's desire for pastor's emphasis on youth and children	.06	.01	
Church school size, percent change 1970–85	.38	.38*	

	Zero-order Correlation	Beta	R^2 for Cluster[3]
Christian education emphasizes faith and contemporary issues	.02	− .01	.14
J. New Membership Recruitment and Integration			
Pastor's weekly hours spent on new member recruitment	.17	.17°	
Percent of session agreeing "quality of preaching" is among 3 top reasons new members join congregation	.14	.10°	
Percent of session agreeing "evangelistic outreach" is the thing congregation does least well	− .09	− .06	.05
K. Theology			
Theological liberalism	.21	.21°	.04
L. Relations to Other Churches			
Joint worship services with non-Presbyterian congregations	− .13	− .09°	
Easy for outsiders to see how congregation differs from other churches in the area	.24	.23°	.06
M. Facilities			
Percent of session agreeing fellowship space is "about right" in size	.26	.07	
Percent of session agreeing sanctuary space is "about right" in size	.25	.14°	
Percent of session agreeing education space is "about right" in size	.32	.22°	.12

	Zero-order Correlation	Beta	R^2 for Cluster[3]
N. Influence in Decision Making			
Pastor's influence in the congregation	.24	.24°	.06
O. Congregational Climate			
Significant conflict in congregation in last two years	−.10	−.05	
Members excited about congregation's future	.34	.33°	.11

[1] All zero-order correlations were significant near or below the .10 level.
[2] Among the regression coefficients (Betas), ° indicates significant at the .10 level. Betas show relationships while controlling for other variables in the cluster.
[3] R^2 shown for each cluster is the adjusted R^2.

Community Context

The predictive power of each cluster is shown in the right column. Cluster A shows that increased affluence of the community is weakly predictive of Presbyterian church growth. Another indicator of social status is educational attainment, in Cluster D. In communities with higher proportions of persons with a college education background, membership growth was more likely.

The strongest contextual factor predicting church growth is population growth in the zip code area (Cluster B). Population growth was also the strongest predictor in the 1975 study.

In Cluster C, an increase in the proportion of persons forty-five and older is positively related to growth, particularly increased numbers of persons age forty-five to sixty-four. A high number of widowed persons in the community is inversely related to membership growth.

Having a high proportion of mothers in the neighborhood working full-time is slightly correlated with decline, rather than growth, in Presbyterian churches (Cluster E). The reasons are unclear but probably have to do with types of families living nearby and with time demands on working mothers. Having new housing in the neighborhood (built after 1970) is strongly associated with church growth. Both an increase in housing in the zip code area and the replacement of old housing by new housing seem to give churches new opportunities for growth (Cluster F).[2] As Cluster G shows, being in the urban South is associated with membership growth. (Other similar measures such as suburban South, urban West, and so on, were tested, but none were important.)

Congregational Demography

In past research on Presbyterian and United Church of Christ congregations, congregational affluence has been found to be a predictor of membership growth (Roof et al., 1979; McKinney, 1979). It is again in the present study (see Cluster H). Based upon the pastor's estimate, the percent of members with annual household incomes over $35,000 is associated with growth.

Having proportionately more members in the thirty-five to fifty-four-year-old age group is conducive to growth; higher percentages of members aged fifty-five to seventy-four is not. Having more families with two parents and school-age children is also conducive to growth.

Institutional Factors

Certain church programs have an effect. Activities regarding children, youth, and Christian education were consistent and positive predictors of membership change (Cluster I). This is particularly so for growth in the church school, the strongest single predictor of church growth in the data.[3] Two items measuring the approach taken by the church school, however, proved not to be predictors. One asked whether the approach stresses faith and contemporary issues (shown in the table). Another measured whether the approach of the church school is more traditional and Bible-centered (not shown in the table).

Membership recruitment activities are important for growth (Cluster J). Congregations that do a poor job of evangelistic outreach are less likely to grow. In the area of evangelism, pastors can make a measurable difference, as many writers on church growth have emphasized (e.g., Wagner, 1979; Johnson, 1989). Pastors who report spending relatively more of their work time on new member recruitment tend to have growing memberships. These findings have a certain consistency: time and energy invested in evangelism are characteristic of growing congregations. Also related is the finding that churches are growing in which session members more often report that "quality of preaching" attracts new members. Other researchers have pointed out the significance of preaching for growing congregations (e.g., Hartman and Wilson, 1989).

Being theologically liberal (as estimated by session members) was a plus for church growth (Cluster K). This finding is contrary to much that is written about church growth today. The session questionnaire also included several measures of theological strictness, but none were related to growth or decline (and are not shown here).

Consistent with the expectations of Kelley (1977), who argued that involvement in ecumenical activities hinders growth, we found (in Cluster L) that participation in joint worship services with other denominations was mildly predictive of decline. Also, being a church that clearly differs from other churches in the area is predictive of growth, and, conversely, being a church like others nearby predicts decline.

The physical facilities of the congregation make a difference in membership change (Cluster M). Member satisfaction with the sanctuary, educational, and fellowship space was clearly conducive to growth. Of the three, satisfaction with educational space is the most important.

Items regarding decision making in the congregation and the congregation's morale were also tested. Among a number of decision makers listed in the questionnaire, only the session's estimate of the degree of the pastor's influence over decision making was positively related to membership change. Greater pastoral influence is positively related to growth (Cluster N).

Cluster O has two measures of congregational climate. The most important is the report by session members that members are excited about the congregation's future. This is a major predictor of church growth.[4] The experience of significant conflict in the congregation during the past two years (reported by the pastor) is associated with declining congregations.[5] The actual question asked, "In the past two or three years, has your congregation experienced any serious conflicts?" so our information does not span all eight years under study. Our analysis probably underestimates the impact of conflict.

Variables That Were Not Significant

It is important to mention some of the variables that proved not to be related to church growth or decline and thus were eliminated from Table 9.1. Many of them have been mentioned by past analysts of church growth.

Among community context measures, the presence of school-age children and adolescents in the zip code area was not significantly related to membership change, contrary to past research.[6] The presence of significant proportions of never married adults was not related to membership change in the 1980s. Also not related to membership change was the proportion of the population that was female, the proportion of housing units that were rented versus owned, the proportion of the population that was nonwhite, and growth in that proportion from 1980 to 1985.

For congregational demographics, nonsignificant predictors of membership change included the ratio of attendance to membership, the proportion of members under age twenty, the ratio of average church attendance to seating capacity, the proportion of lifetime members, the length of time since the congregation began worshiping in its present location, and the ratio of members under twenty and members over seventy-five to their relative proportions in the community.

Among institutional indicators, none of the social justice orientation and activities items were associated with membership change, contrary to much conventional wisdom. We looked at a large number of programs such as food pantries, soup kitchens, scout troops, or renting facilities to community groups, but none were related to church growth. Also, none of the internal programming items were important, except for those related to Christian education, especially for children and adolescents. Attempts to correlate numerous stewardship programs and emphasis items were fruitless. None of the indicators of worship diversity and activity were significantly related to membership change. Finally, pastoral tenure and most of the items measuring how pastors divide their work time were not related to membership change, with the exception noted above for time spent on new member recruitment activities.

Relative Importance of Clusters of Variables

We also wished to assess the overall importance of different kinds of factors. As Table 9.1 showed, our predictor variables are in three categories—community context, congregational demography, and institutional factors, labeled I, II, and III. We made overall regression analyses including all the thirty-two variables in these categories, entering I first, then II, then III, following earlier practice. It would seem likely that community context has a more important causal impact on congregational demography and program than vice versa.

The results are shown in the first line of Table 9.2. The second column of the table shows the proportion membership change (-12% for the total sample), then the last three columns show the adjusted R^2 for category I, I + II, and I + II + III. Community context accounts for 16% of the variance, congregational demography accounts for an additional 4%, and institutional factors account for another 12%, adding up to 32% of the variance explained.

In the 1975 study, the variables measured were more specifically focused on growth and decline, and they explained 26% of the variance—14.6% explained by contextual factors and 11.4% by institutional factors. The new study had more explanatory power. Why? One way to check is by controlling for the regions of the nation studied. In 1975, only the UPCUSA congregations were included—almost none in the South. Therefore in a separate calculation we removed the South from the new data and looked at only the non-South (388 congregations). The result is shown near the bottom of Table 9.2 after "Non-South." (For details see Table

A9.3 in the Supplemental Appendix, available from Hartford Seminary Center for Social and Religious Research.) The explained variance was 9% for the community context, 4% for congregational demography, and 16% for institutional factors, for a total of 29%.

TABLE 9.2

Membership Change in Twelve Subgroups and Variance Explained by Three Sets of Clusters in Twelve Subgroups (Adjusted R²)

	Number	Median Change	Variance Explained (Adj. R²)		
			I (7 clus.)	I+II (8 clus.)	I+II+III (15 clus.)
Total Sample	583	−.12	.16	.20	.32
Church Size:					
1–100	98	−.06	.13	.16	.34
101–250	206	−.10	.08	.15	.27
251–500	135	−.15	.09	.14	.22
501 and over	110	−.11	.43	.49	.57
Community Types:					
Large City	110	−.18	.41	.42	.61
Suburb of City	79	−.10	.29	.29	.40
Small City	112	−.08	.12	.12	.25
Town and Country	237	−.12	.07	.20	.30
Region:					
Northeast	135	−.16	.03	.07	.28
Midwest	165	−.15	.10	.13	.23
West	84	−.08	.00	.01	.36
South	183	−.06	.19	.21	.32
Non-South	388	−.14	.09	.13	.29
Church Age:					
<1901	348	−.12	.19	.22	.31
1901–50	133	−.18	.26	.30	.48
1951–85	102	−.06	.11	.11	.47

Note: The number given is for the regression analysis in the subgroup.
Some cases were lost due to missing data.

In the present study we had three categories of variables, not two, and the most exact comparison of 1975 and the 1990 studies would ignore congregational demography and look only at community context and institutional factors. In 1975 the figures were 14.6% and 11.4%; in the present study they were 9% and 16% in the non-South. The relative importance of context has dropped, and the importance of institutional factors has risen.

Is this a result of the different data used in 1975 and in 1990? That is, do research studies using census data for contextual variables find lower associations between context and church growth than do studies using pastors' ratings of contextual factors? If so, this may explain the changes in findings from 1975 to the present study. Fortunately a Baptist study of church growth used both kinds of measures, providing a comparison. In a study of Baptist congregations from 1981 to 1987, zip code area population change correlated .30 with congregation growth or decline, while pastors' estimates of neighborhood growth or decline within a mile of the church correlated at .37.[7] Pastors' ratings seem to produce an overestimate of the importance of community change. Of the two, census data are the more reliable.

In short, the change in measurement method from the 1975 study to the present study very likely caused the lower estimate of the importance of contextual factors in the non-South. We are led to believe that the earlier estimate was too high and that the estimate in the non-South in the present study is better.

The situation is complicated by the addition of southern churches in the present study. Churches in the South are more influenced by their communities, for better or worse, than those in other regions, as the lower part of Table 9.2 shows. Thus, by adding southern churches to the sample the estimate of contextual influence rises. We are left with a conclusion similar to that in 1975, that contextual factors are slightly stronger than institutional factors in the whole denomination.

Maybe the change in outcomes is due to actual change in society. Has the society itself changed? The answer is not very clear, but we doubt if social change was very great. All census reports indicate that changes in the rate of neighborhood movement and residential mobility in the 1970s and 1980s were small.[8]

Analysis of Influences Within Subgroups

Because we were concerned with how the overall model fares in different types of congregations and locations, we looked at four sets of subgroups:

church size in 1980, community type, region, and the period in which the congregation was founded. Past research has shown that these subgroups vary in congregational growth and decline. The remainder of Table 9.2 shows the statistics for the subgroups.

The smallest congregations, those with 100 or fewer members in 1980, declined the least: an average of 6%. The larger congregations varied in rates of decline with the 251–500 member churches declining the most at 15%. Congregations in large cities were hardest hit by declining membership (-18%), followed by town and country churches (-12%), suburban congregations (-10%), and small city churches (-8%). Congregations in the Northeast and Midwest experienced the steepest declines (-16% and -15%, respectively), while churches in the West (-8%) and South (-6%) declined less.

The total explanatory power of our model for each subgroup is seen in the righthand column. The model is the most effective in explaining growth or decline for three types of churches—large churches, churches in large cities and suburbs, and churches founded since 1900. The reasons are not all the same. The models explain change in large churches, city churches, and suburban churches because contextual factors greatly influence them. For them, as the community goes, so go the Presbyterian churches. The models explain change in churches founded since 1900 for a different reason—for them the influence of institutional factors is much greater.

Our model is weaker for explaining changes in smaller churches. They seem less dependent on community context and deliberate actions, as several researchers have suggested (e.g., Carroll, 1977; Dudley, 1978; and Rothage, n.d.).

The breakdown by church age at the bottom of Table 9.2 does not distinguish between churches founded in recent years. The question arises if churches founded in more recent years have different rates of growth or decline. In Table 9.2 we see that the median decline in churches founded since 1951 was 6%. For churches founded in 1951 to 1960 the decline was 7%, and for churches founded since 1960 it was 5% (not shown in the table). The two periods are similar.

We could not test the overall model statistically for the most recent churches due to the low number of cases, but we could look at correlations with individual measures. There were fifty churches founded in 1951–60 and fifty-one since 1960. The correlations for the latter group were clearly stronger. (The correlations in the 1951–60 group were similar to the total sample.) The correlation between growth-or-decline and educational attainment in the community (Cluster D) for the churches founded since 1960 was .41, compared with .20 in the total sample. The correlation with location in the suburban South versus all others (Cluster G) was .35, compared with .22 in the total sample. The correlation with growth in the church school (Cluster I) was .53, compared with .38 in the total sample. The correlation with hours spent by the pastor in new member recruitment was .47, compared with .17 in the total sample. The correlation with session perception that evangelism is done poorly (Cluster J) was − .32, compared with − .09 in the total sample. The correlation with adequacy of education space (Cluster M) was .41, compared with .32 in the total sample. It is obvious that our model is very effective for recently founded churches, even though we cannot demonstrate it statistically due to the limited number of cases.

The variations by region are surprisingly small. The main finding seems to be the relatively greater impact of community context on churches in the South and the greater impact of institutional factors in the West. (The reader should remember that subgroups with small numbers of cases, like the West with only eighty-four cases, have lowered adjusted R^2 solely for statistical reasons.)

Analysis of Specific Factors Within Subgroups

Although Table 9.2 signals differences in factors supporting church growth in different subgroups, it provides no specifics. We searched for more detail through regression analyses within the subgroups. The analyses are statistically identical to the overall analysis in Table 9.1. The results are shown in Table A9.1 in the Supplemental Appendix. We will summarize them here.

As noted earlier, community context had immense effect on churches with over 500 members. The most powerful predictors for these churches were Clusters B and F, referring to overall population change in the zip code area, the houses built since 1970, and the percent of persons in the community who lived in the same house their whole adult lives. These community changes strongly determined if the largest churches grew or declined, but they had limited impact on other churches.

The impact of institutional factors also varies by size. It is a bit greater for small churches than for large ones. However, the analysis found that two factors are very important for churches over 500 members—the church school and efforts for evangelism (Clusters I and J).

The type of community in which the church is located is also very important. Churches in large cities are the most affected by changes in their context and also by institutional factors. Our analysis is most suitable for explaining their histories. Suburban churches are also greatly affected by community changes. For city churches the most influential factors are change in economic level in the zip code area, population change in the zip code area, and increase in young adults and middle adults in the zip code area. Being in an educated community also is important for growth in city churches.

For churches in suburbs the most influential factors are population change in the zip code area and being in an educated community.

It should be no surprise that city churches also grow or decline more than others depending on their leadership and program—especially their church school, their evangelism efforts, and the adequacy of their physical facilities. These three factors explain a large portion of their growth or decline. The situation for suburban churches, small city churches, and town and country churches is similar but less crucial; institutional factors explain less.

How about variation by region of the nation? Community variables are the most influential on southern churches—especially population change in the zip code area, change in the number of young adults and middle adults in the zip code area, and houses built since 1970. Why these variables have affected southern churches more than others is unclear.

Institutional factors were most important in the Northeast and West—especially the church school, the adequacy of the physical facilities, and the effort given to evangelism.

Finally, does it matter how old the congregation is? Yes, the more recently the church was founded, the more crucial are institutional factors for its growth or decline. The most consequential factors for churches founded since 1950 are church school, adequacy of physical facilities, and effort expended in evangelism. These are the same institutional factors we have found to be important before. Community context is a bit more predictive of growth or decline of churches founded between 1901 and 1950—especially the number of houses built since 1970 and the percentage of people who have lived their whole adult lives in the same house.

In a Declining Church, Context Outweighs Institutional Factors

What can we say about membership growth and decline in congregations of the Presbyterian Church (U.S.A.) in 1980–88 as compared with 1968–74? First of all, the overall picture is one of continuing membership decline. The causes of the earlier decline are probably still in place. From 1980 to 1988 the median change was a decline of 12%. There were some growing congregations: 20% gained 10% or more. Many of these congregations were in the South.

When we tried to account for growth or decline, we used the same strategy as the researchers used in the 1975 study. We looked at correlations of all of our variables with the membership change from 1980 to 1988 and retained those variables correlated with change. They were able to explain 32% of the variance as compared with 26% in 1975.

We arranged the variables in three sets—contextual factors, congregational demography, and institutional factors. As in 1975, contextual factors were a bit stronger than institutional factors. In the non-South the contextual factors were weaker in the present study than in the 1975 study, but for some reason they were stronger in the South, so that our overall estimate of the relative strength of the two is unchanged: contextual factors are a bit more explanatory. The measures of congregational demography added a bit more explanatory power than in 1975. It seems likely that the power of contextual factors weakened a bit from the earlier study to this one.

The factors making for growth and decline of large churches and big city churches are clearest in our data. Being located in areas of *growth* in total population, in per capita income, and in the proportion of middle-aged persons was positive for membership growth, as was being located in areas where there is a high level of education and a greater proportion of newer housing. Growth was also more likely in the urban and suburban South. Growth was negatively affected by having a high proportion of widowed persons, a high number of working mothers, and a low rate of geographical mobility. Taken as a whole, this set of contextual variables suggests the kinds of communities in which PCUSA congregations do best and worst. That they do best in growing, more affluent, better-educated communities where the housing stock is newer, is no surprise given all past research.

Congregational demography variables were less important than contextual or institutional factors, but it is true that congregations with a greater proportion of affluent, middle-aged members, and a higher percentage of members in two-parent households with school-age children are more likely to be growing.

The importance of institutional factors, which the congregation can consciously do something about, is shown in this study. Most important are factors relating to Christian education programs, emphasis on evangelistic outreach (especially by the pastor), and quality preaching. Facilities are also important, especially educational facilities. Congregations described by their sessions as theologically liberal are slightly more likely to be growing. And congregations that have a positive view of their future are growing.

We found much variation in the strength of the various factors from location to location, from small churches to large churches. It is inappropriate to generalize about what makes for growing or declining churches without talking about location, size, region, and age. Unfortunately, many vague generalizations are being spread today, creating more confusion and disappointment than positive results.

To sum up: No single factor explains why some churches grow and others decline. It is a combination of factors, many of which we have isolated and measured. We were able to explain 32% of the variation in growth or decline, which is quite good for sociological research. The rest of the variation is due to peculiar local, accidental, and unmeasured factors we were unable to study. These findings can probably be generalized to congregations of other similar denominations. Churches vary by size, community type, region, and so on. In the future we must learn to specify what affects growth and decline in particular types of congregations in particular locations. That task awaits further study.

Excursus: "Factors Influencing Presbyterian Congregational Growth or Decline in the 1980s"

Details of the 1975 Study

The Presbyterian Special Committee to Study Church Membership Trends was appointed in 1974 to help denominational leaders understand the decline. Its final report, *Membership Trends in the United Presbyterian Church in the U.S.A.*, was published in 1976, and a later analysis of the data was done by Roof et al. (1979), in the *Understanding Church Growth and Decline, 1950–1978* volume. Research methods are described in both reports.

The task force studied congregational growth or decline in the 1968–74 period. It randomly selected 350 churches in the "growth" category (5% or more growth in 1968–74), 350 in the "decline" category (30% or more decline), and 350 in the middle of the spectrum, which was about 15% decline. Of these 1,050 congregations, 802 agreed to take part. In autumn 1975 the task force sent out two kinds of questionnaires: first a "church questionnaire," which asked a number of factual questions about the community, the congregation, the church program, and so on, to be filled out by a knowledgeable person; and second, a packet of six to fifteen "individual questionnaires" to be given to designated categories of active parishioners. More questionnaires were sent to large congregations than to small ones; an average of 6.5 were returned. As a result of this method, the persons filling out the individual questionnaires were relatively active lay members, not a random sample.

The researchers aggregated the data from the church questionnaires and the individual questionnaires for each congregation, resulting in nearly 500 variables covering neighborhood context, characteristics of members, congregational leadership program, leadership, conflict, and so on. No census data on each church's community were available. The unit of analysis was the congregation.

First, the researchers computed a membership change measure, 1968 to 1974, by dividing the 1974 membership figure by the 1968 figure. Then they computed zero-order correlations between all 500 variables and the membership change measure. A majority of the variables were found to be useless because of a weak correlation with membership change, because they unduly overlapped other variables, or because they were on topics (such as evaluation of presbytery or synod staff) on which the respondents lacked knowledge. After initial screening, twenty-three of the contextual, and seventy-two of the institutional variables were retained for further analysis. The contextual variables were organized in four clusters: Affluence, Demographic Change, Community Facilities, and Church Competition. The institutional variables were organized in fifteen clusters, including Membership Satisfaction with Worship and Program, Pastor, Social Action, and Congregational Harmony and Cooperation. Then, through use of multivariate analysis, the researchers assessed the importance of each cluster separately and the overall importance of contextual and institutional factors. Finally, the analysis was repeated within strata of church size (with no useful result) and within each of six community types—growing area in a large city, nongrowing area in a large city, growing area in a suburb of a large city, nongrowing area in a suburb of a large city, small city, and town and country.

Results of Regression Analyses of Subgroups

This section contains detailed regression tables from the new data. The four tables in the Supplemental Appendix (Tables A9.1, A9.2, A9.3, and A9.4) depict betas and adjusted R^2s for analyses within each of four church sizes, four community types, four regions of the nation, and three ages of the congregation (based on founding dates). All the R^2s are adjusted downward using the standard adjustment formula of SPSSX. The formula is based on the number of cases and the number of variables in the regression, and it most deflates the R^2 when N is low and the number of variables is high. In subgroups with N less than 100 the adjustment greatly deflates R^2 when a large number of predictors are being used, even as much as from .20 to .01 and from .61 to .36. The reader should remember this when comparing columns having greatly different Ns.

C h a p t e r   T e n

Congregational Growth and Decline in Indiana Among Five Mainline Denominations[1]

Daniel V. A. Olson

Since the mid-1960s most mainline Protestant denominations have been losing members. This study of churches affiliated with five mainline denominations in Indiana reveals a similar pattern of membership loss. Between 1980 and 1988 all five denominations lost members, but they did so at dramatically different rates. Within Indiana, the Lutheran Church, Missouri Synod, lost only 2% of its members.[2] The United Church of Christ lost 6%, The United Methodist Church lost 10%, the Christian Church (Disciples of Christ) lost 11%, and the Presbyterian Church (U.S.A.) lost a staggering 22% of their members between 1980 and 1988.

Discouraging as these figures may be to mainline church leaders, the denominational totals tell only part of the story. Not all mainline churches are declining. More than a quarter of the congregations included in this study had net gains in membership between 1980 and 1988, and one church grew by more than 1,200%. What accounts for these differences? Why are some mainline congregations growing, while most are declining? Are congregations at the mercy of changing times? Or are there steps a church can take to turn things around even when they belong to denominations that are in decline?

This chapter identifies a variety of factors affecting the growth and decline of congregations. Some are beyond the control of congregations, but others are factors a church can change. Six important conclusions arise from these findings.

1. Congregations that emphasize growth and evangelism can grow (or at least slow their decline), but only 37% of the churches in this study emphasize growth.
2. If churches want to grow, they need to have an openness to change and an orientation to serving the needs of persons outside the local congregation rather than just the needs of current members.

3. Emphasizing social action programs may limit growth somewhat, but this is not a cause of denominational decline for mainline denominations, since only 8% of these churches have such an emphasis.
4. As in previous studies (e.g., Hoge and Roozen, 1979), membership trends are heavily influenced by community population trends. However, the influence of demographic factors declined during the 1980s in Indiana because there was less variation in population growth rates among Indiana communities.
5. The growth rates of small churches and churches in smaller communities are less affected by community population changes than are the growth rates of large churches and churches in larger communities.
6. Denominational differences in growth rates are major, but are not explainable using the variables contained in this study.

Data Sources and Methods

The data for this chapter come from three sources, a survey conducted in congregations, census data at the zip code level, and church yearbook data (including membership and giving statistics). The census data were purchased from National Planning Data Corporation and are organized by zip code for all zip codes in Indiana. The data include actual census data for 1970 and 1980, as well as estimates for 1984 and projections for 1989.

The survey was conducted in early 1986. Questionnaires were mailed to 1,424 congregations in the state of Indiana associated with six denominations (the Christian Church [Disciples of Christ], the Episcopal Church, the Lutheran Church, Missouri Synod, the Presbyterian Church [U.S.A.], the United Church of Christ, and The United Methodist Church). Each church received a single questionnaire to be filled out by the pastor or a knowledgeable church leader. The questionnaire asked for self-descriptions of the congregation, program emphases, methods used by the church to increase membership and giving, presence or absence of church conflicts, subjective assessments of changes in the surrounding community, and similarities or differences between congregation members and people in the local community. The survey did not ask about actual levels of membership or giving since this information is available from church yearbooks.

A total of 641 usable questionnaires were completed for a return rate of approximately 45%.[3] However, most of the analysis below is based on a smaller group of 457 churches for which it was possible to match questionnaire data with census data and membership data for both 1980 and 1988.[4] Because the appropriate annual yearbook data for the Episcopal congregations were not easily available at the time of data entry, the Episcopal churches (only thirty churches) were excluded from this analysis.

This chapter uses regression methods to identify factors related to percentage change in church membership from 1980 to 1988.[5] Following Carroll, Dudley, and McKinney (1986), this chapter examines four types of predictor variables: context, identity, process, and program. Contextual variables include census data for the zip code in which the church is located, as well as estimates of community characteristics made by the questionnaire respondents. Variables having to do with church identity include denominational affiliation, church size, and assessments made by questionnaire respondents concerning where their church fits on a series of seven-point scales in which the two end points of the scales are opposite descriptions of congregations. For example, respondents were asked to indicate whether their congregation is "more influenced by its history and tradition" (coded as a 1) or "more influenced by contemporary ideas and trends" (coded as a 7). The only process variable contained in this study concerns the presence or absence of major church conflicts in the past ten years. The program variables include per capita giving in 1980, sources of church income, and a series of questionnaire items in which respondents indicate how much various types of programs are emphasized at the respondent's church and how effectively these programs are carried out.

The order of these categories (context, identity, process, and program) corresponds to the amount of direct influence a congregation can have over the variables in each category. Congregations can do little, short of relocation, to improve their community context. A church can change its identity, but only slowly. Congregational identity is largely the product of recent history. Thus, to remake congregational identity, one must make new history, a process that takes time.

Churches have even more control over process variables, variables like communication patterns, methods of decision making, and presence or absence of church conflicts. However, such changes require that leaders and members first have an awareness of the current state of these processes and know how to change them.

Among the four categories of variables examined in this chapter, congregations have the most control over church programs. Leaders and members usually know what these programs are. They are clearly reflected in budget statements and weekly bulletins. This explicitness makes programs the easiest to change (assuming change is desired!).

By separating these variables into four types, it is possible not only to see which factors have the most influence on church growth rates, but also to identify those characteristics that a church can most effectively change if it wants to grow.

Factors Related to Growth

Table 10.1 gives an overall view of the relative importance of the various growth-related factors. The variable descriptions in the left-hand column are grouped into the four general categories described above: context, identity, process, and program. Within these categories, similar variables are grouped into clusters. The first numerical column shows the zero-order correlations (without statistical controls) of these variables with percentage membership change (1980 to 1988). While the data set includes many variables that could potentially be included in regression equations, Table 10.1 includes only variables that correlate with congregational growth at the .10 level of significance or less.

The second column shows the standardized betas for regressions using only the variables in each cluster. The third column shows the proportion of total variance in growth rates (adjusted R^2) that is accounted for by the variables in each cluster. The fourth column shows the adjusted R^2 for each of the four categories of variables.[6]

The last column shows the increment in adjusted R^2 added by each category of variables, that is, the additional proportion of variation in growth that is explained by a category of variables above and beyond that which is explained by earlier categories of variables. Thus, the value shown in this column for program variables is .09, indicating that church programs account for an additional 9% of the variation in church growth above and beyond the effects of the other four categories of variables. The final row, at the bottom of Table 10.1, shows that, taken together, the variables "explain" about one-quarter of the variations in church growth rates. That is, the adjusted R^2 for all variables equals .269.

Context

Taken together, the demographic (contextual) variables explain a little less than 9% of the variance in growth rates in this study. Table 10.1 shows that the adjusted R^2 for the contextual variables is .086. This figure is considerably lower than the results reported by Thompson, Carroll, and Hoge (elsewhere in this volume) for Presbyterian churches. Moreover, community context accounts for only about 32% of the total variance explained by all the variables in this study of Indiana churches. This figure is quite low compared to the findings reported in the earlier volume (Hoge and Roozen, 1979) in which contextual variables accounted for more than half of the explained variance in growth rates.

TABLE 10.1

Variables in Final Analysis: Zero-order Correlations, Standardized Regression Betas Within Clusters, and Explained Variance for Clusters and Types

	Zero-order correlation	Standardized Beta	Adj. R^2 for cluster	Adj. R^2 for type	Increment to Adj. R^2
1. Community Context					
A. Census Data					
Percent Change in Population 1980–89	.2123	.130*			
Median Age 1980	−.1199	−.130*			
Percent Hispanic 1980	−.0935	−.074			
Percent of Adults with 9-11 Years of Formal Education 1980	−.1616	−.081	.052		
B. Informant's Assessments of Community					
New Single Family Housing Development	.1739	.153*			
General Business Development	.1339	.095*			
School Closings	−.0936	−.077	.041		
C. Informant's Assessments of Similarity Between Congregation and Community					
Racial Similarity	.1565	.131*			
Economic Status Similarity	.1377	.109*	.031	.086	.086
2. Congregational Identity					
A. Informant's Assessments of Congregation					
Congregation is more influenced by "its history and tradition" than by "contemporary ideas and trends."	−.1788	−.177*			
Congregation is primarily oriented to serving "its own members" rather than "the world beyond its membership."	−.0827	−.014			

Congregation is "known as a prestigious church in the area" more than "not considered one of the status churches in the area."	.03231[1]	.039			
Congregation's approach to individual salvation is "decidedly evangelistic, stressing a definite conversion experience" rather than emphasizing "education, nurture, and gradual growth in faith."	.0400	.036	.028		
B. Denomination			.084		
United Church of Christ	.0717	.055			
Christian Church (Disciples of Christ)	−.0003	−.008			
Lutheran Church, Missouri Synod	.2096	.159*			
Presbyterian Church (U.S.A.)	−.2644	−.208*			
United Methodist Church	.0110	—[2]			
C. Church Size in 1980	−.0474[1]	−.047	.000	.127	.090
3. Process					
Major Church Conflict in Past 10 Years	−.0700	−.070	.003	.003	.000
4. Program					
A. Current Church Program Priorities					
Christian Education (Youth and Adults)	.1086	.100*			
Local Evangelism	.0941	.098*			
Social Action (Study and/or Action by Members)	−.0725	−.082*			
World Mission Support	.0737	.076	.023		
B. Current Effectiveness of Programs					
Worship	.1015	.099*	.010		
Local Evangelism	.0701	.065			

	Zero-order correlation	Standardized Beta	Adj. R² for cluster	Adj. R² for type	Increment to Adj. R²
C. Programs Receiving Greater Emphasis Compared with 10 Years Ago					
Christian Education (Youth and Adults)	.0913	.074			
Local Evangelism	.0542	.073			
World Mission Support	.1258	.130*	.020		
D. Strength of Stewardship Efforts					
Stewardship Education Programs	.0701	.104*			
Overall Emphasis on Stewardship 10 Years Ago	− .0652	− .078	.010		
E. Finances					
Per Member Giving in 1980	.1359	.130*			
Percent of Income from Endowments	− .0848	− .044			
Percent of Income from Regular Offerings	.1456	.111*			
Percent of Income from Special Offerings	− .0672	− .029	.031		
F. Importance of Church Growth					
Overall Membership Recruitment Emphasis	.2074	.175*			
Preaching and Personal Involvement of the Pastor in Membership Recruitment	.1509	.094*	.046	.103	.090
Total Adjusted R² All Variables			.269		

[1]Both congregational prestige and church size become much more important variables when entered into regression along with the denominational dummy variables (see text for explanation).

[2]No Beta is shown for the Methodist dummy variable since dummy variable regression requires that one of the denominations not be included in the regression equation.

The apparent drop in ability of demographic variables to explain church growth may be due to differences in the number and quality of variables (both contextual and noncontextual) used in this, as compared to earlier studies. Alternatively, the importance of demographic variables may actually have decreased since the 1970s. While there are important differences between the variables used in this study and the variables used in previous studies, two pieces of evidence suggest that contextual variables may have lost some of their explanatory power over time.

First, others in this volume report similar declines in the importance of contextual variables. Second, among the 899 Indiana congregations for which I have membership figures in 1970, 1980, and 1989, the correlations between population change and church growth decrease considerably from the 1970s to the 1980s. In the period from 1970 to 1980 the correlation is .253 (R^2 = .064). In the period from 1980 to 1988 it is .186[7] (R^2 = .035), almost a 50% drop in the ability of population change to explain membership change.

What would cause such a drop? A quick study of population trends in Indiana shows that in the communities where these churches are located, average population increases were almost 10% during the 1970s, but fell to only +3% in the 1980s. More importantly, there was less variation in population growth rates during the 1980s,[8] that is, the gap between the most rapidly declining and most rapidly growing areas is not as great. During the same time the means and standard deviations of church growth rates changed little.

In regression and correlation, when one reduces the range of variation of one variable while the variation in the second variable is constant, correlations and R^2 values will diminish even if the underlying causal process is unchanged. This appears to have happened in Indiana. During the 1980s there were fewer differences in community growth rates that could be used to explain differences in church growth rates. Thus, the correlations have diminished even if the potential effects of major community changes have not.

Table 10.1 shows three separate clusters of contextual variables. The first comes from actual census data. Within this cluster, percentage change in population is the most important predictor. Churches are more likely to grow in growing communities. Additionally, mainline churches appear not to grow well in communities with a large proportion of older residents. This is probably because such communities often have fewer new, and as yet unchurched, persons moving in who are available for recruitment. Finally, mainline churches also do not do well in communities in which the residents are dissimilar to most mainline attenders in their race and education. They grow poorly in areas with many Hispanics and where average educational levels are low.

The variables in the second cluster are based on the questionnaire respondent's assessment of community trends. While these assessments are not as objective as the actual census figures, they correlate well with church growth (perhaps because respondents judge community trends by church trends) and moderately well with the actual population changes.

The third cluster of contextual variables differs from most previous studies since the items focus on the degree of similarity between the congregation and the community. Mainline congregations grow best in communities that are racially and economically similar to the congregation.

While the contextual variables appear less important than in earlier studies, their role is still significant. Unfortunately, there is little a church can do, other than relocation, to change its demographic context. However, it is worth noting that large churches and churches in large communities appear to be more affected by contextual variables than small churches and churches in small communities.

Table 10.2 shows the adjusted R^2 values from regressions predicting church growth using only the contextual variables. In the upper part of Table 10.2 the churches have been broken into groupings of approximately equal size (based on membership in 1980). The growth rates of the smallest churches in the study, those with less than 162 members in 1980, are not affected in any measurable way by the contextual variables used here. They neither grow nor decline in response to demographic change.

Similarly, churches in small communities are little affected by the demographic trends of their communities. Table 10.2 shows that the impact of contextual variables increases with the number of people living in the same zip code as the church. Unfortunately the data set does not include the actual populations of the towns or cities in which churches are located. However, a careful comparison of these towns and cities with the population of each church's zip code shows that city size and zip code population are very closely related. There are a few small zip codes located in large cities, but not enough to significantly affect the overall results in Table 10.2. Zip code population is a fairly good proxy measure for community size.

The findings in Table 10.2 are quite robust, that is, they are consistent over time and with different subsets of churches. The same two patterns are apparent in separate analyses (not shown here) for the period of 1970 to 1980. Moreover similar results have been obtained by Thompson, Carroll, and Hoge (in this volume), Roof et al. (1979), and McKinney (1979). Other analyses also not shown here suggest further that church size and community size work together in an additive fashion. Small churches in small zip codes are affected the least by community population changes. Small churches in large communities and large churches in small communities are moderately affected by population change. Finally, large churches in large zip codes are most responsive to population change.

TABLE 10.2
Variance in Church Growth Explained by Contextual Variables by Church and Community Size

	Median Number of Cases	Membership Change 1980–88	Variance Explained by Context Adj. R²
Total Sample	440	− 8.8	.086
Members in 1980			
1–161	106	− 7.2	.000
162–289	114	− 8.0	.115
290–523	110	− 9.6	.204
524 and over	117	− 8.8	.130
Zip Code Population in 1980			
1–4,282	109	− 7.2	.014
4,283–14,166	110	− 5.6	.106
14,167–27,888	113	− 10.4	.132
27,888 and over	116	− 11.2	.198

Identity

Returning to Table 10.1, one sees that of the four categories of variables, the variables measuring congregational identity are the strongest predictors of membership change. They account for nearly 13%[9] of the variance in church growth and about 47% of the total explained variance in this study. This strength is largely due to the denominational affiliation variables (discussed below), but other church identity factors are important.

The first cluster of identity variables includes informants' self-assessments of the congregation. Among this cluster the first variable is most important. Respondents at the most rapidly growing churches say their churches are more influenced by "contemporary ideas and trends" than by "history and tradition." While some might interpret this distinction as a proxy for theological liberalism versus conservatism, the correlations of this item with other questionnaire items suggest a quite different pattern, a pattern that explains why this item is a predictor of membership growth.

Churches that are more influenced by "contemporary ideas and trends" are less likely to say the congregation is primarily oriented to "serving its own members" as opposed to "the world beyond its membership" (r = − .395), more likely to say they engage in social action (r = .224), more likely to place a strong emphasis on church growth (r = .199), more likely to say they have effective evangelism programs (r = .136), more likely to have a minister who puts a high priority on church growth (r = .127), and less likely to say they are "one large family" rather than a "loosely knit association of individuals and groups" (r = − .099).

In other words, an emphasis on "contemporary ideas and trends" as opposed to "history and tradition" reflects an outward rather than an inward focus, a focus on the needs of nonmembers and people outside the church as opposed to current members. Lyle Schaller has consistently argued (e.g., 1968, 1981) that such an outward focus is a necessary prerequisite for membership growth. On the other hand, it is natural for a church with an inward focus to stress "history and tradition," to focus on the past and the practices of the past. Such practices once served current members well and continue to meet their needs (else they would not still be attending). But past practices do not often serve the needs of potential new members. To attract new members, Schaller argues that a church must have an openness to change and an emphasis on programs that serve nonmembers (e.g., evangelism, social action).

Congregational prestige, the third item in the self-assessment cluster, has a low correlation and standardized beta. However, this variable becomes more important when it is included along with the denominational variables in regressions. This is because the denominations differ in the prestige accorded to their churches by the questionnaire respondents. (Respondents in the denomination with the smallest membership losses, the Lutheran Church, Missouri Synod, were least likely to describe their church as "prestigious.") But within each denomination, more prestigious churches fared better than less prestigious churches.

Similarly, Table 10.1 suggests that 1980 church size, the third identity cluster, has little effect on church growth. But like prestige, size becomes important when it is included along with denomination in regression equations. Once the differences in average church size across denominations (due to different definitions and standards of membership) are taken into account, it becomes apparent that, within these denominations, smaller churches declined the least and grew the most. However, one should view this finding cautiously. Marler and Hadaway (1992) found that the relationship between size and growth rates varies by denomination.

Table 10.1 shows that denominational affiliation affects congregational growth more than any other variable in this study. While unsurprising to those who have read Dean Kelley's *Why Conservative Churches Are Growing* (Kelley, 1972), it is perhaps the most puzzling finding of this study. The data examined here suggest that denominational affiliation is very important, but these data reveal nothing about *why* denomination is so important. What is it about belonging to a particular denomination that affects congregational growth rates? In technical language, the variance in church growth rates explained by denominational affiliation is not shared with any other variables in the study (including measures of evangelism and emphasis put on church growth). Including these and other variables into regression alongside denominational variables fails to reduce the betas for the denominational variables. In simpler terms, none of the other variables measured in this study can explain away, or explain why, some denominations are declining faster than others.

Obviously there is something about denominational affiliation that explains the major differences in their growth rates both nationally and in Indiana. Unfortunately, this study contains no variables that account for these differences. Notably, it does not include measures of theological conservatism or strictness, the variables most often thought to explain denominational growth rates (Kelley, 1972; Iannaccone, 1989). Denominational differences are important, but this study cannot tell us why.

Process

As shown in Table 10.1, churches that experienced "serious" conflicts over "theological, social, financial, administrative, interpersonal, or other issues" during the past ten years were slightly less likely to grow than churches without such conflicts. This finding is unsurprising but important. A better measure of church conflict might show an even stronger negative correlation with membership growth.

Program

Churches that want to grow can grow or at least slow their declines. This is the most important finding from among the program variables, and one of the most important findings in this study. This longtime assertion of church growth advocates (e.g., Wagner, 1976) appears to receive strong confirmation even among these mostly declining mainline congregations. This assertion is supported by the adjusted R^2 for the last program cluster, by the betas for variables indicating that evangelism receives a high priority or a higher priority than it did ten years ago,[10] and by the findings of Hadaway and of Thompson, Carroll, and Hoge (in this volume).

The good news is that churches that want to grow can grow. The bad news is that few of the churches studied here emphasize growth. Only 37% of the respondents in the sample say that their church places a "strong" or "very strong" emphasis on membership recruitment. This suggests that membership declines have more to do with a desire for growth than with the techniques of church growth programs. Churches that place a low value on membership growth, compared to other goals, are unlikely to emphasize recruitment programs. If denominational leaders present such churches with elaborate plans for growth, plans that may have worked in more willing congregations, little growth seems likely. As I discuss below, factors related to congregational identity play an important role in determining which churches want to grow and thus the likelihood that they will implement programs that lead to membership growth.

The next most important program cluster concerns finances. Those churches that had higher per capita giving at the beginning of the study period (1980) were more likely to grow in the years that followed. This could mean that higher per capita giving reflects higher member commitment (a quality likely to attract outsiders). Or it could be that higher giving levels enable these churches to fund new staff and programs that attract outsiders.

Interestingly, churches that grew between 1980 and 1988 had *lower* per capita giving in 1988, at the end of the study period. This initially puzzling result confirms a similar observation based on a national sample of Christian (Disciples of Christ) congregations (Meyers and Olson, 1991). What appears to happen is that growing churches necessarily have many new members, members who initially, at least, are likely to give less money to the church, thus lowering per capita giving. Attracting new members probably serves to increase temporarily the number of "free riders" who depend upon the commitment of old-timers to foot the bill.

Results for the stewardship program cluster suggest that growth is also associated with the strength of stewardship education programs. If such programs increase per capita giving, they may encourage growth for the reasons discussed above. The negative relation of growth with strength of stewardship programs ten years ago probably reflects the tendency for growing churches to think they do most things better than they did in the past.

The variables in the first and third program clusters suggest that an emphasis, or an increased emphasis, on evangelism may lead to growth. Similarly, churches that emphasize world mission have higher growth rates. Perhaps this is because such an emphasis is compatible with evangelical activities. Alternatively it may reflect a general concern for nonmembers, a concern that appears to make churches more open to growth. Finally, a strong emphasis on Christian education is also associated with growth.

The correlation and beta for the social action variable in the first program cluster suggests that churches whose members place a stronger emphasis on social action relative to other church programs are somewhat less likely to grow. However, an emphasis on social action cannot explain the membership losses of mainline denominations since very few of the churches in this study have such an emphasis. When respondents were asked to rank seven program areas according to the emphasis each area receives in their church (the source of the variables in the first program cluster), 65% of the respondents said that social action received the least emphasis. Only 8% ranked social action fourth or higher. While these few churches have somewhat lower growth rates, a social action emphasis cannot account for the membership decline of mainline denominations.

The second program cluster includes items asking about the effectiveness of programs rather than the emphasis these programs receive. Not surprisingly, effective evangelism programs are associated with growth. But one cannot tell if respondents estimated the "effectiveness" of evangelism programs by asking themselves whether or not the church had been growing.

The effectiveness of worship is also positively related to congregational growth. Again, respondents may estimate "effectiveness" based on how well their church is growing. Nevertheless, it is worth noting that while only sixteen of the churches rated the effectiveness of their worship as "unsatisfactory," these same churches experienced an average decline of 20% between 1980 and 1988. This compares to an average loss of 5% among the remaining churches. Worship is important for these mainline churches. In fact, 83% of the informants said that worship receives more emphasis than any other church program.

The Critical Role of an Outward Orientation

Table 10.1 highlights the factors that are most strongly associated with membership growth in congregations. However, some of these factors are beyond the control of most congregations. Contextual variables are important, but churches cannot change their context unless they relocate. Similarly, denominational affiliation is important, but most churches are not willing or able to switch denominations (and such a change probably would not help). In contrast, churches have more control over programs. Table 10.1 shows that program variables play an important role in growth. This is an important finding.

Churches that want to grow can take positive steps to improve their membership trends. Stating matters in this way, however, forces the question of growth back one step. Why do some churches want to grow while others do not? The fact that only 37% of these churches place a high emphasis on new member recruitment suggests that many churches place a low priority on growth. Without such an emphasis, churches are unlikely to institute the programs that can foster growth. What separates these churches from those that place a high priority on new member recruitment?

The critical difference appears to be between churches that have an outward orientation (emphasizing the needs of nonmembers) versus churches with an inward orientation (focusing on members' needs more than nonmembers). This difference is reflected in many of the church identity variables, variables that turn out to be good predictors of the emphasis put on new member recruitment.

For example, recruitment programs receive more emphasis in churches that are primarily oriented towards reaching the world beyond the members rather than "serving [their] own members" (r = .209), in churches that are more influenced by "contemporary ideas and trends" rather than "history and tradition" (r = .199), in large churches (r = .165), in churches that take a "decidedly 'activist'" approach to social issues (r = .148), and in churches whose approach to individual salvation is "decidedly evangelistic," stressing a definite conversion experience (r = .074).

Interestingly, both evangelistic and social activist churches are more likely to emphasize growth. What is important is an outward orientation focusing on nonmembers and a willingness to institute programs that serve their needs. Thus, while the presence or absence of certain programs has a direct effect on membership growth, church identity factors have an indirect, and perhaps more decisive effect on church growth. They determine whether a church will institute the programs that make growth possible.

There is a second way that an outward versus an inward focus affects growth. Churches that place a high emphasis on serving the needs of "the world beyond [the] membership" are much more affected by population trends. They grow more when their communities grow and they decline more when their communities decline. The correlation between population change and membership change among these churches is .303. In contrast, this correlation drops to .190 among churches that place a moderate emphasis on nonmembers' needs and drops even further to .134 among churches that put more emphasis on members' needs.[11]

The relationship between population growth and church growth is weakest among the churches with an inward focus. Such churches are less affected by demographic change. They retain more of their members when their community is in decline but they are also unable to recruit many new members when their community is growing. Why is this true?

Elsewhere (Olson, 1989) I argue that inward churches are likely to be churches where members are bound together by strong ties of fellowship (leading to high retention) but where the tightly-knit character of these ties prevents the quick absorption of newcomers (leading to low recruitment). Longtime members (who are usually plentiful in such churches) have many rewarding family-like ties to one another. In fact, Schaller (1982) suggests that such churches, usually small churches, come closest to being a "ministry of the laity." Genuine caring and support is strong in these churches. Strong bonds of fellowship prevent members from leaving even when they become dissatisfied with other aspects of church life. Such churches resemble large families.

But strong fellowship ties are a two-edged sword. The longtime members of such churches, since they already have many rewarding church friendships, have little time, energy, or need to develop additional ties with potential newcomers. Thus newcomers find such churches cliquish, feel unaccepted and unloved, and leave to look for a more welcoming church. The saturation of church fellowship networks lowers recruitment potential, but the rewarding character of these ties keeps retention rates high.

Churches with an inward focus tend not to emphasize growth since growth requires the disruption of the large family of fellowship. After all, how many families would prefer to double or triple in size? And how many children truly rejoice at the birth of a new sibling? Growth requires a focus on non-members' needs and thus threatens to take away resources from current members. Moreover, the possible success of church growth programs threatens to dilute the richly rewarding family-like ties often found in inwardly directed churches.

The inward versus outward dimension may also explain why small churches and churches in small communities are not as affected by population change (see Table 10.2). Such churches are more likely to reveal identity traits characteristic of inwardness. For example, small churches are more likely to be describe themselves as "one large family" ($r = .228$), more likely to be influenced by "history and tradition" ($r = .140$) as opposed to "contemporary ideas and trends," and more likely to be oriented to "serving [their] own membership" ($r = .125$). These identity traits are also more likely to be found in churches located in smaller communities (partly because church size and zip code population are related [$r = .272$]). Thus a tendency towards inwardness among small churches and churches in small communities may also explain why these churches are so little affected by either community growth or decline.

The Will to Grow

This study suggests that churches, even churches in declining mainline denominations, can improve their membership statistics by placing a high emphasis on growth. However, it also finds that many churches do not want to grow because growth threatens to disrupt the many benefits members receive from belonging to an inwardly focused congregation.

Leaders who want a church to grow must be concerned about the types of programs and techniques that best foster growth. But such programs are unlikely to succeed in inwardly focused churches. Thus leaders interested in growth must also think carefully about how to change the identity of such churches from an inward focus on members' needs to an outward vision for the needs of nonmembers. Leaders need to be aware that such changes threaten the loss of many valuable assets common to inwardly focused congregations, assets like strong ties of fellowship and caring. They also risk the loss of long-term members who are alienated by the changing church identity.

It may not be possible to preserve the benefits of inwardness and also have a strong outward focus conducive to membership growth. However, the best church growth plans and the best churches will be those that manage to do both well.

C h a p t e r   E l e v e n

Belief Style, Congregational Climate, and Program Quality

Michael J. Donahue and Peter L. Benson

Much of the empirical literature on congregational growth and decline has centered on sociological and sociodemographic influences (e.g., Hoge & Roozen, 1979). Fewer studies have examined the influence of beliefs and attitudes held by members. A congregation is a collection of believers; does it matter what they believe? Or perhaps belief style or "religious orientation" matters: Are congregations whose members' faith emphasizes love of neighbor more likely to report growth than those who emphasize love of God? Then again, perhaps congregational climate, the impression the members have of how the congregation "feels" ("warm" or "intellectually challenging"), has more influence. Other contributions to this volume suggest just such an effect. Lastly, how does the perceived quality of congregational programming, including worship and education, influence growth or decline?

The study presented here examines each of these domains (demographics, belief, climate, and program quality) to understand their influence on congregational growth and decline. A recent large-scale study of congregational life allows consideration of these questions in a denominationally diverse, nationally representative sample of congregation members.

The Effective Christian Education Study

Effective Christian Education: A National Study of Protestant Congregations (Benson & Eklin, 1990; Rohlkepartain, 1993) was funded by the Lilly Endowment and the participating denominations: Evangelical Lutheran Church in America, Christian Church (Disciples of Christ), Presbyterian Church (U.S.A.), United Church of Christ, and The United Methodist Church.[1] It involved the completion of lengthy survey instruments by nationally representative samples of pastors, Christian education coordinators, Christian education teachers, adults, and youth in each denomination. Among the concepts measured were belief content and style; various forms of religious involvement (e.g., congregation involvement, church attendance, private devotion, monetary contributions, exposure to religious media); congregational "climate"; congregational loyalty; perceptions of congregational emphases (e.g., evangelism, social justice, member support); and characteristics of members (education, income, marital status, racial/ethnic identification, and rural/urban residence).

In addition, ECE included a wide variety of measures concerning Christian education. These included exposure to Christian education across the lifespan, and the availability and quality of various Christian education programs in one's present congregation.

Answers to questions about many of these areas were obtained from all of the participants in the survey. Other ratings—most notably quality of programs, availability of resources and the like—were probed in particular detail with the coordinators and teachers of religious education, and the pastors.[2]

This study examines the relations between this constellation of variables and congregational growth and decline. It focuses on the pastors, Christian education staff, and adult members of the participating denominations.

Method

Survey Sampling

In 1988, lengthy surveys were administered in nationally representative samples of congregations. In each of the five participating denominations, 150 congregations were sampled, stratified by four categories of congregational size. A total of 492 congregations participated (66% of those invited), with participation rates ranging from 73% (ELCA) to 58% (UMC) within denominations.

Nonparticipating congregations tended to be those whose leadership was in transition. The participating congregational samples were compared with the known national characteristics of the participating denominations and found to be proportionally representative on a range of demographic factors. Participation rates (about 60%) were similar to those observed in other large-sample surveys of church bodies (see also Castelli and Gremillion, 1987) as well as those reported by the 1990 U.S. Census before its follow-up procedures (United States GAO, 1990).

Within each participating congregation, a project director was asked to arrange survey administration for the pastor, the coordinator of Christian education, and up to ten Christian education teachers. In addition, ten adult members randomly sampled from the membership rolls were invited to participate. Survey sessions were governed by a set of standardized procedures described in a detailed administration manual. Careful procedures were established to guarantee and preserve confidentiality for each respondent. Survey sessions ranged from one and a half to two and a half hours in length.

In each of the denominational samples of congregations, about 65% of the randomly chosen adults and teachers participated. About one-half of the nonrespondents did not participate due to illness or travel during the survey administration sessions. In all five denominations, samples slightly overrepresent females, and underrepresent inactive members.

Analytical Procedure

Congregations included in the analysis. Our interest in these analyses concerns the congregational characteristics that predict growth or decline in membership. Therefore, each congregation is treated as a single unit. The adults in a congregation are represented by a single mean score on any given question. In order to ensure that such means were based on a reasonable number of respondents, only those congregations in which at least six adults responded were included. This reduced the total number of congregations available for analysis to 384, a 22% reduction. In addition, for some variables, the ratings of the Christian education teachers, the coordinator of Christian education, and the pastor were combined into a single "leadership" mean. This approach was employed primarily to obtain composite ratings of the effectiveness of the individual congregation in particular areas: e.g., overall program quality, or perceived congregational support for Christian education.

Measures of congregational growth and decline. Two measures of congregational growth and decline were employed in these analyses. The first was a question that appeared at the end of the survey completed by pastors: "Compared to 5 years ago, is the size of your church growing, remaining steady, or decreasing?" Possible responses were (1) decreasing significantly, (2) decreasing a little, (3) remaining steady, (4) growing a little, or (5) growing significantly.

This measure obviously has a number of drawbacks. First is the problem of "halo effect," also known as "illusory correlation" (Markus & Zajonc, 1985). Perceptions tend to be altered to form a consistent image, either positive or negative. It might be argued that when congregations have a positive climate and active members, that there is a general tendency to perceive everything as rosy, and to report the congregation as "growing" even if the actual numbers are not increasing.

To address some of these concerns, a second measure of congregation growth/decline was also employed, based on the number of members the congregation reported to the national denominational office for the years 1983 and 1988. National office staff of each of the participating denominations graciously responded to a request that they provide these membership numbers from their 1984 and 1989 yearbooks. These data were then added to the ECE data set.[3] A "percent increase" measure was then calculated by dividing the 1988 membership figure by the 1983 membership figure.

This measure also has a number of drawbacks. As one of the denominational representatives took pains to point out, one cannot tell from these measures whether a particular congregation had decided, during this particular five-year period, to "clean the rolls" and remove names of members who had left the congregation. This measure also varies from denomination to denomination as a function of the definition of "membership" in that denomination. At the same time, it is the one "objective" measure of change in membership.

Relation between the two measures. Initial analyses of the relation between congregational growth and decline as reported by the pastors and that based on the membership figures obtained from the denominational yearbooks were unsettling. The two measures were essentially unrelated. Closer examination, however, indicated that the relation was being strongly influenced by a small number of congregations whose figures reflected either extreme growth or decline. Deleting five extreme cases[4] resulted in the correlation between the two measures rising to .39.

Another data transformation. The issue of the use of change scores in data analysis is a contentious one (see Nunnally, 1983 for a review). In this study, while the pastor's estimate of congregational change is not technically a "change score" (not a difference between two numbers, but a response to a single question), the question of how best to measure change as reported in the denominational yearbooks remains. As noted above, the basic measure employed was a ratio between the two reports of congregation size, five years apart. But the ratio, by itself, leads to certain statistical concerns. The most convenient way to deal with these concerns is to employ base 10 logarithms, a transformation that equates increases and decreases in a way that makes greater intuitive sense than simple ratios.[5]

With the partial support of a supplemental grant from the Lilly Endowment, data files were created for each congregation that included the mean scores for adult members of congregations on the range of variables described above, as well as various data supplied in surveys unique to the pastors, and the "educational effectiveness" measures reflecting the opinions of pastors, coordinators, and teachers. Due to the relatively small number of congregations within each individual denomination, most analyses were conducted after pooling all of the available data into a single data set. When the data were pooled across the five denominations, each congregation's data were weighted in order to make the data representative of the combined national distribution for the denominations. This had the effect of giving the United Methodist congregations a stronger impact on the findings than that of the remaining denominations. Additional by-denominational analyses were also conducted for comparison purposes.

Results

Two sets of analyses were performed, one employing the denominational yearbook data, and the other based on the pastor's ratings of the growth in the size of the "congregational family." The correlation of these two measures of congregation growth/decline and the entire group of variables described above were calculated. After determining the set of variables with high correlations, the relations were further explored through regression analysis.

Zero-order Correlations

Across all participating congregations. Table 11.1 shows the variables that correlated .20 or greater with either the pastor's estimate of congregational growth/decline, or the log of the change ratio derived from denominational yearbooks. They have been arranged in descending order based on the correlation with the pastor's estimate, and those measures that correlated +0.20 or better only with the change ratio are listed at the end.

Most notable about this list is what is absent. The hypothesis that originally motivated these analyses—that either the content or style of belief of a congregation might be related to growth or decline—is rather effectively refuted. No particular religious belief, nor any of the styles of belief or "religious orientations" addressed in these surveys was correlated +0.20 or stronger to congregational growth or decline. These measures included overall faith maturity, growth in faith maturity during the previous two or three years, "orthodoxy," "vertical" religion, "horizontal" religion (see Davidson & Knudsen, 1977), religious centrality, church importance, and God concepts.

The correlations of the variables in Table 11.1 with the change ratio are generally less strong, and whether or not a characteristic is correlated with the change ratio is in fact unrelated to whether is it correlated to the pastor's estimate of growth or decline.[6] The larger number of correlations between the pastor's subjective estimate of change and the various attitudes and perceptions of the other members of the congregation renews concerns that some of the findings here may be influenced by the "halo effects" discussed above. Nevertheless, the remainder of the discussion will concentrate on the correlations based on the pastor measure.

TABLE 11.1

Zero-order Correlations of ± .20 or Stronger Between Measures of Congregational Growth/Decline and Various Congregational Characteristics

Source[1]	Congregational Characteristic	Pastor Estimate	Log Change Ratio
Adult	Helps Members Make Friends	.47	.07
	Supports Members in Hardship	.42	.06
	Teaches Denominational Heritage	.42	.07
	Promotes Intergenerational Contact	.42	.19
	Warm Climate	.42	.12
	Quality of Worship	.41	.15
	Teaches Caring Skills	.41	.08
	Utilizes Members' Talents	.41	.15
	Helps Members Appreciate Rituals	.40	.13
	Helps Members Develop Faith	.37	.12
	Helps Members Apply Faith to Life	.37	.12
	Quality CE[2] for Teens	.36	.19
	Quality CE for Children	.36	.16
Pastor	Year Congregation Founded	− .33	− .25
Adult	Teaches Faith Perspective on Morals	.32	.12
	Congregational Loyalty	.30	.03
Leader	Youth CE Emphasizes Moral Values	.30	.21
Adult	Youth CE Emphasizes Spiritual Development	.30	.11
	Helps Members Examine Global Impact of Life-style	.30	.08
	Quality of Bible Instruction	.29	.11
Leader	Emphasizes Youth CE Teacher Training	.29	.28
	CE Programs Are Publicized	− .29	− .16
Adult	Thinking Climate	.28	.08
	Involves Members in Leading Worship	.28	.07
	Involves Members in Community Service	.27	.04
Pastor	% of Adult Members Attending Weekly	.27	.25
	Mission:[3] CE for Teens	.27	.25
Adult	Helps Members Discuss Faith	.27	.14
Leader	Youth Programs Encourage Questioning	.27	.11
Pastor	% of Membership Active in CE	.27	.22
	Mission: Strength for Daily Life	.26	.08
Adult	Quality CE on Political Issues	.25	.12
	Quality CE on International Issues	.25	.00

Source[1]	Congregational Characteristic	Pastor Estimate	Log Change Ratio
Leader	Youth CE Promotes Intergenerational Contact	.25	.12
	Youth CE Innovative, Creative	.24	.11
Pastor	Mission: Members Find Purpose in Life	.24	.02
	Mission: CE for Children	.24	.13
	Mission: Provide Love, Support	.24	.02
	CE Staff Person Present	.24	.00
	% Age 12-18	.24	.26
	% High School Youth Active in CE	.23	.21
Leader	Youth CE Is Active Learning Process	.23	.10
	Emphasizes Adult CE Teacher Training	.23	.18
	CE Programs for Parents	.22	.13
Pastor	% Adults College Graduate	.22	.03
	Mission: Evangelism	.22	.13
Adult	Quality CE for Adults	.22	.03
Leader	Adult CE Is Active Learning Process	.21	.15
Pastor	% of Children Active in CE	.21	.18
	% of Congregation 70 or Older	− .21	− .31
Adult	Involves Members in Peace and Justice Issues	.21	.02
	Teaches About Other Faiths	.21	− .02
Pastor	% Jr. H.S. Youth Active in CE	.20	.10
	% Annual Budget Devoted to CE	− .14	.26
Leader	Youth CE Program Has Clear Purpose	− .18	− .23
	Leadership Committed to CE	.19	.21

[1]"Adult" indicates information based on the mean response of six to ten adults in the congregation. "Pastor" indicates information drawn from surveys unique to pastors. "Leader" indicates that the measure is based on mean responses of the pastor, coordinator of Christian education, and teachers of Christian education.

[2]CE = Christian Education

[3]"Mission" indicates one of a series of questions concerning the pastor's impression of the degree to which a particular issue is considered important to that congregation.

Note: N varies from 355 to 310; all p < .0001.

The results displayed in Table 11.1 indicate several things. Chief among them is that growth is largely in the hands of the congregation. It is related to trying hard to be a community of faith: supporting the membership, teaching the denominational heritage, utilizing members' talents, helping the members develop their faith and apply it to their lives. This is a picture of a congregation in which the membership is strongly "engaged"; not warm and fuzzy, but warm and focused.

By denomination. The across-denomination analyses displayed in Table 11.1 allowed us to examine the relative impact of characteristics that might be relatively constant (relatively high or relatively low) within a specific denomination. Table 11.2 examines effects within denominations.

TABLE 11.2
Ten Strongest Zero-order Correlations Between Reports of Congregational Growth/Decline and Various Congregational Characteristics, by Denomination

Source[2]	Congregational Characteristic	Denomination[1]				
		DC	ELC	PC	UCC	UMC
Adult	Helps Members Make Friends			.41	.45	.58
	Supports Members in Hardship	.38	.34	.41	.39	.47
	Teaches Denominational Heritage					.58
	Warm Climate			.34	.43	
	Quality of Worship	.43	.38	.39		.46
	Promotes Intergenerational Contact					.62
	Teaches Caring Skills	.36		.43	.39	
	Utilizes Members' Talents	.38			.39	.48
	Helps Members Appreciate Rituals				.34	.53
	Quality CE for Teens	.41				.51
	Quality CE for Children		.34			.46
Pastor	Year Congregation Founded		−.39			
Adult	Congregational Loyalty				.38	
Leader	Emphasizes Training Youth CE Teachers				.34	
Adult	Involves Members in Community Service			.34		
Pastor	% of Adult Members Attending Weekly		.33	.35		
	Mission: Strength for Daily Life			.34		
	Mission: CE for Children	.38				
	% High School Youth Active in CE	.36				
Adult	Quality CE on Political Issues		.32			
Leader	CE Programs for Parents	.38				

Source[2]	Congregational Characteristic	Denomination[1]				
		DC	ELC	PC	UCC	UMC
Pastor	% Adults College Graduate		.38			
Leader	Emphasizes Adult CE Teacher Training		.32			
Pastor	% of Congregation 70 or Older				−.39	
	% Jr. H.S. Youth Active in CE	.36				
Leader	Leadership Committed to CE	.45				
	Youth Included in Worship				.35	
	Adult CE Well-Organized		.37			
Pastor	Mission: Support Members in Crises			.40		
	Average Adult Income		.46	.38		

[1]For denominations, DC = Christian Church (Disciples of Christ), N = 46 to 66; ELC = Evangelical Lutheran Church in America, N = 60 to 69; PC = Presbyterian Church (U.S.A.), N = 46; UCC = United Church of Christ, N = 59 to 67; UMC = United Methodist Church, N = 55.
[2]See Table 11.1 for explanation of labels and abbreviations.
Note: All p < .007.

All of the top nine characteristics from Table 11.1 appear again here, and all but one of the denominations display at least four of the nine. The most distinctive pattern is associated with the Lutherans. In that denomination, the pastor's perception of growth and decline is most strongly associated with the pastor's assessment of the member's income, negatively associated with the year the congregation was founded, and next most strongly associated with the pastor's perception of the member's level of education. Aside from support in hardship, the emphasis on interpersonal contact present in the other denominations is not evident here.

By congregation size. In order to examine the possible influence of congregational size on these correlations, the congregations were divided into three groups: those whose pastors reported their congregation had fewer than 200 members (36%), those reporting 200 to 500 members (38%), and those reporting more than 500 members (26%). These three categories were then designated "small," "medium," and "large," and the ten highest correlates of congregational growth for each of these groups were examined. Table 11.3 presents the findings.

It is clear from Table 11.3 that each size of congregation has its own emphases. The "top ten" correlates for each of the three groups produces a list of twenty-four different characteristics; only four are shared by two of the types, and only one by all three. Perhaps most distinct is the emphasis on personal belief among the mid-sized congregations. It is here that issues of social justice, as reflected in concern for global issues and the poor, and a rejection of "exclusivity," is found to be associated with growth.

TABLE 11.3

Ten Strongest Zero-order Correlations Between Reports of Congregational Growth/Decline and Various Congregational Characteristics, by Congregation Size

| Source[2] | Congregational Characteristic | Congregation Size[1] | | |
		under 200	200–500	500+
Adult	Helps Members Make Friends	.49	.39	.57
	Supports Members in Hardship	.46	.42	
	Teaches Denominational Heritage			.52
	Promotes Intergenerational Contact	.50		.54
	Warm Climate		.38	.57
	Quality of Worship	.61		
	Teaches Caring Skills	.46	.40	
	Utilizes Members' Talents		.32	
	Helps Members Appreciate Rituals	.49		
	Helps Members Develop Faith			.46
	Quality CE for Teens			.48
	Quality CE for Children	.50		
	Teaches Faith Perspective on Morals	.46		
	Helps Members Examine Global Impact of Life-style	.47		
	Quality of Bible Instruction			.49
Leader	Youth Programs Encourage Questioning			.52
Adult	Quality CE on International Issues	.47		
Leader	Emphasizes Adult CE Teacher Training		.34	
Adult	Personal Concern About Global Issues		.57	
	Personal Concern for Poor		.37	
	Congregational Loyalty, Active Adults			.50
	Belief: Only Christians Will Be Saved		− .31	
Leader	Overall Quality of Adult CE			.49
Pastor	CE Programs Emphasize Liberation Themes		.33	

[1]For small congregations, N = 114 to 116; for medium, N = 108 to 125; for large, N = 63 to 79.
[2]See Table 11.1 for explanation of labels and abbreviations.
Note: All p < .001.

Some of the size differences also reflect the different emphases and styles often attributed to various-sized congregations. Small churches tend to emphasize warmth, family, and informal networks, whereas larger congregations place more emphasis on programs and established structures (see Foltz, 1990). This parallel suggests that congregations that accept the dynamic of their size—rather than trying to overcome them—are more likely to grow.

It should be noted that the five denominations that participated in the study varied somewhat in their distribution across the three size categories employed here. While Disciples of Christ, Presbyterian, and United Church of Christ congregations have similar small-medium-large percentage distributions (approximately 45%-35%-20% in each case), Lutheran congregations are more heavily concentrated in the mid-range (26%-49%-25%) and the Methodist congregations in these analyses were more likely to be large (17%-31%-52%).

Regression Analysis

The length and complexity of data displays discussed thus far preclude cogent summary. Such mind-numbing "laundry lists" of variables, while informative for those with interests in specific content areas, becloud larger issues concerning which characteristics are most strongly related to congregational growth and decline. Since many of these variables are interrelated, how much of this is redundant? The way to address this issue is through multiple regression. This allows an analysis of the degree of unique correlation between these congregational characteristics and congregational growth or decline.

As a first stage in conducting these analyses, sets of congregational characteristics were created, "congregational themes" as it were, whose relation with church growth/decline had been demonstrated in the earlier analyses. These themes were:

Demographics (from the pastor survey): (a) Year Congregation Founded; (b) Percent of Congregation Age 12-18; (c) Percent of Congregation 70 or older; (d) Percent of Adult College Graduates.

Congregational impact (from the adult survey): (a) Teaches Denominational Heritage; (b) Helps Members Develop Faith; (c) Helps Members Apply Faith to Life; (d) Helps Members Discuss Their Faith; (e) Teaches Faith Perspective on Morals; (f) Quality of Christian Education on Political Issues.

TABLE 11.4
Partial Multiple Correlations for Regression Models
Predicting Pastor's Perception of Church Growth

Model Employed	Partial R
Demographics (N = 233)	
Pastor: Year Congregation Founded	−.34*
Pastor: % of Congregation Age 70 or older	−.15
Congregational Impact (N = 312)	
Adult: Teaches Denominational Heritage	.42
Adult: Helps Members Develop Faith	.13
Program Quality (N = 321)	
Adult: Quality of Worship	.41
Adult: Quality of CE for Children	.18*
Congregational Climate (N = 321)	
Adult: Helps Members Make Friends	.47*
Adult: Promotes Intergenerational Contact	.19
Congregational Mission (N = 318)	
Pastor: Mission—CE for Teens	.27
Pastor: Mission—Strength for Daily Life	.18*
Educational Programs (N = 304)	
Leader: Emphasizes Adult CE Teacher Training	.26
Pastor: CE Staff Person Present	.17
Leader: Youth Programs Encourage Questioning	.14
Grand "Best Predictor" Model (N = 255)	
Adult: Helps Members Make Friends	.48
Pastor: Year Congregation Founded	−.23
Adult: Quality CE for Children	.17
Pastor: Mission—Strength for Daily Life	.14

Note: Partial R values are reported if they are .10 or greater; all $p < .05$.

Program quality (from the adult survey): (a) Quality of Worship; (b) Quality of Bible Instruction; (c) Involves Members in Community Service; (d) Quality of CE for Teens; (e) Quality of CE for Children; (f) Quality of CE for Adults.

Congregational climate (from adult survey): (a) Helps Members Make Friends; (b) Supports Members in Hardship; (c) Warm Climate; (d) Promotes Intergenerational Contact; (e) Teaches Caring Skills; (f) Utilizes Members' Talents.

Congregational mission (from pastor survey): (a) CE for Teens; (b) Strength for Daily Life; (c) Members Find Purpose in Life; (d) CE for Children; (e) Provide Love and Support; (f) Evangelism.

Educational program (from the pastor and "leadership" surveys): (a) Emphasizes Youth CE Teacher Training; (b) Emphasizes Adult CE Teacher Training; (c) Youth Program Encourages Questioning; (d) Youth CE Program Is Active Learning Process; (e) Adult CE Program Is Active Learning Process; (f) CE Staff Person Present.

Each of these themes was analyzed separately. The congregational characteristics for each "theme" were used to predict the pastor's estimate of church growth and decline. The results of this analysis are displayed in Table 11.4.[7] The table displays only those predictors that had partial R values of .10 or higher, after controlling for all of the other characteristics in that theme.

Each of the themes produced a small set of important characteristics. In general, both age of congregation and member age works against growth, while program quality, congregational impact, climate, mission, and educational program dynamics seem to promote growth. Christian education has a rather robust effect, as its influence is seen in perception of impact (e.g., Teaches Denominational Heritage), perception of program quality (Quality of Education for Children), mission (e.g., CE for Teens), and educational program development (CE Teacher Training, CE Staff Person Present, and Youth Programs Encourage Questioning). This finding is consistent with previous analyses of ECE data, indicating a powerful impact for well-conducted Christian education programs in all areas of congregational life.

Having thus sifted through the variables and obtained a subset of thirteen that are important across these six domains, a "grand model" was constructed. In this analysis, the thirteen congregational characteristics that had emerged as the strongest predictors across the six congregational themes were combined in a single analysis. The results of that analysis are also displayed in Table 11.4. Here again, only the strongest predictors are displayed, those with partial R values of .10 or higher after controlling for each of the remaining twelve predictors.

The "grand model" is composed of four rather different elements. One (Helps Members Make Friends) reflects climate. Strength for Daily Life is a congregational impact variable. And a third (Quality CE for Children) represents a focus of educational effectiveness.

It is important, in considering this last model, not to think that these four areas are the only ones that require attention. Each of these congregational characteristics are correlated with others (e.g., Helps Members Make Friends correlates .77 with our measure of a "Warm" climate), and it is the nature of regression analysis to take the single strongest correlate and disregard other variables to the extent that they are related to those predictors. It is best, then, to think of these four predictors as representative of a broader body of concerns; to think of them as areas of effort that would embody a variety of conceptually related characteristics.

Warm, Focused Christian Education Promotes Growth

Early publications examining findings from the Effective Christian Education project document a strong relation between educational program emphasis and quality and the formation of individual faith (Benson & Eklin, 1990). This analysis demonstrates that the impact of Christian education also extends to congregational growth and decline. High quality Christian education, therefore, appears to support both individual and institutional growth.

From a practical point of view, the findings suggest that much of church growth is in the hands of the membership. While some "fixed" or "unalterable" demographic factors also play a role (e.g., Year Congregation Founded), they are far from dominant in explaining growth. This is good news, indicating that congregations are not at the mercy of prevailing demographics, but can in fact foster growth through program changes that are directly related to their mission as a faith community.

The single strongest "fixed" factor, and the only major negative predictor of congregational growth is the year in which the congregation was founded. It is probable that this is largely a demographic artifact. Churches are founded because populations are growing. New churches founded in growing areas will display relatively rapid growth, at least partially because it is easier for a new, small church to show large percentage growth than for a larger church to show similar percentage growth. Lastly, the absence of this effect for "Year Congregation Founded" when the congregations are analyzed by the three separate size categories suggests that it is not the case that old congregations, per se, are likely to grow.

Finally, a note about climate. Congregational "warmth" is often mentioned as the precursor to growth. This study addresses this issue in several ways:

1. The characteristic "Helps Members Make Friends," so highly correlated with warm climate, was a factor in congregations of all sizes,
   and in three of the five denominations. It was also the strongest predictor in the "grand" model. Thus, climate is important, but not the
   sole issue in church growth.
2. Program quality was found to be an important predictor of growth, even
   in such "traditional" areas as teaching the denominational heritage.
3. Both program quality and fostering a "thinking climate" were found
   to be predictive of growth. This suggests, as we have noted, that
   perhaps congregations interested in growth should not be as concerned about being "warm and fuzzy" as being "warm and focused":
   focused on who they think they are, on their members as individuals
   rather than as a group, on what they have to offer for the new member, and on what their membership as a whole has to offer the wider
   community.

Future Research

It must be noted that one of the hypotheses with which this research was
begun, reflected in the title of this chapter, was not supported. There is little
evidence here, aside from some correlates of growth/decline in mid-sized
congregations, that belief style or content has much relation to the growth or
decline of congregations in the denominations examined here. Churches
with theologically and/or socially liberal members are as likely to grow as
congregations with a more conservative orientation. This finding runs
counter to the oft-cited maxim that associates growth with theological conservatism (e.g., Kelley, 1972).

But perhaps the effects of the content of belief are better expressed, not in
terms of the content, but through their diversity or unanimity. Are congregations in which the majority are in theological agreement with one another
more likely to grow that those congregations that are more heterogeneous?
One congregation may be liberal, another conservative, and both may grow
as theological liberals and conservatives seek them out. In such a circum-
stance, the growth or decline of these congregations are directly related to
the beliefs of their members, but looking for a specific type of belief related
to growth would be ineffective. People who "strongly agree" with a particular
belief statement are making one church grow, while people who "strongly
disagree" are attending another. In the current study, in which we have no
more than ten respondents per congregation, we do not have a sufficient statistical base to examine such a possibility. But perhaps on a later survey, single items or brief scales might be included in large samples of large numbers

of congregations. Such an approach would better measure the influence of beliefs on the climate of the congregation, and thereby the influence of theology on growth or decline. It may yet be shown that it is not any particular theological orientation, but taking a stand (as opposed to being lukewarm) that leads to growth (see Rev. 3:15-16).

Part Three

INDIVIDUALS AND THE CHURCH CHOICE

David A. Roozen and C. Kirk Hadaway

Denominations grow as individuals join local congregations. All three
levels of initiative and response are linked in the overall growth
equation, such that a change in any one has implications for the
other two. The previous sections of the book approached the growth equation
from the perspective of the denomination and the congregation. In
the current section we look at the meaning and motivations of individual
church involvement. For readers whose everyday interests in the dynamics
of growth direct their primary attention to denominations or congregations, let two reminders suffice to suggest the peril of ignoring the individual. First, it was social and value changes in individuals that drove the
church declines of the 1960s—declines that previous chapters have shown
affected all streams of American denominationalism. Second, there is a
consensus in the practical literature on church growth that different kinds
of individuals approach the church differently, and that effective growth
strategies must be sensitive to these differences.

Social research is often frustrating for practitioners. In part, this is
because scholars seldom reach a common conclusion. However, such was
not the case in regard to the causes of the church membership and participation declines of the 1960s. With a rare degree of unanimity, the
research of the late 1970s pointed directly to the then young adult baby
boom generation as the major source of the downturn. Wuthnow's
(1978:143) conclusion is typical:

> [The] losses can be explained to a significant degree as the result of young peo-
> ple being thrust together by a variety of historical events into a countercultural
> generation unit whose values and lifestyles did not include, and were often in
> active opposition to, participation in organized religion.

As Hoge and Roozen (1979:328) put it in slightly broader perspective:

> A broad cultural shift has occurred that has hit the churches from the outside, and it has hit the affluent, educated, individualistic, culture-affirming denominations hardest. The shift occurred much more among the youth than the older adults. It was most visible among the affluent young people, especially those on college campuses. It began in the early 1960s and achieved momentum during the middle and late 1960s.

That the changes "hit the churches from the outside" should not be read to imply that the churches were powerless to respond. Rather, it should be read in the context of Inskeep's prior chapter in this book: that during the 1960s the "outside" changed, and churches did not respond to this change in ways conducive to membership growth.

The "new" values emerging with the baby boom generation included three interrelated dimensions according to Yankelovich's (1974) *The New Morality: A Profile of American Youth in the 70's*. The first was a set of "new moral norms" including changes in sexual morality in a liberal direction and a lessening of automatic respect for and obedience to established institutional authority. The second dimension relates to social values, including a decreasing affirmation of the work ethic, marriage and family, and the importance of money in defining success. The third dimension concerns a change in the meaning of "freedom." Once tied primarily to more utilitarian concerns of economic security and upward mobility, the baby boom generation gave it an expressive twist, redefining freedom as choice and self-fulfillment.

In summary, the value changes of the 1960s were in the direction of individualism, personal freedom as self-fulfillment, and tolerance of diversity. And the effect of the changes on church participation was highly predictable, at least for those with a historical sensitivity. Since at least the turn of the century the ascendance of traditional sexual and family values and traditional free-enterprise values have been associated with high church participation, and the ascendance of "new morality" and civil libertarian values associated with marginal participation (Hoge, 1974).

The research of the 1970s also indicated that the depressing effect of value changes on the church participation of the baby boomers was strengthened by at least two other characteristics of this generation. First, their "postponement" of marriage and family formation, and relatedly low birthrates cut deeply into the historically strong connection between church and family. Second, their high geographic mobility severed connections to the local church in which they were raised (over 90% of boomers were raised with some connection to the church).

With the baby boom generation clearly established as the major source of the church declines of the 1960s and early 1970s, recent research on trends in individual church participation has focused on a new set of questions, including:

1. Whether the boomer's young adult marginality from organized religion would continue as the generation continued through the life cycle, or whether it was "typical" young adult rebellion to be followed by a return to the church as the generation matured; and
2. Whether the value changes so prominent among the boomers were unique to that generation, or whether the value changes were reflective of pervasive cultural changes that would be passed on to future generations.

Unlike the scholarly consensus about boomers' role in the declines of the 1960s and early 1970s, this new set of questions has generated considerable, and at times heated, disagreement (e.g., Hout and Greeley, 1990; Chaves, 1990). Given the centrality of the questions for an understanding of current trends in church participation, they are addressed to varying degrees in each of the five chapters in this section. Indeed, the research reported here suggests that all of the conflicting viewpoints contain a kernel of truth. The "big chill" generation did warm to worship as it moved into mid-life. Nevertheless, the generation's young adult drop-off was more severe than previous generations, and its mid-life return less pronounced. Not only has its mid-life return been less pronounced, but also it has been on different terms. All of the evidence suggests that the boomers' relationship to the church is fundamentally different from that of previous generations of Americans—that it is, to use the varied terminology of recent scholarly discussion, more "voluntaristic," consumer-oriented, and captive to the subjective, expressive dimensions of cultural individualism.

Finally, while the value orientation of the post-boomer generation now in their twenties appears to be somewhat different from that of the boomers (the post-boomers being a bit less anti-institutional; a bit more economically conservative, but equally liberal socially); their church participation patterns are identical to those of the boomers when they were in their twenties. Implication: the boomer legacy of church voluntarism has been passed down to the next generation.

While investing a great deal of energy in the relationship between sociocultural change and religious change, the 1970s' research on religious participation paid scant attention to the relationship between church involvement and religious belief. It assumed that the two were too strongly related and mutually reinforcing to change independently. For a variety of reasons, not the least of them being an increasing diversity in belief and an increasing concern over the potential anti-institutional effects of cultural individualism, research in the 1980s began including personal religiosity in its causal models of church participation (e.g., Hoge and Polk, 1980; Cornwall, 1989; Willits and Crider, 1989; Lee, 1992). Several of the following chapters continue this emerging practice. They show that the relationship is not as strong as traditionally assumed, and that the relationship differs over time and by denominational family. Similar findings are reported for the relationship between one's religious upbringing and one's adult church involvement.

The vast majority of empirical research on religious participation, including most of that reported in the following chapters, uses national survey data and the interpretive techniques of multivariate, statistical inference. It is a powerful combination for examining the relative and changing influence of the diverse motivations and forces that lead different kinds of people into or away from the church. The strengths of such research include: its reliable gauge of the national situation; its ability to identify influences that, if asked about directly, an individual may not be able to articulate; and, particularly for trend studies, its ability to tap into an increasing archive of national surveys. However, because of its broad scope and the quantifiable format of questions used in most large-scale surveys, it misses some of the nuances of particular individual biography. Fortunately, concern about membership declines during the 1970s produced a flurry of more qualitative studies specifically directed at why church dropouts felt they had dropped out, and why recent returnees felt they had returned. Such studies provide rich, narrative detail.

In Hale's pioneering *Who Are the Unchurched?* (1977), for example, we hear over 160 persons living in six diverse counties in the United States talk about why they are unchurched. Hale artfully winds his anecdotal material around a framework of over twenty reasons given by his interviewees for their current location outside the church. Hale's unchurched range all the way from the "burned-out" to the "cop-outs"; and from the "pilgrims" to the "publicans." Hale says he met few "true unbelievers." In Rauff's *Why People Join the Church* (1979) we hear the voices of 180 men and women recall their journeys from outside to inside the doors of the church. Rauff blends the diverse voices around a framework of twelve major themes—ranging from a vague feeling of emptiness to a specific invitation from a relative or church evangelism program. And in Hoge's *Converts Dropouts Returnees* (1981) we are presented with an in-depth examination of religious mobility among Roman Catholics.

Each of these works is a rich complement to the broad sweep of inferential, national survey research. However, one limitation readily acknowledged by the authors of the narrative studies is that such studies do not provide a reliable portrait of the prevalence of the reasons given for or against church involvement. *The Unchurched American* (Princeton Religion Research Center, 1988) fills this void, to some extent, with its blending of national survey scope and qualitative probing. It provided a national sample of 1,027 persons who had stopped attending church or synagogue for two years with a detailed list of possible reasons why, and asked them to note all that applied to them. The list of reasons and distribution of responses is contained in the right column of Table P3.1. It is interesting to note that three of the four most frequently given answers are more indicative of indifference toward the church than of direct confrontation with it. It appears that for the most part, people don't go away angry; rather, they drift away as other things become more important, and/or as one moves through a natural life transition that breaks one's previous connection to a particular local church. If anything, such drift causes one to wonder more about why they attended than to wonder about why they left.

Its name notwithstanding, the "Unchurched American" study surveyed both active and inactive church people, including 1,512 persons who at some time during their life had been unchurched, but were now regular attenders. It asked this large national sample of "returnees" why they decided to attend again. The list of reasons provided and the distribution of responses is presented in the left column of Table P3.1. It is interesting to note that none of the six most frequently cited reasons involve the proactive outreach of the church. Rather, at least as articulated by the returnees, they involve changes in one's "inner" feelings, and/or changes in one's family situation. The church may have been critical for planting the seeds of "inner needs" some time in these returnees' past; and certainly the church was receptive to those returnees who sought it out and continue their involvement. But in terms of both reasons given for involvement and reasons given for noninvolvement, Americans are more likely to locate the initiative for their church involvement (or lack thereof) in self and family than they are to locate it with the church.

Against this backdrop, the following five chapters all deal to varying degrees with the implications for the church of North America's "new" religious voluntarism.

Cautious Optimism

The first chapter in this section, by Marler and Roozen, begins with a tempting invitation to probe what on the surface looks like a very uninteresting ten-year trend in religious participation within the United States. From 1978 to 1988 there was no significant change in overall levels of either church membership or worship attendance for the population as a whole. But prompted by the host of optimistic voices found in all United States denominations, Marler and Roozen proceed to ask whether the surface stability means that nothing has changed, or whether it hides subterranean churnings. They find that the latter is the case, and that "the increasing dominance of religious consumerism, as a form of cultural individualism, is the most important change in the religious marketplace of the late 1980s." But this only raises a further question: given the popular perception that creeping individualism is corrosive of institutional commitment, why haven't church membership and worship attendance declined accordingly?

TABLE P3.1
Reasons for Decreasing and Increasing Church Involvement

For Decreasing		For Increasing	
Found other activities	26%	I felt an inner need to go back to church	40%
Started making my own decisions	25	I felt an inner need to rediscover my religious faith	27
Moved to new community	22	I wanted a child of mine to receive religious training	23
Specific problems with church	20	I felt guilty about not going to church	19
Church no longer a help in finding meaning of life	13	I got older and thought more about eternal life	17
Felt out of place because other members were more affluent and better educated	3	I went with my spouse or relative	17
		I was invited to church at an important time	14
Life-style no longer compatible with church membership	13	I was married	12
		Another reason	9
Poor health	4	I had an important religious experience	8
Work schedule	12	I moved back home	5
Divorced or separated	6	I was divorced or separated	3
Other reasons	18	No opinion	3
No opinion	5	I couldn't go due to illness but I got better	2

Source: Princeton Religion Research Center (1988)

Marler and Roozen's answer comes in two parts. First, that the critical dynamic in individualism is "choice," not anti-institutionalism. "Choice" implies a heightened sense of why one chooses his or her institutional commitments. "Choice" also implies a change in the reasons one uses for "making" the choice—individual priorities take precedence over institutional loyalty. But "choice" in and of itself does not predispose the outcome of the choice. Second, within this context of increasing church consumerism, the empirical data show that traditional institutional loyalties and beliefs have decreased as reasons for making the church choice. But the data also show that in the United States, persons are finding church involvement more responsive to their personal tastes. The number of people making the church choice did not change during the 1980s, but the reasons for making the choice did change.

Marler and Roozen also explore how the negotiation of the church choice is different within different denominational families. Their summary conclusion: "Conservative Protestants are increasingly committed to 'my church'; liberal Protestants are increasingly committed to 'what church?'; and Roman Catholics continue to choose 'The Church.' In each family, however, church consumerism is an increasingly important element. This is especially true for liberal Protestantism, because unlike conservative Protestantism or Roman Catholicism, there is no single coherent liberal Protestant subculture to constrain individual preferences.

The Paradox of Poverty and Potential

The second chapter in the section provides another overview of changing national trends in religious participation, but this time of Canada rather than the United States. Bibby presents a provocatively instructive analysis of the Canadian situation in its own right. But when read together with Marler and Roozen's chapter on the United States one gains the added illumination of comparative perspectives. The "voluntary" nature of religious participation in the North American setting is a dominant theme in both chapters. Marler and Roozen's chapter on the United States analyzes the dynamics of religious voluntarism within a national context of relatively strong religious institutions. In stark contrast Bibby's chapter on Canada analyzes the situation in what he characterizes as a context of "dire institutional crisis." Bibby describes the puzzling relationship between stagnant religious institutions on the one hand, and many signs of individual religious vitality and inquisitiveness. The paradox of religion in Canada is that precisely at a time when organized religion is facing significant problems, the desire for some kind of spirituality is pervasive. From the perspective of religious institutions the chapter explores two alternatives for resolving the paradox: better distribution of the church's current "product," and changing the church's product.

Seventy-five Million Strong

The remaining three chapters in the section return to the situation in the United States, each focusing on a different subgroup of the population. They start with the 75 million Americans who constitute the baby boom generation, then turn to the religious participation of black Americans, and conclude with the most detailed study of Roman Catholic parish involvement yet to appear.

The baby boom generation represents the largest twenty-year birth cohort in the history of the United States; it currently constitutes one-third of the population; and demographers estimate that boomers will continue to dominate consumer markets for another fifty years—until the youngest boomers turn seventy-five in the year 2039. That the baby boom generation was the major source of the declines in religious participation of the 1960s is a matter of virtual consensus among researchers, as already noted. Recent attention to a rekindled interest in the church among some of the boomer dropouts has softened judgments about the enduring effect of this generation's movement into young adulthood and out of the church. Nevertheless, Figure P3.1 should serve as a reminder of how dramatic and persistent the jolt of the sixties was and is. The figure shows not only the depth of the declines, but also: (1) that any mid-life church bounce for the boomers is, at least up to the present, a relatively minor blip among the trend lines; and (2) that the post-boomer generation appears to have inherited the boomers' predisposition toward low rates of church involvement. On the positive side, the post-boomers' relationship to the church is no worse than that of the boomers; and the boomer mid-life bounce, although small, is real.

An in-depth look at the baby boomers, therefore, presents both a look into the future and an interesting picture of the conflicting positive and negative religious impulses currently at play in American religion. Roof and Johnson's chapter on "Baby Boomers and the Return to the Churches" addresses four major questions: (1) Is there a return? (2) Who are the returnees? (3) What kind of a return is it? and (4) Will the return make any difference for patterns of church growth and decline in the decade ahead?

Roof and Johnson's answers? Yes, there has been some return. But there are more dropouts who remain outside the church than there are returnees. Return rates are highest for conservative Protestants, lowest for liberal Protestants, and just slightly better for Roman Catholics than for liberal Protestants. Who are the returnees? They disproportionately consist of parents; of persons who had relatively strong connections to the church prior to dropping out; of persons who are relatively conservative in life-style, moral values, and political attitudes; and of persons who had relatively little direct, personal involvement in the counter-cultural activities of the 1960s.

What kind of return is it? Roof and Johnson conclude that it is a return characterized by a fluid consumer mentality, personal concerns, and spiritual quests. What about the future? Younger boomer dropouts appear more pre-disposed to return than were older boomers, which might "portent an even greater return to organized religion in the 1990s than in the 1980s." But this return would be only to congregations that have adapted or can adapt to the highly voluntaristic norms of belonging characteristic of both younger and older boomers. The key to such adaptation, Roof and Johnson suggest, is a congregation's ability to create religious narratives that encompass one or another segment of the boomer generation's diverse subcultural groupings.

Churched and Unchurched Black Americans

A leading demographic periodical introduces a feature story this way: "you'll know it's the 21st Century when everyone belongs to a minority group" (Waldrop, 1990). Estimates are that by the year 2010 Asians will out-number Jews in the United States by a margin of two to one, and Hispanics will inch ahead of blacks to become the country's largest racial/ethnic minor-ity group. The significance of the latter comes into more stark relief when it is further noted that the growth rate of the black population will be nearly double that of the white population. Next to the continuing movement of the baby boom generation through the life cycle, the increasing racial/ethnic diversity of the United States will be the major demographic trend through at least the first quarter of the new century.

Unfortunately, research on the religious participation of American racial/ethnic groups pales in comparison to their demographic significance. Religious data on Hispanic and Asian Americans are almost nonexistent, and regrettably no major study has yet to appear from which a contribution to this volume could be culled. The situation is not all that much better for black Americans. But the past decade has seen the publication of *The Black Church in the African American Experience* (Lincoln and Mamiya, 1990)—the first major empirical study of the black church in thirty years. It has also seen the appearance of several national surveys of religion that include sig-nificant subsamples of black Americans. Nelsen and Kanagy's chapter on churched and unchurched black Americans contained in this section takes advantage of the latter to provide an extensive analysis of the situation in the late 1980s, and to draw comparisons with the more limited national survey available from the late 1970s.

FIGURE P3.1
Membership and Attendance Trends by Age

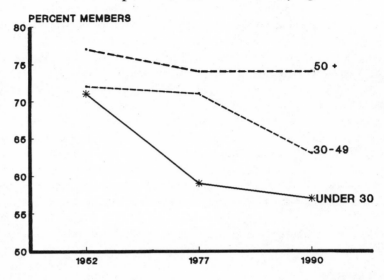

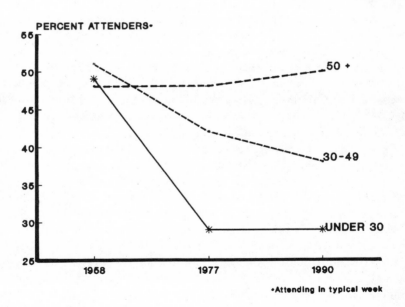

•Attending in typical week

Sources: Marty, Rosenberg and Greeley (1968)
Princeton Religion Research Center (1981. 1991)

Nelsen and Kanagy's point of departure is E. Franklin Frazier's 1963 prediction that domination of the black church in the black community would decrease as blacks became "integrated into the institutions of the American community." The good news of the study is that blacks have realized some upward mobility over the last thirty years, but Frazier's prediction has yet to materialize. In fact, the proportion of churched black Americans increased slightly from 1978 to 1988. Nelsen and Kanagy demonstrate that the slow and sometimes halting movement of blacks out of the rural South, through the major cities of the North and South, and into middle-class suburbs has added new layers of complexity to our understanding of how blacks relate to the church. Specifically, they show a progressive movement from communal to voluntaristic motivations for church participation as one moves from rural to city to suburban locations. Nelsen and Kanagy also document a radical polarization in church membership by age in the major industrial cities of the North. In fact, within an otherwise optimistic assessment of the emerging future of the black church, Nelsen and Kanagy point to the black church's increasing disconnection with urban young adults as its greatest and least understood challenge.

Religious Participation Among Roman Catholic Parishioners

The scholarly community has directed a great deal of attention in the last decade to the eclipse of old-line Protestantism, the public revitalization of conservative Protestantism, the spreading dominance of Mormonism throughout the mountain states of the West, the rise and fall of the "new religious movements," and the amorphous ascent of the equally amorphous "New Age." However, the public consciousness appears to be ambivalently silent about how Roman Catholicism fits into the changing mosaic of religion in the United States. In reading Harold Bloom's best-selling, *The American Religion: The Emergence of the Post-Christian Nation* (1992), for example, one would never realize that Roman Catholicism is the largest denomination in the United States—three times larger than the Southern Baptists, its nearest competitor; and over twenty times larger than such old-line Protestant anchors as the Episcopals or such Pentecostal rising stars as the Assemblies of God. Nearly three of every ten adults in the United States currently identify themselves as Roman Catholic, up from 20% in the late 1940s. And there are two strong indications that the Roman Catholic share of the American religious marketplace will continue to inch up in the foreseeable future. First, the Roman Catholic plurality is greater among young adults than older adults. Second, upwards to 90% of Hispanics in the United States are Roman Catholic. Combining these two demographic drivers with the strong upward social mobility of Roman Catholics since mid-century leads us to concur with Roof and McKinney's (1987) contention that Roman Catholicism is the very center of the newly emerging mainstream of American religion.

Welch's chapter in this section on the religious participation of Catholic parishioners is, therefore, absolutely essential for a comprehensive understanding of church growth and decline in the United States. In addition, Welch introduces several new conceptual considerations to the study of individual religious participation, as well as underscoring the centrality of several others. It is one of very few studies that examines how the characteristics of a local church influences the participation of its members. Welch looks at four types of church involvement and finds that each is responsive to different factors. He reminds us that many, but not all, of the strongest influences on involvement are beyond the control of church leaders. Among those influences over which church leaders have some control, Welch makes a strong case for the importance of specialized ministries, genuine social integration, and the level of faith-sharing within the fellowship.

Welch's chapter will be of natural interest to Roman Catholics. But its lessons have a broader urgency. One of the ironies of the Roman Catholic movement from sideline to mainline is that the church participation of Roman Catholics, once the envy of Protestant denominations, has dropped over the last thirty years to near parity with that of the latter.

Chapter Twelve

From Church Tradition to Consumer Choice:

The Gallup Surveys of the Unchurched American

Penny Long Marler and David A. Roozen

There are many reasons for expecting that church membership and attendance should have been on the upswing during the 1980s: the "revival" of the Religious Right; the conservative swing in the national mood; the baby boomers finally settling into traditional adult roles; and denominational preoccupation with evangelism and church renewal. In fact, an article by Herb Miller (1989), written for the National Evangelistic Association, lists thirty-four reasons for optimism concerning church trends. In the context of such optimism a comparison of the membership and worship attendance figures from the 1978 and 1988 Gallup surveys of the Unchurched American (Princeton Religion Research Center, 1978, 1988) appears rather enigmatic. While supporting at least some of the reasons given for optimism, the surveys nevertheless show *no* statistically significant change in either church membership or worship attendance over the ten-year period. In fact, as will be seen in Table 12.2, the comparative figures show, if anything, a slight decline; and in this regard the Unchurched American Surveys are consistent with other national surveys (Hout and Greeley, 1987; Chaves, 1989; Princeton Religion Research Center, 1990).

Given the general stability in religious participation found in national surveys over the last ten years, the purpose of this paper is to use the 1978 and 1988 Gallup Unchurched American Surveys to probe beneath the apparent surface calm for possible subterranean churning. Our informing question is whether the overall stability is the result of "nothing having changed," or the result of identifiable positive and negative changes that cancel each other out. In pursuing this question our analysis moves through four stages. First, we look for potential increases and decreases over time in characteristics traditionally related to membership and attendance. For example, if we find that commitment to Christ (a traditionally positive correlate of participation) increased, but that confidence in organized religion decreased, the two changes could cancel each other out in terms of overall rates of membership and worship attendance.

Second, we look for possible positive and negative changes over time in membership and attendance within different subgroups of the population. For example, if we find that the religious participation of the baby boom generation increased over the last ten years, but that of the depression generation decreased, the positive and negative changes of the these two groups may cancel each other out in terms of the overall level of membership and worship attendance.

Third, we explore the extent to which the relationships may have changed over time in a multivariate model of membership and attendance. In a sense, this is a more powerful and nuanced means of pursuing the same kinds of questions addressed in phase one and two. It allows us to explore changes in the meanings of and motivations for religious membership and participation, even if the overall levels did not vary.

Roof and Hoge's (1980) study of the 1978 Unchurched American Survey provides a helpful point of departure for our multivariate analysis. Building on Hoge and Roozen's (1979) review of research on religious commitment, Roof and Hoge tested five theories of religious participation. The reader is referred to Hoge and Roozen, and Roof and Hoge for a comprehensive discussion of the theories. In brief they include:

1. **Deprivation theory:** As summarized by Roof and Hoge, "it is actually a group of related theories, all stating that persons suffering deprivation look to religion as a means of compensation" (1980:406). The theory has been used with both objective measures of deprivation such as socioeconomic status, and subjective indicators such as "satisfaction with life."

2. **Child rearing theory:** As its name suggests this theory proposes that parents become actively involved in the church for the sake of their children and the quality of family life.

3. **Social learning theory:** Roof and Hoge note that this theory can be applied at both the subcultural and individual level. At the subcultural level the theory argues that normative expectations for religious participation differ among different subcultures such as denominations and regions. Such a perspective has been used, for example, to account for religious participation being higher in the South than in the West, and being higher for Roman Catholics than for mainline Protestants. At the individual level, social learning theory proposes, in its most concrete application to religion, that the strength of church-related reli-

gious socialization during childhood is a major determinant of one's adult religious attitudes and behavior.

4. **Localism theory:** Most forcefully articulated by Roof (1978), it is a specific application of the sociological notion of "plausibility structures" (Berger, 1967). In Roof's view, because of the increased pluralism of cultures in contemporary society, the plausibility of church religion is increasingly restricted to those persons with a high investment in traditional, local community affairs, and those local social networks in which they are embedded.

5. **Value structure theory:** In its most general formulation this theory argues that there will be a congruence between the individual's religious beliefs and values, and other beliefs and values that the individual holds. Specifically in regard to social and religious changes in the United States since the 1930s, empirical applications of the theory consistently find traditional sexual and family values and traditional free-enterprise values to be associated positively with church participation, and "new morality" and civil libertarian values to be associated with marginal participation.

In applying these theories to the 1978 Unchurched American Survey data, Roof and Hoge found no support for the deprivation theory, minimal support for the child rearing and social learning theories,[1] and strongest support for the localism and value structure theories. They also found that most of the affect of age and education on religious participation is mediated through localism and value structures, and that their multivariate model had more explanatory power for liberal Protestants and Roman Catholics than it did for conservative Protestants.

The careful development of the 1978 Unchurched American Survey and insightful analysis of Roof and Hoge provide a solid grounding for comparative analysis. Unfortunately, the 1988 survey either omitted or radically changed several of Roof and Hoge's key variables so that an exact replication of their analysis was not possible. Consequently, our analysis uses a multivariate model constructed from variables available in both surveys, including several used by Roof and Hoge, and two new dimensions. Our model includes variables related to Roof and Hoge's child rearing, social learning, and value structure theories. Localism is not included because a comparative variable is not available across surveys.[2] Deprivation theory was not included because, like Roof and Hoge, we found minimal support for it in a preliminary analysis of the 1988 data.

Two dimensions not included in the Roof and Hoge analysis have received increasing attention in discussions of American denominational religion over the last ten years. They include:

1. ***Religious individualism:*** Although discussed in various ways in the literature, religious individualism has at least two major components. First, in the form of "Sheilaism" (Bellah et al., 1987), it is decidedly anti-institutional. Second, as a manifestation of the "new voluntarism," it reflects a growing consumer orientation in American religion (Stark and Bainbridge, 1985; Roof and McKinney, 1987).

2. ***Religious commitment, particularly spirituality:*** A common theme in the emerging literature on the religiosity of the baby boom generation is a distinction between personal spirituality and organized religion. The critical implication for our purposes is that many in this generation do not make a direct connection between their personal religiosity and their participation in religious institutions (Roozen, Carroll, and Roof, 1990).

Building on current theory, therefore, our multivariate analysis of the Unchurched American Surveys adds items that test various dimensions of commitment to religious institutions per se, in distinction from belief and devotional practices. Importantly, these additional variables provide new insights into the veracity of the popularly perceived, increasing consumerism of American religion.

We first apply our multivariate model of membership and attendance to our entire sample, and discuss the implications of this third stage of our overall analysis. We then move to the fourth and final stage of our analysis: the application of our model to examine the different patterns, and changes in patterns, of membership and attendance among conservative and liberal Protestants, and Roman Catholics.

Data and Measures

Our data are from the 1978 and 1988 Unchurched American Surveys conducted by the Gallup poll for ad hoc coalitions of religious instrumentalities. Full descriptions of the sample designs can be found in the survey reports (Princeton Religion Research Center, 1978, 1988). Each of the surveys contains the standard Gallup organization cross-sectional sample of the adult, noninstitutionalized population, eighteen years of age and over; and a variety of supplemental subsamples. Our analysis disregards each year's supplemental subsamples and uses only the standard Gallup poll cross-sectional sample.

Operational definitions of variables included in our analysis are listed in Table 12.1. Of particular note are three variables that measure church consumerism—a special case of religious individualism. The first variable in this category is a single item that measures whether or not church attendance is optional for standing as a "good Christian." We label this item "church voluntarism." The second variable is a scale that measures the degree to which the church is perceived as warm, spiritual, and meaningful. This scale is labeled "church personalism." The third variable is the church organization scale. This scale measures the degree to which the church is perceived as too organized, too restrictive about morality, or not concerned enough about social justice issues.

In Support of Optimism

Table 12.2 shows the change (or lack thereof) from 1978 to 1988 in the percentage distributions of key variables in our analysis. At the top of the table the reader will note that both church membership and attendance remain virtually unchanged over the ten-year period. The remaining sixteen variables in the table are all "traditional" correlates of religious participation. Of these traditional correlates, half show no significant change from 1978 to 1988; the other half show significant changes.

Among the eight traditional correlates that changed over the ten-year period, five changed in a direction that should have a positive impact on membership and attendance. In 1988 there are higher levels of commitment to Christ, and "warm" perceptions of the church (church personalism scale[3]); there are lower levels of negative organizational perceptions of the church; there are lower levels of "new morality" values; and there is an aging population. In each of these cases, the movement from 1978 to 1988 is from categories of traditionally lower membership and attendance to categories of higher participation.

The 1978 to 1988 changes for prayer and region are neutrally mixed in regard to their possible effect on religious participation. For frequency of prayer, there is movement over time from both the high participation "daily prayer" category and the low participation "never pray" category to the middle range "less than daily" prayer category. Regional change is from areas of moderate participation—the Northeast and Mid-Atlantic—to both the high participation South and the low participation West. The change in education is dramatic, but education itself has a complex relationship to religious participation with little direct effect.

The Confounding of Optimism

Overall, the changes apparent in Table 12.2 support an optimistic view vis-à-vis church membership and attendance. Other things being equal, the changes should have been accompanied by increases in membership and attendance. Why weren't they? Table 12.3 provides an initial answer and moves us into the second phase of our analysis.

TABLE 12.1
Definitions of Variables and Scales

Member:
  "Are you, yourself, a member of a church or synagogue?"   Yes/No

Attendance:
  "About how many times would you say you attended a church or synagogue in the *past six months*—would you say at least once a week, two or three times a month, or once a month or less?"

Denominational Family:
  Followed coding used by Roof and Hoge (1980). "Liberal Protestant" (UCC, UMC, Episcopal, United Presbyterian, LCA, Disciples, American Baptist); "Conservative Protestant:" (Southern Baptist, Latter-Day Saints, Other Baptists, Baptists—Don't Know, Missouri Synod Lutheran); "Roman Catholic"; and "Other."

Belief Scale: (1978 alpha: .45; 1988 alpha: .50)
  "What do you believe about Jesus Christ?" Plus, "Do you believe there is life after death?"

Commitment to Christ: (Single item)
  "Would you say that you have made a commitment to Jesus Christ, or not?"

Religious Experience: (Single item)
  "Have you ever had a religious experience—that is, a particularly powerful religious insight or awakening?"

Church Personalism Scale: (1978 alpha: .66; 1988 alpha: .68)
  Three likert items: most churches and synagogues (1) are warm and accepting of outsiders; (2) have a clear sense of the real spiritual nature of religion; (3) are effective in helping people find meaning in life. (Note: the 1978 items were asked in a negative direction, and are reversed in our scale to make them comparable to the positive direction of the 1988 items.)

Church Organization Scale: (1978 alpha: .54; 1988 alpha: .42)
  Three likert items: most churches and synagogues (1) are too concerned with organizational, as opposed to theological or spiritual, issues; (2) are not concerned enough with social justice; and (3) are too restrictive in the rules preached about morality.

Church Voluntarism: (Single item)
  "Do you think a person can be a good Christian or Jew if he or she doesn't attend church or synagogue?"   Yes/No

Traditional Values Scale: (1978 alpha: .46; 1988 alpha: .50)
  Two likert items: Would you welcome or not welcome (1) more emphasis on traditional family ties; (2) more respect for authority.

New Morality Scale: (1978 alpha: .58; 1988 alpha: .47)
  Two likert items: Would you welcome or not welcome (1) more acceptance of sexual freedom; (2) more acceptance of marijuana usage.

Religious Socialization: (1978 alpha: .62; 1988 alpha: .68)
  Four items: importance of religion when growing up; Sunday school or church attendance when in grade school; religious training as a child; and confirmation training during one's youth.

TABLE 12.2

1978–1988 Change in Marginal Percentage Distributions

	1978	1988	NS
Church Member	66.7%	65.8%	NS
Church Attendance			
Once a week or more	34.7	33.9	
2–3 times a month	14.7	15.2	
Once a month or less	14.8	16.8	
None in the last 6 months	35.9	34.1	NS
Denominational Family	Not Sig.		
Belief Scale	Not Sig.		
Religious Experience	Not Sig.		
Frequency of Prayer			
Daily	57.2	51.9	
Less than daily	29.5	37.2	
Never	13.0	10.9	
Commitment to Christ			
Yes	61.1	67.5	
Don't know	6.2	5.7	
No	32.8	26.9	
Church Personalism Scale			
Low	47.4	21.0	
Moderate	30.8	36.9	
High	21.8	42.1	
Church Organization Scale			
High	44.8	32.2	
Moderate	38.3	47.6	
Low	16.9	20.1	
Church Voluntarism	Not Sig.		
Traditional Values Scale	Not Sig.		
New Morality Scale			
High	12.0	4.4	
Moderate	24.0	20.9	
Low	64.0	74.6	
Religious Socialization Scale	Not Sig.		
Sex	Not Sig.		
Age			
21 and under	8.6	5.4	
22–32	26.9	21.8	
33–42	18.1	20.7	
43–52	14.7	14.4	
53 +	31.6	37.8	
Education			
Less than high school graduate	31.0	20.3	
High school or some college	56.1	56.9	
College graduate	13.0	22.8	
Region			
Northeast and Mid-Atlantic	27.8	23.2	
South, Midwest, Mountain	60.0	62.0	
West	12.0	14.8	
Family Cycle	Not Sig.		

Table 12.3 shows the percentage of church members and the percentage of regular church attenders for both 1978 and 1988 within categories of our traditionally hypothesized correlates of religious participation. The "church personalism scale" section of the table provides a clear example of why what should have been a positive demographic change for levels of religious participation did not result in an overall increase in participation. Table 12.2 showed a significant increase from 1978 to 1988 in the proportion of the population who had positive perceptions of church personalism.

Table 12.3 shows that in both 1978 and 1988 such positive perceptions and membership are positively related—i.e., the "warmer" one's perceptions of the church the more likely one is to be a church member. However, Table 12.3 also shows that membership rates for the high personalism category in 1988 are not as high as they were in 1978. In fact, there is a decline in church membership from 1978 to 1988 within each category of church personalism. There are more people in 1988 with a positive image of the church, but such people are less likely to be members in 1988 than in 1978. The net result is that the two changes cancel each other out. The same dynamic can be seen for the new morality and the commitment to Christ sections in Table 12.3.

A more complex set of dynamics is at work in the age/cohort section of Table 12.3, but with the same overall effect. There is some of the above dynamic—i.e., an increase over time in the proportion of the population over fifty-five years old, but a decrease over time in the participation of this age group. Additionally, there is a mix of some cohorts and age groups that increased their participation and some that decreased. For example, the religious participation of the twenty-one and under age group increased over time, but the participation of the forty-three to fifty-two age group decreased; and, the religious participation of the cohort born between 1946 and 1956 (this cohort was twenty-two to thirty-two years old in 1978 and thirty-three to forty-two in 1988) increased over the ten-year period, but the participation of the cohort born between 1926 and 1935 decreased.

Overall, Table 12.3 shows that more subcategories of our traditional correlates declined in participation than increased, thus neutralizing the positive demographic changes noted in Table 12.2.

We began our analysis with the question: Is the overall stability in church membership and attendance during the 1980s the result of "nothing having changed," or the result of identifiable positive and negative changes that cancel each other out? It is clear from Tables 12.2 and 12.3 that it is the latter. Additionally, Table 12.2 suggests that a significant portion of the subterranean churning has to do with why a person chooses to get involved in the life of a religious institution. We now turn to the third stage of our analysis—a more in-depth exploration of the changes from 1978 to 1988 in the meanings of and motivation for church participation.

TABLE 12.3
1978–1988 Membership and Attendance Change Within Categories of Independent Variables°

	1978–1988 Change in % Church Member		1978–1988 Change in % Attending Twice a Month or More	
	1978	1988	1978	1988
Frequency of Prayer	Not Sig.°°		Not Sig.°°	
Commitment to Christ				
Yes	81.5	80.5		
Don't know	50.0	43.5	Not Sig.°°	
No	42.2	33.7		
Church Personalism Scale				
Low	57.9	53.2		
Moderate	66.5	59.8	Not Sig.°°	
High	85.8	77.2		
Church Organization Scale	Not Sig.°°		Not Sig.°°	
New Morality Scale				
High	37.9	35.1		
Moderate	57.0	54.8	Not Sig.°°	
Low	75.7	70.6		
Age and Cohort°°°				
21 and under	55.6	59.3	43.4	46.2
22–32	56.2	55.4	39.7	41.0
33–42	58.5	65.3	43.2	46.1
43–52	80.0	68.1	58.2	47.8
53 +	75.2	71.8	57.8	55.9
Education	Not Sig.°°		Not Sig.°°	
Region	Not Sig.°°		Not Sig.°°	

°   Only variables showing significant marginal changes in Table 12.2 are included.
°° Not significant at p > .01.
°°° A╲connects a cohort's 1978 membership and attendance with its 1988 membership and attendance.

The Changing Meaning of Religious Participation

The meanings of and motivations for religious participation are varied and complex. Therefore, analysis requires a relatively sophisticated statistical technique that simultaneously examines a variety of relationships (a model). We opted for a block-step multiple regression approach. Individual explanatory variables in our model are grouped into "blocks," and each block is entered into the regression analysis in successive "steps." The regression analysis shows the relative influence of the various blocks on religious participation for 1978 and 1988. Our major interest is a comparison of the influence of these blocks across the ten-year period. The variables and blocks in our model, and the order in which they were entered in our regression analysis are listed in Table 12.4.[4] Because of our interest in both membership and worship attendance, we first apply our explanatory model to membership, and then apply the same model to worship attendance, adding church membership as the first block-step in the analysis.[5]

TABLE 12.4
Step Descriptions

Step #	Describes	Items/Scales
1	CHURCH MEMBERSHIP	Church Member
2	CHURCH CONSUMERISM	Church Voluntarism Church Personalism Church Organization Scale
3	TRADITIONAL RELIGIOSITY	Commitment to Christ Frequency of Prayer Belief Scale Religious Experience
4	VALUE ORIENTATION	Traditional Values Scale New Morality Scale
5	SOCIAL BACKGROUND	Religious Socialization Scale Gender Age Education Region: Non-West, West Family Cycle: 　　Married with kids, 　　married without kids, 　　and never married

We report the major findings of our analysis through a series of figures, graphically displaying the total explanatory power of our model (R^2 = percent of variance explained), and the incremental increase in explanatory power associated with the addition of each block-step (R^2 change). A more complete set of statistical results is contained in Tables A12.1 to A12.3 in the Appendix and A12.4 in the Supplemental Appendix.[6]

The Individual and Choice: Increasing Religious Consumerism

Figure 12.1 summarizes the results of the analysis for the total 1978 and 1988 samples. Beginning with membership, the figure shows little change from 1978 to 1988 in the meanings of and motivations for church membership. Traditional religiosity has the strongest effect in both years, followed by church consumerism. Beyond their strong influence, social background and general value orientations add little explanatory power.[7] But religious socialization (early contact with the church) by itself remains a strong predictor of membership.

FIGURE 12.1
What Affects Church Participation in America?
Step Summaries, 1978–1988

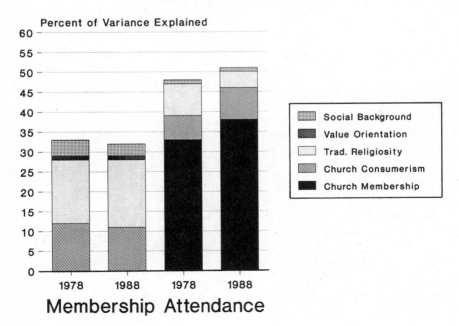

In essence, Americans join a church primarily because it "fits" their particular beliefs about Jesus, the Bible, life after death, and their accustomed devotional practice. Secondarily, Americans tend to choose and join a church they like—one that is warm, meaningful, and not too strict or organized. In fact, these reasons for joining have changed very little over the past decade. Such is not the case for worship attendance, however.

Figure 12.1 shows notable changes from 1978 to 1988 in the pattern of relationships for worship attendance. In 1978, church membership and traditional religiosity have the strongest influence on attendance, followed by church consumerism. In 1988, the importance of church membership for predicting attendance increases by 5 percentage points and church consumerism replaces traditional religiosity as the second most powerful explanatory block. Social background factors have little direct influence on church attendance in either 1978 or 1988, and general value orientations have no significant direct effect.[8]

Changes in the relationships of two individual variables in the church consumerism block are particularly interesting. The effects of church personalism and church voluntarism on worship attendance increase from 1978 to 1988 (see Table A12.1). But the increase in church voluntarism is especially dramatic. Indeed, the largest single change from 1978 to 1988 is the increasing influence on attendance of the conviction that it is necessary to attend church to be a good Christian or Jew.[9] This shift is important because the proportion of the American population feeling one way or another on this issue did not change (see Table 12.2). Nevertheless, the influence of church voluntarism on worship attendance did increase significantly. What does this mean? Simply, that those who believe church attendance is necessary to be a good Christian or Jew in 1988 are more likely to participate regularly than those who felt it was necessary in 1978. The trend is clear: Americans who attend church regularly in the late eighties do so because church attendance is a priority. They feel that churchgoing is an important—yes, even a necessary—thing to do. And when they do attend, they increasingly choose a "warm" and meaningful church.

To summarize, from 1978 to 1988 Americans who joined a church were primarily influenced by their religious beliefs and practice. Yet over that same period of time, motivations for church attendance shifted. The importance of church membership increased, and church consumerism replaced traditional religiosity as the strongest predictor of church attendance. The result? Americans who attended church regularly in the eighties did so because they felt that churchgoing is necessary to be a good Christian or Jew. Frequent attenders are also more likely to perceive the church as warm, spiritual, meaningful, and properly social-justice minded. Those who attend church less frequently are more likely to feel that it is *not* necessary to go to church to be a good Christian or Jew. They also do not like a lot of specific things about the church—finding it cold and/or irrelevant.

The ascendance of church consumerism, then, cuts both ways. "Emancipation of the self"—as Roof and McKinney (1987) put it—is increasingly accompanied by anti-institutionalism for some. However, the obverse is also true: increased institutional commitment is markedly characteristic of the very active. Here we see the two faces of religious individualism. First, as a kind of self-emancipation, religious individualism loosens institutional moorings (Merelman, 1984:30ff.). The result is a religion functionally and spatially located in the self. Like Bellah et al.'s (1985) Sheila Larson, individuals are free to create their own religious faith (tenets and all) and consecrate their own personal "sacred space." In the radically individualist case, they themselves become their "temples." This kind of religious individualist neither wants nor feels the need for formal religious institutions. Religion is more than a "matter of personal choice"; as a self-created thing, it is the essence of a personal taste.

Second, it is clear that individualism also means something else. "Choice" includes both the choice to participate as well as the choice not to participate in the life of religious institutions. Our data suggest that the emancipation of the self works to "tighten up" or clarify commitments to institutions. It shows, for example, that worship attendance in the eighties was less a case of particular religious beliefs, parental legacy, or social habit than it was in the seventies. In a world of busy-ness and multiple organizational options, traditional reasons are less compelling. Church consumerism and personal satisfaction increasingly provide such reasons for making the "church choice."[10]

Significantly, the majority of Americans still choose church (66%—see Table 12.2). Still, the data indicate that denominational executives and local clergy can depend less on tradition and social convention to people the pews. Indeed, American church attendance is increasingly influenced by a concrete, local connection (church membership) and consumer satisfaction. Institutions exist primarily to serve the individual, and not vice versa. In this context, careful programming and local marketing become important. So while the incidence of religious participation has remained constant, the meaning of religious participation and implications for church response have changed.

Thus, it is curious that most discussions of the effects of increasing individualism or voluntarism focus on the negative implications for institutional life (e.g., Jacoby, 1975; Lasch, 1978; Robertson, 1980; Bellah et al., 1985; Roof and McKinney, 1987). Such discussions are frequently grounded in the kind of pro-institutional, social paradigm of American religion Herberg described in his 1955 classic, *Protestant-Catholic-Jew*. From this perspective, individualism almost inevitably erodes participation in voluntary organizations. As individualism tightens its grip on American culture, the argument goes, the church will experience increasing decline. Eventually, the only people left in the church are those who resist the influence of American individualism and continue to operate out of a social locus of control. There is little evidence for this kind of conclusion, however.

Quite the opposite: recent research suggests that individualism is a culture-wide phenomenon that affects the way everyone interprets and re-interprets their daily lives—including the majority of those making the church choice. In *The Inner American*, Verof, Douvan, and Kulka (1981:529) examine the results of two national surveys of the American population's subjective mental health. The initial survey was conducted in 1957 and replicated in 1976. The most significant change, as described by the authors

> has been a shift from a socially integrated paradigm for structuring well-being, to a more personal or individuated paradigm for structuring well-being. We see the 1957 population taking much more comfort in culture and the 1976 population gathering much more strength in its personal adaptations to the world. We see this very general theme in a number of different ways . . . (1) the diminution of role standards as the basis for defining adjustment; (2) the increased focus on self-expressiveness and self-direction in social life; (3) a shift in concern from social organizational integration to interpersonal intimacy.

If Verhof and company are correct, then the basic change from a social to an individual locus of control in American culture began prior to the surveys of religious participation presented here. That being the case, what we are reading in the Unchurched American Surveys is how this individuated paradigm is permeating the way persons approach religious institutions. Consequently, an individualistic approach need not lead to decreased institutional commitment as much as a change in how that commitment is interpreted, and then, lived out—as, for example, through Yankelovich's "ethic of commitment" (1981:250ff.).

An increasing individual locus of control simply means that an individual gets "more picky" about what options he or she chooses out of the many. In the church choice, there are the options to participate or not to participate. And if persons choose to participate, there are additional choices about "how"—under what conditions—they will participate. Traditions of the past give way to concerns for self-expression ("I will decide to go, how often to go, or not to go at all based on my particular needs and interests") and interpersonal intimacy ("If I do choose a particular church, and go, I expect that it will provide meaningful experiences and warmth"). The increasing dominance of religious consumerism, as a form of cultural individualism, is the most important change in the religious marketplace of the late eighties.

Denominational Differences in the Meaning of Church Participation

Cultural individualism as church consumerism is a pervasive force in the religious marketplace of the late 1980s. Next we consider its interaction with another distinguishing feature of American religion—denominational pluralism. Specifically, we turn to an examination of the changing meaning of church participation within liberal and conservative Protestantism, and Roman Catholicism. As before, changes in the meanings of and motivations for church membership and worship attendance are analyzed using the block-step regression model outlined in Table 12.4. Results are graphically presented in the text (Figures 12.2–12.4) with more detailed tables included in the Appendix (Tables A12.2–A12.3).

Not surprisingly, our analysis shows that the "church choice" is negotiated in different ways by each of the three denominational groups. In summary, conservative Protestants are increasingly committed to "my church"; liberal Protestants hold allegiance to "what church?"; and Roman Catholics continue to choose "THE church."

The Conservative Protestant Choice: "My Church." Conservative Protestants are very clear about what church they belong to and attend. It is "my church," and for membership among conservative Protestants traditional belief and religious socialization became increasingly important during the 1980s. As shown in Figure 12.2, the most powerful effects on church membership among conservative Protestants in 1988 are traditional orthodoxy (explaining 14% of the variation), church consumerism (9%), and social background characteristics (4%). Within these blocks, single variables with the strongest effects in 1988 include: church voluntarism, commitment to Christ, religious belief, and religious socialization (see Appendix, Table A12.2). From 1978 to 1988, the incremental effect of traditional religiosity on membership increased 4% and social background factors gained slightly (1%).

Conservative Protestant membership is increasingly characterized by a set of inherited, biblically focused beliefs. One might argue, as Ammerman (1990) does, that a population shift from the Frostbelt to the Sunbelt has forced large numbers of southern conservatives to define themselves more sharply against "foreign" religious and cultural influx. This "circle the wagons" mentality is reinforced by: (1) a high level of orthodox dogmatism among conservative Protestants—particularly evangelicals (Jelen, 1990; Jelen and Wilcox, 1991); and (2) a longtime investment in the religious education of adults and children that emphasizes biblical knowledge and traditional evangelical beliefs more than civic or moral education (Benson and Eklin, 1990).

In general, conservative Protestants differentiate themselves from liberal Protestants on doctrinal grounds (Balmer, 1989; Hunter, 1983).[11] Thus, membership—while still influenced by loyalty to a particular conservative Protestant denomination or church—is increasingly typified by allegiance to the generic category of "evangelicals" (Marsden, 1987). In fact, Hadaway and Marler (1993) show that "bred and raised" religious conservatives are much more likely to remain within the broader conservative Protestant camp than liberal Protestants are to stay in the broader liberal Protestant camp. In the late eighties, "my church" is a church that upholds evangelical beliefs.

What membership means for conservative Protestants is especially important because membership is highly predictive of church attendance, and increasingly so. Figure 12.2 shows that from 1978 to 1988, church membership's effect on church attendance among conservative Protestants rose from 23% to 31% (explained variance). The figure also shows that the effect of church consumerism on attendance increased by 6%, and social background factors by 2%. Strikingly, the effect of traditional religiosity on worship attendance decreased 11% between 1978 and 1988. Membership and church consumerism, together, explain 42% of the variance in church attendance in the late eighties (compared to only 28% in 1978).

FIGURE 12.2
What Affects Church Participation Among Conservatives?
Step Summaries, 1978–1988

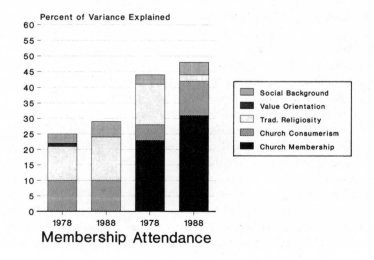

Belonging to a church that holds traditional evangelical beliefs is still important for attendance. But what increasingly determines the level of active involvement for conservative Protestants (over and above belonging) is church consumerism. Conservative Protestants choose a church, join it, and go frequently because they like it. They perceive their church as warm, meaningful, and not too strict or too organized (for examples, see Ammerman, 1987:59 and Marsden, 1991:81). Conversely, conservative Protestants who belong but do not attend regularly are dissatisfied with their church—not so much because it is not conservative enough, but because it does not meet their personal needs for warmth, meaning, and "spirituality," or it is perceived as "too strict" or "too organized."

The Liberal Protestant Choice: "What Church?" Liberal Protestants negotiate the church choice very differently from their conservative Protestant counterparts. These differences became increasingly stark from 1978 to 1988, especially in regard to the general significance of church membership. Figure 12.2 shows that during the 1980s the influence of both traditional religiosity and social background factors on church membership increased for conservative Protestants, as did the overall explanatory power of our membership model. Figure 12.3 shows that the exact opposite is true for liberal Protestants. For liberal Protestants traditional religiosity and social background factors have less influence on church membership in 1988 than in 1978, and the overall explanatory power of our membership model decreases (explaining 31% of variance in 1978, but only 26% in 1988). Perhaps not coincidentally, liberal Protestant denominations have lower rates of membership retention and growth (Marler and Hadaway, 1993; Hadaway and Marler, 1993).

Not only does Figure 12.3 show that the predictability of church membership declined from 1978 to 1988, it also shows that membership's influence on worship attendance declined across the ten-year period (from an incremental effect of 23% to 18%). Whether liberal Protestants are members or not has much less impact on frequency of attendance than it used to. Overall, membership is a factor of diminishing importance.

The declining significance of membership among liberal Protestants may be partially explained by less effective Christian education. For example, in a study of six American Protestant denominations, Search Institute found that mainline bodies exhibited low rates of church school attendance, high rates of dissatisfaction with present Christian education efforts, and low scores on "denominational loyalty." Of particular concern were very low scores on faith maturity among liberal Protestant youth (Benson and Eklin, 1990).[11]

But even more generally, the diminishing significance of membership among liberal Protestants and the declining effectiveness of Christian education appear to be part of a broader erosion of all the traditional, institutional purveyors of liberal Protestant culture. As Carroll and Roof (forthcoming) note in their conclusion to a collection of twenty essays on the subject:

> Mainline Protestantism has moved "beyond establishment" in the sense of an unofficial hegemony which mainline Protestants exercised at the cultural and social level in nineteenth- and early twentieth-century America. The combined impact of pluralism and privatization in matters of religion and culture has eroded much of this hegemony. This erosion, together with the serious hemorrhaging at the level of membership, has left mainline Protestants with a severe crisis of identity and purpose.
>
> We know that mainline Protestant denominations are in serious trouble. Here we are not speaking only of membership decline. Many of the cultures of particular denominations are out of touch with the changed realities that the church confronts in late twentieth-century America. Many of the plausibility structures on which the churches have relied to transmit and sustain cultures are no longer effective.

The emerging consensus in the late 1980s is that liberal Protestants go less to church school, know less about their denominational traditions and beliefs, and are less loyal to their denominations (Roof and McKinney, 1987:85ff.).

Liberal Protestants embody a consumer orientation toward religion to a much greater extent than either conservative Protestants or Roman Catholics. This is especially evident in the worship attendance model in Figure 12.3. It shows a significant decline from 1978 to 1988 in the effect of traditional religiosity on attendance (from 10% to 4%). And it shows an equally significant increase in the effect of church consumerism on attendance—almost doubling from 8% to 14%. Indeed, in the 1988 analysis, each variable in the church consumerism block shows a strong direct effect on church attendance (see Appendix, Table A12.3). It is especially telling that the relationship of church voluntarism to worship attendance is stronger than any other single variable in the entire model, including church membership.

The religious marketplace for liberal Protestants is wide open today. Less motivated by denominational or theological loyalty in the church choice, liberal Protestants attend church because it is warm, provides personalized meaning, has a clearly "spiritual" focus, is not "too organized," is not "too restrictive," and has just enough—but not too much—social justice emphasis. Like conservative Protestants, active liberal Protestants demonstrate commitment to the institutional church as an avenue for expressing and cultivating personal religiosity. But unlike conservative Protestants, the influence of church consumerism among liberal Protestants is increasingly unconstrained by traditional religious beliefs and practices or by social background factors.

FIGURE 12.3
What Affects Church Participation Among Liberals?
Step Summaries, 1978–1988

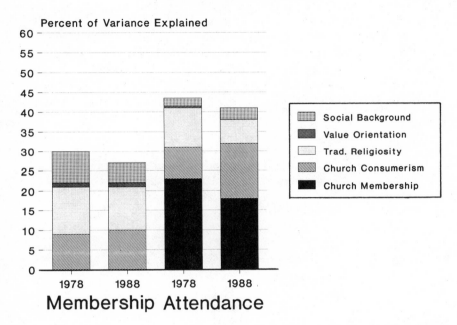

The pivotal question for active liberal Protestants is not whether church is important—but "what church?" This consumer-oriented pattern of choosing is reinforced in various ways. It may be encouraged by liberal Protestant denominations that place fewer demands for joining on persons who attend but are not "official" members (Stone, 1990). Or, in an opposite way, freedom from the ties of denominational loyalty may be reinforced by less convincing reasons (and less compelling demands) to stay in the liberal Protestant family. Indeed, Hadaway and Marler (1991) have found that barely half of those who are raised in liberal Protestant denominations remain "in the fold" through adulthood.

The Catholic Choice: "THE (Vatican II) Church." Roman Catholics present yet another picture. As shown in Figure 12.4, from 1978 to 1988 Roman Catholic membership is increasingly influenced by traditional religiosity (up 3% in variance explained) followed closely by church consumerism (up 2%). In both these respects, Roman Catholic changes are similar to those for conservative Protestants. Considering changes in individual variables over time, however, there are notable differences between Roman Catholics and conservative Protestants (see Appendix, Table A12.2, and Supplemental Appendix, A12.4). In the traditional religiosity block, the effect of commitment to Christ on membership increases from 1978 to 1988 for both denominational groups. For Roman Catholics this is combined with an increase in the effect of prayer, while for conservative Protestants it is combined with a surge in the effect of belief. In the church consumerism block, the major factor responsible for its increased overall effect on conservative Protestant membership is church voluntarism, while for Roman Catholics it is satisfaction with the organizational side of the church—feeling that the church is neither too organized nor too strict, with just enough social justice emphasis.

FIGURE 12.4
What Affects Church Participation Among Catholics?
Step Summaries, 1978–1988

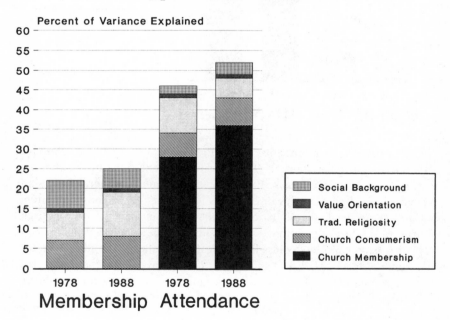

Such findings are consistent with recent programmatic changes as well as continuing institutional tensions within post-Vatican II Catholicism. The increasing relationship between traditional religiosity and Catholic membership, for example, may be a consequence of the adult catechists and religious education movement of Vatican II (Raferty and Leege, 1989). More particularly, the strong effects of commitment to Christ and prayer are corroborated by the findings of Searle and Leege (1985). Their research shows, for example, an increasing incidence of "prayers to the Godhead exclusively" among Roman Catholics under forty. Gremillion and Leege (1989) conclude that this is directly related to the "Christocentric reemphasis" of Vatican II.

But Vatican II has also left a wake of unresolved tensions. As D'Antonio et al. observe, "Before Vatican II, the Church appeared to many as a monolith in its religious beliefs and practices" (1989:13). In fact, they argue that "democratization" has permeated the church since Vatican II resulting in tensions "between the newer pluralistic tendencies and the traditional, hierarchical, authoritarian structure" (1989:14). It is not surprising, then, to discover that concerns about organizational issues increasingly define Roman Catholic membership.

Perhaps the most distinctive feature in the Roman Catholic negotiation of the church choice appears in regard to worship attendance. Most visible is the increasing importance of membership for attendance. For Roman Catholics, even more so than for conservative Protestants—and in both cases in clear contrast to liberal Protestants—membership and attendance go hand in hand. And as already noted in the Roman Catholic and conservative Protestant cases, membership is increasingly defined by a specific set of beliefs and practices. Both traditions teach, and individuals within both traditions accept, that "my church" or "THE church" represents the "right" choice—whether on biblical or traditional grounds. As a result of historically important concerns about ecumenism and inclusivity, liberal Protestants are less dogmatic about the church choice; thus, individualism, personalism, and local organizational factors weigh more heavily than membership for attendance.

Nevertheless, the increasing influence of church consumerism on participation is also evident in Figure 12.4 for Roman Catholics. Its effects are even more vivid in the detail of Table A12.4 (Supplemental Appendix). Although no single institutional variable in 1978 had a significant direct effect on church attendance, all items and scales in the church consumerism block have significant effects in 1988. Additionally, whereas satisfaction with the organizational side of the church characterizes membership among Roman Catholics, the adjudged warmth or personalism of a parish is the most critical for attendance.

In sum, active Roman Catholics are members who believe that it is necessary to go to "THE" church to be a good Christian, and who feel that the parish they attend is warm and meaningful with a clear spiritual focus. Roman Catholic religious participation in the late 1980s, therefore, exhibits an interesting blend of loyalty to the tradition, and a filtering of this tradition through individual choice.

Cautious Optimism: The Individual Prevails

The subterranean churning beneath the surface calm of national church membership and attendance trends presents the proverbial dilemma of how to interpret half a glass of water. The glass can be seen as half-full, and such optimistic assessments are supported by concrete evidence of vitality. During the 1980s:

- Commitment to Christ and perceptions of the church as warmly personal increased.
- The percentage of adults never praying and negative perceptions of the church's organizational structure declined.
- Church membership and worship attendance increased for the baby boom generation.
- The South continued to grow at a disproportionate rate; there was a decrease in counter-cultural values; and large segments of the population moved into both the family formation and the post-retirement phases of the life cycle—all of which, traditionally, have been associated with high levels of religious participation.
- Increasing cultural individualism did not result in a decrease in overall levels in church membership or worship attendance.

Such signs should be received as encouraging. At the very least, they point to strengths upon which to build. Still, an overly optimistic assessment can act as an anesthetic, muting awareness of painful changes as they occur and delaying necessary attention to the changes until it is too late.

Our analysis also provides objective grist for pessimists who prefer to see the glass as half-empty. During the 1980s:

- The percentage of Americans praying daily declined.
- Church membership and worship attendance decreased among those over fifty-five years old.
- Worship attendance became less dependent upon denominational loyalty and personal religiosity, and more dependent upon church consumerism.
- The population of the West—a region with traditionally low levels of church involvement—continued to grow disproportionately.

Pessimism, like optimism, can have positive and negative effects. On the negative side, the pessimist often gives up, dismissing the possibility of building on current strengths and circling the wagons to take a final, and inevitably diminishing, stand. On the positive side, a pessimist's caution often leads to a deeper probing of the situation.

Indeed, probing beneath the apparent surface calm of American religious life led us to a deeper and more foundational issue. Our analyses show that the increasing dominance of religious consumerism, as a form of cultural individualism, is the most important change in the American religious marketplace of the late 1980s. The finding is important because it represents a paradigm shift away from traditional social-scientific assumptions of a social locus of control and typical theological idealizations of religion as "total commitment." At a fundamental level, it represents a change in the way Americans relate to religious institutions.

There are many social analysts and religious leaders who view cultural individualism as indicative of a church glass half-full, and rapidly emptying. Do not count us among them. The data do not warrant it. Church consumerism is not necessarily corrosive of institutional involvement. There are two faces to choice: choice implies an option, not a predetermined choice. Americans can choose to participate or not to participate in the life of religious institutions. And during the 1980s, Americans continued to choose church. The reasons for the church choice, however, did change. Americans attend regularly because they feel that churchgoing is necessary to be a good Christian or Jew and because they happen to like the church they frequent. Increasingly, positive institutional qualities like warmth and a spiritual focus draw Americans to church.

Nevertheless, we do believe that the increasing influence of individualism presents a significant challenge for America's religious institutions. The challenge has at least two dimensions. First, and perhaps most obvious, the increasing dominance of cultural individualism tilts the balance of power in the negotiation of the church choice in the direction of the individual. This is not so much because there are more church options; current generations of Americans have always lived within easy commuting distance of many and varied local churches. And it is not due solely to the influence of church voluntarism. Rather, the data suggest that the balance of power in making the church choice "tips" toward the individual because within a longstanding context of multiple church options and against the backdrop of growing conviction about church voluntarism, Americans are increasingly acting on the options as choices. They are more conscious of their institutional commitments; more reflective about the reasons for investing their commitments in any particular institution; and more concerned that the church of choice is responsive to their personal commitments. Individual tastes and priorities take precedence over institutional loyalty.

The second, and closely related, dimension of challenge in the contemporary negotiation of the church choice is that an increasing emphasis on reflective commitment and personal satisfaction tilts the balance of power in the direction of the immediate and the concrete. In the competition between abstract dogma and concrete embodiment, the subjective-expressive possibilities of the latter are clearly most compelling. In the struggle between past loyalties and present needs or wants, feeling takes precedence over memory. What increasingly counts is the immediate relevancy of more traditional church norms and forms to my personal situation, my personal interests.

The strategic response to church consumerism is specialized and personalized programming. In the church choice, program is product. As such, church programming itself must diversify to fit the interests and needs of a variety of consumer groups or market niches. After all, it is product that delivers value to an increasingly discriminating consumer.

The American religious situation is becoming a more consumer-oriented marketplace. Some have even argued that the individualistic underpinning of the consumer orientation is a functional necessity in a modern society of diverse life-styles and segmented life worlds (e.g., Walrath, 1987). Nevertheless, there is really no such thing as a "pure" individualist. Identifiable and quite formidable social constraints still exist—particularly in the religious sector. Despite the fact that church consumerism is increasingly influential for predicting who goes to church, traditional religiosity and religious socialization remain strong predictors of who joins. Americans who hold traditionally orthodox beliefs and who were raised in the church are still more likely to join. Although, at least for liberal Protestants, such subcultural pressures have become significantly less important for both joining and attending.

The formative effect of subcultures is critical to understanding the differences found in our analysis among liberal Protestants, conservative Protestants, and Roman Catholics. The latter two maintain strong subcultures. Relatively clear, traditional stances on religious belief and practice, as well as religious socialization are key ingredients in the maintenance of both subcultures. Conservative Protestant and Roman Catholic subcultures both contain and sustain a predisposition toward church membership as an adult. Membership in either "my" church or "THE" church is an important component of individual biography. That does not mean, however, that church consumerism has no effect. For persons embedded in either subculture, individual tastes (or choice) and the quality of the local church product (or program) increasingly determine how active a member they will be.

In stark contrast, the strength of the liberal Protestant subculture has seriously eroded. As a consequence, the influence of all traditional correlates of membership and participation have declined. At the same time, the influence of consumerist impulses increased. The combined effect is that the responsiveness (or nonresponsiveness) of local churches becomes an issue of critical importance. For liberal Protestants, church consumerism is increasingly predictive of both membership and activity. In this sense, liberal Protestantism represents the purest stream of consumerism within American denominationalism.

What is the likely effect of these changes for the future of denominational growth? Other things remaining equal (e.g., rates of new church development, or dramatic swings in birthrates), future national membership trends for conservative Protestants and Roman Catholics will be largely dependent upon subcultural strength. At the same time, future attendance trends for conservative Protestants and Roman Catholics will be dependent upon the ability of local congregations and parishes to respond to the immediate needs and wants of their members. To the extent that they are able to embody their traditions and practices in user-friendly ways, conservative Protestants and Roman Catholics can count on an active (and increasingly cohesive) membership. In contrast, both future national membership and attendance trends for liberal Protestants will be largely dependent upon the ability of local congregations to fend for themselves in the absence of strong subcultural norms.

Chapter Thirteen

Religion in the Canadian 1990s:

The Paradox of Poverty and Potential[1]

Reginald W. Bibby

B y virtually every imaginable measure, organized religion in Canada is in serious trouble. Membership and attendance have been steadily declining since at least the beginning of the 1950s. The inclination of Canadians either to place a high value on religion or see it as having a significant impact on life also has been decreasing in the past fifty years. And differences in involvement and commitment by age suggest that the problems facing organized religion will only get worse in the immediate future.

Yet, in the midst of this apparent demise of faith, there are signs that the market for religion remains extensive. Far from abandoning the country's dominant religious groups, the vast majority of Canadians continue both to identify with them and to rely on them for pivotal rites of passage. Belief in supernatural phenomena and interest in questions of meaning remain widespread.

The paradox is that, precisely at a time when organized religion is facing significant problems, the desire for some kind of spirituality is pervasive. In the face of apparent religious poverty, there appears to be so much religious potential. The critical theoretical question is why such disparity exists between what the public seems to want and what organized religion seems to be doing. The critical practical question is what—if anything—can be done to close the gap.

The State of Organized Religion

Decreasing Involvement

The steady decline in the proportion of Canadians who attend services regularly is continuing. The weekly attendance figure that stood at six in ten in the late 1940s dropped to four in ten in 1970, and now stands at just over two in ten.

The attendance decline has been pervasive. Regular attendance that characterized over 80% of Roman Catholics as recently as the mid-1960s now describes only 33%. Just 22% of Protestants are now attending weekly, while attendance among those who identify with no group, along with "Others" has remained fairly stable (see Table 13.1).

TABLE 13.1
Percent Weekly Service Attenders in Canada: 1975–1990*

	1975	1980	1985	1990
TOTAL NATIONAL	31%	28%	26%	24%
ROMAN CATHOLIC	45	41	36	33
PROTESTANT	26	24	25	22
Anglican	24	20	15	15
United Church	28	18	16	15
Conservative	38	52	64	49
NONE	<1	<1	<1	<1
OTHER	17	11	13	15

*Percent who say they attend services "Almost every week" or more. "Other" includes religious non-respondents.
Source: *Project Canada* Survey Series.

Regular weekly attendance is particularly low for the country's two largest mainline bodies, the United and Anglican churches (about 15% attend regularly). It is highest for conservative Protestant groups (46%). Yet even the conservative Protestant attendance boom of the 1980s could be over. As they become more urbanized and upwardly mobile, increasing numbers of these Protestant evangelicals show signs of treating weekly attendance as optional, following the pattern of other Canadians. The sample size is fairly small, however (some 100 cases); further examinations of the attendance patterns for conservative Protestants are required.

Beyond attendance, professed membership in local churches and other kinds of religious groups now stands at 29%—down dramatically from a 1975 level of 48%. Particularly striking is the sharp decline in local parish membership for Roman Catholics in the past fifteen years, from 56% to 28% (see Table 13.2). During that period, Protestant membership has shrunk from 51% to 37%, yet it now exceeds the level for Roman Catholics. The proportion of Canadians who identify themselves as Anglican or United Church, and say they are members of local churches has dropped from about 50% to 35% since 1975. Conservative Protestants, at over 50%, are still far more likely than others to claim membership in local churches; they do, however, show signs of slipping from their lofty membership heights of the 1980s.

The Marginal Role of Religion

The latest 1990 survey has found that only about one in four Canadians say that religion is "very important to them" (see Table 13.3). This is in sharp contrast to the importance accorded areas such as family life (82% "very important"), a comfortable life (63%), or a rewarding career (50%).

It is not surprising, therefore, to find that large numbers of Canadians do not think that religion should inform either social or personal morality. Some four in ten people say that "ministers should stick to religion and not concern themselves with social, economic, and political issues." Almost five in ten Roman Catholics express this opinion, along with more than three in ten Protestants, and nearly four in ten evangelicals.

As for the personal realm, the widespread cultural emphasis on individualism is readily evident. A resounding 65% of Canadians say that "everything's relative," with one in two maintaining that "what is right or wrong is a matter of personal opinion." When specific areas such as premarital sex and abortion are probed, we find that very large numbers of Roman Catholics and evangelicals are among those who voice approval for these actions—defying the positions taken by their churches (see Table 13.3).

When the vast majority of Canadians turn to religion, they are inclined to be highly selective customers who see religion playing a fairly peripheral role in everyday life.

TABLE 13.2
Percent Religious Group Membership in Canada: 1975–1990*

	1975	1980	1985	1990
TOTAL NATIONAL	48%	42%	36%	29%
ROMAN CATHOLIC	56	47	38	28
PROTESTANT	51	45	43	37
Anglican	50	44	34	30
United Church	52	44	37	35
Conservative	56	53	73	56

Source: *Project Canada* Survey Series.

TABLE 13.3
Percent Religious Correlates by Denomination: 1990

	NAT (1249)	RC (505)	PROT (535)	ANG (142)	UC (189)	CONS (100)
RELIGION is very important to me	27%	31%	28%	20%	20%	52%
Ministers should STICK TO RELIGION and not concern themselves with social, economic, and political issues	41	46	34	30	31	37
Everything's relative	65	69	58	64	60	52
What is RIGHT OR WRONG is a matter of personal opinion	50	56	43	51	40	35
Approve of PREMARITAL SEX	80	82	73	85	76	50
Approve of LEGAL ABORTION availability when mother's health endangered	95	93	95	97	97	87

Source: *Project Can90* national survey.

The Loss of Confidence

The national surveys through 1990 document a critically important trend. In the face of scandals involving televangelists and sexual charges involving priests, along with the controversy concerning the ordination of homosexuals in the United Church, there has been a dramatic drop in public confidence in religious leaders in the last decade.

In 1980, approximately 60% of Canadians said that they had "a great deal" or "quite a bit" of confidence in religious leaders, a level virtually unchanged from the early 1970s. By 1985, in part reflecting the spillover into Canada of the effects of the troubles of American television evangelists, the confidence level dropped to about 50%. Today, on the heels of further American and Canadian scandals and sexual charges in the Roman Catholic Church, the confidence level has plummeted to 37%. No other Canadian institution— with the sole exception of the much-maligned federal government—has experienced such a severe loss of public confidence.

The confidence drop in merely five years has been 15 percentage points for Roman Catholics, 23 points for United Church adherents, 22 points for

Anglicans and 18 percentage points for conservative Protestants (see Table 13.4). In the case of those with no religious ties, confidence in religious leaders has not fallen, but remains fairly low.

In the light of current attitudes toward leadership, Canadians are highly pessimistic about religion's influence. In 1980, 29% said that they expected religion would gain influence by the end of the century, while another 29% predicted religion would lose influence. Reflecting a noteworthy loss of confidence, in 1990, those people expecting religion to gain influence by the year 2000 dropped to 19%, while those who believe it will lose influence rose to 38%.

TABLE 13.4
Confidence in Religious Leaders: 1985–1990°

	1985	1990
TOTAL NATIONAL	51°	37
ROMAN CATHOLIC	62	47
PROTESTANT	52	32
Anglican	46	24
United Church	50	27
Conservative	68	50
OTHER	30	41
NONE	10	15

°Percent indicating having "A Great Deal" or "Quite a Bit" of confidence.
Source: *Project Can85* and *Project Can90* national surveys.

Age Structure Realities

An analysis of the foregoing findings by age underlines the crisis facing organized religion in Canada. Membership and attendance, along with the value placed on religion and confidence in leadership, differ significantly by age (see Table 13.5). Only conservative Protestants appear to be experiencing a fair measure of success in instilling involvement and interest in their younger people.

Looking at the nation as a whole, it is clear that Canadians fifty-five and over are, by far, more "committed and confident" than others. Given such age variations, barring major, unforeseen changes in the behavior and outlook of younger Canadians, the writing is on the wall: the aging of the population will bring with it an accelerated decline in the country's interest in organized religion.

TABLE 13.5
Percent Religious Involvement and Importance by Age for Select Religious Groups: 1990

	NAT	RC	PROT	ANG	UC	CONS
MEMBERSHIP						
18-34	17%	18%	27%	20%	18%	49%
35-54	31	32	32	31	21	50
55+	42	38	49	39	58	70
WEEKLY ATTENDERS						
18-34	13	16	14	4	5	45
35-54	22	30	19	14	10	40
55+	40	60	31	27	27	64
RELIGION IMPORTANT						
18-34	16	18	20	12	8	44
35-54	23	28	22	13	9	55
55+	45	57	40	32	40	61
CONFIDENCE IN LEADERS						
18-34	28	38	24	14	16	45
35-54	35	44	29	29	23	47
55+	47	62	39	30	38	47

SOURCE: *Project Can90* national survey.

Given that (1) most people who will return to churches after an adolescent hiatus have done so by their mid-thirties, and (2) the involvement levels of teenagers in Canada is even lower than young adults, the membership and attendance patterns of the present eighteen- to thirty-four-year-old cohort give us clues regarding the future of religion in Canada. Projecting their membership and attendance levels some twenty-five years ahead, to approximately the year 2015, this is how the picture would look.

The importance that Canadians will place on religion, along with their inclination to be members of local groups, will drop from today's 30% levels to around 15%. By 2015, weekly attenders will have tumbled from the current 23% level to about 15%.

Such declines will not be minor for the country's religious groups. The percentage drops in membership and attendance will translate into significant numerical losses for Canada's religious denominations. By the year 2015 religious groups in Canada may have only about 5 million members—

compared to a current 7.5 million, and just over 4 million weekly attenders—versus today's 6 million (see Table 13.6).

Although the Roman Catholic Church will remain Canada's largest religious body, it will experience large membership and attendance losses. Relative to the population, conservative Protestants will manage to hold their own, but will not significantly increase their market share.

What looms is a particularly dramatic alteration of the religious landscape of Canada. By around 2015 the previously dominant mainline Protestant denominations will have less local church members than the conservative Protestants. Even more important, their combined weekly attenders will be about one-third of the conservative's total.

The resource implications, in terms of the loss of people, finances, and power with which to engage in ministry, are nothing less than staggering. Life in Canada's twenty-first century looks extremely grim for organized religion.

TABLE 13.6
Membership and Attendance Projections for Select Religious Groups
Based on Membership and Attendance Levels
of Current 18- to 34-years-olds

		NAT	RC	PROT	ANG	UC	CONS
MEMBERS							
1990	% of pop. 26 million	29	13	15	3.0	5.6	3.9
	Number (in 1000s)	7,540	3,422	3,944	780	1,456	1,019
2015	% of pop. 32 million	17	9.0	11	2.0	2.9	3.4
	Number (in 1000s)	5,440	2,707	3,542	640	922	1,098
WEEKLY ATTENDERS							
1990	% of pop. 26 million	23	16	9.0	1.5	2.4	3.4
	Number (in 1000s)	5,980	4,033	2,345	390	624	892
2015	% of pop. 32 million	13	8.0	6.0	.4	.8	3.2
	Number (in 1000s)	4,160	2,406	1,834	128	256	1,008

SOURCES: *Project Can90* and *The Canadian Almanac*, 1991.

The percentage of population estimates for religious groups for 2015 are computed using their sizes as of 1990. Assuming their percentage of the population will shrink by 2015, these projected membership and attendance figures are, if anything, generous.

Meanwhile, Back in the Culture

If that were all that there is to the Canadian religion story, those who value faith and are in touch with reality would be in a state of despair. There is little doubt that organized religion is in serious shape, with its golden years apparently relegated to history. (See Table 13.7.)

But as one looks out on the cultural landscape and watches the dust settle on the grey ruins of much of organized religion, an interesting spectacle can be seen. In the midst of the debris and desolation, a large number of green patches of spirituality can be detected. The temples may be disintegrating, but the grass is far from dead.

At least four indicators of latent spirituality can readily be observed.

Identification

Despite the fact that just over two in ten Canadians now are regular weekly attenders, and just under three in ten profess church membership, over nine in ten nonetheless continue to identify with a religious group. Forty-five percent identify themselves as Protestants, 41% say that they are Roman Catholics, while 4% identify with other groups. Only 10% indicate that they have no religious preference, and past research suggests that as many as half of these are "temporary nothings" who will eventually "re-identify" with the group in which they were raised. Some 95% of Canadians, then, have not relinquished a religious identification.

Some fast facts on these "affiliates":

- They don't lack for religious backgrounds: 78% say they attended monthly or more when they were growing up, with 66% accompanied by their mothers and 54% by their fathers.
- Close to 90% of those raised as Protestants, Catholics, or Others have retained the religious ties of their parents.
- While only two in ten attend weekly, six in ten do sometimes; just two in ten never attend—and that proportion hasn't changed since at least 1975.
- Almost 90% of nonweekly attending Protestants and Catholics say they have no intention of abandoning their religious traditions. They mean it. Even the 3% who indicate interest in a new movement such as New Age continue to identify with Protestantism and Catholicism.
- Although just 27% may say that religion is very important to them, another 29% add that it is somewhat important; only 19% say that it's not important at all.

- Similarly, religious group heritage is seen by only 20% as very important, but another 28% acknowledge that it is somewhat important; the not important at all figure is just 21%.

TABLE 13.7
Value Placed on Religion and Religious Group Heritage: 1990*

	Religion					Religious Heritage				
	VI	SW	NV	NI	TOT	VI	SW	NV	NI	TOT
TOTAL NATIONAL	27%	29%	25%	19%	100%	20%	28%	30%	21%	100%
ROMAN CATHOLICS	31	36	26	7	100	24	37	29	10	100
PROTESTANTS	29	29	25	17	100	18	27	32	23	100
Anglican	20	27	33	20	100	16	24	35	25	100
United Church	20	31	31	18	100	12	27	37	24	100
Conservative	52	27	10	11	100	35	31	18	16	100
OTHER	36	31	19	14	100	46	24	23	7	100
NONE	2	2	20	76	100	1	2	23	74	100

*Percents Very Important, Some What, Not Very, Not Important at all.
SOURCE: *Project Can90* national survey.

Rites of Passage

Of considerable significance, virtually all of the nine in ten Canadians who identify with religious groups say that they plan to turn to these groups when they need weddings, funerals, and birth-related ceremonies carried out—if they haven't already done so. Further, a national survey of youth conducted in late 1987 found that they anticipate turning to religious groups in the future: 75% for birth-related ceremonies, 80% for weddings, and over 85% for funerals.

Undoubtedly such a desire for rites of passage sometimes reflects cultural habit, on other occasions the seeking out of the appropriate professional who "does such jobs." But clergy are among those who also report that, frequently, the desire for these passage ceremonies also reflects a poorly articulated sense that "God needs to be brought in on this."

The widespread, ongoing demand for religious rites of passage appears to be a second indicator of the fact that the need to satisfy a spiritual dimension of life continues to characterize large numbers of Canadians.

TABLE 13.8
Conventional and Less Conventional Beliefs and Practices*

	NAT (1249)	RC (505)	PROT (535)	OTHER (44)	NONE (122)
CONVENTIONAL					
Existence of God	82%	92%	86%	76%	25%
Divinity of Jesus	75	87	80	45	12
Heaven	70	82	75	50	18
Life after death	68	74	71	61	31
Hell	46	44	58	49	8
Have experienced God	43	54	43	37	7
LESS CONVENTIONAL					
Psychic powers	59	56	65	59	48
ESP	59	56	62	57	58
Precogition	47	55	38	39	49
Spirit world contact	38	41	38	49	26
Astrology	34	39	33	26	22
Will be reincarnated	26	31	21	36	20
Communication with dead	23	29	18	20	16

*Percent indicating they "Definitely" or "Think" they believe in the beliefs and practices listed.
SOURCE: *Project Can90* national survey.

Beliefs and Practices

At a time when religious leaders are decrying the loss of faith, it is significant that religious beliefs and practices are thriving. Canadians, young and old, continue to endorse traditional beliefs about God, the divinity of Jesus, and life after death. Close to half of the population maintain that they have experienced God's presence, with the same proportion saying that they pray privately weekly or more. A quarter say they read the Bible or other scriptures at least once a month.

To the consternation of many religious leaders, older and younger Canadians also continue to embrace less conventional beliefs. (See Table 13.8.) Yet most appear to treat them, not as alternatives to traditional religion, but rather as "add-ons." About 60% of Canadians indicate that they believe in ESP, while the same proportion maintain that some people have special psychic powers that enable them to predict events. Almost 50% report that they themselves have experienced precognition. Approximately one in three say they believe in astrology; for the record, 88% know their astrological sign and half the population read their horoscopes at least once a month—outnumbering scriptural readers two to one.

Acknowledgment of the reality of things beyond the observable world is remarkably high. Some 40% of Canadians believe that "we can have contact with the spirit world," while 23% maintain that "it is possible to communicate with the dead." And as they themselves contemplate what will happen to them after they die, about one in four Canadians say that they expect to be reincarnated.

Belief in a supernatural dimension of reality is widespread in Canada, and shows no signs of abating. On the contrary, in recent decades, supernatural ideas have gained considerable credibility. They are held without apology by virtually everyone, and viewed as worthy of the attention of filmmaker, journalist, and scientist. It is therefore strange that organized religion has been so inept at capitalizing on such an apparent opportunity.

The Quest for Meaning

A fourth indicator of the interest Canadians have in the spiritual dimension of life is the ongoing inclination to raise questions of meaning and purpose. The author's latest 1990 national survey has found that one in two people express concern about the question of life's purpose. The 1980 survey found that eight in ten reported that they reflect on why there is suffering in the world, while seven in ten reported that they fairly frequently wonder about what happens after death. Further, six in ten said they raise the academic question of how the world came into being, along with the immediate question of how they can find real happiness.

In addition to specific questions of meaning, the 1990 survey has found that the third most prevalent personal concern—behind concerns about money and time—is the feeling Canadians have that they "should be getting more out of life." Such a sentiment may well suggest a receptivity to "something more" than day-to-day existence, offering another signal that the desire to have spiritual needs met does not belong to history. (See Table 13.9.)

Resolving the Paradox

This brings us back to the paradox mentioned at the outset—that at a time when organized religion is facing very serious problems, the interest in spirituality, whether verbalized as such or not, appears to be extremely pervasive. Canadians continue to identify psychologically with religious traditions, feel a need for religious rites, be intrigued by the supernatural realm, and look for answers to questions of meaning.

TABLE 13.9
Percent Select Religious Characteristics by Religious Service Attendance: 1990

	Non-Weekly (934)	Weekly (288)
IDENTIFICATION		
Identify with a religious group	87%	99%
Not inclined to leave the group	81	**
Religion important	44	97
Religious group heritage important	36	89
RITES OF PASSAGE		
Plan have birth ceremonies performed	28	21
Plan have wedding ceremonies performed	30	21
Plan have funeral(s) carried out	60	64
BELIEFS AND PRACTICES		
Believe in God	78	97
Think have experienced God	34	74
Believe in ESP	64	41.
Believe in contact with spirit world	41	33
QUEST FOR MEANING		
Concerned about the purpose of life	54	42
Feel should be getting more out life	72	55

**Not asked of regular attenders.
SOURCE: *Project Can90* national survey.

In short, there appears to be a considerable market for the very things that religion historically "has been about." Given what seem to be almost ideal market conditions, the obvious question needs to be raised: why are religious groups facing such a crisis? Why can't the companies "sell" their products when there is every reason to believe that the customers want them?

Two rather obvious possibilities exist. The first is that the companies are not doing a very good job of distributing the products. The second is that they aren't offering the right ones.

Distribution Problems

There is good reason to believe that organizational means-end inversion is fairly common. Simply put, the companies have frequently become preoccupied with themselves as organizations, rather than with ministry to the population.

Historically, religious groups have been called to be more than communities in which faith is experienced. They also have been expected to be the means by which faith is shared with outsiders. While being a resource to the initiated, the religious group ideally also ministers to others—providing meaning for those who are raising questions about life's purpose, addressing issues concerning the supernatural realm, giving significance to life's passages.

The problem is that it is easy to lose sight of such an externally-directed role. Since at least Max Weber, observers have drawn attention to the reality of routinization, whereby groups tend to become turned inward, focusing upon themselves as organizations, rather than on the original purposes that brought them into being.

Canadian religious groups, like their counterparts elsewhere in much of the Western world, have often fallen into such a pattern of self-interest. Ask religious leaders about the problems facing organized religion today and chances are good that most will bemoan numbers and finances—rather than their failure to minister effectively to the Canadian populace. Concerns often center upon "church growth" and "church planting," rather than on addressing the spiritual needs of the people across the country. Success often is measured in terms of simply putting people into a physical building so many days a month, and expecting them to subscribe to belief and behavioral norms, including giving fairly generously of both their time and money.

Further indicative of their insular nature, most local congregations in Canada, conservative or mainline, are highly homogeneous, socially and ethnically. In some rural and small urban churches they have come to resemble "extended family shrines." Outsiders are not generally attracted to such settings. Equally important, it seems that outsiders also have not been particularly wanted, prior to appropriate socialization, that is.

The net result in the Canadian 1990s is that organized religion has not particularly aimed its ministry at outsiders for more than membership recruitment purposes. Even then, growth by recruitment of insiders has been preferred. Frankly, it is far more cost-effective. Bringing in "sinners" is both tough and hard on resources.

It seems clear that the organization has been prized over addressing the spiritual needs of the country. It therefore is no surprise that a population that is receptive to the major themes of religion has been only superficially touched by Canadian religious groups.

In a literal sense, the two seem to be living in two different worlds.

Product Problems

A second reason for the apparent disparity between spiritual interest and group decline is the abdication of the supernatural and spiritual realms by religious denominations. Part of this problem can be found in the emphasis on rational thought, which has led some to regard the sheer exploration of the supernatural as inappropriate. In lieu of the gods, a spirit world, and life after death, now it seems that highly subjective inward journeys are the stuff of religious quests. The result is a limited connection to churches by Canadians, both young and old, who say in larger numbers that they are puzzled about the purpose of life, think it might be possible to communicate with the dead, and increasingly believe that they themselves will be reincarnated.

In addition to some religious groups downplaying and disowning the supernatural, the old dichotomy between the social and the spiritual has again plagued religion in Canada in recent decades. There has been a very strong social justice emphasis in Canada in the post-1960s. Responding to such a theme, the leaders of the country's largest denomination, the United Church, have led the way in calling for a more just society. Along with other mainline groups, including the Anglicans, Lutherans, and Presbyterians, the United Church has joined voices across the country in championing the rights of women, cultural minorities, and natives. The United Church has also engaged in a highly divisive debate over the ordination eligibility of homosexuals.

While justice attempts are highly commendable, if they are not accompanied by a strong emphasis on things spiritual, large numbers of people are left feeling vacuous. The obvious problem is this: justice issues are being promoted by a wide variety of Canadian institutions and interest groups. People consequently need to be able find a clear fusion of "God and society" when they deal with religious groups. Otherwise, religious groups say nothing to society that society is not already saying to itself.

Significantly, there has been extensive dissension in the United Church over the failure to achieve an adequate justice-spiritual synthesis. That conflict may provide an important tip-off as to why so many Canadians with mainline roots are not bothering much with the churches. Ironically, many find that the attempts at relevance are largely irrelevant.

Toward Turning Things Around

There does, however, appear to be considerable hope in sight. There is a great need for Canadian religious groups to stop blaming the culture, and seize the opportunity at hand. Such a turnaround will include an effort to rethink what churches are for and to rework expectations as to what is worth pursuing. Some starting places in reaching out to the population might include capitalizing on the ongoing tendency of people to identify with religious groups, along with their desire for rites of passage. Groups also need to be responsive to the widespread interest in the supernatural, as well as to the highly pervasive quest for meaning.

Effective strategies will undoubtedly include recovering a holistic message that speaks to God, self, and society; recognizing the centrally important role of relationships in fostering both commitment and involvement; and being flexible about the use and non-use of physical facilities.

The Market Exists

The paradox characterizing the religious situation in Canada is not something that is unique to this country. Evidence from other highly developed countries, including the United States, suggests that interest in areas historically addressed by religion—the supernatural, the significance of life passages, spiritual quest, the meaning of life—surpasses interest in organized religion. Consequently, there is good reason to believe that problems of means-end inversion and irrelevant relevancy contribute to the apparent anomaly of high spiritual interest and low religious group involvement in many other societies.

Still, religious participation and commitment in the U.S. appears to exceed that of most other countries. Following the rationale just offered, there might be a very good reason. Unlike countries such as Canada, Britain, France, Germany, the Netherlands, and Sweden, for example, the United States has a very large evangelical Protestant presence. About 7% of Canadians identify with conservative Protestants, compared to over 30% of Americans.

To the extent that American evangelicals have the resources, the vitality, and "a product" that is in touch with ongoing spiritual and supernatural concerns, they may be playing an important role in meeting the market demand for such emphases. They thereby may be a key source of the higher attendance and commitment levels in the United States.

Currently, Canada is among the many countries that lack a functional equivalent. The market for religion exists; but the gods have yet to arrive.

Chapter Fourteen

Baby Boomers and the Return to the Churches

Wade Clark Roof and Sr. Mary Johnson

W ith babes in arms and doubts in mind, a generation looks to religion," is the caption of a *Newsweek* cover story (December 17, 1990) on young Americans returning to God. The post-war "baby boom" generation, having transformed American society in so many ways, is now reshaping the religious landscape. Youth born between the years 1946 and 1964— perhaps better thought of as two cohorts, the older and younger boomers—are at an influential age. The older boomers are now in their mid-forties, the younger ones are in their thirties. All together, 75 million strong—roughly one-third of the American population—-they are what sociologists call the "lead cohort" of contemporary society, setting trends that include moral values, political attitudes, family life, career patterns, and religious life.

Because of their sheer size—the largest cohort of youth ever in our nation's history—baby boomers have impacted religious institutions since the time they were children. In the 1950s, the swelling numbers of school-age children combined with economic prosperity led to the suburban expansion of churches and synagogues. Religious membership increased as parents sought religious instruction for their children. "A Little Child Shall Lead Them," argued Dennison Nash (1968) at the time, suggesting that the very presence of so many children helped to account for the so-called religious revival of the 1950s. Symbolism of religion, family, and country was pervasive, buttressed no doubt by rising affluence and the cold-war ideology of the times.

Then, beginning in the mid-1960s, when large numbers of this generation were spread between their adolescence and early twenties, they greatly altered the cultural climate of the country. Trauma surrounding the civil rights movement and later the Vietnam War, and the changing moral, sexual, and familial values of the counter-cultural years, all combined to produce a youthful defection from the religious establishment. Cults and new religious movements of all kinds flourished, as did more secular human potential movements and "alternative life-styles." Trends persisted into the 1970s, although social activism dissipated and the counter-cultural values of the "new morality"

293

became an individualistic "drop out and turn on" regression to drugs, sex, and self. And throughout this period, many youth did just that—drop out of religious institutions. Just as in earlier times they swelled the membership rolls of mainline Protestant, Catholic, and Jewish congregations, now they left in record numbers, adding to the malaise that had set in upon these institutions.

And now, once again, we are at a critical phase in the life of this generation—the time of their "second coming," as Annie Gottlieb (1987) puts it. Many boomers are approaching mid-life and the kinds of assessment that often accompany that phase of life. To the extent that there is a dominant direction to changes within the post-war generation in the 1990s, it is into family formation and parenting, mid-life career concerns, and some re-examination of value commitments, the latter often in a more conservative direction. According to the *Rolling Stone* Survey (see Sheff, 1988), many in this generation who once endorsed sexual freedom and altered consciousness now say "no" to their children with respect to casual sex and drugs.

With respect to boomers and religion, there is considerable speculation today—far more speculation than actual research. Conflicting views are found in the statements by religious leaders and in the media and popular writings. Three views, or some version of them, often get stated:

1. **Return to Religion.** It is said that boomers are returning to organized religion after a lengthy absence. Media reports of a return to greater religious involvement became commonplace in the late 1980s and early 1990s. The return is presumed to be in the conservative direction, that is, to evangelical and fundamentalist congregations. Religious return accompanies a "conservative drift" in social and political attitudes, and family formation and parenting patterns.

2. **Secular Generation.** Diametrically opposite, this view suggests that baby boomers are perhaps the most secular, most materialistic of generations yet. Many of the stereotypes and caricatures of the baby boom generation encourage such thinking: labels like Yuppies and Dinks, and descriptive terms such as narcissistic and self-serving. The truth is only a small proportion of baby boomers fit the Yuppie and Dinks descriptions, but they have a disproportionate influence in shaping public opinion.

3. **Privately Religious, but not Institutionally Involved.** A third view seeks to reconcile the two above by implying that baby boomers are religious—perhaps, very religious—but they don't express it in traditionally institutional religious ways. Their religion is privatized, invisible, deeply personal and spiritual. One thinks of Jack Simms' consulting service in California that goes by the name of B.O.O.M.E.R.S.,

Inc., i.e., Believers Outside of Most Every Religious System. Boomers are religious and spiritual but not in ways that you might easily identify.

The purpose of this chapter is to examine current boomer trends in religion, and to try to sort out the validity of these possible explanations. We are concerned primarily with the trends as they relate to organized religion. Accordingly, we look at four topics pertinent to church life in the 1990s: (1) Is there a return to the churches? (2) Who are the returnees? (3) What kind of return is it? and (4) Will the return make any difference for patterns of church growth and decline in the decade ahead?

Is There a Return?

The NORC General Social Survey Series indicates—at least in the case of worship attendance—that there is a return. These surveys based on representative samples of the adult American population were conducted throughout the 1970s and 1980s, and are probably the most reliable source of trend data on the American population. Questions on religion, especially beliefs and attitudes, are limited but worship attendance is included in all the surveys.

Roozen, McKinney, and Thompson (1990), for example, using the General Social Survey series for the early 1970s and the early 1980s, document an increase from 33.5% to 42.8% in regular worship attendance for persons born between 1945 and 1954 (the older boomers). They speak of the "Big Chill" generation warming to worship, suggesting that the number of older boomers regularly involved in the worship life of their religious communities has increased by 3 to 4 million.

In a follow-up analysis, Roof and Roozen (1989) reexamined the NORC data adding a third time period. Specifically the pooled NORC samples used in their analysis covered: the "early seventies" (1972, 1973), the "early eighties" (1982, 1983), and the "late eighties" (1987, 1988). Similarly, the baby boomer population was split into two waves, the "older baby boom," born from 1945 to 1954, and the "younger baby boom," born from 1955 to 1965. There are both substantive and practical reasons for this split. Aside from obvious life-cycle differences, older boomers came of age during the sixties and hold values that still set them apart from those growing up in the more sedate seventies. And practically, there were too few cases of younger boomers in the 1972–73 sample, thus forcing us to pay attention primarily to the older half of the generation.

The results of this analysis are shown in Table 14.1. Several observations can be drawn. First, worship attendance increased from the early 1970s to the early 1980s, and remained at elevated levels for older boomers throughout the 1980s. Data for the two time periods in the 1980s thus add support to the thesis of a return to organized religion. Second, among younger boomers, there was an increase in religious attendance from 1982–83 to 1987–88, especially a shift from low to moderate involvement. This pattern adds further support to the "return to religion" argument.

TABLE 14.1

Worship Attendance for Older and Younger Baby Boom Cohorts in 1972–1973, 1982–1983, and 1987–1988

	1972–73	1982–83	1987–88
Older Cohort°			
Worship Attendance			
Low	39.6%	37.0%	35.9%
Moderate	26.9	20.2	23.3
High	33.5	42.8	40.8
N =	(1015)	(1124)	(721)
Younger Cohort°°			
Worship Attendance			
Low	—	41.5	35.6
Moderate	—	22.8	27.9
High	—	35.6	36.5
N =		(1151)	(825)

°Born 1945–1954
°°Born 1955–1965

Another study inquiring into boomers is the Lilly Endowment-funded survey of 1,579 baby boomers, born between 1946 and 1962, carried out in 1988 and 1989 in four states—California, Massachusetts, North Carolina, and Ohio. In this study, for which we were principal investigators, 96% of all boomers identified a religious tradition in which they were raised. Almost 90% said they had attended Sunday school, or had some type of religious training as a child. We were interested in knowing what had happened to them since childhood. How many remained in the faiths in which they grew up, or had switched to other faiths or simply dropped out? If they had dropped out, how many had returned to active religious involvement later in their lives?

A partial answer is found in Table 14.2. It shows the traditions in which the respondents were raised and their current religious preferences. Americans tend to have high levels of religious switching between denominations and even denominational families, and it was expected that boomers would have equally high, if not higher, switching levels. It was also expected that switching would be greater for mainline Protestants than conservative Protestants, in keeping with all that is known about the Protestant establishment's malaise and weaker claims upon the individual's commitment (Hoge and Roozen, 1979; Roof and McKinney, 1987). The findings as shown here are consistent with this prediction: only 65% of the boomers raised in mainline Protestantism today claim a similar affiliation; 83% of conservative Protestants remain in the same affiliation.[1] Of those reared in the Protestant mainline, 15% are now conservative, whereas, the conservatives have lost only 4% to the mainliners. Of those raised as Protestant mainliners, 13% are now "Nones" (no religious affiliation) as compared to 9% of conservatives.

Worth noting are the horizontal rows in the table for the two large Protestant constituencies. Here it is apparent that conservative Protestants have picked up sizable numbers of boomers in the switching process from all religious groups but Jewish. For mainline Protestants, the numbers switching in are all considerably lower, except for Jews who do drift in their favor.

TABLE 14.2
Switching Patterns: Religion Reared and Current Religion

Current Religion	Religion Raised					
	Mainline Protestant	Conservative Protestant	Catholic	Jewish	Other	None
Mainline Protestant	65%	4%	2%	3%	2%	6%
Conservative Protestant	15	83	9	—	10	25
Catholic	6	2	76	—	—	6
Jewish	—	—	—	81	—	—
Other	2	3	1	3	70	—
None	13	9	12	14	17	64
Total %	101	101	100	101	99	101
N =	(369)	(460)	(542)	(36)	(41)	(52)

Of interest, Catholics fall midway between mainline and conservative Protestants in holding on to their own: 76% reared Catholic still identify as Catholic. Those who leave Catholicism tend to go either to the "Nones" or to the conservative wing of Protestantism. Jewish boomers who have switched have largely disaffiliated from religion. Those reared in nonaffiliated homes are the least stable, a big proportion of them switching to the conservative Protestants. Looking at the horizontal row for the nonaffiliated, we see large numbers in all the groups who have abandoned religious affiliations. Growing up in the sixties and seventies, many in this generation dropped out of organized religion altogether.

But switching tells only a part of the story, and in some respects the least interesting part. What about movement in and out of religious institutions, or a change in the level of religious involvement, without a change of affiliation? To get a breakdown on involvement in organized religion, a three-fold classification was used:

Loyalists: Those persons brought up in a religious tradition and who remained involved in one tradition or another.

Dropouts: Persons once involved but who were inactive for a period of two years or more, and were still inactive at the time of the interview.

Returnees: Persons once involved, then dropped out for a period of two years or more, and then returned to active involvement.

As shown in Table 14.3, 42% of the respondents report having remained religiously involved during their teenage and young adult years. They were still involved at the time of our interviews. These loyalists may have switched congregations, possibly even switched denominations or faiths, but they have maintained an institutional religious connection. We do not know how this compares with previous generations in a strict statistical sense, but it appears that the proportion of loyalists coming out of the sixties and seventies is lower than for earlier generations of this century.[2]

Fifty-eight percent have dropped out at one time or another, at least once and often more than once. More than a third of those who dropped out, however, have returned to active involvement. Still this leaves a large proportion of persons who might be thought of as truly dropping out. The three-fold distribution of the boomers then is as follows: 42% Loyalists, 22% Returnees, and 36% Dropouts. Another way of reading the data is that 64% are currently involved in religious institutions, and 36% are disaffiliated and show little sign of re-affiliating with religious institutions.

Of interest are the trends by religious family. Much previous research suggests that the defections of the 1960s and 1970s were greatest in the more liberal Protestant and Jewish traditions. The "religious depression" of the period was brought about largely as a result of young people who dropped out of the so-called "mainline" religious congregations (Hoge and Roozen, 1979; Roof and McKinney, 1987). Some turned to the new religious movements, some turned to evangelical faiths, but most, it seems, just dropped out. Many explanations of why the more liberal, mainline congregations suffered have been given: too much emphasis on social activism, an identity-crisis brought on by a close association with American middle-class culture—which was in turmoil in the 1960s, and the loss of religious vitality within the Protestant establishment. Whatever the underlying religious and cultural reasons, for many baby boomers the religious mainline had become spiritually stale and unsatisfying. As one of our respondents said about leaving the Methodists in search of a more experiential type of religion: "There was no meat, I got fed a lot of Twinkies."

As Table 14.3 shows, the losses have been greatest for boomers growing up in the more liberal Protestant and Jewish traditions, especially the latter. Eighty-four percent of Jewish boomers have, at one time or another, dropped out of religious participation for a period of two years or more. We have only aggregate figures for Jews and cannot break out patterns for Reform, Conservative, and Orthodox constituencies because of the small size of the sample. More reliable are the data for Protestants and Catholics. Sixty percent of mainline Protestant boomers have dropped out at one time or another—a larger figure than for conservative Protestants or Catholics. Jews can drop out religiously, but are still Jews culturally, and thus still able to sustain a Jewish identity. Conservative Protestants and Catholics who drop out are perhaps better able to sustain a religious identity than mainline Protestants, given the stronger social and psychological bonds holding them to religious beliefs and values. In comparison, liberal Protestantism suffers because there is much less of a cultural boundary separating the tradition from the larger culture. As Martin Marty is fond of saying, liberal Protestants have "alumni associations," which mark their weaker and rather tenuous connections with their religious past.

Overall, men have dropped out more than women, and older boomers more so than younger boomers. The greater defection of males is common. Age differences reflect the periods in which the boomers grew up. The relation of education to dropping out is complex: dropout rates are higher for those with less than a high school education and for post-graduates, and less so for high school and college graduates. Dropping out of religious institutions in the sixties and seventies was not simply a middle-class phenomenon; it occurred at both ends of the class spectrum, among the privileged and the not-so-privileged.

The crucial question has to do with the return to active religious participation. In keeping with the patterns for dropping out, fewer Jewish and mainline Protestant dropouts have returned to their synagogues and churches: 17% and 34%, respectively. The return is considerably greater for conservative Protestants, 10 percentage points higher than for mainline Protestants. A greater return combined with fewer losses to begin with, along with net gains from switching, means that conservative Protestants enjoy a considerable advantage over mainline Protestants in sustaining their congregations. Catholics fall somewhere in the middle, with a higher return than for mainline Protestants and lesser than for conservative Protestants.

TABLE 14.3
Patterns of Institutional Involvement for Major Traditions

	Total	Mainline Protestant	Conservative Protestant	Catholic	Jewish	Other
Percent ever dropping out:	58%	60%	54%	57%	84%	50%
Of these: Percent who have returned	38	34	44	37	17	23
Current Profile:						
Loyalist	42	39	46	43	16	50
Returnee	22	21	24	21	14	12
Dropout	36	39	30	36	70	38
Total	100	99	100	100	100	100
N =	(1448)	(369)	(460)	(542)	(36)	(41)

Looking at the return in the broader context of religious family profiles, we find the following: conservative Protestants stand out among the major religious families for having the highest proportion of Loyalists, the lowest proportion of Dropouts, and the highest proportion of Returnees—-a winning combination for maintaining a vital religious tradition. Probably more than any other large religious group, conservative Protestants have been better able to withstand the corrosive influences of modern culture—the greater religious individualism and voluntarism—undermining institutional loyalty. Roman Catholics are fairly well positioned regarding their young adults, with 43% Loyalists, 21% Returnees, and 36% Dropouts. Mainline Protestants have the weakest profile among Christian groups with only 39% Loyalists, 21% Returnees, and 39% Dropouts. Jews have the weakest profile overall.

Men and women are returning in about equal proportions. Older boomers are returning more than younger boomers, consistent with their greater family and parenting obligations. With education, there is a more consistent pattern for returning than with dropping out: the higher the level of education, the lower the rate of return. One-half of dropouts with less than a high school education have returned to church or synagogue; 46% of high school graduates; 40% of college graduates; and only 30% of post-graduates. So we see that social class is a very important factor for boomer involvement in organized religion. Working-class boomers drop out, but are more likely to return to church, whereas well-educated, middle-class boomers who drop out are more likely to join the ranks of disaffiliated. This is especially the case for post-graduates, many of whom belong to the professional and "New Class" sectors.

Is there a return to organized religion? Unquestionably, there is a return. We have no historical estimates of how many youth in the past have dropped out, and then after a while, returned to active involvement. If the proportion dropping out was greater in the sixties and seventies, then there is a large pool of potential returnees. Given the sheer size of the baby boomer generation, it follows that returnees would account for a sizable proportion of the young adult population. Media accounts of a "return to religion" are not incorrect; however, the trend should be kept in perspective—returnees are a smaller proportion than the dropouts who are still outside organized religion. Only for conservative Protestants does the proportion returning come at all close to matching the figures for dropping out.

Who Are the Returnees?

Next we explore the major social and religious background characteristics of the Returnees.

Family Cycle

The most obvious explanation put forth for the return of boomers to organized religion has to do with changes in the family cycle. Boomers dropped out as individuals, but when they return, they often are married with children. There is considerable evidence in the research literature to support this argument (Carroll and Roozen, 1979; Schroeder, 1975; Roozen, McKinney, and Thompson, 1990). Married people are more settled than unmarried, and the presence of children is a stabilizing influence on young couples. The presence of school-age children especially encourages parental religious involvement. Concern for the moral and religious training of children is a factor of some importance across all religious traditions, resulting in more active participation in churches and synagogues.

A follow-up telephone interview to the Lilly Endowment boomer survey with 536 respondents showed that parenting and family situation are crucial variables. This smaller survey found that married persons with children are far more likely to be Loyalists, that is, not to have dropped out of church or synagogue at any time, and even more significantly, to have returned to active religious participation if they had dropped out. Forty-one percent of married people with children are Loyalists and 50% of all who have dropped out are Returnees—much higher than for any of the other constituencies. And it is the case that married people with children are more religious of the several constituencies on a wide array of beliefs, experiences, and attitudes toward organized religion. Data not shown here reveal them to have had less exposure to counter-cultural influences—46% say they have smoked marijuana, whereas considerably more than half have done so in all the other constituencies. They hold far more conservative views on moral issues such as abortion, unmarried couples living together, the legalization of marijuana, respect for authority, and for a return to stricter moral standards.

In contrast, married people without children are the mirror opposite. Only 16% of those who have dropped out in this category are Returnees, considerably lower than for the divorced/separated or even the singles. They rank lower than singles on all the religious items, on some items considerably lower. These findings suggest a changing subculture for married couples who have postponed having children, many of whom have dual careers. Their lower levels of religiosity fit with their more liberal views, more liberal than for singles, on such matters as the legalization of marijuana, legal abortion regardless of reason, unmarried couples living together, and acceptance of alternative life-styles. Age interacts with family situation: within the total baby boom generation married persons without children are generally older than singles, and perhaps surprisingly, tend to be less conservative than the younger wave of boomers, especially on moral and political values.

The divorced/separated are a changing profile group. Past research has often described this constituency as having low rates of religious participation. Traditional family norms are deeply ingrained in all the major religious communities, and for a long time, those whose life-styles deviated from these norms often did not feel accepted in church services and activities. Our research shows them to have the highest numbers who had left organized religion, yet are returning at levels higher than for either married persons without children or singles. That they may be returning in greater numbers is no doubt explained partly by the large proportion who have children—that is, they are single parents. As the size of the single-parent population has increased, and the norms surrounding single-parenting have changed, so have patterns of religious participation. Churches have increasingly accommodated these trends toward more diverse family-type subcultures with new ministries aimed at the needs of singles, the separated and divorced, and single parents.

Conservative Drift

Another explanation of the return to the churches is the conservative shift in social and political values during the eighties. Roozen, McKinney, and Thompson (1990) argue that a broad shift in values and attitudes was of greater impact on worship attendance than the effects of aging and family changes. By means of test factor standardization, they conclude that more than 70% of the increase in church attendance on the part of older boomers can be accounted for by a turn to more conservative social and political views. Without making a causal argument about the directionality of change, nonetheless they offer incontrovertible evidence that the religious and attitudinal changes have occurred simultaneously.

Unquestionably, there has been a shift in this generation's values and attitudes. The *Rolling Stone* Survey (see Sheff, 1988), for example, shows that attitudes of boomers have changed drastically in three areas: drug usage, sexuality, and family life. Whereas 46% in this survey admitted to using drugs when they were growing up, 74% (and 94% of parents) now say they disapprove of their children experimenting with drugs. A generation that was extremely active sexually now holds to much less permissive views for their children in the age of AIDS. But even without this new plague, the emphasis on sexual freedom would likely have diminished. Permissive attitudes on sex are incompatible with the strong emphasis on family life now expressed by boomers. Families and friendships are now both high priorities, contrary to an earlier emphasis on self as suggested in stereotypes such as the "Me Generation."

The Lilly Endowment boomer survey underscores as well the importance of changing values and priorities. Returnees are considerably more conservative in life-style issues, moral values, and political attitudes than those who dropped out. But more is involved than simply changing attitudes and priorities. If it were just that, then we would expect a more uniform, across-the-board shift in churchgoing. The research suggests that the sixties had a deep and lasting impact: those most affected by the counter-cultural trends of that era are the ones least likely now to return to the churches. Those who were exposed to drugs and rock music, who have endorsed sexual freedom, and who have engaged in demonstrations and marches during the civil rights and anti-war movements at the time are much less likely to be affiliated with organized religion today. Even if their attitudes and values have shifted in more recent times in the conservative direction, the scars from that earlier period have not vanished.

Religious Background

Returnees—unlike Dropouts—did not, for the most part, make a clean break with religious institutions when they were growing up. They dropped out but never totally left. During their adolescence and early adulthood, the age at which most religious defection occurred, they remained more involved in churches and synagogues than did Dropouts. In the Lilly Endowment boomer survey, 41% of those who have returned were attending religious services once a month or more during their youth; in contrast, among Dropouts the figure was 25%. However, Returnees are only slightly more likely to have parents who were religiously involved than Dropouts. More important than parental religiosity in predicting return to active involvement was the person's own experience and involvement during the critical period of institutional disengagement: many made a total break with organized religion, others simply took leave for a while but did not really break with their traditions.

What Kind of Return?

We know there is a return to religion on the part of boomers as described above. But what kind of return is it? How committed are the returnees to the churches and synagogues? These are crucial questions considering the social and cultural changes of the sixties and seventies. Two lines of thinking point to reduced levels of commitment for returnees: changing attitudes toward public social institutions, and high levels of cultural and religious individualism on the part of this generation. Briefly, we examine these two arguments.

There is ample evidence to suggest that members of this generation are less trusting of public social institutions. Starting in the sixties and lasting into the present, the baby boomers led the way in raising questions about the government in particular, but not just the government. Asked in 1985 by the Gallup Poll to rate a list of ten major social and political institutions without reference to their leaders, the baby boomers emerged as the least trusting of all age groups toward eight: organized religion, the military, banks/banking, public schools, Congress, newspapers, big business, and organized labor (Light, 1988:161). Asked by the Harris poll to rate the leaders of fifteen institutions in 1985, the baby boomers were the least trusting toward eight: organized religion, the military, the press, TV news, major companies, the White House, Congress, and the Executive Branch (Light, 1988:160). The trauma surrounding civil rights, the Vietnam War, Watergate, and one after another environmental disaster all heightened levels of distrust and suspicion of people in authority.

The "distancing" from institutions that many members of this generation experienced continues to shape loyalties and commitments. Data from Table

14.4 show rather convincingly that on a range of indicators of institutional religious commitment Returnees consistently score lower than Loyalists. They are somewhat less likely to consider themselves religious, to believe in God, to hold church membership, to view the congregation as important, to attend regular services, to have a strong denominational identity, and to feel closer to others of the same religion than to other people. These patterns hold for Catholics and Protestants, and for older and younger boomers.

TABLE 14.4
Religious Indicators for Loyalists and Returnees

	Loyalist (N=174)	Returnees (N=128)
Consider yourself religious	98%	92%
Definitely believe in God	94	86
Church member	88	82
Congregation important in life	91	83
Attends services once a week or more	63	56
Strong denominational identity	63	53
Feel closer to others in the same religion than to other people	45	41

A second argument is that high levels of cultural and religious individualism erode traditional religious authority. For Americans generally, religious individualism is of course quite high. But even more so for boomers, the "culture of choice" as reflected in great tolerance of diversity, open-mindedness, and respect for personal life-style preferences, has reached unprecedented proportions. The post-war generation is, in the sense in which Karl Mannheim spoke, the major carrier of cultural changes stemming from the sixties, described variously as "expressive utilitarianism" (Bellah et al., 1985) and the "new voluntarism" (Roof and McKinney, 1987). The changes reach deep in the human psyche re-ordering outlooks and orientations, away from social conformity to greater emphasis on self: wants, feelings, preferences, fulfillments, and inner experiences all get priority in a shift from an "objectivist" to a more "subjectivist" locus of control.

What this all means for religious commitment is open for considerable speculation. Yet there is reason to think that this shift, in many subtle ways, is reshaping institutional religious norms. For example, among Catholic baby boomers, 88% say that one can be a "good Catholic" without contributing money regularly to the Church; 85% say the same about going to Church every Sunday; 81% with respect to obeying the Church's teaching on divorce and remarriage. Interestingly, however, only 19% of boomers say one can be a "good Catholic" without being concerned about the poor. Boomers reject the Church's historic obligatory practices and moral teachings, yet at the same time demonstrate overwhelming support for the Church's teachings on social justice. This points less to a wholesale rejection of the Church's teachings than to a redefinition of a good Catholic now evolving among members of this generation. That the Church must increasingly listen to this generation is apparent: 95% of Catholic boomers think that the development of Church teachings should be in the hands of both the hierarchy and the laity, not just in the hands of the hierarchy alone.

We examined shifts in approaches to religious participation and found, for Catholics as well as Protestants, some changes associated with religious individualism. Because Returnees were (and still are) more caught up in the cultural whirlwinds of the sixties, we expected their institutional orientations to be even more pronounced in the individualistic, voluntaristic direction. We constructed two measures trying to get at subtle differences in orientations. One was a question on how going to church or synagogue was viewed, as a "duty and obligation" or as "something you do if you feel it meets your needs." Boomers overwhelmingly endorse the latter, and Returnees, as expected, are especially strong in endorsing this more expressive, self-oriented view in greater proportion (see Table 14.5). A second question touched upon a highly normative view about families attending church and synagogue as a unit versus the possibility of family members making individual choices about their participation. Boomers overwhelmingly endorse the normative model of family and religion, but Returnees are more caught up in the individualistic culture than Loyalists. A third of Returnees subscribe to this latter as compared to 21% of the Loyalist constituency. Returnees in the mainline religious traditions are even more individualistic in outlook than are conservative Returnees, further intensifying an already-existing problem of institutional commitment for mainline Protestantism.

That there are qualitative changes in the commitment of many boomers returning (or at least exploring the possibility of returning) to churches and synagogues appears to be unquestionable. Boomers are returning, but that doesn't necessarily mean they are joining congregations. More so than their parents, they are apt to "shop" with a consumer mentality for both a congregation and denomination that meets their personal, ideological, and family needs. There is considerable fluidity, of people switching denominations and selecting congregations because of an exciting worship leader, good music, social action program, shared concerns, self-help recovery

TABLE 14.5
Religious Individualism for Loyalists and Returnees

	Loyalist	Returnee
Which expresses your view:		
(a) Going to church/synagogue is a duty and obligation, or	23%	16%
(b) Going to church/synagogue is something you do if you feel it meets your needs	62	73
(c) both	15	11
	100%	100%
Is it important to you to attend church/synagogue as a family or should family members make individual choices?		
(a) As family	79	65
(b) Individual choice	21	32
(c) Don't know	—	3
	100%	100%

groups, religious education programs, even a large and convenient parking lot. Once boomers start attending a particular church, for whatever reason, others often come simply because of the presence of large numbers of their own generation. Quality of services offered to individuals and families is far more important than denominational heritage for most of our respondents. Personal concerns and spiritual quests shape the character of religious discourse in congregations where boomers are numerous. There is considerable yearning on the part of many to find out more about religious traditions, to explore spirituality, and to find in the great smorgasbord of religious possibilities that America offers, new spiritual insights that are meaningful and worthy of their commitment. Many are looking not only for insights, but also for ways to be of service, for opportunities to give of their time and support to causes and projects that seem worthwhile.

Future Trends

What about future trends? Can we make any projections about the religious involvement of boomers? Projections are of course risky, but we do get some clues from the age-based differences among the boomers.

Age is a major division within the boomer population: those born at the front end of the generation in the late forties are quite different from those born at the very back in the early sixties. Fifteen years apart, the two constituencies have had differing cohort experiences. Older boomers remember freedom marches and the assassination of President Kennedy; they came of age in a period of counter-cultural and political turmoil and were deeply affected by the Vietnam War. People now in their late thirties and early forties experienced the sixties head-on and were the most transformed by that momentous decade. In contrast, younger baby boomers are more likely to remember gas lines in the seventies, Three Mile Island, and Chernobyl; they came of age in a quieter time marked less by social protest than by scarcity and a return to greater inwardness; generally they have achieved an easier blend of pragmatism and idealism than those of their generation who are older. Douglas Walrath (1987) speaks of older boomers as "challengers," prone to question authority and conventionality, and the younger ones as "calculators," more inclined to see life as involving hard choices and calling for priorities.

Cohort experience and life-cycle factors interact to create distinctive religious patterns in any generation (see Roof and Walsh, 1993), and certainly this is the case for the boomers. As already observed with the NORC data, older boomers are returning to organized religion in greater numbers proportionately than younger boomers. But simply because the older boomers are returning does not mean that they are the most religious in other ways (see Table 14.6). Younger boomers are more religious on measures of personal faith and practice: they consider themselves more religious and affirm traditional Judeo-Christian beliefs and practices more so than do older members of the generation. This is true across a wide spectrum ranging from belief in the Devil to conflict between religion and science. Interesting, also, they are more inclined to say they would call upon religious institutions for "rites of passage" for themselves or for family members—for baptisms, weddings, and funerals. To say this does not of course mean that they will necessarily follow through with such rites, but it does suggest a higher level of normative religious expectations. Their greater religious traditionalism goes hand in hand with a more conservative stance generally. Younger boomers voted for Bush in 1988 in greater numbers than did older boomers, view themselves more as political conservatives, and hold to more conventional views on moral issues than older boomers.

All of this might portend an even greater return to organized religion in the 1990s. As the younger boomers grow older and assume family and parenting responsibilities, they might return to congregations in larger numbers than have the older boomers. Much depends, of course, on the churches themselves. If the churches can effectively relate to the values, life-styles, and concerns of this generation, boomers will return. Churches that are effective in this, we would expect, will be those that can create a climate where boomers

TABLE 14.6
Religious Characteristics of Older and Younger Baby Boomer Cohorts

	Older	Younger
Institutional Involvement		
Percent Loyalist	35%	32%
Percent Dropping Out		
Of these:	65	86
Percent Returnee	43	38
Percent Dropout	57	62
Personal Beliefs and Practices		
Consider to be religious	83	89
Say grace at meals	36	39
Believe in eternal life	80	83
Believe in Devil	61	67
Born again	43	45
View religion and science in conflict	53	63
Attitudes toward Organized Religion		
Consider church membership important	67	60
Would expect to call upon institution for rites for self or family:		
Baptism	71	82
Wedding	74	86
Funeral	85	90

feel comfortable and where the religious narratives encompass their own life stories. Tex Sample (1990) is surely right when he says that programming will greatly differ, depending on whether the constituency aimed at is on the cultural left or the cultural right. Upper middle-class, cultural-left people relate to journey theology and spiritual quests, whereas working-class, cultural-right people relate more to traditional family values and conventional moral and religious thinking. Multi-layered spirituality combining themes from across religious traditions will characterize the former (as one of our respondents said, "I am a Presbyterian into wholistic thinking); more orthodox Christian interpretations are held to among the latter.

Whether the boomer's religious questions and concerns will carry over to institutional commitment is the big question. Despite all the media attention to the "return of the boomers," regular religious attendance in the polls does not appear to have significantly increased. Highly voluntaristic norms of religious belonging are deeply ingrained in this generation, among younger as well as older members, and this will likely be the predominate shaping influence on styles of congregational involvement in the future. Reginald Bibby's (1987) "a la carte" style of religious belief seems to be the wave of the future for this generation, which probably means that we can expect a great deal of continued shopping around for religious themes, and even within a religious community considerable picking and choosing of what to believe and how to practice what one believes. Every congregation has its own ethos, and the extent and style of commitment will vary depending on whether or not boomers can relate their lives to what is going on in a particular locale. The congregations attracting boomers will be those that can discern the spirit of the times, and are able to respond in ways that are genuinely real, authentic, and deemed meaningful.

Chapter Fifteen

Churched and Unchurched Black Americans

Hart M. Nelsen and Conrad L. Kanagy

Three decades ago, E. Franklin Frazier (1963:85-86) predicted that the domination of the black church in the black community would decrease as blacks became "integrated into the institutions of the American community." In the ensuing thirty years the civil rights movement, court action, and federal legislation have, in fact, lowered barriers to education, jobs, and housing. Many members of the growing black middle class have migrated to the suburbs of the North and West (Roof and Spain, 1977:17). But despite the opportunity for upward mobility and integration, uncertain economic times and less government support minimized the breadth and endurance of such opportunities. According to the authors of A Common Destiny (Jaynes and Williams, eds., 1989:194-200), some blacks have reacted to both the opportunity and the uncertainty in their efforts to retain their cultural identity, and to pursue better housing, more education, and higher incomes. But others have had fewer opportunities and have been frustrated by low educational levels, poverty, and isolation within the inner cities.

This chapter will focus on recent and possible future changes in the church participation levels of black Americans, particularly in relation to social change in the black community. Frazier's thesis suggested the eventual abandonment of the black church by those who achieved integration into society's mainstream. Nelsen and Nelsen (1975:137) observed, however, that even "as conflict over basic values grew, the black church prospered" in the 1960s. Black cultural identity and its connection to the black church had remained important, irrespective of social-economic integration, so there was no reason to expect abandonment of the black church by the middle class. (See Roof and McKinney, 1987, on communal ties and sustaining beliefs.)

The black church had prospered in the South, in part because it has been the center of black community life, addressing multiple needs, not just religious concerns. The urban North, however, presented special challenges to the church; life-styles were more diverse and there was greater competition from other agencies and institutions relative to meeting community needs.

The central cities of the North, in particular, have experienced decline subsequent to Frazier's study. With increased joblessness in the inner city, upwardly mobile individuals have moved to the suburbs, resulting in social isolation for those left behind. The institutions (including churches) of the inner cities have lost the viable support they had when the community was more class-integrated (Wilson, 1987:56-57). Given the greater likelihood of middle- rather than lower-class people to participate in organizations, the decline in being churched should not be displayed by blacks in the suburbs, but rather, by the young and poorly educated in the cities of the North.

Our primary focus is the comparison of black church attendance rates across residential and regional contexts, with attention given to the differences in motivation for participation. Specifically, does the church still have strong communal ties or is it facing greater dependence upon the religious motivations of people? In the rural and urban South, blacks have been expected to belong to the church, and at least occasionally participate. In the urban North participation has been more voluntary, and more likely to be linked to the fulfillment of religious needs.

While Frazier's predictions that church participation would decline have not materialized, there are important differences in rates of participation by context, that is, by region and residence. Hard empirical data generally do not exist for carefully examining changes in black church participation since the 1950s and 1960s. We are fortunate, however, to now have two national Gallup samples—from 1978 and 1988—of unchurched and churched Americans, including significant subsamples of black Americans.[1] This allows us to look at change in black church participation over the last decade, and permits an in-depth analysis of motivations for participation across different regional and residential contexts.

In looking at the overall change in black church participation across the Gallup surveys, many will be delighted that the percentage of churched black Americans has increased from 57% to 62% over the decade. The less encouraging news is that this increase is due primarily to heightened rates among older, northern city blacks. The rates remain basically unchanged in other areas. Importantly, little has been done to correct the disproportionately great disaffiliation of young adult blacks in the northern cities, of whom about only one in three are churched.

Both past theoretical speculation and empirical data suggest that the black church is a diverse institution that has met and continues to meet different kinds of personal and community needs. This diversity is largely related to differences in the regional and residential locations of black churches. Lincoln and Mamiya (1990:15), for example, cogently argue that there can be no single view of the black church since it addresses various needs, issues, and social conditions. Our task is to employ the Gallup surveys to examine the motivations people have for being churched, and how they might differ in different social contexts. Differences in motivation of black religious participation can be understood to represent a continuum from communal/involuntary on the one end, to voluntary/personal on the other. Movement toward the voluntary end should be evident as one moves from the South to the North.

Relationship Between the Black Church and Society: Differences by Context

Historically, settings for the black church ranged from the rural South to nonsouthern urban centers. In the rural South, blacks had low educational levels, and church and religion could provide some escape from an oppressive society. In the southern city, the theodicy could shift somewhat to mastery of this world. The church in the nonsouthern city imperfectly met the needs of migrants who came from various types of church settings. (On the roles of black churches in Chicago from 1910–30, see Grossman, 1989.) In some settings and times, especially in the cities of the 1930s, some black churches withdrew from community involvement, and revivalistic, sectarian storefront churches prospered. (See Lincoln and Mamiya, 1990:209 who summarize this "deradicalization thesis.")

But the contexts and the churches have changed. The civil rights movement demanded that churches in all settings address race issues. The rural church and the southern urban church have deep roots in the community, providing significant networks and resources for leadership. The black church in the nonsouthern city was not as successful at dominating the community or in attracting as high a proportion of residents for participation in either religious or extra-religious functions.

Lincoln and Mamiya (1988:364-65, also 1990) identify the rural church as the "historical and cultural reservoir of the 'black folk' religious experience." Today this experience is affected by changes in occupational distribution, with many of the young leaving rural areas as small, individual farms decline in number. They also observe the growing class split in the black community. Those now in the middle class have experienced the benefits of civil rights politics, while those in the lower class continue to have needs that the rural church should meet.

In the inner cities of the North, in particular, conditions are not favorable for the church. Factories have closed in the central cities, and upwardly mobile residents have moved to the suburbs. Those left behind, subject to persistent poverty and sometimes identified as the "underclass," have become increasingly isolated. The traditional institutions of help—schools, churches, social agencies, police, and the ward and precinct political system—have been greatly weakened. (For the changing conditions of the Chicago inner city from the 1940s to the present, see Lemann, 1991.)

Participation: Communal Versus Voluntary Motivations

Nelsen, Yokley, and Nelsen (1971:10) have noted how the entrenchment of the church in the black community can secure nearly involuntary membership. This is particularly evident in the rural South (Nelsen and Nelsen, 1975:61-62, 84). The migration to the northern cities meant greater choice among life-styles, as well as less social control by the churches. The northern, urban church became one institution among many, and increasingly focused on meeting religious needs, whereas the southern church traditionally performed economic, educational, and social functions, as well. Stump (1986:312) observed that church attendance depends more on strength of belief and less on a sense of social obligation in areas where denominational affiliation is diverse and rates of membership are low. Where there is greater cultural pressure to attend, a weaker association exists between personal religious orientation and participation. According to Stump (1987:145-46), "In the more secular North . . . many black social institutions rival the church in importance, and frequent attendance consequently tends to be limited to individuals possessing high levels of religiosity."

Analyzing data from 1978, Nelsen (1988:407) wrote that participation in the black church is more likely to occur for personal religious reasons in the metropolitan non-South than in the South. An important variable accounting for church membership and attendance in the non-South was the subjective importance of religion to the individual—Nelsen's best predictor of whether individuals were involved in the church. Only about half of the metropolitan residents in the non-South indicated that religion was very important to them, compared to three-fourths of their southern counterparts and about 85% of the nonmetropolitan Southerners. Since personal religiousness is especially important in the nonsouthern setting for church participation, and since religion is not very important to as many individuals there, we can understand the lower level of church participation.

In contrast, the southern socialization pattern, especially in rural areas, is to encourage, even demand, participation in the church. Individuals are churched as part of fitting into communal networks. Carmichael and Hamilton (1967:103) identified middle-aged women who were especially influential in the black community as "staunch church members." The civil rights movement drew upon this characteristic and, no doubt, further strengthened the power of the black church in the rural areas and cities of the South.

Participation in the black church in the South is related to the building and retention of community there; it is semi-involuntary. Involvement in the church in the urban North more directly reflects personal religious interest or expression; it is voluntary. Given the greater diversity of life-styles in the cities, the lower rates of personal religiousness in the North, and the historical pattern of the church dominating the community in the South, church participation on the part of blacks should be higher in the South than in the North.

The suburbanization of blacks in both the South and North introduces a new consideration for the black church.[2] In the North, suburbanization has occurred as an element of class mobility, with the central cities retaining especially lower-class, poorer, and isolated blacks. Hence, the participation rate ("churched") should be higher in the northern suburbs than in the northern central cities. A prediction about the southern suburban areas would be less certain because suburban residences around southern cities have generally included agricultural areas. Such areas have lower educational, occupational, and income levels on the part of blacks than is true for the cities, according to Roof and Spain (1977:15-17). Given the high churched rate expected for both the southern cities and the rural South, movement to the southern suburbs should lead to a lower rate of participation. While northern suburban areas should have lower rates than such areas in the South, these rates should still be higher than those of the northern central city. A higher degree of personal (or voluntary) reasons for participation should exist for the southern and northern suburbanites and the northern central city residents, while a more involuntary, or communal, basis for participation should exist for the rural and central city residents of the South.

Gender differences in rates of being churched should be tied to communal reasons for involvement, with women more likely than men to be churched. Hence, we would expect gender differences particularly in the nonmetropolitan areas and central cities of the South. Where the basis for participation is more voluntary we would also expect educational and age differences in rates of being churched. Especially important for voluntary participation would be personal religiousness.

Given our theorizing, we would rank the various region-residence areas according to their projected levels of church attendance in the following order from high to low: the rural South, the central cities of the South, the suburban South, the suburban North, and the central cities of the North. The rural South and central cities of the South have been identified as having a strong communal basis for participation (semi-involuntary), while the other three places of residence should be more associated with voluntary participation.

Data and Definitions

Using face-to-face interviews, the Gallup Organization has now collected two sets of data on "unchurched" and "churched" Americans—in April 1978 and March 1988. We use the unweighted data sets in our analysis. In 1978 a second survey added additional unchurched Americans. Since the unchurched were not oversampled in 1988, our reanalysis of the 1978 data set—for comparisons with 1988—excludes the unchurched oversample of 1978. The 1988 data set oversampled blacks and Hispanics. We exclude the Hispanic oversample, but include the additional blacks who were interviewed.

To be "churched" means to be a member of a church and to have attended in the past six months, apart from weddings, funerals, or special holidays. Individuals without data for this measure were excluded from the study.

Our regional and residential categories for reporting the 1988 data will be the rural (nonmetropolitan) South, southern (central) cities, suburban South, suburban North, and northern (central) cities. We exclude the rural (nonmetropolitan) North because there are only fifteen blacks in the sample with that residence. When we use the term "North" or "northern" we are referring to non-South or nonsouthern.

TABLE 15.1

**Demographic Differences in the Percentage of Churched
Black Americans, 1978–1988**

	Year of Study	
Demographic Categories	1978	1988
Total black American	57%	62%
Residence		
Metropolitan	46	59
Rural (nonmetropolitan)	91	81
Metropolitan by region		
North	40	51
South	60	70
Northern metropolitan by age		
Age 40 and older	43	63
Under 40	38	37

Findings: Rates of Being Churched

As noted earlier, the percentage churched has increased from 1978 to 1988, and this increase is especially visible among urban blacks (suburban and central city) age forty and older (see Table 15.1). As drugs and drug-related crime increasingly trouble the inner city, it should not be surprising to find older blacks involved in churches for the comfort that can be found there (see Anderson, 1990).[3]

There are substantial differences in rates of being churched across the five regional-residential categories (see Figure 15.1). The highest rate of being churched in 1988 occurs in the rural South (85%), followed in order by the southern city (76%), the southern suburb (64%), the northern suburb (57%), and the northern city (49%). In examining the effects of different motivations for church participation, we will see in Table 15.2 that their strength varies with context. That is, the strength of any particular motivation's relationship to church participation will be different in different regional-residential categories—or, in statistical language, there is a significant interaction between motivation and context.

FIGURE 15.1
Percent Churched by Region-Residence

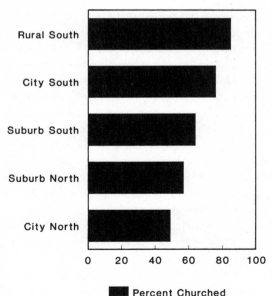

Religious motivations should be significantly related to being churched in areas where church involvement is voluntary, that is, where individuals are churched for personal rather than communal reasons. In Nelsen's analysis of the 1978 data, "importance of religion" was the most powerful predictor of being churched, especially in the metropolitan non-South. For the 1988 analysis we are dividing the "metropolitan" category into suburb and city. We also have two different measures of religiosity: importance of religion and belief in life after death. Table 15.2 presents the percentages of churched across the five residential categories for each of our two religious motivation measures.

The table shows that importance of religion and belief in an afterlife are significantly related to being churched in the three regional-residential areas that depend on voluntary participation—the southern suburbs, the northern suburbs, and the northern cities. In these three contexts, religious motivations for church participation are strongly evident. In the other two locations—the rural South and the cities of the South—importance of religion and belief in an afterlife are not significantly related to being churched. In these two settings individuals participate less out of a personal religious orientation and more because being churched is expected—on a communal, or semi-voluntary basis.[4]

Consistent with the latter, Table 15.2 also shows that gender is significantly related to being churched in the rural South and in the cities of the South; women being more affected by the tug of communal ties toward church participation than men.

Table 15.2 also shows the differential effect on church participation across region-residence for education and age—both of which should show a more voluntary pattern if our thesis is correct. As shown in the table, high school graduates are more likely to be churched, but the power of the education variable (dichotomized in the table as high school graduate or not) is relatively low. An analysis not shown in the table (with education trichotomized—less than high school, high school diploma, and some college or more) and employing the five residential-regional categories and age, (dichotomized), produced a stronger effect for education (beta = .18). Without being controlled, age tends to suppress the impact of education on being churched (older blacks tend to have lower educational levels and are more likely to be churched). The percentages churched with education trichotomized are: less than high school, 50%; high school diploma, 67%; and some college or more, 71%.

Of all the blacks under forty years of age, 52% are churched, compared to 71% of those forty years and older. Looking at age differences within each place of residence, we find that significance is obtained only for the residents of the northern cities, although significance is approached in the northern suburbs as well.

TABLE 15.2
Percent of Churched Black Americans in 1988 by Selected Religious and Demographic Predictors, Within Regional and Residential Categories

Selected Predictor	South Rural	South City	South Suburb	North Suburb	North City	Total	Eta/ Beta°	R°
Region/Residence°°	84.6	76.4	63.8	57.4	48.7	61.9	− .27	
	(52)	(72)	(69)	(54)	(158)	(404)	− .21d	.46
Importance of Religion								
Less than very	85.7	68.4	20.5	30.8	22.4	33.9		
important	(7)	(19)	(15)	(13)	(67)	(121)		
Very important	84.4	79.2	75.9	65.9	67.8	73.9	.38	
	(45)	(53)	(54)d	(41)a	(90)d	(283)	.34d	.46
Believe in afterlife								
No/Undecided	77.8	64.7	47.8	35.5	27.6	41.1		
	(9)	(17)	(23)	(17)	(58)	(124)		
Yes	86.0	80.0	71.7	67.7	61.0	71.2	.29	
	(43)	(55)	(46)a	(37)a	(100)d	(281)	.25d	.38
Age								
Under 40	76.5	74.3	60.0	50.0	32.9	52.1		
	(17)	(35)	(40)	(24)	(76)	(192)		
40 and older	88.6	78.4	69.0	66.7	61.5	70.9	.19	
	(35)	(37)	(29)	(27)	(78)d	(206)	.18d	.35
Gender								
Men	75.9	64.1	65.6	53.8	42.5	56.3		
	(29)	(39)	(32)	(26)	(80)	(206)		
Women	95.7	90.0	62.2	60.7	55.1	67.8	.12	
	(23)a	(33)b	(37)	(28)	(78)	(199)	.13b	.32
Education								
Not high school	82.8	70.0	55.6	50.0	41.2	57.4		
graduate	(29)	(20)	(27)	(14)	(51)	(141)		
High school	87.0	78.8	69.0	60.0	52.3	64.4	.07	
graduate	(23)	(52)	(42)	(40)	(107)	(264)	.10a	.29

°ANOVA and MCA were used to test the three-way relationship, including interactions, among churched, region-residence, and the selected religious and demographic, second predictors. Eta is for the relationship between the second predictor and being churched, *without* controlling for region-residence. Beta is for the relationship between the second predictor and being churched, controlling for region-residence. "R" reports the strength of the two predictors together. One-Way ANOVA was used to test the significance of differences in the percentage churched within each of the five regional-residential categories for each predictor.

°°Significant (c) interaction occurred between residence-region and importance of religion in predicting being churched; the Eta and Beta for region-residence and "R" are from that analysis.

Significance: (a) p < .05;   (b) p < .01;   (c) p < .02;   (d) p < .001.

Using the importance of religion, age, and education as predictors, we find that all three of these variables were significantly related to being churched in northern cities. Older blacks, those who report religion to be important to them, and the better educated are more likely to be churched. Each of these three predictors relates to voluntary participation, a characteristic of the suburban and northern experience.

Our two Gallup surveys included six statements about the church that neatly capture criticisms that blacks have made about the church over the years, for example, that "there's no real religion among the members" or that the "church places too much emphasis upon money" (see Drake and Cayton, 1944:418-19). The 1978 data on these statements were analyzed by Nelsen (1988). Not all of the statements, however, describe characteristics of the black church that further develop the distinction between communal and voluntary bases for church participation. One exception to this is the following statement: "Churches today have a clear sense of the real spiritual nature of religion." This statement measures the likelihood that an individual would participate in a church based on his or her perception of the religious or spiritual nature of the church. Overall, 53% were churched if they disagreed with the statement, and 69% were churched if they agreed with it (this difference remains significant when place of residence is controlled, as can be seen in Table 15.3). Of those who disagreed with the statement, about three-fourths of the rural and central city southerners were churched compared to less than half of suburbanites and those residing in the central cities of the North. But in the northern cities the most significant differences exist in the

TABLE 15.3

**Percent of Churched Black Americans by Response to:
"Churches Have a Clear Sense of the Real Spiritual Nature of
Religion," Within Regional and Residential Categories**

| | South | | | North | | | Eta/ | |
	Rural	City	Suburb	Suburb	City	Total	Beta°	R°
Disagree/	78.9	73.9	57.7	57.1	36.4	52.6		
Undecided	(19)	(23)	(26)	(28)	(77)	(173)		
Agree	87.9	77.6	67.4	57.7	60.5	69.0	.17	
	(33)	(49)	(43)	(26)	(81)a	(232)	.13°°	.32

°See Table 15.2 note for an explanation of eta, beta, and R. Agreement or disagreement was one predictor, and region-residence the second predictor. Significant interaction was not present for these two variables in predicting the rate of being churched.
°°Significant @ $p < .01$.

rates of being churched by view of the statement: 36% of those not identify-ing churches as especially religious were churched, compared to the 61% being churched of those believing that churches have a clear sense of what is religious.

Future Needs and Dreams

It has been observed that regional contrasts persist in black religion even though conditions associated with escapist, otherworldly religion have declined overall (Nelsen, 1988; see also Stump, 1987:150-51). One explana-tion examines "important adaptive changes" that have taken place in the black church (Glenn and Gotard, 1977; see also Lincoln, 1974; Ellison and Sherkat, 1990:553). Furthermore, black churches in different regions have adapted differently in response to their region's unique changes. Seculariza-tion theory, as it addresses the differentiation of the black church and reli-gion vis-à-vis other institutions, proposes that individuals increasingly partici-pate in organized religion because of religious commitment, rather than out of communal pressures or because of nonreligious functions performed by religious institutions.

With increased levels of education, religion would not thrive as an escapist orientation but, rather, as one that affirms experiences in the here-and-now. (See Mukenge, 1983:204, on the role of the church in "maintaining mental health and psychological stability.") Some individuals would find special meaning conveyed by churches, while others would not. Religious participa-tion is now more a matter of personal choice, particularly in the suburban areas and the northern cities.

The secularization and differentiation of the black church (with member-ship increasingly related to religious commitment), seems to occur in an ever-evolving fashion. Nevertheless, the black church meets various needs in diverse settings. Lincoln and Mamiya (1990:11) point out that "black churches are institutions that are involved in a constant series of dialectical tensions." As black Americans adjust to changes, including reversals, in eco-nomic prosperity and access to mainstream America, the black church offers differing expressions of needs and dreams.

The 1988 data set allowed us to examine differences within the metropoli-tan areas, between suburbs and central cities. There are similarities between these two places of residence in the non-South, with importance of religion and belief in an afterlife the best predictors of being churched. These are not significantly related to being churched in the rural South or in the cities of the South. An especially interesting aspect of the 1988 data set is the similar-ity between the suburban South and the North in terms of patterns that predict being churched. Furthermore, the percentage churched in the suburban South more closely resembles that in the suburban North than in the southern cities.

Even though blacks in the rural South or the central cities of the South are more likely to indicate that religion is very important to them, to believe in an afterlife, and to be churched; being churched is not related to personal religiousness in these regions. This is not because otherwise religiously oriented persons in the rural and urban South are not churched, but rather because in these areas otherwise nonreligiously oriented persons are also churched. We characterize religious participation in these locales as being communal—blacks are expected to participate and they do (particularly women). In the other three locations—the two suburban areas and the central cities of the North—participation is more voluntary and is related to the personal religiousness of the individuals.

Considerable literature documents the finding that younger Americans are less likely to be involved in churches (Hoge and Roozen, 1979). For blacks in 1988, one-half of those under forty years of age were churched, compared to seven-tenths of those forty years and older. In each of the five residential categories, when age is related to being churched there is a dramatic decline in the percentage of those under forty years old being churched (see Table 2). Three-fourths of the rural Southerners and those of the central cities in the South under forty are churched, but only one-third of those in the central cities of the North are so. While the data are not shown here, younger blacks with lower educational levels in Northern cities display particularly low rates.

Lincoln and Mamiya (1990:397) call attention to "the growing class divide between the coping sector of middle income blacks and the working poor, and the crisis sector of the dependent poor," noting that this is a major challenge facing the black church. In their word, a "reconnection" must occur between the black church and the urban black poor, given the increased isolation that characterizes the residents of the inner cities. The growing problems of the inner city suggest that the unchurched young adults of today will not easily become churched tomorrow, despite a considerable increase in the rate of being churched from 1978 to 1988 for blacks forty years and older in the cities of the North.

In the rural South and in the cities of the South, participation will remain high as church and black community remain firmly intertwined. Future participation trends in these areas, therefore, will be driven largely by demographics—more specifically, general population growth or decline. Future rates in the suburbs are difficult to predict because the driving force in these areas will be the local black churches. Attendance will depend on the ability or willingness of the local church to link its religious message to issues of meaning associated with new social status, and a continued search for a black identity within this new status.

The situation in the northern cities is not encouraging. Participation among older adults should remain relatively high as increasingly marginalized blacks continue to remember the church, and turn to it for traditional piety and refuge. But the future of the black church in the city is really dependent in the long term on the black church's ability to involve the less educated, younger adults who currently have little predisposition—and possibly even disdain—for the church. This is perhaps the greatest and least understood challenge for the black church. Whether the established churches in the central cities—many with members who commute from their new residences in the suburbs—can be successful on a large scale remains to be seen. Their success will depend on programs designed to reach youths in the inner cities, to encourage their education, to mentor, and to be a bridge for their eventual church participation. The racial crisis that erupted in Los Angeles in 1992 has spurred middle-class blacks to reconsider their commitments (or the lack of these) to the poor of the inner city, and discussion has emerged about the need to reinvest there. It might be hoped that the black churches of the middle class will lead the initiative to provide resources and leadership for such a development. It is also possible that inroads into the inner city might be made by streetwise evangelists. Strenuous efforts by both types of religious organizations would testify to the diversity of mission and functions of the black church.

Chapter Sixteen

Participation and Commitment Among American Catholic Parishioners[1]

Michael R. Welch

This chapter will help church leaders understand the factors that influence the participation of their parishioners. Such an understanding is important, given the changes that have occurred among the largest and most prominent religious denominations during the past thirty years. As transformations in mainline American Protestant denominations become increasingly evident (Chaves, 1989; Greeley, 1989:21-66; Iannaccone, 1990; Roof and McKinney, 1987; Wuthnow, 1988) and signs of some convergence between these mainline bodies and American Catholicism appear (Caplow, 1991:71), questions about the nature of Catholic piety and types of institutional religious commitment have also resurfaced. Many of these questions center around changes in the devotional practices of Catholics (e.g., the apparent decline in the use of "confession"). Several researchers (D'Antonio, Davidson, Hoge, Wallace, 1989; Hoge, 1981, McNamara, 1985), particularly Greeley (Greeley, 1989; 1991; Greeley, McCready, and McCourt, 1976), have focused on the historical declines in Mass attendance that occurred during the late 1960s through the middle 1970s (more specifically, 1968–75) to assess the impact and meaning of these events. In summary, Greeley indicates that Catholics' attendance rates have "restabilized" since 1975 and offers primarily a life-cycle explanation to account for the observed trends (1989:42-56).

Beyond these broad-scale interpretations of changes in Catholics' religious behavior, much remains to be learned about how specific aspects of parish and community environments influence the religious participation of parishioners. This task is complicated, however, by the fact that participation takes different forms, with some being more meaningful than others for certain parishioners; that some forms of participation receive greater emphasis, depending on the specific type of parish; and that many distinctly different influences on participation can be identified.

Taking these complexities into account, this chapter focuses on four kinds of religious participation that Catholic parishioners display, and on three different types of influences on participation—characteristics of individuals themselves, characteristics of their parishes, and characteristics of the community in which a parish is located. In particular, questions about the effects of such contextual properties, as the last two factors are called by sociologists, are important for at least two reasons.

First, parishes and their surrounding community environments are the central locus of religious activity for most Catholics. It is in these units that Catholics are schooled, worship, wed, and have fundamental moral values instilled and behaviors reinforced (see, Greeley, Durkin, Shea, Tracey, and McCready, 1981, for a supporting view). Thus, if we wish to understand better what shapes the religious behavior of parishioners, we cannot ignore the unique attributes displayed by specific parishes.

Second, the connection between contextual attributes and parishioners' religious participation helps pastors, church planners, and administrators understand what factors influence the vitality and mission of parishes. Without precise knowledge about those aspects of parish life that are most likely to foster the religious participation and commitment of parishioners, church leaders may be led to invest scarce resources in unproductive or marginally beneficial programs.

Because of the substantive and methodological complexity of the analysis, the sections that follow flow in what may strike some as a rather peculiar order. Specifically, I begin with the conclusions and then invite the reader to proceed through the detailed analysis that produced them. That is, I first summarize the findings' implications for church leaders, and then discuss the sources of information and measures of religious participation used in the study. Next, I summarize and test simple hypotheses about factors that relate to church participation and commitment among Catholic parishioners. Finally, I turn to an analysis of the relative importance of contextual and personal factors, concluding with an overview of the major influences on each of the four kinds of participation that were studied.

Implications for Church Leaders

The findings of the following analysis have several important implications for pastors and other church leaders. Although the conclusions listed here do not exhaust all possible implications that may bear on the development of church programs or pastoral practice, they do identify the more important sets of factors that relate to participation in the life of the parish.

1. Different aspects of religious behavior are not equally responsive to the same sets of forces. Thus, Catholic leaders should clearly recognize which aspects of religious commitment they wish to nurture when they design programs to enhance parishioners' levels of involvement. As will be seen from the data reported, particularly in the discussion of Table 16.4, few factors show uniform influence across the four religious behaviors that were analyzed.

2. Among the sets of variables that pastors or other church leaders can control most easily, two stand out as key factors for promoting the increased involvement of parishioners: the presence of specialized ministries and programs within a parish, and the level of faith sharing that occurs. Compared with other sets of institutional variables that leaders can manipulate, these variables make statistically significant and relatively important contributions in predicting different aspects of involvement when the remaining factors have been controlled. It might be advisable, therefore, to identify specific programs and ministries parishioners find most fulfilling and to implement activities, such as adult faith-sharing groups, which focus on the discussion of religious beliefs or other related issues. Although this mechanism is presently incorporated in some adult religious education programs, it may merit more serious attention on the part of pastors or diocesan administrators.

3. Most of the sets of variables that have the strongest linkages to religious behavior are not under the control of church leaders. We should be realistic and not expect substantial increases in parishioners' levels of involvement to flow from many changes that pastors initiate. In short, it appears that altering relatively ineffectual programs in a variety of ways is probably wasted effort.

4. If pastors or church planners wish to increase parishioners' involvement, they should focus on maximizing the overall social integration of parishioners within their parishes. This one set of individual-level variables, more than any other, appears to be the most critical factor for increasing commitment and involvement among rank-and-file parishioners. Thus, any efforts that enhance an authentic sense of belonging and a connection to fellow parishioners are not misdirected. However, such goals are sometimes difficult to implement. Too often merely a transitory illusion of gemeinschaft is achieved. A more enduring community evolves only after years of interaction have produced an abiding trust among parishioners, and between priest and people. Forced attempts at "easy" intimacy achieved through such simplistic, fash-

ionable mechanisms as after-Mass coffeehouses probably do little more than run up the parish's bill for doughnuts. Because efforts to build an authentic sense of community take time, it might also be wise for dioceses to reconsider mandatory policies that stipulate a pastor's maximum length of tenure in a specific parish.

5. All of the preceding suggestions underscore the benefits to be gained from conducting more frequent and intensive needs assessment studies within parishes. Such studies can help pastors assess the value of current programs, activities and ministries, and identify new opportunities for service. Only by collecting this type of empirical evidence can a local pastor reach informed judgments about how programs really work and whether they effectively promote involvement or commitment.

Measuring Religious Participation and Related Factors

Data and Measures

Information on the levels of religious participation and commitment displayed by American Catholics in and through their local parishes was obtained from the Notre Dame Study of Catholic Parish Life (hereafter abbreviated as CPL). This study, funded by the Lilly Endowment, collected several kinds of information (e.g., surveys of individuals and parishes, ratings drawn from participant observations, census data for a subset of sampled parishes, and so on) on a representative cross-section of parishes within the United States during the winter and spring months of 1983–84 (see Leege and Welch, 1989, for a more complete description).[2]

The following four measures of religious participation constitute the dependent variables for all of the analyses: (1) number of parish activities in which a parishioner is involved (Parish Activities), (2) estimated amount of money the parishioner's family contributed to the parish during the year (Financial Giving), (3) frequency of participation in basic worship (e.g., Sunday Mass and Communion) activities (Basic Devotion), and (4) frequency of participation in traditionalistic (e.g., Stations of the Cross, Novenas, and so on) religious rituals (Traditionalistic Devotion).[3]

Because of the extensiveness of the data (more than 700 variables) a series of preliminary analyses was conducted to reduce the sets of predictor variables to a more manageable number that could be incorporated into the final analyses.[4] These initial procedures were governed by both empirical and theoretical considerations. A complete list of variable wording and coding is available in the Supplemental Appendix.

Measures of Local Contextual Variables: Properties of the Community

Following Roof et al. (1979), several measures of the community environment in which a parish is located were included in preliminary analyses, and designated as "local contextual" variables. Only measures displaying significant and theoretically interpretable correlations with the measures of participation were retained. As a set, five variables were used to represent factors ranging from community ecology (e.g., urban environment), to factors that shape local community culture (e.g., number of families, decreases in younger segment of population) and opportunities for choosing a place of worship (e.g., presence of another Catholic church in the community). Measures of these variables are described in the Supplemental Appendix (Table A16.2).

Measures of Local Institutional Variables: Aggregate and Global Properties of the Local Parish

"Local institutional" variables refer to characteristics of the local parish church and its congregation (Roof et al., 1979:212). In some instances these variables represent congregations' attributes that are reflected in the mean scores (or relevant percentages) of individual members of each parish; hence, they refer to aggregate properties of the congregation. These properties differ from the constituent characteristics of individual parish members from which they are derived and represent aspects of the encompassing social or psychological "climate" of a parish (e.g., the social class standing of an individual parishioner compared to the socioeconomic composition of the parish as a whole). Other variables, however, represent institutional properties of the parish that are distinct from such congregational attributes (e.g., the presence of a parish school). Twenty-six simple measures of local characteristics are included in the final analysis, along with three more complex measures (see Supplemental Appendix, Table A16.1 for a complete description).[5]

Measures of Individual-Level Variables: Personal Attributes of Parishioners

Individual-level variables represent personal attributes of parishioners, such as race, gender, marital status, involvement in community organizations, and level of satisfaction with aspects of the parish—to name but a few. These, and other characteristics like them, shape the behaviors and activities of parishioners in both secular and religious spheres. Thus, twenty measures of these characteristics are included in the final analysis (see Supplemental Appendix, Table A16.1).

Selected Hypotheses Under Study: A Multi-level Approach

The sets of variables described in the preceding sections are linked to patterns of religious participation that American Catholic parishioners display. But the nature of these linkages remains to be formalized. In the remainder of this section I present several selected hypotheses, grouped by the kind of variables involved in the predicted relationship and by the theory from which the prediction derives. Simple hypotheses drawn from extant theories, or whose derivation is obvious, will simply be presented and not discussed, so I can devote sufficient space to new hypotheses.

Because the principal goal of this chapter is to examine the predictive ability of different types of variables related to religious involvement in one's parish, hypotheses are framed to reflect simple zero-order relationships. Examination of more complex (e.g., conditional or net) relationships involving specific predictors is beyond the scope of the chapter.

Selected Hypotheses Involving Individual-Level Variables (H1–H7)

Correlations between the measures of the individual-level variables and the four measures of religious participation are reported in Table 16.1 (only relationships in which $r > \pm .10$ and significant at $p < .05$ are reported).

Considering only the statistically and substantively significant correlations in the table, it is clear that all of the following individual-level hypotheses (H1–H7) receive support—but to varying degrees.

Child-rearing Theory (H1). Building on previous research (e.g., Carroll and Roozen, 1975; Hoge and Carroll, 1978; Nash and Berger, 1962), it is predicted that parishioners who have at least one child under the age of eighteen should be more involved in religious activities and show higher levels of commitment than parishioners who are childless or have older children. Support for this theory in our analysis, however, is rather weak (see Table 16.1), with only one relationship attaining the criterion levels of substantive and statistical significance. Among Catholics, the presence of younger children within a family is only moderately associated with participation in parish activities.

Boomer Cohort Hypothesis (H2). Because of the historical experiences that shaped their lives during a critical period in the process of religious development (teenage years to the middle twenties), parishioners who are members of the "baby boom" birth cohorts should be less committed and religiously involved than parishioners who are members of earlier cohorts (H2). Although some might contend that cohort effects do not explain variations in religious involvement among Catholics (see Greeley, 1989:42–56)

TABLE 16.1

Zero-order Correlations Between Individual-Level Variables and Measures of Religious Participation[*]

Hypo-theses	Individual-Level Variables	Measures of Participation			
		Basic Devotion	Tradition-alistic Devotion	Parish Activities	Financial Giving
H_1	Have child under 18			.108	
H_2	WWII Cohort				.121
	Baby Boomers	−.147	−.253		−.167
H_3	Moral Traditionalism	.180	.271		.151
H_4	Theological Progressivism		−.203		
H_5	Geographic Mobility		−.245		
	Conversations: Pastor	.223	.356	.289	.151
	Conversations: Parishioners	.226	.232	.344	.132
	Community Attachment	.264	.304	.301	.171
H_6	Non-Catholic Spouse	−.161			−.131
H_7	Satisfies Spiritual needs	.174	.210	.201	
	Rated quality: Liturgies				
	Rated quality: Homilies	.122	.194		
	Rated quality: Pastoral Care				
Demographic Variables					
	Gender (Male=1)				.147
	Presently married		−.137		.138
	Race (Black=1)		.106		
	Education		−.152	.111	.182
	Voluntary organizational memberships	.128	.111	.241	.133

[*]Only coefficients ≥ ± .10 and p < .05 are reproduced.

Roof and McKinney (1987) suggest that the Boomer cohorts function as carriers of a "new voluntarism" that may be reflected in the religious behavior of several denominations, including, perhaps, Catholicism.

This hypothesis (H2) receives a relatively high degree of support from the data presented in Table 16.1: the baby boomer cohorts show consistently lower levels of participation (on three of four measures of participation) compared to their Catholic counterparts of earlier generations.

Value Structure Theory (H3). Parishioners holding more traditionalistic social values should display higher levels of participation in religious activities and higher levels of commitment than parishioners holding less traditionalistic values (H3). We tested this prediction by examining relationships between the Moral Traditionalism scale and our four measures of religious participation. Support for the hypothesis is generally consistent, with positive relationships ranging from moderate to substantial (see Table 16.1).

Doctrinal Belief Theory (H4). Parishioners who hold the most conservative, orthodox beliefs about church doctrine or practices should be more religiously involved and committed than those who adopt more progressive, heterodox beliefs (H4). Support for this prediction should be manifest in a negative relationship between the Theological Progressivism scale and the measures of participation. Given the single significant relationship presented in Table 16.1, it seems clear that this hypothesis is only weakly supported. It appears only to be true for Traditionalistic Devotion.

Social Integration Hypothesis (H5). Parishioners who are more strongly integrated into the parish community should be more religiously active and committed (H5). This hypothesis predicts positive relationships between the variables representing Conversations with Pastor, Conversations with Other Parishioners, Community Attachment, and our measures of participation. Because migration disrupts social integration (Welch and Baltzell, 1984) a negative relationship between Geographic Mobility and our religious participation measures would also support the hypothesis. Results from our analyses provide relatively strong support for this hypothesis across each of the four types of participation (see Table 16.1).

Reinforcing Values Hypothesis (H6). Compared to nonmarried parishioners or those married to Catholic spouses, parishioners who are married to non-Catholic spouses should display lower levels of commitment and participation in religious activities (H6). The relative absence of shared religious values within a "mixed marriage" is thought to diminish intra-familial pressures toward Catholic participation of the Catholic partner. Actual conflicts over religious practices might also dissuade the Catholic partner from participating in religious activities more fully (see Welch, Johnson, and Pilgrim:188). As can be seen in Table 16.1 , there is moderate support for H6. Respondents having non-Catholic spouses are less likely to show high levels of basic devotionalism and financial giving than Catholics who are married to Catholic spouses or who are single.

Member Satisfaction Hypothesis (H7). Parishioners who are more satisfied with the parish and its worship activities should be more likely to show high levels of religious participation and commitment within that parish (H7). This hypothesis, framed at the individual-level, is simply a corollary of aggregate-level hypotheses that were formalized and tested earlier by Roof, Hoge, Dyble, and Hadaway (1979:202). At the operational level positive relationships between the four measures of participation and commitment and the following variables would constitute supportive evidence: Parish Satisfies Spiritual Needs, Parish Satisfies Social Needs, Rated Quality of Liturgies, Rated Quality of Homilies, and Rated Quality of Pastoral Care.

There is very modest support for this hypothesis: only seven of the relevant twenty relationships are in the predicted direction and sizable enough to warrant consideration. In general, parishioners who feel that their social needs are being satisfied within a parish are more likely to participate at higher levels than less satisfied peers. Satisfaction of spiritual needs and the rated quality of preaching also show a moderate relationship to devotional styles parishioners display (Table 16.1).

Correlations representing relationships between several basic measures of demographic characteristics (gender, level of education, marital status, and race) and religious participation are also reported in Table 16.1, as are correlations between the number of memberships in voluntary organizations a parishioner reports and the levels of participation he or she displays. Education shows the strongest positive relationships to Parish Activities and Financial Giving, but shows a nearly equally strong negative relationship to Traditionalistic Devotion, as might be expected. Variables representing race, gender, and marital status also show a varying pattern of relationships to the different measures of participation. In contrast, however, parishioners who report a tendency to join various civic organizations are also consistently more likely to participate in a variety of devotional practices (both basic and traditionalistic) and parish activities, and to donate more of their annual family income to the parish.

Selected Hypotheses Involving Local Contextual Variables (H8–H9)

In this section, the focus shifts from hypotheses involving characteristics of individual parishioners (e.g., whether they are members of the "baby boom" generation, or are married to a non-Catholic, and so on) to hypotheses that predict how characteristics of the local community culture relate to the level of participation parish members exhibit. As a result, these hypotheses address questions about the extent to which geographically defined environments may shape the religious behavior of parishioners. Relevant correlations are presented in Table 16.2.

TABLE 16.2

Zero-order Correlations for Relationships Between Local Contextual Variables and Measures of a Parishioner's Level of Religious Participation°

Hypotheses Represented	Local Contextual Variables	Measures of Participation			
		Basic Devotion	Tradition-alistic Devotion	Parish Activities	Financial Giving
H$_8$	Parish Competition				−.110
	Decline in % Population Under 18	−.102			−.131
	% Growth in Number of Families				
H$_9$	% Growth in school-age population		−.173		
Community Type Variables					
	Urban		.101		.123
	Suburban		−.173		

°Only coefficients $\geq \pm .10$ and $p < .05$ are reproduced.

Opportunity-for-Selection Hypothesis (H8). Parishioners living in an area in which more than one Catholic parish is located should display higher religious participation and commitment than parishioners who live in a town or place in which there is only a single parish (H8). The presence of multiple parishes within a single town allows Catholics the opportunity to select the one parish that best meets their needs. If individual members are most likely to attend the parish that offers greatest overall satisfaction, it seems equally likely that their participation and commitment will be enhanced. This reasoning does not ignore canonical parishes and the status of parish boundaries, it merely recognizes what may be an important tendency among some younger and middle-aged Catholics to engage in "parish shopping" (see, Leege and Welch, 1989:142–44). Positive relationships between the Parish Competition variable and the measures of participation and commitment are predicted.

The results from Table 16.2 provide at best weak and mixed support for H8. Only one correlation is sizable and that relationship is negative rather than positive, suggesting that the availability of multiple parishes within a community may actually have an adverse influence on parishioners contributions to their "home" parish.

Family/Youth-oriented Subculture Hypothesis (H9). Parishioners who are served by parishes located in areas that are experiencing a growth in the school-age population and the number of resident families should be more religiously active and committed than their counterparts living in parishes not located in such an area (H9). This hypothesis posits that increases in the school-age population and the number of families residing in an area give rise to a salient familistic/youth-centered subculture that emphasizes involvement in community organizations (ostensibly to advocate the interests of families in the earlier stages of the family life cycle); intergenerational transmission of moral and religious values; and the promotion of a bourgeois, hygienic social environment favorable to family life. The normative focus of such a subculture should directly and indirectly reinforce churchgoing and religious commitment among all members within the area who are exposed to it. In addition, such cultural pressures may induce parishes to increase their repertoire of religious and social services, making them more attractive to all types of parishioners and not merely those with younger children. Such attractiveness would seem likely to promote relatively high levels of participation and support. Note, this is not a hypothesis about the individual participation of young families, but rather posits that the presence of young families creates an atmosphere that positively influences everyone's participation.

This hypothesis also receives only weak and mixed support: only three of twelve relevant correlations surpass ± .10 and the relationships vary considerably in both magnitude and direction across the different types of participation. Growth in the school-age population within a community is linked to lower levels of Traditionalistic Devotion, as might be expected; but such growth shows only negligible relationships to other measures of participation. Declines in the younger segment of the population (those under 18) are also linked to lower levels of Basic Devotion and Financial Giving; however, growth in the number of families present within a community bears no substantial relationship to these or any other forms of participation.

Although no specific hypotheses were presented regarding the type of community in which parishes are located, correlations relating urban and suburban location to levels of participation are also reported in Table 16.2. In general, parishioners from suburban parishes show higher levels of giving than their counterparts in rural and small town parishes (the comparison category) and lower levels of traditional practices. Parishioners from urban parishes tend to display slightly higher levels of Traditionalistic Devotion than their suburban contemporaries.

Selected Hypotheses Involving Local Institutional Variables (H10–H20)

Institutional parish variables denote characteristics of specific parishes, such as organizational features (e.g., number of registered members), parish programs, or aspects of the parish subculture (e.g., the level of moral traditionalism that exists within a parish). These variables represent a third level of factors that can affect the degree to which parishioners participate. Correlations involving these variables are presented in Table 16.3.

Status Group Theory (H10). Parishioners located in parishes whose congregations are characterized by high levels of socioeconomic status (SES) should display higher levels of religious participation than their counterparts in congregations having lower levels of SES (H10). Following Weber (Gerth and Mills, 1958:186), the aura of high status that attaches to such parishes may foster high levels of participation among many individual members principally because of their desire for vicarious identification with the life-style of the higher social classes.

The two substantial correlations reported in Table 16.3 provide moderate, but mixed, support for H10. Parish-level SES is positively related to Financial Giving, but the substantial, negative correlation between the measure of parish-level SES and Traditionalistic Devotion indicates that parishioners in parishes characterized by high status tend to show lower levels of traditional devotional activities than parishioners in lower status parishes.

Boundary-Maintenance or Closed Community Hypothesis (H11). Parishioners who are members of a parish congregation that is characterized by high levels of homogeneity and a concern for boundary-maintenance should display higher levels of religious participation and commitment (H11). Derived from Kelley's (1972) arguments, this hypothesis suggests that a strong sense of group boundaries and relative cultural homogeneity should promote a heightened group distinctiveness, and, accompanying it, an intensification of commitment expressed in higher levels of participation among parishioners.

Support for this hypothesis would be represented by positive relationships between the Index of Ethnic Homogeneity Within Parish, the Level of Religious Endogamy Within Parish, the Aggregate Level of Religious Boundary-Maintenance Within Parish, and our four measures of participation and commitment. As can be seen in Table 16.3, H11 receives little support. Only the measure of parish boundary-maintenance is positively related to one of the participation measures (Traditionalistic Devotion); the remaining eleven correlations are negligible in magnitude and mixed in their direction.

TABLE 16.3
Zero-order Correlations for Relationships Between Local Institutional Variables and Measures of a Parishioner's Level of Religious Participation[*]

Hypotheses Represented	Local Institutional Variables	Measures of Participation			
		Basic Devotion	Tradition-alistic Devotion	Parish Activities	Financial Giving
H_{10}	Parish Level SES		−.190		.192
H_{11}	Ethnic Homogeneity				
	Religious Endogamy				
	Religious Boundary-Maintenance		.210		
H_{12}	Geographic Immobility among Parishioners		.202		
	Attachment to Parish		.168		
	Frequency of Conversations among Parishioners		.157	−.118	−.109
H_{13}	Of Moral Traditionalism		.113		
H_{14}	Theological Progressivism		−.222		
H_{15}	Parish Complexity				.139
	Organized Planning Process Used in Parish				
	Number of Registered Families		−.109		.133
H_{16}	School in Parish				.103
H_{17}	RCIA				.162
H_{18}	Evangelization Programs				
	Faith Sharing			.128	
H_{19}	Bible Study				
	Ministry to Sick				
	Ministry to Elderly				
	Ministry to Divorced		−.153		
	Social Programs				
H_{20}	Satisfaction with Religious Education		.150		
	Satisfaction with Spiritual Needs		.150		
	Satisfaction with Social Needs		.152		
	Satisfaction with Pastoral Care		.188		

		Measures of Participation			
Hypotheses Represented	Local Institutional Variables	Basic Devotion	Tradition-alistic Devotion	Parish Activities	Financial Giving
	Rating of Homilies		.131		
Other Measures of Parish Climate					
	Mean Age		.177	− .106	
	Average Organization Memberships			.100	
	% of Parishioners Holding Leadership Positions in Organizations			.109	

°Only coefficients ≥ ± .100 and p < .05 are reproduced.

Group Cohesion/Gemeinschaft Hypothesis (H12). Parishioners who are members of parishes characterized by relatively high levels of group cohesiveness should display higher levels of religious participation and commitment (H12). Parishes that are characterized by stable networks of interacting parishioners have a greater opportunity both to transmit religious norms and to enforce them (see, Welch and Baltzell, 1984:77, 80; White, 1968; Wald, Owen, and Hill, 1990, for evidence in support of this reasoning), thus promoting higher levels of participation among members. Parishes that display such social integration are also likely to generate collective bonds of attachment that promote a gemeinschaft-like environment. This type of parish environment may, in itself, promote greater involvement because it is satisfying to many members who are searching for a sense of community. Indicators of group cohesion such as the Aggregate Level of Geographic Immobility, Mean Level of Attachment to Parish, and Mean Frequency of Conversations Among Parishioners should display positive relationships to the four measures of participation if the hypothesis is supported.

Five of the twelve correlations representing this hypothesis (see Table 16.3) are at least moderate in magnitude (± .10 ± .20) and four of the five correlations are in the predicted direction. Measures such as the frequency of communications among members that reflect the extent of in-group interaction within a parish seem to be central in maintaining group integration— and are ultimately linked to religious participation. Overall, it would appear that H12 is at least moderately well supported by the data.

Subcultural Traditionalism Hypothesis: General Values (H13). Parishioners who are members of parishes characterized by relatively high levels of traditionalistic values should have higher levels of religious participation and commitment (H13). In parishes where highly traditionalistic moral values predominate, the normative climate should incline members toward high levels of involvement. This parish-level corollary to H3 is tested by the relationship between the Climate of Moral Traditionalism Within Parish and the four measures of religiosity. Positive relationships are predicted.

This hypothesis gains some weak support from the analysis, with parishioners from parishes that display a highly traditionalistic climate showing higher levels of Traditionalistic Devotion. None of the other three relevant relationships are both statistically significant and substantively important.

Subcultural Traditionalism Hypothesis: Doctrinal Values (H14). Parishioners who are members of parishes characterized by conservative or highly orthodox beliefs about church doctrine or practices should be more religiously involved and committed (H14). Conservative parishes should promote and enforce subcultural norms that reflect their orthodox views: e.g., frequent Mass attendance, reception of the sacraments, and a generally high level of involvement in parish life. The potential intolerance of these types of parishes may give them considerable normative power. A negative relationship between Aggregate Level of Theological Progressivism Within Parish and our participation measures would provide support for the hypothesis.

Again, there is only weak support for this hypothesis: one of four relevant relationships is in the predicted direction and sizable enough to merit examination (see Table 16.3). The linkage involves the climate of doctrinal progressivism and patterns of traditional devotion.

Anti-bureaucracy/Anti-impersonalism Hypothesis (H15). Parishioners who are members of larger parishes that have a more bureaucratic form of organization should be less religiously involved or committed than their counterparts in small, less bureaucratic parishes (H15). Consistent with elements in Dudley's reasoning (1977), parishioners may be repulsed by what they perceive to be the impersonalism and inauthenticity of larger, more complex parishes that often develop an emergent bureaucratic character. Thus, the relatively unattractive organizational aspects of these parishes may depress involvement and lead to defection on the part of some parishioners.

This hypothesis leads to the prediction that indicators of high levels of bureaucratic organization (Level of Parish Complexity and the presence of an Organized Planning Process Used Within Parish) would be negatively related to the participation and commitment measures. The Number of Reg-

istered Families in Parish should also be negatively related to the four religiosity variables. H15 receives only mixed and weak support from the data in
Table 16.3. Only three of twelve relationships are at least modestly strong
and one relationship is even inverse (Table 16.3).

Parish School-as-Magnet Hypothesis (H16). Parishioners who are members of parishes that have a school should be more religiously active and
committed than their counterparts in parishes without schools (H16).
Despite some ambivalence about the costs and relative drain that parish
schools place on parish resources, it is often argued that schools produce a
dynamism that attracts members and increases their involvement in parish
activities. The extent of this involvement, however, is not well understood. Is
this dual process of attraction and enhancement confined to the sector of
social activities or does it extend to more purely religious activities as well?
At the operational level, the hypothesis predicts a positive relationship
between Presence of School in Parish and the measures of religious participation and commitment.

Support for H16 is also somewhat weak. The presence of a parish school is
positively related, to a moderate degree, to higher levels of giving among
parishioners, but it is not meaningfully connected to the other three types of
participation.

Level of Demand Hypothesis (H17). Parishioners who belong to parishes
that make relatively significant demands on their members should display
higher levels of religious participation and commitment than their counterparts in less demanding parishes (H17). Kelley (1977) emphasizes the importance of a congregational environment that places demands on its members
and he believes that such demands actually enhance commitment. In studying group dynamics, social psychologists have also contended that groups
that impose relatively severe initiations on new members as evidence of their
commitment often succeed in engendering a highly intense commitment.
This enhanced commitment is usually viewed as a by-product of rationalizations used to relieve any cognitive dissonance that was associated with meeting the original demands. In short, many members may convince themselves
that their initial effort was worthwhile by devoting even more time and energies to the group. Conversely, groups that require less of their members may
be perceived as less worthwhile and, as a result, will be less likely to evoke
strong commitment from members.

Only one indicator of demands placed on members by a parish is available
in the data: whether the parish has a program for the Rite of Christian Initia-
tion (RCIA). Although this program applies to converts, its presence in a

parish provides at least partial evidence for assessing the membership requirements a parish imposes. As with H16, support for H17 is weak and rests on a single substantial positive relationship linking the presence of the RCIA program to financial contributions (see Table 16.3).

Faith Sharing and Outreach Hypothesis (H18). Parishioners who belong to parishes in which members frequently discuss religious beliefs should show higher levels of participation and commitment (H18). Discussing one's faith with others, usually in the context of small Bible study groups or other similar groups that operate within a congregation, has been viewed by some church growth scholars (e.g., Raines, 1961; Schaller, 1975) as a singularly important mechanism for promoting a dynamic congregational environment. In Catholic parishes, where faith-sharing practices have changed markedly since the influence of Vatican II reforms on parish life at the grass-roots level, the same patterns may now be promoting greater involvement among rank-and-file parishioners.

Two measures in our data can be used as indicators to test this hypothesis: whether Evangelization Programs (are) Used in Parish and the Aggregate Level of Faith Sharing Within Parish. Both measures should display positive relationships to the measures of religious commitment and participation.

This hypothesis receives only very weak support from the data. The use of evangelization programs within a parish is not connected to any of the measures of participation, at least not in any important way. Moreover, even a climate that promotes faith sharing among parishioners shows only a single, important, moderately positive relationship to one form of participation—Parish Activities (Table 16.3).

Program Specialization Thesis (H19). Parishioners who belong to parishes that offer a variety of specialized programs or ministries should display higher levels of religious participation and commitment (H19). The availability of specialized programs or ministries within a parish increases the likelihood that individuals will have their particular religious needs met and, as a result, are more likely to exhibit high levels of involvement.

This hypothesis leads one to predict positive relationships between the measures of religious commitment and participation and five binary variables that represent the presence or absence of the following parish programs: Bible Study, Ministry to Sick, Ministry to Elderly, Ministry to Divorced, and Presence of Social Service Programs Within Parish.

In Table 16.3, only two of twenty relevant correlations are of sufficient magnitude to consider, and only one of these correlations is positive. As a result, one can conclude that H19 receives only very weak support. A specialized program may enhance the activity level of the target group served by the program; but there is no evidence in our data that any particular kind of specialized programming creates a more general climate of participation.

Satisfying Parish Hypothesis (H20). Parishioners who belong to a parish that is viewed as highly satisfying by its members should be more religiously involved and committed than their counterparts from less satisfying parishes (H20). This hypothesis is simply the parish level corollary to H7 presented earlier. It predicts positive relationships between all sets of parish level measures of congregational satisfaction (e.g., Congregation's Level of Satisfaction with Religious Education, Satisfaction of Congregation's Spiritual Needs, Satisfaction of Congregation's Social Needs, Congregation's Level of Satisfaction with Pastoral Care, Congregation's Rating of Homilies) and our measures of religious participation and commitment.

Table 16.3 reveals an interesting, but weak, pattern of support for this hypothesis. Four of the five measures of satisfaction display moderately positive relationships as predicted, but with only a single type of participation: Traditionalistic Devotion. No other forms of participation are linked to the group-level measures of satisfaction in a consistent way.

Finally, Table 16.3 also presents correlations between the measures of participation and three other measures of parish climate: the average age of parish members, the average number of organization memberships held by parishioners, and the percentage of parish members who hold leadership positions in voluntary organizations. As can be seen from the table, each of these variables is related to an individual's participation in parish activities, but not to most of the other types of participation (the exception being the relationship between the average age of members and Traditionalistic Devotion). Mean age of parish members also exhibits a moderate negative relationship to Parish Activities, although the two measures that tap voluntary organization membership are positively related to this activities variable.

Comparing the Relative Explanatory of the Different Sets of Variables

To assess the relative importance of the different sets of variables for explaining variations in parishioners' patterns of religious participation and financial contributions, a hierarchical regression model was used. The model effectively summarizes the relative contributions made by each set of variables after the preceding sets of variables have been included in the analysis. Although this approach has some limitations, it is well suited to our analytical task.[6]

Sets of variables were entered into the analysis based on measurement level and presumed causal primacy. For this analysis, sets representing attributes of local community contexts were treated as "givens" and entered into the regression analyses first, followed by sets representing characteristics of individual parishioners. Sets of variables representing characteristics of the local parish (i.e., local institutional variables) were entered last, because these characteristics seem to be most often shaped by the preceding blocks of variables and not vice versa. Within the larger blocks of individual-level, contextual, and institutional variables, the order of entry for the separate sets of constituent variables was again based on assumed causal primacy, but relative to variables within the same general category (e.g., individual-level variables were compared to other individual-level variables, local contextual variables were compared to other local contextual variables, and so on).

Results of these multiple regression analyses are summarized in Table 16.4. A more detailed reporting is contained in Supplemental Appendix A16.2.

TABLE 16.4
Variance Attributable to Sets of Individual, Contextual, and Institutional Variables (Incremental Change in Adjusted R^2)[*]

Sets of Variables	Basic Devotion	Traditionalistic Devotion	Parish Activities	Financial Giving
Local Contextual Variables	.019	.009	.015	.040
Individual Level Variables	.168	.260	.268	.176
Local Institutional Variables	.024	.026	.304	.250
Total R^2 for Model Including all Blocks of Variables	.211	.295	.304	.250

[*]Blocks listed in the same order of entry used in the analysis.

Predicting Participation: What Influences Matter Most?

Several patterns in these results are most interesting. Overall, the multilevel models reported in Table 16.4 appear to do best in accounting for an individual's level of involvement in parish activities (total R^2 = .304) and participation in traditionalistic worship (total R^2 = .295), although the models are also fairly successful in explaining levels of basic devotion (total R^2 = .211) and the financial contributions one's family makes to a parish (total R^2 = .250). But it is also apparent that the eight sets of individual-level variables as a total block exert by far the greatest impact on all the measures of religious behavior. Data in Table 16.5 indicate that the individual-level variables account for between 70% to more than 88% of the total adjusted variance explained for each of our participation measures. By comparison, selected features of the local context in which parishes are situated generally have the least impact on parishioner's religious behavior relative to the blocks of individual-level and local institutional variables (with only one exception). Institutional variables representing characteristics of the local parish exhibit more impact, but even then these sets of institutional variables do not account for much more than 12% of the total adjusted variance associated with any of the four models.

TABLE 16.5
Percentage of Adjusted Total Variance in the Measures of Religious Behavior Explained by the Set of Individual-Level, Local Contextual, and Local Institutional Variables°

Sets of Variables	Basic Devotion	Traditionalistic Devotion	Parish Activities	Financial Giving
Local Contextual Variables	9.0%	3.1%	4.9%	16.8%
Individual-level Variables	79.6	88.1	88.6	70.4
Local Institutional Variables	11.4	8.8	6.5	12.8

°Based on increments to adjusted R^2 reported in Table 16.4.

It is also clear that particular sub-blocks of variables are more important for explaining some aspects of participation than others. For example, although a parishioner's demographic characteristics and level of social integration into the parish community are important predictors of all types of religious participation (see Table 16.6), one's satisfaction with his or her parish is important, surprisingly enough, only for understanding a parishioner's involvement in parish activities.

Table 16.6 actually reveals more commonalities than differences, however, in those sets of factors that shape different kinds of participation. For each of the types of participation, individual characteristics of parishioners are by far the most influential predictors we can identify. Local context variables such as Family/Youth Culture Orientation and Community Type, appear to be helpful only for understanding variations in basic devotion and giving, but their explanatory contributions for the other participation measures, though often statistically significant, are rather inconsequential. Finally, relative to the other blocks of variables, measures of institutional characteristics appear to be relatively unimportant for predicting participation.

TABLE 16.6

Specific Blocks of Variables That Are the Strongest Predictors of Religious Participation (Only Blocks That Account for ≥ 1% of the Total Adjusted Variance Are Represented)

	Measures of Religious Participation						
	Basic Devotion		Traditionalistic Devotion		Parish Activities		Financial Giving	
Variables	Variance Explained	Variables	Variance Explained	Variables	Variance Explained	Variables	Variance Explained	Variables
Social Integration	8.6%	Social Integration	10.5%	Social Integration	15.6%	Democratic Characteristics	8.4%
Demographic Characteristics	3.2	Birth Cohort	5.3	Voluntary Organization Memberships	5.1	Social Integration	3.6
Birth Cohort	2.6	Demographic Characteristics	4.4	Demographic Characteristics	4.0	Birth Cohort	3.4
Family/Youth Culture Orientation	1.4	Moral Traditionalism	2.1	Satisfaction with Parish	1.6	Moral Traditionalism	1.2
Voluntary Organization	1.2					Family/Youth Orientation	1.0

In summarizing the more specific patterns that appear for each of the types of participation represented in Table 16.6, it is clear that basic devotional participation is most responsive to such things as the parishioner's level of social integration, demographic characteristics and birth cohort, number of voluntary organizations to which he or she belongs, and prominence of youth and younger families within the local community. Traditionalistic devotion, however, is more strongly influenced by purely individual factors, such as a parishioner's degree of social integration, demographic characteristics, birth cohort, and the traditionalism of his or her moral values. Characteristics of individuals, particularly level of social integration, demographic characteristics, organizational memberships, and one's overall satisfaction with the parish, are also most influential in shaping participation in parish activities. Finally, although financial giving is indeed most responsive to individual-level factors (namely, demographic characteristics, social integration, birth cohort, and traditionalistic moral values), some influences from the local community context (type of community and the prominence of familial or youth-oriented segments of the community) are important in influencing what parishioners contribute.

Chapter Seventeen

Church Growth in North America:

The Character of a Religious Marketplace

C. Kirk Hadaway

What is happening?" So Hoge and Roozen (1979) begin their conclusion to *Understanding Church Growth and Decline: 1950–1978.* I could start similarly. Or, the question could be posed in the past tense: "What *happened* to churches and denominations over the past decade?" The present tense still seems appropriate because the changes that began with the first rumble of Martin Marty's "seismic shift" continue to shape religion today.

The studies in this book examine denominations, congregations, and individual religious participation from many angles. Taken together, this research tells us much about the nature of religion in America. The studies also are linked by a common concern with growth (or the lack of growth). This final chapter draws from all three sections and related literature to describe how churches and denominations grow or fail to grow in the current religious marketplace.

The Times, They *Were* A-changin'

The 1960s were a watershed decade for mainline denominations. In the first few years, mainline denominations were growing numerically—as they had since the colonial era. By the mid-1960s, however, the mainline began to decline in membership. These declines slowed in the mid- to late-1970s, but did not stop. In fact, mainline denominations continue to lose more members than they gain. Historians suggest that this downturn is nothing new. And it is true, in several other eras Protestant denominations failed to keep up with the growth of the American population. But in the 1960s, mainline Protestant denominations not only failed to pace population growth, they also experienced membership *decline*. This was new, and its effect on the collective psyche of mainstream American Protestantism was profound.

Since only mainline denominations declined numerically and since the declines began in the 1960s, explanations for membership loss tend to focus on conservative/mainline differences and on the impact of the sixties counter-culture. This approach sheds some light on the problems of the mainline, but paints a somewhat distorted picture of conservative denominations and cultural/demographic change. The chapters in this volume present a more balanced perspective.

The shape of American society and American denominations during the 1950s, 1960s, and 1970s sets the stage for understanding the current religious scene. A quick survey of major changes across these decades provides needed clarity.

Denominational growth rates dropped in the 1950s as a direct result of declines in the birthrate.

Rates of membership growth surged in the 1940s for all denominational families (see Hunter 1987:205). It was an atypical era in many respects. During this decade marriage rates climbed to record levels, and the baby boom began. The church capitalized on these changes by following new families to the suburbs and providing family oriented programming.

The birthrate peaked in the early 1950s and began to decline before the end of the decade. This decline accelerated as more women entered the work force and oral contraceptives became available in the 1960s. At the same time, rates of denominational membership growth dropped. The declines were steep and parallel.

Changes in social and religious values influenced the church in the sixties.

The cultural ethos of the 1960s affected churches in several ways. Changing values regarding divorce, birth control, age of marriage, and optimal family size led to *additional* declines in the birthrate. The birthrate eventually dropped below replacement level fertility for white Americans. Further, birthrates were especially low among highly educated persons—the primary constituency of the mainline.

Churches also were affected by changing values regarding church membership, church attendance, and the proper role of religious authority. Young adults, in particular, were more likely to question the value of religious institutions. They were less likely to participate in churches. In fact, many young adults dropped out of religion altogether (Glenn, 1987).

We can speculate that declining birthrates would not have led to actual membership losses in the mainline if additional cultural and demographic changes had not occurred in American society during the sixties. The rising divorce rate, dramatic increases in labor force participation among women, as well as delayed marriage and child-rearing were all linked to changing cultural values. Smaller families, for example, were not only considered to be more practical from an economic perspective, they also were considered a morally appropriate response to the "population explosion."

> **Conservative denominations were affected by cultural and demographic changes, although not to the extent of the mainline.**

Declining rates of membership growth affected all denominational families in the 1950s and early 1960s. This fact did not register with denominational leaders at the time because net increases in membership remained substantial. In fact, as pointed out in the first chapter, mainline membership losses were seen as aberrations in the early years of decline. At the same time, growth concerns were considered less important than other church priorities. Serious efforts to understand the declines and reverse them did not start until the mid-1970s—a decade after the losses began.

Because of close ties to mainstream culture, the liberal mainline was hit harder by social change than other denominations. Mainline families had fewer children on average than conservative Protestant families. In addition, the children of mainline families were more likely to drop out of the church once they became adults. Mainline denominational programs also were affected. In the 1960s and 1970s, church planting and evangelism became lower priorities for the mainline (see Greer, chapter 3).

This Church Shopper Went to Market; This Church Member Stayed Home

The counter-culture "cooled" long ago, although the values of the sixties' generation did not die. Instead, they were absorbed into the value structure of the dominant culture. As a consequence, two counter-cultural values persist: a distrust of institutions (formerly, the establishment) and the importance of "doing your own thing."

Hardly anyone says they are against the "establishment" anymore, nor is the phase "do your own thing" part of everyday speech. Yet, these orientations still survive. Baby boomers, in particular, retain little taken-for-granted respect for institutions and traditions. They also believe people should be free to live life on their own terms—so long as no one gets hurt. When fused with the long-standing tradition of individualism in America, these changes lead to a kind of "religious consumerism."

According to Roof and Johnson (chapter 14), "More than their parents, they (boomers) are apt to 'shop' with a consumer mentality for both a congregation and denomination that meets their personal, ideological, and family needs." Similarly, Marler and Roozen state in chapter 12, "Our analyses show that the increasing dominance of religious consumerism, as a form of cultural individualism, is the most important change in the American religious marketplace of the late 1980s." Bibby (chapter 13) makes similar observations about the Canadian situation. In fact, the consumerist approach of "religion a la carte" in Canada is further developed than it is in the United States.

To use Marler and Roozen's terminology, North Americans feel free to choose church or not, and the "church choice" is increasingly dependent on personal tastes more than a background of traditional belief and practice. This context of increased freedom of choice "cuts both ways" in relation to church involvement. "'Choice' includes both the choice to participate, as well as the choice not to participate in the life of religious institutions" according to Marler and Roozen (chapter 12). Indeed, many have chosen to opt out of religion altogether. Yet for others, religious individualism as church consumerism works to clarify commitments. Those who choose church in the nineties do so more for their own satisfaction and interest than social habit, parental legacy, or ethnic tradition.

The social and cultural changes we describe are neither "bad" nor "good" for churches in North America—at least from an organizational perspective. They do present a challenge, however, because churches historically are slow to change. Yet in this religious marketplace, change is essential because successful churches are churches that respond quickly to the preferences of increasingly careful church shoppers. This aptly describes the approach of a new breed of entrepreneurial congregations. Churches like Willow Creek Community Church in Illinois and Saddleback Valley Community Church in Southern California were organized from their inception to appeal to consumer oriented baby boomers. Their growth is nothing short of phenomenal. Perhaps it goes without saying that the theological and ethical implications of such approaches will be the subject of much debate among theologians and church leaders.

The Situation in the Denominations

Given the changing demographic and cultural context of the United States (and Canada), what is the situation in the denominations and their churches? Clearly, these shifts affected everyone. Yet the religious sector not only was influenced, it also responded. A few of these reactions made the situation worse from a growth perspective. For example, the mainline went with the flow of the culture and de-emphasized evangelism. Other responses, like the emergence of megachurches and the parachurch movement, are clear evidence of the resilience of American religion.

Considering the diversity of denominations and their churches, it is likely that some churches will always be growing somewhere. The mainline may now be on the sideline, but there are many mainline congregations that buck the trends and grow. Conversely, many conservative congregations are in decline. Nevertheless, it is possible to characterize the situation in each denominational family from the perspective of that denomination as well as the local church or parish.

Mainline Protestants

Mainline Protestantism has many growth related problems. Oddly enough, however, a few denominational leaders insist that the liberal mainline—in particular—is poised for growth. These leaders suggest that denominations like the Episcopal Church and the United Church of Christ now have a clearer sense of identity (strongly liberal—rather than theologically mixed) and are ready to move forward. Few admit a possible scenario: that persons who didn't fit the new liberalized denomination left or chose not to join in the first place. Although, continuing liberal-conservative clashes within mainline denominations even raise questions about such liberal unanimity. Theologically conservative members remain, even in liberal denominations, and usually are very active in their churches.

Put bluntly, mainline denominations retain few visible characteristics that suggest a future of growth. Birthrates remain extremely low among the predominantly white, middle-class constituency of most mainline churches. And as the "baby bust" generation enters childbearing years, the prospects for a new surge in the number of young white families with children are not promising. It is also an open question whether boomers who returned to church because of their children will remain active once their children reach confirmation age (Marler and Hadaway, 1993).

Rates of denominational switching and disaffiliation are high for mainline Protestants (Roof and McKinney, 1987; Hadaway, 1991*b*; Hadaway and Marler, 1993). Denominational loyalty is low. Mainline baby boomers are less active in church than their parents were and the children of boomers are receiving much less exposure to church traditions and beliefs than the boomers themselves.

According to Marler and Roozen (chapter 12), liberal Protestants "embody a consumer orientation toward religion to a much greater extent than either conservative Protestants or Roman Catholics." Many liberal Protestants attend infrequently. Some have gotten the message from their churches that infrequent attendance is acceptable (Marler and Hadaway, 1993). But for liberal Protestants who do attend, the church choice is best characterized by the phrase, "what church?" Marler and Roozen find that liberal Protestants are less motivated by denominational or theological loyalty. Instead, they choose a church and attend "because it is warm, provides personalized meaning, has a clearly 'spiritual' focus, is not 'too organized,' is not 'too restrictive' and has just enough—but not too much—emphasis on social justice." Unburdened by guilt or communal restraint, mainliners are free to attend wherever (and whenever) they want without making a specific commitment.

At the national and the judicatory level, evangelism and new church development were re-emphasized in the 1980s (Greer, chapter 3). Yet, these programs still do not receive the priority (or funding) they did prior to the 1960s. Consequently, their impact on growth is limited. The number of new churches started annually, for instance, does not nearly equal the number of churches lost.

If mainline denominations are serious about reversing their declines, greater effort must be made. New church planting strategies must be created, and leaders in existing congregations must learn to appreciate the value of evangelism and adult Christian education. New priorities mean renewed programmatic actions. Thus, training and resources are necessary. Finally, it seems clear that one key for future growth is the ability of mainline denominations to reach beyond their traditional white constituency—without losing it. As Green and Light have shown, the ABC has been successful at the former, but not the latter.

Both the liberal and moderate mainline have large numbers of strong, stable churches. Some of these churches responded to cultural and demographic changes and grew. Few, however, harnessed the kind of entrepreneurial spirit that seems necessary for rapid growth. Mainline denominations would benefit from a greater variety of church types (including innovative entrepreneurial churches).

Simply trying to be "the church for all people" in a community is no longer enough in the new religious marketplace. The day of the generalist is gone. The market savvy specialist is more in keeping with the times. Openness to change is required, as is an open orientation to the world. That means acceptance (something that mainline churches often do well) and the willingness to tell others about one's product. Implied in this statement is the fact that the churches must have products—that is, something specific to sell. Churches in conservative denominations are programmatically oriented. They provide programs fashioned to meet people's needs and interests. Mainline churches, by and large, do not. They must provide people oriented programs if they are to compete—not with conservative congregations, but for their own constituencies.

Conservative Protestants

The differences between some conservative denominations and the mainline are only a matter of degree. The conservative branches of the Lutheran family (Lutheran Church, Missouri Synod and Wisconsin Evangelical Lutheran Synod) certainly resemble the Evangelical Lutheran Church in America (which is considered mainline) more than they resemble the Southern Baptist Convention. The same is true for the Cumberland Presbyterian Church. These conservative branches of mainline denominational families, along with the Southern Baptist Convention, share three traits: slow growth, bureaucratic structure, and biblical conservatism. They vary greatly in other respects: polity, evangelistic orientation, and theological heritage.

Two questions are of most interest regarding these denominations. Why are they growing, and why are they growing so slowly? One obvious reason for their growth is that mainstream conservative denominations have a considerably larger percentage of congregations that are growing rather than declining. Some of this is due to the context. The United Methodist Church and the Episcopal Church, for instance, might have grown rather than declined over the past few years if over 80% of their churches were located in the South (as is the case for the Southern Baptist Convention). Even considering contextual factors, however, mainstream conservative denominations are more growth oriented than liberal/mainline denominations. Particularly in the Southern Baptist Convention, new church development and evangelism receive strong emphasis. Such actions flow from an evangelical ideology.

Mainstream conservative denominations also tend to be programmatically strong—they provide excellent training and abundant resources for their churches. A high priority on adult Christian education programs is part of this, as is the effort of denominational agencies to provide resources with a clear doctrinal agenda at modest cost. Denominational seminaries reinforce this emphasis by offering training in specialized program areas.

Considering all these strengths, why are mainstream conservative denominations not growing faster? These denominations share something else with the mainline. Their largest group of churches are plateaued—neither growing nor declining rapidly. By and large, these stable congregations are neither innovative nor market driven. Instead, they are supported by tradition and a clear sense of the way things "ought" to be done. Many baby boomers find such churches rather stilted, dull, and even unfriendly. They lend stability to a denomination, but they prevent rapid growth.

Another reason for the slow growth of mainstream conservative denominations may be simply their high level of expectations. These denominations expect their members to be involved. They are not "strict" in Kelley's sense, but the norms for active membership are different from those of the mainline. Therefore, Marler and Roozen conclude that "Conservative Protestants are very clear about what church they belong to and attend" and "Conservative Protestant membership is increasingly characterized by a set of inherited, biblically focused beliefs." The result is an active, committed core membership. Southern Baptist and Lutheran churches tend to hold onto their members. Lacking the spiritual fervor and lively worship of charismatic churches, however, mainstream conservatives are less able to replace those they lose. Their growth remains heavily dependent on relatively high birthrates and membership retention.

The Southern Baptist Convention differs from other mainstream conservative denominations in that it has many entrepreneurial churches that seem only peripherally "denominational." These churches are market driven, innovative, and quite conservative. In this respect the Southern Baptist Convention resembles the Assemblies of God, rather than the Lutheran Church, Missouri Synod. These megachurches often see themselves as benefiting the denomination more than the other way around. And this may be true. Such churches are a major source of growth in both the Southern Baptist Convention and the Assemblies of God (see Marler and Hadaway, chapter 2; and Hadaway, 1991c).

The Assemblies of God, and many smaller evangelical sects, share the theological conservatism and evangelistic orientation of the Southern Baptist Convention. They share few other characteristics, however. They have fewer heavily institutionalized, nongrowing congregations, higher rates of new church development, more additions through denominational switching, and higher rates of denominational growth.

Indeed, Pentecostal/Holiness groups exhibit a movement quality. Members tend to be "true believers" who attend "religiously" and give generously. True sectarians, they are less influenced by the culture. Thus, they are able to grow in very unlikely circumstances. The unique combination of doctrinal clarity and organizational flexibility increases the chances that these churches will grow in good times and bad. Further, parachurch resourcing has made them market-wise and their experiential theological framework has made them, curiously enough, "touch points" of expressive individualism.

Nevertheless, with flexibility and responsiveness comes volatility. These denominations exhibit a "boom or bust" pattern of growth or decline. The vast majority of their congregations are growing or declining. They do not have a large base of stable churches that checks wide swings in denominational growth rates. Decline is possible, almost overnight, as the Assemblies of God found in the late 1980s. In general, however, these denominations and fellowships are growing. Given the segmentation of American society, the fact that they seem "out of step" with the dominant culture may be to their advantage.

Catholics and Black Protestants

Despite growth in the sheer numbers of self-identified Catholics, the average Roman Catholic attends Mass much less frequently today than was the case in past decades. Self-reported attendance may have stabilized in the 1970s, but poll data on religious affiliation suggest that membership problems are not over. Disaffiliation is high and switching to other denominational families is increasing (Roof and McKinney, 1987; Hadaway and Marler, 1991). The situation is even worse among Catholic baby boomers (see Roof and Johnson, chapter 14). People are still born into the Catholic Church and continue to see it as "THE church." Yet the Catholic subculture is changing. As Marler and Roozen note in chapter 12, Catholics who attend regularly are institutionally committed and feel their parish "is warm and meaningful with a clear spiritual focus." In other words, they are acting more and more like religious consumers rather than a captive audience.

The growth charts in chapter 1 present a misleading picture of health. The Catholic Church counts all persons assumed to be baptized Catholics in each parish, whether or not they have ever received Mass in that parish. The Catholic Church may be growing in terms of affiliates, but any growth in active membership is likely the result of immigration and high birthrates among Hispanics.

What conclusions can be made about the black church in America? Unfortunately, the largest black denominations are not able to collect systematic membership records from their churches; so research is limited. Nevertheless, it is clear that many black churches are healthy and growing. As was true for Holiness/Pentecostal churches, worship is the key to growth in the black church. Programs such as Christian education and organized evangelism are secondary. Indeed, evidence of such worship based institutional health is easily observed by driving past black churches in almost any city at noon or 1:00 P.M. on Sundays. Black churches and Pentecostal churches are often packed—with standing room only. This is in great contrast to the typical mainline or traditional conservative church.

Are black denominations growing? The apparent health of black churches suggests so. In addition, Hadaway (1991c) and Marler and Hadaway (chapter 2) find that black churches in historically white denominations are growing much faster on average than white churches. Other sources of growth include the almost "involuntary" nature of church participation among blacks in the South and continued high levels of attendance in the North (see Nelsen and Kanagy, chapter 15). The evidence also suggests that cultural changes in the 1960s and 1970s had less effect on black denominations than white denominations. Birthrates remained high for blacks, and anti-institutionalist attacks did not target the black church. According to Nelsen and Nelsen (1975), even "as conflict over basic values grew, the black church prospered in the 1960s."

The only troubling signs for the black church are extremely low levels of church participation among youth in northern inner cities. According to Nelsen and Kanagy, "the future of the black church in the city is really dependent in the long term on the black church's ability to involve the less educated, younger adults who currently have little predisposition—and possibly even distain—for it." For the present, however, the black church appears considerably vital.

Growth Futures

What does the future hold for denominations in the United States in the 1990s? The easy answer, and the answer that is most likely to be accurate, is "more of the same." In other words, no dramatic "seismic shift" is in the offing, but the gentle rumblings of decline will continue. Still, the example of Canada presented by Reginald Bibby in chapter 13 should serve as a warning to churches and denominations in the United States. A "great American drop-off" could occur in the United States, just as it did in Canada (Bibby, 1987).

The danger is that no one will recognize the meaning of the warning, and American denominations will continue to "do church" in the same way. Perhaps more baby boomers will return to the church; perhaps the next generation of young adults will be more religious than their parents; perhaps revival will come to America. Perhaps. Hoping will not change present realities, however.

The reality is that individuals are approaching the church in a much different way than they did in the past. Religious choices were always available, but now Americans are acting on those choices. Several chapters in this volume used "religious consumerism" or a similar term to describe this orientation. Denominational loyalty is down as a result. A church choice is made increasingly on the basis of personal likes and dislikes. For some Americans this means increased church commitment, and for others it means no commitment at all—at least to the institutionalized church. Yet recent research suggests many have chosen a third option: marginal commitment. This group has decided to withhold judgment. It is the "soft underbelly" of the church, a group that retains a denominational identity, but rarely attends. The eventual decisions of this group (and their children) may determine the growth future of Protestants and Catholics in America (Marler and Hadaway, 1993).

What about the local church? Obviously some churches will be more successful than others in a deregulated religious economy. The research in this book tells us that evangelistic churches are most likely to grow. It also tells us that growth is rapid in new churches and in large entrepreneurial congregations. The religious consumer wants a friendly, warm, caring church where he or she can worship God in a meaningful way. Churches that have these qualities and that work for new members tend to be growing congregations.

Most churches could grow if they were more responsive to the needs of their members and potential members. Few Americans are hostile toward the church. Even the most critical persons think that the church has something to offer someone. Entrepreneurial churches understand that they must be interesting and inviting. Ministries are provided to meet needs, and needs are discovered through actually talking with and listening to people.

We began this book by focusing on denominations. Now I end with them. How must they respond to the current religious economy? Denominations must acknowledge that they exist in a deregulated religious market. There are no more monopolies and not much brand loyalty. An open market means greater competition. Churches and individuals are free to choose products from a much wider variety of sources. In fact, parachurch organizations capitalized on this trend earlier by catering to the needs of independent churches and denominations without publishing houses. Now the market is wide open. In this environment denominations must provide better products or they will lose market share.

Who is the denomination's target? In the past, the proper target was church leadership. In the days of strong, almost taken-for-granted denominational loyalty, clergy and selected lay leadership served—quite functionally—as representatives of church membership in denominational forums. Yet as Marler and Roozen observe, a cultural shift toward a more individual locus of control raises questions about "trickle down" denominationalism. Indeed, denominational loyalty is reduced because denominations remain a mystery to many church members. Members see and hear little other than controversial pronouncements, news of conflict, and appeals for funds. Denominational staff complain that the laity don't understand, and the laity think denominational staff are out of touch.

In a real sense, denominations must rediscover their constituency and allow their constituency to rediscover them. How can this be done? First steps would include reconceiving the role of local church clergy as *links to* rather than *proxies for* the membership. The denominations need to take their message in clear ways directly to the individual church member. Better programs of denominational education for local congregations would not hurt. Focus groups with laity are another way, as are national and regional gatherings—where the business is not business.

Despite slow and erratic growth in denominations and congregations, the picture is not entirely bleak. Church growth is possible because churches grow. Denominational growth is possible because denominations grow. America has a very rich and strong religious economy. Obviously there are no easy answers during almost inevitable periods of religious disinterest and stagnation. If leadership were a little more imaginative and farsighted, growth would happen faster. But not much faster.

NOTES

Chapter One
Denominations Grow as Individuals Join Congregations

1. The extent to which membership growth is indicative of denominational vitality is, of course, arguable on both organizational and theological grounds. But because the very concept of "membership" is more vague in Roman Catholicism than it is within most of denominational Protestantism, the relationship is especially tenuous within Roman Catholicism.

2. For those interested in broader historical interpretations of American religion in the last half of the twentieth century, there are many to commend, including: *American Evangelicalism: Conservative Religion and the Quandary of Modernity* (Hunter, 1983), *The New Charismatics II* (Quebedeaux, 1983), *Understanding American Jewry* (Sklare, 1983), *Bible Believers: Fundamentalism in the Modern World* (Ammerman, 1987), *American Mainline Religion* (Roof and McKinney, 1987), *The Restructuring of American Religion* (Wuthnow, 1988), *The Changing Parish: A Study of Parishes, Priests and Parishioners After Vatican II* (Hornsby-Smith, 1989), *Between the Times* (Hutchison, 1989), *The Catholic Myth* (Greeley, 1990), and *The Black Church in the African American Experience* (Lincoln and Mamiya, 1990).

3. Appendix Table A1.1 shows the individual membership trends for the three liberal and five moderate denominations included in the family aggregates. They are the only denominations in these families for which membership figures across the forty-year span are readily available.

4. The term "evangelical" figures prominently in most recent scholarly treatments of the increasing diversity within "conservative" Protestantism. Unfortunately, different scholars use the term in different ways, and these differences confound the term's usefulness as a label for either of our two families. Some scholars use it as a theological descriptor of a moderated fundamentalist adaptation to modernity (e.g., Hunter, 1983; Ammerman, 1987; Wuthnow, 1988). Other scholars, drawing heavily on the work of Marsden (1984) use it as an organizational descriptor of those denominations that emphasize parachurch networks over denominational centralization. Although there is some relationship between the two, it is far from perfect. Denominations that stress authoritative doctrine have a predisposition toward organizational centralization, especially as they get large. Denominations that emphasize the present-day operation of the Spirit tend to have loose national denominational organizations. Many smaller denominations that stress authoritative doctrine, however, are not organizationally centralized. Indeed, many identify themselves as "fellowships" rather than denominations.

   In addition, in neither of the scholarly delineations of "evangelicalism" noted above is the critical issue "evangelism" in the sense of witness. Evangelism in this latter sense remains a strong characteristic of all denominations typically identified with the broader stream of conservative Protestantism. We therefore do not feel it appropriate to use the label "evangelical" for either of our two "conservative" Protestant families.

5. Appendix Table A1.1 lists the nine conservative and six Pentecostal/Holiness denominations included in the families, and shows their individual membership trends.

6. That the relationship between membership growth and denominational vitality within Roman Catholicism is more tenuous on conceptual grounds than it is within most of Protestantism has already been noted. Particularly in the Roman Catholic case, therefore, worship attendance (or some other direct measure of involvement in the life of the institutional church) presents a more accurate gauge of denominational vitality. Empirically, this is suggested in the fact that there is a much greater discrepancy between membership trends and worship attendance records for Roman Catholics than for Protestants. National survey trend data shows that Roman Catholic worship attendance declined sharply in the late 1950s and early 1960s, declined moderately through the 1970s, and changed little during the 1980s.

7. Chapter 12 includes a more detailed discussion of the dynamics of cohort replacement in relationship to changes in religious participation during the 1980s.

PART ONE
DENOMINATIONAL GROWTH AND DECLINE

1. The conservative and mainline denominations are the same as those used in the chapter by Marler and Hadaway.

2. The fourteen denominations are the same as those used in the chapter by Marler and Hadaway to estimate the "period effect." The white birthrate is the number of births per 1,000 persons in the white population.

Chapter Two
New Church Development and Denominational Growth (1950–1988): Symptom or Cause?

°This chapter appeared earlier in Monty L. Lynn and David O. Moberg, eds. *Research in the Social Scientific Study of Religion, Vol. 4* (Greenwich, Conn.: JAI Press), pp. 29-72. It is reprinted here in slightly altered form with the permission of JAI Press, Inc.

1. Aggregate membership data and new church development data were obtained from 1950 to 1988 for five denominations: The United Methodist Church, the Southern Baptist Convention, the Lutheran Church, Missouri Synod, the Presbyterian Church (U.S.A.), and the Assemblies of God. For years prior to the Presbyterian merger in 1983, data are combined for the United Presbyterian Church in the United States of America and the Presbyterian Church (US). New church data were obtained through correspondence with church extension executives and denominational researchers over the past fifteen years.

2. Denominational reporting is notoriously problematic—for example, many ethnic congregations typically go unreported or report irregularly. Still, for most denominations the problems have remained relatively constant. For this reason, membership curves are quite smooth for most periods. When they are not the reasons can be found in mergers, schisms, and changes in counting procedures. Adjustments have been made for major changes in denominational trend data when such events occurred. For additional discussion of problems with denominational data see "Methodological Issues in Congregational Studies" (1989).

3. The Lutheran Church, Missouri Synod is viewed as a conservative denomination. It is not generally seen as evangelical, and from a cultural perspective it would seem closer to the American mainstream than the Southern Baptist Convention or the Assemblies of God.

4. The Lutheran Church, Missouri Synod had begun to plateau in membership prior to the relatively minor schism that occurred in the late 1970s. This conflict cost the denomination 100-130 congregations and around 100,000 baptized members. Following rather abrupt losses in 1977 and 1978, the denomination once again settled onto a plateau.

5. According to a research representative for the Assemblies of God, in 1971 the denomination changed its reporting to the National Council of Churches from full members to Sunday school enrollment. Membership and "the numbers game" have been less important for Assemblies of God churches than for most other Protestant denominations (no individual church listing of membership is permitted), so Sunday school enrollment was typically higher than full membership. In 1979, the denomination began systematic data collection on "inclusive" membership. At this time the inclusive membership figure (which is similar to the adherent concept) replaced Sunday school enrollment in reporting to the *Yearbook of American and Canadian Churches* (see Jacquet, 1991).

6. The rate of SBC growth is now at its lowest point in terms of a sustained pattern of membership change. Actual declines were experienced in the mid-1800s, but there was no period of sustained loss or even very slow growth.

7. This estimate was made by a research representative of the Lutheran Church, Missouri Synod.

8. The percentage change for 1950 reflects change from 1949 to 1950.

9. Denominations included the Christian Church (Disciples of Christ), the Church of God (Anderson, Indiana), the Church of the Brethren, the Church of the Nazarene, the Episcopal Church, the Evangelical Lutheran Church in America, the Reformed Church in America, the Seventh-day Adventists, the United Church of Christ, the Assemblies of God, the Southern Baptist Convention, the Presbyterian Church (U.S.A.), The United Methodist Church, and the Lutheran Church, Missouri Synod. Each denomination contributed equally to the average membership change for each year.

10. Although the shift in values was not consistent (in some ways the public is now more liberal than it was in the 1960s), there was a definite conservative shift in many areas. Further, anything that was labeled "liberal" became suspect as fewer and fewer Americans were comfortable with using that term to describe themselves.

11. For instance, it has been suggested that the recent slowdown in membership growth experienced by the AOG resulted (at least in part) from the Jim Bakker/Jimmy Swaggart scandals.

12. Data are for reporting churches only. No adjustments have been made for churches that are listed as Southern Baptist churches, but have not reported membership statistics in several years.

13. Membership data supplied to the authors for this project was full membership for each church. These figures are much lower than those reported to the National Council of Churches.

14. Older churches were those organized in 1983 or earlier.

15. Expected frequencies are based on the proportion of the U.S. population residing in those states in 1980.

16. "Where they are not" refers to states where the SBC has a low proportion of its churches relative to the proportion of the U.S. population in those states.

17. States are shaded from lowest to highest, according to levels on the criterion variable. For older church concentration, the percent of a denomination's churches in a state is compared to the percent of the U.S. population in that state. States where the denomination has a larger percentage of members than would be expected (given the concentration of the U.S. population) are shaded. Levels vary according to the magnitude of the difference. Shading for new church rates vary for each denomination. To receive shading on a new church map a state must have had at least two new churches formed from 1983 to 1988, and have a NCD rate that is greater than the mean for all states. Darker shadings reflect larger deviations (positive) from the national mean for the denomination.

18. This state has relatively few ABC churches, so even a small number of new churches produces a high NCD rate.

19. Demographic data for each church were available at the zip code level through a tape from CACI. However, this data set lacked the 1980 census variable for population mobility (percent of persons who lived in a different state in 1975). Still, as noted in the text, the average new church tends to have a larger proportion of renters in its zip code territory than does the average older church. Areas with a larger proportion of renters tend to have a higher rate of population mobility than areas that are overwhelmingly owner-occupied.

20. Many African-American congregations have affiliated (joined) the ABC rather than having been started as ABC congregations. In this chapter we deal only with churches with recent dates of organization (rather than recent dates of affiliation). Thus, whether the churches were started as ABC churches or affiliated shortly after organizing, all are new congregations.

21. Data from the 1990 Uniform Church Letter reveals that ethnic and black SBC churches were considerably more likely to grow than Anglo churches between 1985 and 1990.

22. Due to missing values on the race/ethnicity variable it is not possible to directly compare these percentage gains and losses to those for the entire denomination reported earlier. This is true for the American Baptist Churches, as well.

23. The Assemblies of God are the youngest denomination in terms of the average age of churches. Age of denomination can also be measured by the date that the churches in the denomination coalesced as a group apart from other churches in the United States. In the case of the UCC, two traditions are involved—one with direct links to the Pilgrims, the other much more recent.

24. Additional analysis (not shown here) was conducted on the percentage of churches with growth between 1983 and 1988 among those churches reporting at least one member in both years (this excluded new churches, nonreporting churches, and churches that died, merged, or left the denomination).

25. This analysis does not focus on shifts in policy, priorities, denominational organization, or funding committed to new church development. In addition, differences in theology are not addressed. More information on how the denominations vary and/or are similar on these points would shed light on the statistical patterns presented in this chapter.

The issue of local congregational initiative versus denominational initiative in new church starts also is important. However, we are unable to examine this issue with the data provided. There is some suggestion in the literature that congregational initiative is a "livelier" option for successful new church development. In the past, there has been some tendency away from local initiative to national (or regional) initiative. In recent years the pendulum may have swung back toward local initiative.

In addition, the relationship between "adoption" of existing (older) congregations versus new church starts is not explored. Denominational data, again, is not available for this level of analysis and comparison. The issue, however, is important as growing numbers of ethnic and independent congregations venture into "dual alignment" and "affiliation." Is the relationship to overall denominational growth and resilience similarly affected by these kinds of churches? These and other issues remain to be explored.

Chapter Four
Growth and Decline in an Inclusive Denomination:
The ABC Experience

1. A comparison of American Baptist, Assemblies of God, Disciples of Christ, Presbyterian, Southern Baptist, United Church of Christ, and United Methodist denominations (Roy Howard Beck, *The United Methodist Reporter*, February 14, 1986) documented that numbers and percentages of ethnic minorities were greater in the ABC than the other denominations studied. Also see chapter 2 in this volume.

2. Although the ABC was not included, a comparison of growth and decline (up to 1980) for other denominations can be found in *American Mainline Religion* (Roof and McKinney, 1987).

3. The counts of churches reported in this research are those certified by Regional Executive Ministers as churches in good standing in each region. The racial/ethnic category for each church is represented by the currently reported racial or ethnic majority of the congregation. The method of coding this factor in the data base precludes more definitive distributions of membership, worship attendance, and giving among the racial/ethnic groups. It has also not been possible to account for the racial/ethnic transitions that some congregations have experienced. It has been necessary to credit the data to the same racial/ethnic grouping that characterized the congregation's majority in 1990 (or the last such recorded category for deceased churches.)

4. Roughly two-thirds of ABC African-American churches are aligned with one or more other denominations. Four percent of white ABC churches are aligned with another denomination. For all ABC churches, 16% are dually aligned.

5. This economic benefit is attractive to all pastors and churches, but the effect of the attractive-

ness on whites is to keep them in the denomination when other factors would cause them to leave. The benefit is not great enough to attract independent Baptist churches if moderate to liberal theological stands and social justice issues are not attractive.

6. Data used in this study were analyzed for each of the thirty-five "Regions" that make up the middle level administrative units of the denomination. Data were summed from these "Regions" to produce data for sections of the U.S. that generally coincide with the regional designations of the U.S. Bureau of the Census. In this study, reference will be made to differences for those broad sectional areas, but not to the "Regional" units of the denomination.

7. The ABC has a continuing problem with nonreporting churches, and with churches skipping reporting years. This situations calls for estimating procedures. Resident membership for nonreporting churches is estimated by regional executives. This is carried forward in subsequent years with adjustments taking place at five-year intervals.

8. Because of the need to estimate membership for nonreporting churches, the "stable" category is probably overrepresented in Figure 4.3 for each racial/ethnic cohort, but to a greater degree for African-American and other churches.

9. Worship attendance for nonreporting years by churches providing some attendance data has been calculated by averaging. Where there was insufficient worship attendance data reported to establish a meaningful trend, worship attendance was calculated at 50% of resident membership for white and most African-American congregations, at 150% for Hispanic and some other ethnic congregations, and at 33% to 40% for exceptionally large African-American congregations. It is believed that the resulting data tends toward "reality" in a way that is far superior to any other methodological approach to the problem of nonreporting.

PART TWO
THE GROWTH AND DECLINE OF CONGREGATIONS

Chapter Five
A Short History of Church Growth Research

1. This conceptual approach to studying congregations—looking at both contextual and institutional factors—was introduced by Dean R. Hoge and David Roozen, *Understanding Church Growth and Decline, 1950–1978.*

2. Other factors are also important. For example, most of these researchers were trained as sociologists and their professional predisposition was to look first to the social context for causal explanations.

Chapter Seven
The Effect of a Church Growth Strategy on United Church of Christ Congregations

1. At least one survey was received from 259 congregations (43.2%), including surveys from 213 pastors and 226 laypersons (representing 144 congregations). An additional 25 pastors (4.2%) stated that they could not complete the surveys, either because they did not remember participating, or, more often, that because of a pastoral or lay leadership change no one was available who was knowledgeable about the workshops. Because a significant number of items came only from the clergy survey, only the 213 congregations with clergy returns (35.5%) were retained to avoid statistical problems with large amounts of missing data. The sample thus is probably biased toward congregations in which more activity occurred, and for some variables, restriction in range may have attenuated the relationship with church growth. Where responses from both clergy and laity were available, means of clergy-lay responses were computed for all questions that appeared on both surveys to decrease the error variance for these questions.

2. The area defined as a parish varied in size from a few census tracts to a township or an entire city or country. For this area, the 1980 census population count and the 1986 estimate were

obtained from the National Planning Data Corporation, and the percentage change was calculated. Percentage, rather than numerical, change was used to correct for the effect of very different parish sizes.

3. The "new members since 1985" measure was used, rather than change in church size or attendance, for two reasons. First, membership figures are notoriously inaccurate and often inflated. In fact, one of the first efforts in a church growth program often is to "clean the rolls" of inactive members, resulting in greater apparent membership loss among participating churches than among nonparticipating churches. Second, the workshops' main goal was to bring new members into the congregations, with secondary goals of increasing attendance and spiritual growth of existing members and decreasing losses through inactivity. Because numbers of new members may fluctuate widely from year to year, a sum of three years was chosen, rather than the figure for 1987, the year of the study, even though some of the congregations had not begun the program in 1985.

4. In the analyses of churches grouped by amount of community change, the effect of community change was not removed in the partial correlation, because grouping by amount of community change had already removed much of its effect. In the analyses of churches grouped by size of church, however, the effect of church size on number of new members was removed because, empirically, even within the subgroups, it was significantly related to numbers of new members received.

5. An alternative explanation for the relationship between efforts to form and involve newcomers in groups and the number of new members could be that churches that had received many new members in 1985 and 1986 needed to form new groups by 1987. Partial correlations between group activity (collected in early 1987) and new members received in 1987 alone (collected in 1988) were similar, however, suggesting that the relationship was not all due to new members prompting new groups.

6. Because so many congregations have their facilities used by community groups, these correlations may have been attenuated by limited variance in the measure of facility use.

Chapter Eight
Is Evangelistic Activity Related to Church Growth?

1. The significance level for inclusion was .01. Principal components factor analysis was used with varimax rotation.

2. Variables were chosen that had factor loadings of ± .40 or more.

3. All of the items used to create the scale were recoded so that low scores indicated high evangelistic activity and high scores indicated low evangelistic activity. Not all items contributed to the scale in an equal manner. Questions that were correlated with growth at .20 (Pearson's r) or lower were recoded into categories 2 to 4, while questions that were correlated with growth at .21 or higher were recoded into five categories (1 to 5). Yes/no questions were coded so that yes = 1 and no = 5 if the correlation was high, and yes = 2 and no = 4 if the correlation was low. After recoding, a scale score for each church was computed by adding responses to all the items. Two items, one that rated the church in evangelism, and another that dealt with programmed evangelistic campaigns were added twice.

4. The Uniform Church Letter is a yearly survey sent to all Southern Baptist Churches. Its purpose is to collect membership, participation, program, and giving data. Around 98% of SBC churches respond on the Letter.

5. The significance level for inclusion was .01.

6. In this case the dependent variable was percent membership change from 1981 to 1987, rather than the three-category growth/plateau/decline variable.

7. Stepwise multiple regression was employed.

8. A high ratio implies a strategy, encouraged by denominational agencies, to enroll as many persons in Sunday school as possible, whether they participate or not.

9. Significance was determined at the .05 level.

Chapter Nine
Growth or Decline in Presbyterian Congregations

1. We had data available from 1970, 1980, 1985, and 1988, thus allowing us to experiment with analyses over various time spans. We did not use the 1970 figures due to the excessive time span, but we did experiment with 1980–85 and 1985–88. Neither produced as clear outcomes as the eight-year span we adopted. Measurement error, reporting, and chance events obscured the analyses over fewer years.

2. In Roof's (1973) dichotomy, following Merton's classification, these persons are "locals." They usually have strong ties to the local community. Past research shows that "locals" participate in their congregations more often than do "cosmopolitans." Yet Presbyterian congregations located where higher proportions of of "locals" reside tend to be losing members faster.

3. The measure of change in church school size is from 1970 to 1985, thus overlapping with the membership change variable, which is 1980 to 1988, by five years. This raises the possibility of autocorrelation—that is, of incorrectly explaining one variable by another not totally independent of it. We explored using church school change from 1970 to 1980 rather than 1970 to 1985, and we found that it had similar, but weaker relation to church membership change (the beta was .20, not .38). The weaker beta may have resulted from substantive distance between the two time periods being related, not just the avoidance of any autocorrelation. We decided to use the 1970–85 change measure. The autocorrelation is not large, judging from the betas for Cluster I in the analyses of subgroups, which drop to near zero for small churches. If autocorrelation had been large, the betas would never drop this low.

4. The question of causal ordering arises here. Which causes which? In our model we are assuming that the institutional variable are causal for growth or decline. Yet good feelings about the congregation could be argued to be a *consequence* of growth. Both are probably true. The measure of good feelings stated, "There is a sense of excitement among members about our church's future." It asked in 1985, roughly midway in the 1980–88 period of growth or decline. We believe that in reality, church growth and a sense of excitement about the future feed each other, so causation goes both ways. We are justified in using this measure of good feelings about the church's future because all research shows that good feelings have an effect on church growth. The only statistical issue is how strong the effect is. We cannot measure it. Possibly the betas in our tables overestimate the true causal power of this factor for church growth or decline.

5. See Hadden (1969:120) and Wood (1986) for treatments of the negative effects of conflict over pastoral leadership on congregations. The next question in the form following this question about conflict asked about specific areas of conflict. Twenty-seven percent of the congregations had experienced significant conflict, and the overwhelming majority of those conflicts were over pastoral leadership (over 90%).

6. Roof et al. (1979) found that the presence of children was an important indicator of membership growth in Presbyterian congregations in the 1968 to 1974 time period. However, as pointed out above, community data on each church was supplied subjectively by the pastor.

7. We thank Kirk Hadaway for sharing data from a 1989 study of Baptist congregations in metropolitan areas.

8. Annual rates of changes of residence varied little from 1968 to 1988, according to census data. See U.S. Bureau of the Census (1989).

Chapter Ten
Congregational Growth and Decline in Indiana Among Five Mainline Denominations

1. Special thanks to Hartford Seminary for support to the author during the final stages of data collection and to the Indiana University Summer Faculty Fellowship Program for partial support during the early stages of data processing necessary to create analyzable files. Thanks to the Lilly Foundation, which supported the collection of the survey data. Thanks to Jackson Carroll and John Hiller, who collected and made the questionnaire data available to me. Special thanks also to Sheryl Wiggins of Hartford Seminary for rapid and accurate data entry of the church yearbook data.

2. The membership changes presented in this paragraph are based on those churches for which membership figures were available in 1970, 1980, and 1988. This excludes those churches that closed during the 1970s or 1980s, newly formed churches, and churches that make infrequent reports of membership to their denomination.

3. Compared with other Indiana churches in these denominations, the churches that completed the questionnaire and met other selection criteria have larger average memberships in 1980 (407 versus 340 members), are in somewhat larger communities, and have somewhat better growth rates.

4. Seven churches were excluded because they had growth rates greater than 10% per year (or an 80% increase from 1980 to 1988). Some readers may be surprised at this. Wouldn't one want to study these extremely fast-growing churches to find out how they do it? In regression terminology such churches are "outliers." They have an extreme effect on regression results, just as an extremely wealthy person has a very large effect on calculations of average income. Had they been included in the analysis, the results would not be typical of the experiences of most churches.

5. For some denominations, the most recent membership figures available in early 1989 were for 1987, not 1988. To adjust for these differences among denominations, the dependent variable actually used in these regressions is the percentage change from 1980 to 1987 or 1988 (depending upon denomination) divided by the number of years covered in the measure of membership change. I did not account for "compounding" membership change in these calculations since there is no strong evidence that churches grow or decline at compounding rates.

6. Throughout this chapter, I report adjusted R^2 values rather than simple R^2 values. This is because there are few cases relative to the number of predictor variables used in the regressions. In Tables 10.1 and 10.2, the adjusted R^2 values come from regressions that often do not include all of the predictor variables for a given category. Regressions with many predictor variables and few cases tend to yield low adjusted R^2 values. Thus, I first used stepwise regression to select the best predictors of growth within a variable category (those variables with statistically significant betas at the .15 level of probability). I then used these variables in a new regression to obtain the adjusted R^2 values reported in Tables 10.1 and 10.2. Because of missing values, these new regressions are often based on different numbers of cases. Thus, the adjusted R^2 values for an entire category sometime exceed the sum of the adjusted R^2 values from the clusters.

7. This figure is different from the correlation reported in Table 10.1, since it is based on a larger number of cases. The correlations reported in this paragraph include churches that did not return questionnaires.

8. The standard deviation of population change rates decreased from 19% to 12%.

9. Sharp-eyed readers will notice that the total adjusted R^2 value for all identity variables is greater than the sum of the adjusted R^2s for the three clusters. This discrepancy is due to the way these R^2 values were calculated (see earlier note) and the different numbers of cases used to calculate the R^2 values in different parts of Table 10.1.

10. It is possible that these findings could reflect some autocorrelation (respondents only say the church puts high emphasis on membership recruitment when a church is growing), but

the questions merely ask about the importance and emphasis put on these activities, not whether they are effective.

11. The first correlation is based on the ninety-eight churches in which respondents checked a one, two, or three on a seven-point scale indicating that the church is more oriented to serving the needs of the "world beyond [the] membership" than the needs of current members. The second correlation is based on 251 churches in which respondents checked four or five on this same scale. The third correlation is based on 106 churches in which respondents checked a six or seven indicating a focus on members' needs.

Chapter Eleven
Belief Style, Congregational Climate, and Program Quality

The authors wish to thank Eugene Roehlkepartain, Kirk Hadaway, David Roozen, and the members of the Congregational Studies Working Group for their comments on earlier drafts of this chapter, and the Lilly Foundation for their support of this research, the Working Group, and a great many important research projects in the area of North American religious life.

1. The original ECE study included the participation of congregations from the Southern Baptist Convention. Given the unique characteristics of that denomination (their scores on many measures were markedly higher than those of the five "mainline" denominations, as a group) their data were not included in this analysis.

2. This brief listing of the contents of the ECE study gives some idea of the scope of the project. For further information, see Benson and Eklin (1990).

3. Support for this augmentation of the data set was provided in part through an additional grant from the Lilly Foundation.

4. Cases deleted were those in which the "growth ratio" was either less than 0.3, or greater than 2.5.

5. For example, if a congregation's size remains unchanged for a given period of time, this is reflected in a change ratio of 1.0. If it doubles in size, this produces a change ratio of 2.0. If it then declines by half (returning to its previous size), the change ratio is 0.5. Adding 2.0 and 0.5 gives 2.5, which does not convey the lack of any net change over the period observed. Consider, however, the log transform of these measures. $\log 2 = 0.3$; $\log 1 = 0.0$; $\log 0.5 = -0.3$. To return to the "doubling and halving" example, the net change is $0.3 + (-0.3) = 0.0$.

6. The correlation between the "pastor's estimate" correlation with a particular characteristic and the "change ratio" correlation with that same characteristic is $-.07$, nonsignificant.

7. The particular regression procedure used is invariant with respect to order of entry (SAS, 1987). All other variables in the model are controlled for, and all regression weights are reported as if the particular predictor had been entered "last."

PART THREE
INDIVIDUALS AND THE CHURCH CHOICE

Chapter Twelve
From Church Tradition to Consumer Choice: The Gallup Surveys of the
Unchurched American

1. Unfortunately, Roof and Hoge's analysis did not include childhood religiosity. Several recent studies have found strong, although largely indirect, effects for religious socialization on church involvement (e.g., Cornwall, 1989). Recent studies have also found stronger regional effects than those reported by Roof and Hoge (e.g., Stump, 1986).

2. The 1988 survey did include a measure of "localism," but not comparable in wording to that used in the 1978 survey. In an analysis of just the 1988 data, not reported here, we found

that the 1988 measure of localism had nearly the same positive effect on religious participation as Roof and Hoge (1980) report for the 1978 measure and data.

3. The items in our "church personalism" scale had a positive wording in the 1978 survey and a negative wording in the 1988 survey. We reversed the coding of the 1988 items to create comparability; and given the location of the items within a larger block of otherwise positively worded questions in the survey, our reversal probably overestimates the actual positive change from 1978 to 1988 in our church personalism scale. However, other "perception of the church" items that had identical wordings in both surveys changed in a positive direction, and this increases our confidence that at least some of the positive change over time in our church personalism scale was real. For present purposes, our interpretation is only dependent upon positive change, not the magnitude of change. For detailed statistical reasons, the reversal of coding in the church personalism scale, while not ideal, should not affect our later regression analysis.

4. A major consideration in a stepwise multiple regression is the order in which blocks are entered into the analysis. This order is dictated both by the researcher's interpretive purposes, and by theoretical assumptions about causal priority. Our model assumes that social background affects general value orientations; both of which affect traditional religiosity; all of which affect church consumerism; all of these four, in turn, affecting church membership; and all of these five affecting worship attendance. However, because we were primarily interested in (a) the direct effect of our blocks (as opposed to their total effect—i.e., direct and indirect), and (b) comparing the strength of the most immediate effects across denominational groups, we enter them in reverse causal order. That is, we enter what we assume to be the most immediate "causes" first, and the "causes of causes" last.

5. While membership may strike some as being autocorrelated with attendance, as will be seen, the relation of membership to attendance acts differently from year to year and across denominational categories—especially for liberal Protestants.

6. In addition to the step summaries upon which the textual graphs are based, the Appendix tables contain the controlled R and part-R for each individual variable in the model. A comparison of the uncontrolled and part-R's provides a gauge of how much of the total effect (uncontrolled R) of any given explanatory variable on either church membership or attendance is direct (part-R), and how much is indirectly mediated through associations with other explanatory variables (R minus part-R).

7. However, the latter does not mean that these individual variables have no effect on membership. Rather, as indicated in the detailed Table A12.1 (Appendix), they show modest effects consistent with the findings of past research. In the multivariate model, however, the explanatory power of the blocks themselves is muted, because their effects are mediated through the relationship of these items to current religiosity and church consumerism. Interestingly, of the variables in our value and social background blocks, religious socialization exhibits the strongest relationship to membership—controlled and uncontrolled.

8. We again caution that this does not mean that they have no effect. Rather, it means that the effect they do have is mediated through their influence on the first three blocks. Further, as was the case for church membership, religious socialization has the strongest overall effect on worship attendance (see Table A12.1 in the Appendix). Also in relationship to current discussions of the baby boom generation's return to active religious participation, it is interesting to note in Table A12.1 that family cycle had a greater influence on worship attendance in 1988 than it did in 1978.

9. This is true in regard both to its direct effect on attendance and to its mediated effect through church membership (see Table A12.1 in the Appendix).

10. This way of understanding religious individualism was presented by the authors at a conference in February, 1991. In a personal communication, Wade Clark Roof acknowledged that his discussion, "Reconsidering Religious Individualism," in *A Generation of Seekers*

(HarperCollins, 1993) draws from Marler and Roozen's insights about the positive implications of individualism for religious institutions.

11. And as Ammerman describes, fundamentalist believers perceive "profound differences" between themselves and other Christians at many levels: in life-style, worship, theology, and authority. In fact, the perception is that "liberal churches are not 'real churches'" (1987:79).

Chapter Thirteen
Religion in the Canadian 1990s: The Paradox of Poverty and Potential

1. The research upon which this chapter is based has been made possible in part through grants from the Lilly Endowment, the Social Sciences and Humanities Research Council of Canada, and the University of Lethbridge.

Chapter Fourteen
Baby Boomers and the Return to the Churches

1. For purposes of this analysis, Protestants were classified as "mainline" or "conservative" using the denominational scheme of Roof and McKinney, 1987. "Liberal Protestant" and "moderate Protestant" affiliations from that work are here combined into a single category called "mainline."

2. On the basis of a content analysis of the expressed concerns of religious publications about youth dropping out of the church, decade by decade in this century, the "Youth Problem" was a recurring theme. It reached critical proportions in the twenties and early thirties, though at no point did the crisis seem to reach the magnitude of the sixties. These results are found in Jonathan A. Dorn, "Sodom and Tomorrow: Will the Younger Generation Really Be Good?" unpublished paper, 1989.

Chapter Fifteen
Churched and Unchurched Black Americans

1. We wish to thank the Roper Center for making the 1978 data set available.

2. In the 1978 data set there were only eleven black respondents residing in the suburban South and nineteen in the suburban non-South. The 1988 data set included a larger number of suburban residents. Massey and Denton (1988:592) report the "rapid suburbanization between 1950 and 1970 radically changed the spatial structure of U.S. cities, transforming them from concentrated, highly centralized agglomerations into scattered, decentralized metropolitan areas." This was chiefly due to white suburbanization—the central cities became blacker and the suburbs whiter during this period. In 1980 blacks were less suburbanized than other minorities, and even in suburbs segregation remained quite high (see also Stahura, 1986:140). As noted in A Common Destiny, 57% of American blacks reside in inner cities: "many are poorly educated, and low-skill and blue-collar jobs have been leaving the inner cities for the suburbs" (Jaynes and Williams, 1989:396). Higher rates of unemployment and substantial levels of persistent poverty increasingly characterized America's central cities over the 1980s.

3. A high percentage of older, urban blacks grew up in contexts favorable to religious socialization—they were likely to have attended Sunday school, for example. That they would turn to the church when older and when times are troubled is not surprising.

4. As can be seen in Table 15.2, significant interaction existed between place of residence and importance of religion in predicting rates of being churched. The thesis of this chapter was that in the three places of residence characterized by voluntary participation we would find personal religiousness (importance of religion to the individual) positively related to being churched, and that these settings would be significantly different from the other two (com-

munal) contexts. The significant interaction and the examination of the presence or absence of relationships across the five settings give support to this hypothesis. A similar pattern exists for the afterlife as a predictor, but the interaction is not significant; had we dichotomized place of residence into the communal and voluntary settings, we would have had an easier test for interaction. (The same could have been done for testing the interaction between each of the other selected predictors and place of residence, that is, communal versus voluntary context).

Chapter Sixteen
Participation and Commitment Among American Catholic Parishioners

1. Data reported in this chapter were first collected with the aid of a grant from the Lilly Endowment. Hartford Seminary, and the Institute for Scholarship in Liberal Arts, University of Notre Dame, also provided support for this research. Finally, I would like to thank Chengang Zhu for providing assistance with computer analyses.

2. Selected data from Phase I and Phase II were merged to provide measures of organizational structure that characterize individual parishes and affect the religious beliefs and actions of parishioners. Individual-level data from the surveys of parishioners and staff were also aggregated to create measures of salient social or psychological features that shape the climate of the parish. Finally, selected census data that reflect aspects of the local environment in which the parish is situated were incorporated into this multilevel data base. These data allow us to study and compare relationships between measures reflecting the levels of commitment and participation shown by parishioners and other relevant characteristics of these individuals, their specific parishes, and the surrounding local environment. This type of multilevel analysis (see Van den Eeden and Huthner for more extensive discussions of multilevel or contextual analyses) offers notable advantages for theorizing (Leege and Welch, 1985).

3. Each measure was selected because it reflected a unique and separate component of a parishioner's institutional participation or commitment to the local parish. In addition, the factor-based scales representing Basic and Traditionalistic Devotion were derived from previous research (Welch and Leege, 1989) that identified several distinct styles of worship by Catholic parishioners. These scales have since been shown to be reliable (e.g., alphas > .70) and valid measures, with notable relationships to a variety of important variables (Welch and Leege, 1991).

4. Once the dependent measures were determined, I examined intercorrelations between the other individual-level variables and these measures. All potential predictor variables that displayed statistically significant (at $p < .05$ level) and theoretically meaningful correlations were retained and grouped into several subsets.

   I further examined intercorrelations among and within these subsets of predictor variables and, whenever appropriate, factor analyzed several of these subsets to reduce further the number of variables. Item analyses were also used to construct simple indices. These procedures minimized redundancy among the predictors and thus ultimately reduced statistical problems that might afflict later analyses. Data reduction procedures yielded four individual-level, factor-based scales (see Kim and Mueller), one summated index, and fifteen single-item measures representing the complete block of individual-level predictor variables. Although one or two variables from a set of dummy variables representing region did display a few weak, but statistically significant, zero-order relationships to the measures of participation and commitment, these relationships were reduced to nonsignificance in later preliminary analyses. As a result, I will not discuss these variables in the following sections.

5. The first of these measures, an index representing the primary socioeconomic composition of a parish, was itself created from measures of parish income level and the level of education characterizing a parish. This summated four-item index exhibited a high level of internal consistency (alpha = .71).

A second index, representing the level of ethnic homogeneity within the parish congregation, was based on a parishioner's principal self-identification with one of twenty-four specific ethnic groups. Marginal distributions on this ethnic self-classification were obtained for each parish and an index of parish-level ethnic homogeneity was computed, using Lieberson's (1970) coefficient of similarity. Values for this index range from zero (indicating complete ethnic diversity—i.e., each respondent falls into a different ethnic category—within the parish) to 1.00 (indicating complete ethnic homogeneity—i.e., all repondents are classified in the same ethnic category).

An index reflecting the extent of religious endogamy within a parish was the final measure included in the set of local institutional variables. This ratio measure represents the percentage of parishioners within each parish who have Catholic spouses, and it is based on the aggregated responses of parish members to a marital status item. Values for this measure extend from 0% (indicating no religious endogamy with a given parish) to 100% (indicating complete religious endogamy—i.e., all respondents within a parish are married to Catholic spouses). The formula is represented below.

$$RE = MPCS/TMP$$

Where,

RE = Level of Religious Endogamy;
$MPCS$ = Number of parishioners married to Catholic spouses;
TMP = Total number of married parishioners within parish

6. As is well known (Kerlinger, 1973:71-72; see also Roof et al., 1979: 220-21, 368), the magnitude of the coefficients representing percentage change in explained variance is contingent on the order in which blocks of variables are introduced into the multiple regression analysis. Thus, empirical results are strongly influenced by the theoretical assumptions reflected in the model. Furthermore, because of the extremely large number of variables included in the analysis, I report only change in the adjusted ("shrunken") R^2 statistic for each block. This adjusted coefficient is more difficult to interpret than a simple R^2 change statistic, but it is more appropriate and does allow for an easier comparison of results with other studies that conducted similar analyses and focused on Protestant denominations (e.g., Roof et al., 1979).

REFERENCES

Amberson, T., ed.
   1979   *The Birth of Churches.* Nashville: Broadman Press.

Ammerman, Nancy Tatom
   1987   *Bible Believers: Fundamentalists in the Modern World.* New
            Brunswick, N.J.: Rutgers University Press.

Anderson, Elijah
   1990   *Street Wise: Race, Class and Change in an Urban Community.*
            Chicago: University of Chicago Press.

Balmer, Randall
   1989   *Mine Eyes Have Seen the Glory: A Journey into the Evangelical Sub-
            culture of America.* New York: Oxford University Press.

Bellah, Robert N., Richard Madsen, William M. Sullivan, Ann Swidler, and Steven
   M. Tipton
   1985   *Habits of the Heart: Individualism and Commitment in American Life.*
            Berkeley: University of California Press.

Benson, Peter L., and Carolyn H. Eklin
   1990   *Effective Christian Education: A National Study of Protestant Congre-
            gations: A Summary Report on Faith, Loyalty, and Congregational
            Life.* Minneapolis, Minn.: Search Institute.

Berger, Peter L.
   1967   *The Sacred Canopy: Elements of a Sociological Theory of Religion.*
            Garden City, N.Y.: Doubleday & Company.

Bibby, Reginald W.
   1978   "Why conservative churches really are growing: Kelley Revisited."
            Journal for the Scientific Study of Religion 17:129-37.

   1987   *Fragmented Gods: The Poverty and Potential of Religion in Canada.*
            Toronto: Stoddart.

Bibby, Reginald W., and Donald C. Posterski
   1992   *Teen Trends: New Directions, New Responses.* Toronto: Stoddart.

Bibby, Reginald W., and Merlin B. Brinkerhoff
   1973   "The Circulation of the Saints: A Study of People Who Join Conserva-
            tive Churches." *Journal for the Scientific Study of Religion* 12:273-83.

   1983   "Circulation of the Saints Revisited: A Longitudinal Look at Conserva-
            tive Church Growth." *Journal for the Scientific Study of Religion*
            22:253-62.

Bloom, Harold
   1992   *The American Religion: The Emergence of the Post-Christian Nation.*
            New York: Simon and Schuster.

Bouma, Gary D.
    1979   "The Real Reason One Conservative Church Grew." *Review of Religious Research* 20:127-37.

Bradley, Martin B., Norman M. Green, Jr., Dale Jones, Mac Lynn, and Lou McNeil
    1992   *Churches and Church Membership in the United States 1990.* Atlanta: Glenmary Research Center.

Brock, C.
    1981   *The Principle and Practice of Indigenous Church Planting.* Nashville: Broadman Press.

Brooks, J. L.
    1990   "Reaching Out: A Study of Church Extension Activity in Mecklenburg Presbytery, North Carolina." In Milton J. Coalter, John M. Mulder, Louis B. Weeks, eds. *The Mainstream Protestant "Decline": The Presbyterian Pattern.* Louisville: Westminster/John Knox Press.

Bullock, Robert H., Jr.
    1991   "Twentieth Century Presbyterian New Church Development: A Critical Period, 1940–1980." In Milton J. Coalter, John M. Mulder, Louis B. Weeks, eds. *The Diversity of Discipleship: The Presbyterians and Twentieth Century Christian Witness.* Louisville: Westminster/John Knox Press.

Callahan, Kennon, L.
    1983   *Twelve Keys to an Effective Church.* San Francisco: Harper & Row.

Caplow, Theodore.
    1991   *American Social Trends.* San Diego: Harcourt Brace Jovanovich.

Carmichael, Stokely, and Charles V. Hamilton
    1967   *Black Power.* New York: Random House.

Carroll, Jackson W., ed.
    1977   *Small Churches Are Beautiful.* New York: Harper & Row.

Carroll, Jackson W., Carl S. Dudley, and William McKinney
    1986   *Handbook for Congregational Studies.* Nashville: Abingdon Press.

Carroll, Jackson W., and David A. Roozen.
    1975   *Religious Participation in American Society: An Analysis of Social and Religious Trends and Their Interaction.* Hartford: Hartford Seminary Foundation.

    1979   "Continuity and Change: The Shape of Religious Life in the United States, 1950 to the Present." In Carroll, Johnson and Marty, *Religion in America: 1950 to the Present.* New York: Harper & Row.

    1990   "Congregational Identities in the Presbyterian Church." *Review of Religious Research* 31 (4):351-69.

Carroll, Jackson W., and Wade Clark Roof, eds. (forthcoming)
    Beyond Establishment. Louisville: Westminster Press/John Knox Press.

Castelli, Joseph, and Jim Gremillion
    1987   *The Emerging Parish: The Notre Dame Study of Catholic Life Since Vatican II.* San Francisco: Harper & Row.

Chaney, Charles
    1982   *Church Planting at the End of the Twentieth Century.* Wheaton, Ill.: Tyndale House.

Chaves, Mark
    1989   "Secularization and Religious Revival: Evidence from U.S. Church Attendance Rates, 1972–1986." *Journal for the Scientific Study of Religion* 28 (4):464-77.

    1990   "Holding the Cohort: Reply to Hout and Greeley." *Journal for the Scientific Study of Religion* 29 (4):525-30.

Coalter, Milton J.
    1991   "Presbyterian Evangelism: A Case of Parallel Allegiances Diverging." In Milton J. Coalter, John M. Mulder, Louis B. Weeks, eds. *The Diversity of Discipleship: The Presbyterians and Twentieth Century Christian Witness.* Louisville: Westminster/John Knox Press.

Coalter, Milton J., John M. Mulder, Louis B. Weeks, eds.
    1990   *The Mainstream Protestant "Decline:" The Presbyterian Pattern.* Louisville: Westminster/John Knox Press.

Cornwall, Marie
    1989   "The Determinants of Religious Behavior: A Theoretical Model and Empirical Test." *Social Forces* 68 (2):572-92.

Costas, Orlando
    1974   *The Church and Its Mission: A Shattering Critique from the Third World.* Wheaton, Ill.: Tyndale House.

    1979   *The Integrity of Mission.* New York: Harper & Row.

D'Antonio, William, James Davidson, Dean Hoge, and Ruth Wallace.
    1989   *American Catholic Laity in a Changing Church.* Kansas City: Sheed & Ward.

Dale, Robert D.
    1981   *To Dream Again.* Nashville: Broadman Press.

Davidson, James D., and Dean D. Knudsen
    1977   "A New Approach to Religious Commitment." *Sociological Focus* 10:151-73.

Dorn, Jonathan
    1989   "Sodom and Tomorrow: Will the Younger Generation Really Be Good?" Unpublished paper.

Drake, St. Clair, and Horace R. Cayton
    1945   *Black Metropolis: A Study of Negro Life in a Northern City.* New York: Harcourt, Brace and World.

Dudley, Carl S.

 1977   *The Unique Dynamics of the Small Church.* Washington: The Alban
         Institute.

 1978   *Making the Small Church Effective.* Nashville: Abingdon Press.

Elliott, Ralph
 1982   *Church Growth that Counts.* Valley Forge, Pa.: Judson Press.

Ellison, Christopher G., and Darren E. Sherkat
 1990   "Patterns of Religious Mobility Among Black Americans." *Sociological
         Quarterly* 31 (December):551-68.

Fackre, Gabrie
 1973   *Do and Tell: Engagement Evangelism in the '70s.* Grand Rapids: Eerd-
         mans.

 1975   *Word in Deed: Theological Themes in Evangelism.* Grand Rapids:
         Eerdmans.

Foltz, Nancy
 1990   "Overview of Religious Education in the Small Membership Church."
         In Nancy Foltz, ed. *Religious Education in the Small Membership
         Church.* Birmingham, Ala.: Religious Education Press.

Frazier, E. Franklin
 1964   *The Negro Church in America.* New York: Schocken Books.

General Assembly Mission Council
 1976   *Membership Trends in the United Presbyterian Church in the U.S.A.*
         New York: United Presbyterian Church, U.S.A.

Gerth, Hans H., and C. Wright Mills, eds.
 1958   *From Max Weber: Essays in Sociology.* New York: Oxford University
         Press.

Glenn, Norval
 1987   "The Trend in 'No Religion' Respondents to U.S. National Surveys,
         Late 1950s to Early 1980s." *Public Opinion Quarterly* 51:293-314.

Glenn, Norval D., and Erin Gotard
 1977   "The Religion of Blacks in the United States: Some Recent Trends and
         Current Characteristics." *American Journal of Sociology* 83 (Septem-
         ber):443-51.

Gottlieb, Annie
 1987   *Do You Believe in Magic? The Second Coming of the 60's Generation.*
         New York: Times Books.

Graham, Ron
 1990   *God's Dominion: A Sceptic's Quest.* Toronto: McClelland and Stewart.

Grant, John Webster
 1988   *The Church in the Canadian Era.* Burlington, Ont.: Welch.

Greeley, Andrew
    1989   *Religious Change in America.* Cambridge, Mass.: Harvard University Press.

    1990   *The Catholic Myth: The Behavior and Beliefs of American Catholics.* New York: Scribner's.

Greeley, Andrew, Mary Durkin, David Tracy, John Shea, and William McCready.
    1981   *Priest, Parish and People.* Chicago: Thomas Moore Press.

Greeley, Andrew, William C. McCready, and Kathleen McCourt.
    1976   *Catholic Schools in a Declining Church.* Kansas City, Mo.: Andrews and McMeel.

Gremillion, Joseph, and David Leege
    1989   *Post-Vatican II Parish Life in the United States: Review and Preview, Notre Dame Study of Catholic Parish Life.* Report 15. Notre Dame, Ind.: University of Notre Dame.

Grossman, James R.
    1989   *Land of Hope: Chicago, Black Southerners, and the Great Migration.* Chicago: University of Chicago Press.

Gunnemann, Louis H.
    1977   *The Shaping of the United Church of Christ.* New York: United Church Press.

Hadaway, C. Kirk
    1978   "Denominational Switching and Membership Growth: In Search of a Relationship." *Sociological Analysis* 39:321-37.

    1980   "Conservatism and Social Strength in a Liberal Denomination." *Review of Religious Research* 21:302-14.

    1981   "The Demographic Environment and Church Membership Change." *Journal for the Scientific Study of Religion* 20:77-89.

    1982   "Church Growth (and Decline) in a Southern City." *Review of Religious Research* 23:372-90.

    1985   "Learning from Urban Church Research." *Urban Mission* 2 (January): 33-41.

    1988   "The Metropolitan Distribution of the 17 Largest U.S. Religious Bodies." *Research Information Report* Series 2, Number 1. Nashville: Baptist Sunday School Board.

    1990   "The Impact of New Church Development on Southern Baptist Growth." *Review of Religious Research* 31:370-79.

    1991a   *Church Growth Principles: Separating Fact from Fiction.* Nashville: Broadman Press.

1991*b* "Denominational Switching, Social Mobility and Membership Trends." In Newell Williams, ed. *Twentieth Century Disciples*. Grand Rapids: Eerdmans.

1991*c* "Five Sources of Growth in the Southern Baptist Convention." In *Southern Baptist Handbook*. Nashville: Baptist Sunday School Board.

Hadaway, C. Kirk, and Penny L. Marler
1993 "All in the Family: Religious Mobility in America." Review of Religious Research (Forthcoming).

Hesselgrave, D. J.
1980 *Planting New Churches Cross-Culturally*. Grand Rapids: Baker Book House.

Hale, J. Russell
1977 *Who Are the Unchurched?* Washington, D.C.: Glenmary Research Center.

Harrison, Paul
1959 *Authority and Power in the Free Church Tradition: A Social Case History of the American Baptist Convention*. Carbondale, Ill.: Southern Illinois University Press.

Hartman, Warren
1976 *Membership Trends: A Study of Decline and Growth in The United Methodist Church 1949–1975*. Nashville: Discipleship Resources.

Hartman Warren, and Robert Wilson
1989 *The Large Membership Church*. Nashville: Discipleship Resources.

Heidinger, James V., II
1987 "The United Methodist Church." In Ronald H. Nash, ed. *Evangelical Renewal in the Mainline Churches*. Westchester, Ill.: Crossway Books.

1988 *United Methodist Renewal: What Will It Take?* Wilmore, Ky.: Bristol Books.

Hine, Leland
1982 "Evangelism: Interpreting the Principle Mandate." Unpublished paper.

Hodges, M. L.
1973 *A Guide to Church Planting*. Chicago: Moody Press.

Hoge, Dean R.
1974 *Commitment on Campus: Changes in Religion and Values Over Five Decades*. Philadelphia: Westminster Press.

1981 *Converts Dropouts Returnees: A Study of Religious Change Among Catholics*. New York: Pilgrim Press.

Hoge, Dean R., and David A. Roozen

    1979*a*   "Research on Factors Influencing Church Commitment." Chapter 2 in Dean R. Hoge and David A. Roozen, eds. *Understanding Church Growth and Decline: 1950–1978.* New York: Pilgrim Press.

    1979*b*   "Some Sociological Conclusions about Church Trends." Chapter 14 in Dean R. Hoge and David A. Roozen, eds. *Understanding Church Growth and Decline: 1950–1978.* New York: Pilgrim Press.

Hoge, Dean R., and David A. Roozen, eds.

    1979   *Understanding Church Growth and Decline: 1950–1978.* New York: Pilgrim Press.

Hoge, Dean R., and David T. Polk

    1980   "A Test of Theories of Protestant Church Participation and Commitment." *Review of Religious Research* 21:315-29.

Hoge, Dean, and Jackson W. Carroll

    1978   "Determinants of Commitment and Participation in Suburban Protestant Churches." *Journal for the Scientific Study of Religion* 17:107-28.

Holsinger, James W., Jr., and Evelyn Laycock

    1989   *Awaken the Giant: 28 Prescriptions for Reviving The United Methodist Church.* Nashville: Abingdon Press.

Hornsby-Smith, Michael P.

    1989   *The Changing Parish: A Study of Parishes, Priests and Parishioners After Vatican II.* New York: Routledge.

Hout, Michael, and Andrew M. Greeley

    1987   "The Center Doesn't Hold: Church Attendance in the U.S., 1942–1984." *American Sociological Review* 52 (June):325-45.

    1990   "The Cohort Doesn't Hold: Comment on Chaves." *Journal for the Scientific Study of Religion* 29 (4):519-24.

Hudnut, Robert K.

    1975   *Church Growth Is Not the Point.* New York: Harper & Row.

Hunt, Earl G., Jr.

    1987   *A Bishop Speaks His Mind: A Candid View of United Methodism.* Nashville: Abingdon Press.

Hunter, George G., III

    1979   *The Contagious Congregation: Frontiers in Evangelism and Church Growth.* Nashville: Abingdon Press.

    1980   *Finding the Way Forward.* Nashville: Discipleship Resources.

    1987   *To Spread the Power: Church Growth in the Wesleyan Spirit.* Nashville: Abingdon Press.

Hunter, James Davison
　　1980　　"The New Class and the Young Evangelicals." *Review of Religious Research* 22:155-59.

　　1983　　*American Evangelicalism: Conservative Religion and the Quandary of Modernity.* New Brunswick, N.J.: Rutgers University Press.

　　1987　　*Evangelicalism: The Coming Generation.* Chicago: University of Chicago Press.

　　1988　　"American Protestantism: Sorting Out the Present, Looking Toward the Future." In J. Richard Neuhaus, ed. *The Believable Futures of American Protestantism.* Grand Rapids: Eerdmans.

Hutchison, William R.
　　1986　　"Past Imperfect: History and the Prospect for Liberalism." In Robert S. Michaelson and Wade Clark Roof, eds. *Liberal Protestantism: Realities and Possibilities.* New York: Pilgrim Press.

Hutchison, William R., ed.
　　1989　　*Between the Times: The Travail of the Protestant Establishment in America, 1900–1960.* Cambridge: Cambridge University Press.

Iannaccone, Lawrence R.
　　1989　　"Why Strict Churches Are Strong." Paper presented at the annual meeting of the Society for the Scientific Study of Religion, Salt Lake City, Utah, October 1989.

　　1990　　"Religious Practice: A Human Capital Approach." *Journal for the Scientific Study of Religion* 29 (3):297-314.

Jacoby, Russell
　　1975　　*Social Amnesia: A Critique of Conformist Psychology from Adler to Lang.* Boston: Beacon Press.

Jacquet, Constant H., Jr., ed.
　　1991　　*Yearbook of American and Canadian Churches.* Nashville: Abingdon Press.

Jaynes, Gerald David, and Robin M. Williams, eds.
　　1989　　*A Common Destiny: Blacks and American Society.* Washington, D.C.: National Academy Press.

Jelen, Ted
　　1990　　"Aging and Boundary Maintenance Among American Evangelicals: A Comment on James Davidson Hunter's 'Evangelicalism: The Coming Generation.'" *Review of Religious Research.* 31 (3):268-79.

Jelen, Ted, and Clyde Wilcox
　　1991　　"Religious Dogmatism Among White Christians: Causes and Effects." *Review of Religious Research.* 33 (1): 32-46.

Johnson, Douglas W.
　　1989　　*Vitality Means Church Growth.* Nashville: Abingdon Press.

Johnson, Douglas W., and Alan K. Waltz
1986   A Study of New Churches, 1966–1984. New York: National Program Division, General Board of Global Ministries, The United Methodist Church.

1987   Facts & Possibilities: An Agenda for The United Methodist Church. Nashville: Abingdon Press.

Johnson, Emmett V.
n.d.   Church Growth: ABC Style. Valley Forge, Pa.: Board of National Ministries, American Baptist Churches in the USA.

Johnson, R. Alan, with Robert L. Burt
1987   "Thirty Years of Evangelism in the United Church of Christ 1957–1987." In Evangelism & Membership Resources Growth Resources. New York: United Church Board of Homeland Ministries, Division of Evangelism and Local Church Development.

Jones, Ezra Earl
1976   Strategies for New Churches. New York: Harper & Row.

Jones, Richard M.
1989   "Marks of a Growing, Caring Church." American Baptist Quarterly, VIII (3):164-66.

Kelley, Dean M.
1972   Why Conservative Churches Are Growing. San Francisco: Harper & Row.

1977   Why Conservative Churches Are Growing. Updated edition. New York: Harper & Row.

Kerlinger, Fred. N., and Elazar J. Pedhazur
1973   Multiple Regression in Behavioral Research. New York: Holt, Rinehart, and Winston.

Kim, J., and C. W. Mueller
1978   Factor Analysis. Beverly Hills, Calif.: SAGE.

Lasch, Christopher
1978   The Culture of Narcissism. New York: Norton.

Lee, Richard R.
1992   "Religious Practice as Social Exchange: An Explanation of Empirical Findings." Sociological Analysis 53 (1):1-35.

Leege, David C., and Michael R. Welch
1985   "Social Context and Individual Measurement in the Study of Religiosity: Some Innovations from the Notre Dame Study of Catholic Parish Life." Paper presented at the Annual Meeting of the American Political Science Association, New Orleans.

1989 "Catholics in Context: Theoretical and Methodological Issues in Studying American Catholic Parishioners." *Review of Religious Research* 31 (2):132-48.

Lemann, Nicholas
1991 *The Promised Land.* New York: Alfred A. Knopf.

Leonard, Charles R.
1984 "A Study of Some Multiethnic Congregations in Light of Church Growth and the Homogeneous Unit Principle." Doctor of Ministry Thesis, Eastern Baptist Theological Seminary, Philadelphia.

Lieberson, Stanley
1969 "Measuring Population Diversity." *American Sociological Review* 34(6):850-62.

Light, Paul C.
1988 *Baby Boomers.* New York: W.W. Norton and Company.

Lincoln, C. Eric
1974 *The Black Church Since Frazier.* New York: Schocken Books.

Lincoln, C. Eric, and Lawrence H. Mamiya
1988 "In the Receding Shadow of the Plantation: A Profile of Rural Clergy and Churches in the Black Belt." *Review of Religious Research* 29 (June):349-68.

1990 *The Black Church in the African American Experience.* Durham, N.C.: Duke University Press.

Lindberg, Carter
1988 "Pietism and the Church Growth Movement in a Confessional Lutheran Perspective." *Concordia Theological Quarterly* 52:129-47.

Markus, Hazel and Zajonc, R. B.
1985 "The Cognitive Perspective in Social Psychology." In Gardner Lindzey and Elliott Aronson, eds. *Handbook of Social Psychology (3rd ed.). Vol. I: Theory and Method.* New York: Random House.

Marler, Penny Long
1993 "Lost in the Fifties: The Changing Family and the Nostalgic Church." Forthcoming in Nancy T. Ammerman and Wade Clark Roof, eds. *Work, Family, and Faith: New Patterns Among Old Institutions.*

Marler, Penny Long, and C. Kirk Hadaway
1992 "New Church Development and Denominational Growth (1950-1988): Symptom or Cause?" In Monty L. Lynn and David O. Moberg, eds. *Research in the Social Scientific Study of Religion, Volume 4.* Greenwich, Conn.: JAI Press.

1993 "Toward a Typology of Protestant 'Marginal Members.'" Review of Religious Research (forthcoming)

Marsden, George
1984 "The Evangelical Denomination." In G. Marsden, ed. *Evangelicalism and Modern America.* Grand Rapids: Eerdmans.

Marty, Martin E.
1979 Foreword. In Dean R. Hoge and David A. Roozen, eds. *Understanding Church Growth and Decline 1950–1978.* New York: Pilgrim Press.

Marty, Martin E., Stuart E. Rosenberg, and Andrew M. Greeley.
1968 *What Do We Believe? The Stance of Religion in America.* New York: Meredith Press.

Massey, Douglass S., and Nancy A. Denton
1988 "Suburbanization and Segregation in U.S. Metropolitan Areas." *American Journal of Sociology* 94 (November):592-626.

McClintock, Wayne
1988 "Sociological Critique of the Homogeneous Unit Principle." *International Review of Mission* 77:107-16.

McGavran, Donald A.
1970 *Understanding Church Growth.* Grand Rapids: Eerdmans.

McGavran, Donald A., and George G. Hunter III
1980 *Church Growth Strategies That Work.* Nashville: Abingdon Press.

McGavran, Donald A., and Winfield C. Arn
1974 *How to Grow a Church.* Glendale, Calif.: Regal Books.
1977 *Ten Steps for Church Growth.* New York: Harper & Row.

McGaw, Douglas B., with Elliott Wright
n.d. "A Tale of Two Congregations: Commitment and Social Structure in a Charismatic and Mainline Congregation." Hartford: Hartford Seminary.

McIntosh, Duncan, and Richard E. Rusbuldt
1983 *Planning Growth in Your Church.* Valley Forge, Pa.: Judson Press.

McKinney, William J.
1979 "Performance of United Church of Christ Congregations in Massachusetts and in Pennsylvania." Chapter 10 in Dean R. Hoge and David A. Roozen, eds. *Understanding Church Growth and Decline 1950–1978.* New York: Pilgrim Press.

McKinney, William J., and Daniel V. A. Olson
1991 "Protestant Church Decision Makers: A Profile." In Constant Jacquet, ed. *Yearbook of American and Canadian Churches.* Nashville: Abingdon Press.

McKinney, William J., and Dean R. Hoge
1983 "Community and Congregational Factors in the Growth and Decline of Protestant Churches." *Journal for the Scientific Study of Religion* 22:51-66.

McNamara, Patrick H.
 1985 "American Catholicism in the Mid-80s: Pluralism and Conflict in a Changing Church." *Annals of the American Academy of Political and Social Science.* 480 (July):63-74.

Merelman, Richard M.
 1984 *Making Something of Ourselves: On Culture and Politics in the United States.* Berkeley: University of California Press.

Methodological Issues in Congregational Studies
 1989 *Review of Religious Research,* special issue edited by M. Welch, 31:113-74.

Metz, D. L.
 1965 *Goal Subversion in New Church Development.* Berkeley: Survey Research Center.

 1967 *New Congregations: Security and Mission in Conflict.* Philadelphia: Westminster Press.

Meyers, Eleanor, and Daniel V. A. Olson
 1991 "A Contemporary Profile of the Christian (Disciples of Christ) Church." In Newell D. Williams, ed. *A Case Study of Mainstream Protestantism: The Disciples Relation to American Culture 1890–1989.* Ed., Newell D. Williams. Grand Rapids: Eerdmans.

Millar, William R., ed.
 1989 "Grow by Caring." *American Baptist Quarterly,* VIII (3):162-215.

Miller, Herb
 1987 *How to Build a Magnetic Church.* Nashville: Abingdon Press.

 1989*a* *Which of These Evangelistic Programs Should We Use?* Lubbock, Tex.: Net Press.

 1989*b* "Will Mainline Churches Reverse Their Membership Decline?" *Net Results* 10 (August):7-9.

Moorhous, C.
 1975 *Growing New Churches.* Self-published.

Morikawa, Jitsuo
 1963 "The Nature and Purpose of Mission." Unpublished paper.

Motz, Arnell, ed.
 1990 *Reclaiming a Nation.* Richmond, B.C.: Outreach Canada.

Mukenge, Ida Rousseau
 1983 *The Black Church in Urban America.* Lanham, Md.: University Press of America.

Nash, Dennison
 1968 "A Little Child Shall Lead Them: A Statistical Test of the Hypothesis that Children were the Source of the American 'Religious Revival.'" *Journal for the Scientific Study of Religion* 7:238-40.

Nash, Dennison, and Peter Berger.
    1962   "The Child, the Family, and the 'Religious Revival' in Suburbia." *Journal for the Scientific Study of Religion* 2:85-93.

Nash, Ronald H., ed.
    1987   *Evangelical Renewal in the Mainline Churches.* Westchester, Ill.: Crossway Books.

Nelsen, Hart M.
    1988   "Unchurched Black Americans: Patterns of Religiosity and Affiliation." *Review of Religious Research* 29 (June):398-412.

Nelsen, Hart M., and Anne Kusener Nelsen
    1975   *Black Church in the Sixties.* Lexington: University Press of Kentucky.

Nelsen, Hart M., Raytha L. Yokley, and Anne K. Nelsen, eds.
    1971   *The Black Church in America.* New York: Basic Books.

Nelson, Lynn D., and David G. Bromley
    1988   "Another Look at Conversion and Defection in Conservative Churches." In David G. Bromley, ed. *Falling from the Faith: Causes and Consequences of Religious Apostasy.* Newbury Park, Calif.: Sage Publications.

Newman, William M., and William V. D'Antonio
    1978   "'For Christ's Sake'; A Study of Key '73 in New England." *Review of Religious Research,* 19:2 (Winter):139-53.

Norwood, Frederick A.
    1974   *The Story of American Methodism: A History of the United Methodists and Their Relations.* Nashville: Abingdon Press.

Notre Dame Study of Catholic Parish Life
            Reports no. 1-14, December, 1984 to March, 1989. University of Notre Dame.

Nunnally, Jim C.
    1983   "The Study of Change in Evaluation Research: Principles Concerning Measurement, Experimental Design, and Analysis." In Elmer L. Struening and Marilyn B. Brewer, eds. *The University Edition of the Handbook of Evaluation Research.* Beverly Hills, Calif.: Sage Publications.

Olson, Daniel V. A.
    1989   "Church Friendships: Boon or Barrier to Church Growth." *Journal for the Scientific Study of Religion* 28:4.

Peck, George
    1983   *A Theological Environment for Effective Evangelism.* Valley Forge, Pa.: American Baptist National Ministries.

Perry, Everett L.
1979   *Historical Overview of the New Church Development Policies of the United Presbyterian Church in the United States of America.* New York: General Assembly Mission Council.

Perry, Everett L., and Dean R. Hoge
1981   "Faith Priorities of Pastor and Laity as a Factor in the Growth or Decline of Presbyterian Congregations." *Review of Religious Research* 22:221-32.

Poloma, Margaret M.
1989   *The Assemblies of God at the Crossroads: Charisma and Institutional Dilemmas.* Knoxville: The University of Tennessee Press.

Princeton Religion Research Center
1978   *The Unchurched American.* Princeton, N.J.

1981   *Religion in America: 1981.* Princeton, N.J.

1988   *The Unchurched American—10 Years Later.* Princeton, N.J.

1990   *Religion in America—Approaching the Year 2000.* Princeton, N.J.

1991   *Emerging Trends* 13(4). Princeton, N.J.

1992   *Emerging Trends* 14(3). Princeton, N.J.

Quebedeaux, Richard
1983   *The New Charismatics II.* San Francisco: Harper & Row.

Quinn, Bernard, Herman Anderson, Martin Bradley, Paul Goetting and Peggy Shriver
1982   *Churches and Church Membership in the United States 1980.* Atlanta: Glenmary Research Center.

Raferty, Susan, and David Leege
1989   *Catechesis, Religious Education, and the Parish.* Notre Dame Study of Catholic Parish Life. Report 14. Notre Dame, Ind.: University of Notre Dame.

Raines, Robert A.
1961   *New Life in the Church.* New York: Harper & Row.

Rauff, Edward A.
1979   *Why People Join the Church.* New York: Pilgrim Press.

Redford, J.
1978   *Planting New Churches.* Nashville: Broadman Press.

Reeves, R. Daniel, and Ronald Jenson
1984   *Always Advancing.* San Bernardino, Calif.: Here's Life Publishers, Inc.

Robbins, Thomas, Dick Anthony, and James Richardson
1978   "Theory and Research on Today's 'New Religions.'" *Sociological Analysis* 39 (1):95-122.

Robertson, James Oliver
    1980   *American Myth, American Reality.* New York: Hill and Wang.

Roehlkepartain, Eugene
    1993   *The Teaching Church: Moving Christian Education to Center Stage.* Nashville: Abingdon Press.

Roof, Wade Clark
    1978   *Community and Commitment: Religious Plausibility in a Liberal Protestant Church.* New York: Elsevier.

Roof, Wade Clark, and C. Kirk Hadaway
    1979   "Denominational Switching in the Seventies: Going Beyond Stark and Glock." *Journal for the Scientific Study of Religion* 18:363-79.

Roof, Wade Clark, and Daphne Spain
    1977   "A Research Note on City-Suburban Socioeconomic Differences Among American Blacks." *Social Forces* 56 (September):15-20.

Roof, Wade Clark, and David A. Roozen
    1989   "Are Baby Boomers Returning to Church?" Unpublished paper presented to American Academy of Religion meetings (December).

Roof, Wade Clark, and Dean R. Hoge
    1980   "Church Involvement in America: Social Factors Affecting Membership and Participation." *Review of Religious Research* 21 (Supplement):405-26.

Roof, Wade Clark, Dean R. Hoge, John E. Dyble, and C. Kirk Hadaway
    1979   "Factors Producing Growth or Decline in United Presbyterian Congregations." Chapter 9 in Dean R. Hoge and David A. Roozen, eds. *Understanding Church Growth and Decline 1950–1978.* New York: Pilgrim Press.

Roof, Wade Clark, and Karen Walsh
    1993   "Life Cycle, Generations, and Participation in Religious Groups." In Hadden and Bromley, eds. *Handbook on Cults and Religious Movements.* Greenwich, Conn.: JAI Press.

Roof, Wade Clark, and William McKinney
    1987   *American Mainline Religion: Its Changing Shape and Future.* New Brunswick, N.J.: Rutgers University Press.

Roozen, David A.
    1979   "The Efficacy of Demographic Theories of Religious Change." Chapter 5 in Dean R. Hoge and David A. Roozen, eds. *Understanding Church Growth and Decline 1950–1978.* New York: Pilgrim Press.

Roozen, David A., and Jackson W. Carroll
    1979   "Recent Trends in Church Membership and Participation: An Introduction." Chapter 1 in Dean R. Hoge and David A. Roozen, eds. *Understanding Church Growth and Decline: 1950–1978,* ed. D. Hoge and D. Roozen. New York: Pilgrim Press.

1989   "Methodological Issues in Denominational Surveys of Congregations."
           Review of Religious Research 31:115-31.

Roozen, David A., Jackson W. Carroll, and Wade Clark Roof
1990   "The Post War Generation and Establishment Religion: A Window to
           50 Years of Religious Change in the United States." Hartford: Hartford
           Seminary Center for Social and Religious Research.

Roozen, David A., William McKinney, and Wayne Thompson
1990   "The 'Big Chill' Generation Warms to Worship." *Review of Religious
           Research* 31 (March):314-22.

Rothauge, A. J.
n.d.   *Sizing Up a Congregation for New Member Ministry.* New York: The
           Episcopal Church Center.

Sample, Tex
1990   *U.S. Lifestyles and Mainline Churches.* Louisville: Westminster/John
           Knox Press.

Sanders, Gerald M.
1987   "The United Church of Christ." In Ronald H. Nash, ed. *Evangelical
           Renewal in Mainline Churches.* Westchester, Ill.: Crossway Books.

SAS Institute, Inc.
1987   *SAS/STAT Guide for Personal Computers, Version 6 Edition.* Cary,
           N.C.: Author.

Schaller, Lyle E.
1968   *The Local Church Looks to the Future.* Nashville: Abingdon Press.

1971   *Parish Planning.* Nashville: Abingdon Press.

1975   *Hey, That's Our Church!* Nashville: Abingdon Press.

1979   *Effective Church Planning.* Nashville: Abingdon Press.

1981   *Activating the Passive Church: Diagnosis and Treatment.* Nashville:
           Abingdon Press.

1982   *The Small Church Is Different.* Nashville: Abingdon Press.

1983   *Growing Plans.* Nashville: Abingdon Press.

1991a   *Forty-four Questions for Church Planters.* Nashville: Abingdon Press.

1991b   *Create Your Own Future.* Nashville: Abingdon Press.

Schroeder, Widick
1975   "Age Cohorts, the Family Life Cycle, and Participation in the Volun-
           tary Church in America: Implications for Membership Patterns,
           1950–2000." *Chicago Theological Seminary Register* 65:13-28.

Schuller, David S., Merton P. Strommen, and Milo L. Brekke, eds.
1980   *Ministry in America.* San Francisco: Harper & Row.

Searle, Mark, and David Leege
  1985   *The Celebration of Liturgy in the Parish.* Notre Dame Study of Catholic
             Parish Life. Report 5. Notre Dame, Ind.: University of Notre Dame.

Sheff, David
  1988   "Portrait of a Generation." *Rolling Stone Magazine,* May 5.

Sklare, Marshall, ed.
  1982   *Understanding American Jewry.* New Brunswick, N.J.: Transaction Books.

Stahura, John M.
  1986   "Suburban Development, Black Suburbanization, and the Civil Rights
             Movement Since World War II." *American Sociological Review* 51
             (February):131-44.

Stark, Rodney, and William Sims Bainbridge
  1985   *The Future of Religion.* Berkeley: University of California Press.

Starr, Timothy
  1978   *Church Planting—Always in Season.* Self-published.

Stone, Jon R.
  1991   "The New Voluntarism and Presbyterian Affiliation." In Milton J. Coal-
             ter, John M. Mulder, and Louis B. Weeks, eds. *The Diversity of Disci-
             pleship: Presbyterians and Twentieth Century Christian Witness.*
             Louisville: Westminster/John Knox Press.

Stump, Roger W.
  1986   "Regional Variations in the Determinants of Religious Participation."
             Review of Religious Research 27 (March):208-25.

  1987   "Regional Contrasts Within Black Protestantism: A Research Note."
             Social Forces 66 (September):143-51.

Tidsworth, F.
  1979   *Planting and Growing Missions.* Durham, N.C.: Moore Publishing
             Company.

Torbet, Robert G.
  1973   *A History of the Baptists* (Third edition), Valley Forge, Pa.: Judson Press.

Towns, E.
  1975   *Getting a Church Started in the Face of Insurmountable Odds with
             Limited Resources in Unlikely Circumstances.* Nashville: Impact
             Books.

Towns, Elmer, John Vaughan, and D. Seifert
  1987   *The Complete Book of Church Growth, second edition.* Wheaton, Ill.:
             Tyndale House.

Tricules, Homer
  1987   "American Baptist Churches in the U.S.A." In Ronald H. Nash, ed.
             Evangelical Renewal in the Mainline Churches. Westchester, Ill.:
             Crossway Books.

United Church Board for Homeland Ministries

1972   *Evangelism for a New Day: Building and Renewing Christian Community in the 1970's*. New York: United Church Board for Homeland Ministries.

1989   "It's a Priority!" *Growing Plans* (Fall):1.

1991   "A National Strategy for Church Development: 1992–2001." Unpublished paper.

United States General Accounting Office

1990   *1990 Census: Costs Are Uncertain Because Wage Rates May Be Uncompetitive*. Report to the Chairman and Ranking Minority Member, Subcommittee on Census and Population, Committee on Post Office and Civil Service, House of Representatives. Document No. GAO/GGD-90-78. Washington, D.C.: Author.

United States Bureau of the Census

1989   *Population Profile of the United Staes, 1989*. Current Population Report P-23, No. 159.

Van den Eeden, Pieter, and Harry J. M. Huthner.

1982   "Multi-Level Research." *Current Sociology* 30:1-179.

Verhof, Joseph, Elizabeth Douvan, and Richard Kulka

1981   *The Inner American: A Self-Portrait from 1957 to 1976*. New York: Basic Books.

Wagner, C. Peter

1976   *Your Church Can Grow: Seven Signs of a Healthy Church*. Glendale, Calif.: Regal Books.

1979*a*   "Church Growth Research: The Paradigm and Its Applications." In Dean R. Hoge and David A. Roozen, eds. *Understanding Church Growth and Decline 1950–1978*. New York: Pilgrim Press.

1979*b*   *Our Kind of People: The Ethical Dimension of Church Growth in America*. Atlanta: John Knox.

Wagner, C. Peter, Win Arn, and Elmer Towns, eds.

1986   *Church Growth: State of the Art*. Wheaton, Ill.: Tyndale House.

Wald, Kenneth D., Dennis E. Owen, and Samuel S. Hill, Jr.

1988   "Churches as Political Communities." *American Political Science Review* 82 (2):531-48.

Waldrop, Judith

1990   "You'll Know It's the 21st Century When . . ." *American Demographics*, December:23-27.

Walrath, Douglas A.

1979*a*   "Social Change and Local Churches: 1951–1975." Chapter 11 in Dean R. Hoge and David A. Roozen, eds. *Understanding Church Growth and Decline 1950–1978*. New York: Pilgrim Press.

1979b   *Leading Churches Through Change.* Nashville: Abingdon Press.

1987   *Frameworks: Patterns of Living and Believing Today.* New York: Pilgrim Press.

Warner, R. Stephen
1983   "Research Note: Visits to a Growing Evangelical and a Declining Liberal Church in 1978." *Sociological Analysis* 44:243-54.

1988   *New Wine in Old Wineskins: Evangelicals and Liberals in a Small-Town Church.* Berkeley: University of California Press.

Weiss, Michael J.
1988   *The Clustering of America.* New York: Harper & Row.

Welch, Michael R., C. Lincoln Johnson, and David Pilgrim
1990   "Tuning-In the Spirit: Exposure to Types of Religious T.V. Programming Among American Catholic Parishioners." *Journal for the Scientific Study of Religion* 29 (2):185-97.

Welch, Michael R., and David Leege
1989   "Religious Predictors of Catholic Parishioners' Sociopolitical Attitudes: Devotional Style, Closeness to God, Imagery, and Agentic/Communal Religious Identity." *Journal for the Scientific Study of Religion* 27 (4):536-52.

1991   "Catholic Evangelicalism and Political Orientations: A Case of Transcended Group Boundaries and Distinctive Political Values." *American Journal of Political Science* 35 (1):28-56.

Welch, Michael R., and John Baltzell
1984   "Geographic Mobility, Social Integration, and Church Attendance." *Journal for the Scientific Study of Religion* 23 (1):75-91.

Werning, Waldo J.
1977   *Vision and Strategy for Church Growth.* Chicago: Moody Press.

White, Richard
1968   "Toward a Theory of Religious Influence." *Pacific Sociological Review* 11:23-28.

Wiebe, Robert H.
1975   *The Segmented Society: An Introduction to the Meaning of America.* New York: Oxford University Press.

Wilke, Richard B.
1986   *And Are We Yet Alive: The Future of The United Methodist Church.* Nashville: Abingdon Press.

Willimon, William H., and Robert L. Wilson
1987   *Rekindling the Flame: Strategies for a Vital United Methodism.* Nashville: Abingdon Press.

Willits, Fern K., and Donald M. Crider

    1989   "Church Attendance and Traditional Religious Beliefs in Adolescence and Young Adulthood: A Panel Study." *Review of Religious Research* 31 (1):68-81.

Wilson, William Julius

    1987   *The Truly Disadvantaged.* Chicago: University of Chicago Press.

Winter, Gibson

    1962   *The Suburban Captivity of the Churches.* New York: Macmillan.

Woodbury, Walter E.

    1956   "Evangelism." In *Yearbook of the American Baptist Convention.* New York: American Baptist Convention.

Wuthnow, Robert

    1978   *Experimentation in American Religion: The New Mysticisms and Their Implications for the Churches.* Berkeley: University of California Press.

    1988   *The Restructuring of American Religion.* Princeton, N.J.: Princeton University Press.

    1989   *The Struggle for America's Soul.* Grand Rapids: Eerdmans.

Yankelovich, Daniel

    1974   *The New Morality: A Profile of American Youth in the 70s.* New York: McGraw-Hill.

    1981   *New Rules: Searching for Fulfillment in a World Turned Upside Down.* New York: Random House.